The making of the GREAT WESTERNS

William R. Meyer

Manufactured in the United States of America

Library of Congress Cataloging in Publication Data

Meyer, William R. 1949-
The making of the great Westerns.

Bibliography: p.
Includes index.
1. Western films—History and criticism. I. Title.
PN1995.9.W4M47 791.43'0909'32 79-11113
ISBN 0-87000-431-X

For my wife Antoinette,
who put up with a lot
while this book was being written

Acknowledgments

Dominick Abel
Joseph Behm
Steven Bernhardt
Larry C. Bradley
Niven Busch
Minard Coons
Olivia de Havilland
Directors Guild of America
Film Favorites
William Gray
Rusty Hancock
Burt Kennedy
Henry King
Stanley Kramer
Lincoln Center Library for the Performing Arts
Joel McCrea
Arthur Miller
Lee O. Miller
Michael Moore
Movie Star News
Darcy O'Brien
George O'Brien
Jerry Perchesky
Hal Polaire
David Ragan
Robert Relyea
Real West (Bill Anderson, Ed Doherty)
Martin Ritt
George Stevens, Jr.
John Sturges
Don Walker
Writers Guild of America

Table of Contents

Introduction

From the time when the first great cowboy movie, *The Great Train Robbery,* flickered on the screen in 1903, to the rugged sentimentality of William S. Hart, the white-hatted, fancy-shirted, slick heroics of Tom Mix, the prairie poetry of John Ford, the power of John Wayne, the slow-motion blood and guts of Sam Peckinpah, to the rawhide looks of quiet but dangerous Clint Eastwood, the Western has been a vital force in filmmaking.

Westerns big and small paid for a studio's prestige productions and occasional gambles. If the big-budgeted epics flopped at the box office, a mogul could look with relief to a cache of Western stories he knew could fill his pockets with the stuff which buys palatial estates and limousines.

But what about the Westerns themselves? They were certainly more than a means to an end. With the decline of the studios and the emergence of a conglomerate Hollywood which features moviemaking as just another corporate enterprise alongside shoe factories and expansive hotels, the Western continues to flourish, if on a narrower plain. The reduction in numbers is primarily a result of fewer films being made.

The Western, like the Broadway theatre, has been kicked around a lot for the past half-century, but it's still alive. Filmgoers still eat up Westerns with their popcorn, and television viewers dial them as often as video programmers put them on the schedule.

The Making of the Great Westerns examines thirty of the screen's most enjoyable, from their inception to release, and beyond. The films and the people who made them are explored: Who they were and are. How directors worked with the producers, writers, actors, and technicians. How they came together to make the film. And the status of the work in screen history. Here the making of the production is emphasized more than its quality, although an informal history of the genre is provided through the selected works. As such, a "B" Western like *Hit the Saddle* is included not owing to its classic greatness, but because the oater—as the cowboy movie has come to be known—is a workmanlike, fun picture which exemplifies in general how such low-budget action films were made.

As the Western has been shooting from the screen since the movies began, it truly represents Hollywood, and, in a way, all America.

When people sought to escape the shattering effects of the World War, they turned from the realistic Westerns of William S. Hart to the escapist films of Tom Mix. And when it was time for the sound Western to "grow up," to be part of the adult sphere of political corruption and light-hearted intrigue in *Mr. Smith Goes to Washington* and *Ninotchka,* the complex hilarity of *Bringing Up Baby,* the often white-washed history of *Juarez,* and the socially significant action of *The Roaring Twenties,* "poverty row" cowboy veteran John Wayne was chosen to ride the oater into respectability in *Stagecoach.* The coming of age reflected the new awareness brought on by the conflicts of the international crisis of the late 1930s.

When the Cold War retrenched battles from the land, air, and sea to the mind, the psychological "thinking man's" Western became popular. And in the 1960s when it was time to satirize archetypal Western values, yet embrace their single-minded sense of action, and even examine the death of the old West, the end of the cowboy as free spirit, the signal was given for many Americans to reappraise accepted ideas. Reappraisals of legends often crumbled them—as in *The Man Who Shot Liberty Valance, The Wild Bunch,* and *The Shootist.*

Yet the making of the Western is also the making of Hollywood. It evokes the earliest days when moviemakers trekked for miles to the right locations, made do with what was around them, without having the luxury of the multi-faceted studio machines which emerged in the 1920s.

In 1955 director Anthony Mann journeyed with a cast and crew of 142 to the Pueblo Indian country of New Mexico to shoot *The Man from Laramie.* In order to film scenes in an 1800-foot canyon, Columbia workers had to bulldoze a road from the main highway seven miles across hard plains and volcanic formations. The making of the production, starring James Stewart, was as tough as the film itself.

When MGM, Fox, Paramount, Warner Brothers, and the other studios became institutions a half century ago, much of the rugged individualism was stamped out of Hollywood. Bill Hart had been making movies his way for a dozen years, yet one of his greatest, *Tumbleweeds,* was unable to obtain bookings in many of the big city theatre chains throughout America. Just the result of one man trying to fight a celluloid city hall.

The battles between filmmakers' artistic integrity and moguls' economic desires are well represented in the Western. More recently Sam Peckinpah went through heartbreaking episodes over *The Wild Bunch.* His epic of the dying of Western legends was cut soon after release, with director Peckinpah fighting all the way. In 1972 Warner Brothers offered a "TV version" sanitized of Peckinpah's blood and gore to the networks, with no pretense that they were getting the original classic.

Director John Sturges had his share of troubles simply trying to shoot *The Magnificent Seven* on location in Mexico. Local censors didn't care for the way the script portrayed the natives. The original story—"Westernized" from a Japanese movie classic—concerns seven men hired to protect a Mexican village from bandits. Authorities wanted the film to show the peons trying to buy weapons, and only employing the gunfighters when they begged for work. Fortunately, Sturges got his way and went on to make one of the finest Westerns of the last twenty years.

There was at least as much good news on the set of the Western as bad. John Wayne had stagnated in tightly budgeted sagebrush sagas at Monogram and Republic for a decade until his old friend John Ford chose him to play the Ringo Kid in *Stagecoach.* But Wayne still had to prove himself. Ford mercilessly hounded the actor, criticizing his walk, line readings, and facial expressions. The tactics worked. Wayne gave a fine performance. And it seems that Ford didn't want the other, more established players to think "B" performer Wayne was getting special treatment just because he was a friend.

Director Budd Boetticher can attest to the opportunities available in making economic pictures with the blessing of a studio. A number of his 50s Westerns have come to be respected as some of the finest genre art since World War II. And Boetticher knew of the need for quality over quantity in even the more modest productions. By the time John F. Kennedy became President, the average American had more entertainment diversions than in any other time in history.

Yet the Western marches on.

William S. Hart and Barbara Bedford

CHAPTER ONE

Tumbleweeds

Year Released: 1925
Studio: United Artists
Producer: William S. Hart
Directors: King Baggott, William S. Hart
Screenplay: C. Gardner Sullivan, based on a story by Hal G. Evarts
81 minutes

Cast:

Don Carver	WILLIAM S. HART
Molly Lassiter	BARBARA BEDFORD
Noll Lassiter	J. GORDON RUSSELL
Bill Freel	RICHARD R. NEILL
Kentucky Rose	LUCIEN LITTLEFIELD
Bart Lassiter	JACK MURPHY
Mrs. Riley	LILLIAN LEIGHTON
Old Woman	GERTRUDE CLAIRE
Old Man	GEORGE F. MARION
Cavalry Major	CAPTAIN T. E. DUNCAN
Hinman	JAMES GORDON
Hotel Proprietor	FRED GAMBLE
Riley Boy	TURNER SAVAGE
Hicks	MONTE COLLINS

Tumbleweeds is a hybrid. It combines the best of the realist style of the films of William S. Hart and the spectacle which typified most silent Westerns after *The Covered Wagon* in 1923.

"Boys, it's the last of the West," laments cattle drover Don Carver, while he and other men of the Box K Ranch ponder their final cattle drive. As Carver, Hart stares at the departing herd as if watching the lowering of his best friend in a coffin into the earth.

The theme of *Tumbleweeds* is the transformation of the frontier into civilization. The story is set against the backdrop of the Oklahoma Land Rush of 1889 in the Cherokee Strip, and begins with the removal of livestock from the territory soon to be thrown up for grabs among eager settlers. With sidekick Kentucky Rose, Carver rides into town and stops a man named Noll from beating up a boy, whom he later discovers is Noll's half-brother, Bart. Carver meets and falls in love with Molly Lassiter, Noll's half-sister. Noll and Bill Freel consort to stake out land before the settlers can. Freel's price for cooperating is Molly's agreement to marry him. Carver is asked by his old boss to search the Strip for stray cattle. Since Carver is registered to ride in the rush, Freel has him arrested as a "Sooner," one who has attempted to secure land illegally, which is exactly what he and Noll plan to do. Kentucky follows the criminal pair into the Strip and, seeing them murder a soldier, informs the authorities in a vain effort to free Carver. But the rush has begun. In order to save the Box K from the clutches of Noll and Freel, Carver fashions a pole and vaults over the walls of the pen which imprison him. Riding hard, he heads for the Box K, while Molly and her young brother gallop for land in a buggy. While Carver defeats the conspirators, Freel tries to convince Molly that the drover is dishonest. When the pair then attempt to steal land from an old couple, Carver once again comes to the rescue. The truth reunites Carver and Molly. Fade out.

In *Tumbleweeds,* Hart does not break with his tradition of making realistic Westerns with historically correct environments. The town, the costumes, the wagons, the artifacts of frontier existence, and the land rush itself are all accurately shown. Hart's penchant for melodramatic plots that vibrate with realism is an active ingredient in the power of *Tumbleweeds.* The "coincidence" that Noll, Molly, and the boy are all related is a potentially corny plot element, certainly, going back to biblical times, where Cain kills Abel, where Joseph is sold into slavery by his brothers. But the familial situation also symbolizes a community growing apart, ultimately being swallowed up by civilization. Here the genesis is just hinted at. This is the beginning.

It is as if Carver and Molly are in effect Adam and Eve, starting the world all over again, going from the things that used to be too

Lucien Littlefield, J. Gordon Russell, Barbara Bedford, William S. Hart, and Jack Murphy

good to an uncertain future. In between there are the Nolls and the Freels attempting to subvert the course of progress.

Balancing the archetypal Hart traits in *Tumbleweeds* are the spectacular land rush and the presence of comic player Lucien Littlefield. Both of these additions were made in the name of a progress of another sort: United Artists wanted to make a film starring Hart which would reflect the tone of the popular cowboy vehicles of the 1920s; *Tumbleweeds* would be a large-scale Western, with plenty of riding sequences and comic relief along the way.

King Baggott is officially credited with directing *Tumbleweeds.* Actor/director Baggott's credits though make it appear unlikely that he was hired to shoot Hart's Western because of his extensive background in the genre, or action productions in general. Although Baggott did lens Universal-Jewel's *The Kentucky Derby* in 1922, which included some horse-racing, the panoramic land rush which climaxes *Tumbleweeds* is all Hart's, in its greatness as well as its flaws.

"Ready for the signal for the maddest stampede in American history," flashes the screen title as the settlers get ready for the race. As the clock strikes noon, a cannon is fired. Carver's horse reels, then there is a cut to an expansive shot of the apparently thousands of frontier families with their buckboards, buggies, horses, or bicycles. The images of the Western faces, the hard-bitten men and women, the hopeful children, dressed in their "homespuns," clothes brought from the East and patched many times throughout the years of struggle with soil and weather, show Hart the realist at work. The montage of the anxious contestants, bored soldiers, clocks, and watches, and more panoramic images heighten the tension which is then only slightly muted by the shadow of the cannon, an ominous intruder.

Since Hart disliked stunting of any kind, there is little crashing of wagons, falling off of horses, or similar occurrences which could have added to the run. Those included are awkward and tend to distract from a very rhythmic scene, like a skip on a record. However, there is one image which stands as a haunting summation of Hart's legendary stature. The lower part of the frame rises slightly over the land on which Hart is riding. In the distance, there is Hart on his horse Fritz, galloping against the backdrop of a beautiful sky, almost taking off into the clouds, as if the moviemakers knew the actor had reached his greatest heights as a star and was riding away for the last time.

Tumbleweeds is representative of many of the finest aspects of the silent Western. It has the rugged realism inherent in the films of William S. Hart, the spectacle of *The Covered Wagon* and *The Iron Horse,* and the work of such celluloid heroes as Tim McCoy and Fred Thomson. *Tumbleweeds* is a throwback to the days when Hart was the Western and the Western was Hart.

The Making of *Tumbleweeds*

William S. Hart retired from the screen three times. The first was primarily due to a paternity suit, the second to Paramount's efforts to regulate his vision of the West. The third and final retirement came when Hart found he could not fight a celluloid city hall—the Hollywood studio system.

In the silent film, Hart was the middle man in a trio of Western stars responsible for projecting the growth of the genre to millions of adoring fans. In turn-of-the-century baseball, enthusiasts celebrated the famous Chicago Cubs double-play combination of Tinker to Evers to Chance. In the Western movie genre, it was Anderson to Hart to Mix. Bronco Billy Anderson was *the* first Western star, acting the part to help create the fundamentals of all action movies—action, movement, suspense, heroics, love. Anderson's West was far from real—a bullet could literally dance around a corner to kill a black-hearted villain. But Bronco Billy brought the nerves of steel, the courage, and the morality to movie cowboys. William S. Hart came on the scene fresh from triumph on Broadway in 1914 to give the Western realism, that touch of Americana only noticed by the French critics in the early years. "Rio Jim," as Hart was affectionately dubbed in France, made sure slices of nineteenth-century Western life found their way into such admittedly melodramatic vehicles as *The Return of Draw Egan, Hell's Hinges, The Toll Gate,* and the other Westerns he made between 1914 and 1921. Hart created the cinema's anti-hero, playing the outlaw eventually reformed by the love of a good woman. Hart's characters could be righteous, but they were always right, and their Western ambiance, from towns to gunplay to hats, chaps, and boots, was invariably authentic. Whether playing Draw Egan, Blaze Tracey, or Singer Jim McKee, Hart evoked the Good Bad Man, a cowboy operating against the grain of written law, only to instinctively support and sometimes die for unwritten codes of Western conduct. Thou shalt not steal another man's horse, thou shalt not collude with the Indians, but sometimes it was necessary to shoot another man, to live the life of an outlaw because you were wronged many years ago. This great contradiction in the Hart Westerns motivates their narratives and brings their characters a reality, an area of grey in the human soul rarely touched in pre-World War I cinema.

When the forty-four-year-old Hart made his film debut in a 1914 two-reel Ince Western called *His Hour of Manhood,* Tom Mix had already been in the movies for five years. From 1909 to 1916, Mix worked for Colonel William N. Selig. Like Hart, Mix learned filmmaking inside and out. Unlike Hart, Mix was rarely given any help with scripting or anything else by the economical Selig. Finally in 1917 Mix moved over to Fox, and broke loose from the one-, two-, three-, and four-reel films he'd been making for Selig. From then on Mix's star escalated under the watchful eyes of William Fox. By 1920, Tom Mix had replaced Hart as top cowboy in Hollywood. Between 1918 and 1920, Mix made twenty films, all fast, furious, and full of the things he did best, namely hard riding, stunts, and a great deal of showmanship. Duded up in fancy Western outfits, guns drawn to right any and all wrongs, Tom Mix was anathema to Hart as a performer. Mix was a Jazz Age cowboy, a daredevil on horseback, a hero who thrilled and chilled his audiences. He was a white-hatted sagebrush star all the way, from the romancing of leading ladies such as Colleen Moore to the lawful wiping out of bad guys everywhere. Mix was omniscient on screen, and his films happily rode all over reality. That's what audiences wanted in the Western, or so thought movie moguls Adolph Zukor, Jesse Lasky, and Joseph Schenck.

By 1921 Tom Mix was only one of the names which could be related to Hart's fall from the saddle of premier Western star. In

William S. Hart

1918, Hart was slapped with a paternity suit from one Elizabeth MacCulley, alleging that he was the father of her fifteen-month-old baby. Two years earlier the star and his sister Mary had met the woman, who claimed to be a fan of Hart's, for a casual evening of dinner and talk. That was the last they heard from her until that cold morning in November 1918. Hart was innocent but couldn't prove it. What would this do to his movie image, everyone wondered.

Famous Players-Lasky, to whom Hart was under contract, decided to avoid a possible scandal by paying Miss MacCulley fifty dollars per month child support, without telling the alleged father.

When the star's Paramount contract ended, he decided to gracefully retire from the screen, rather than battle Tom Mix at the box office and Elizabeth MacCulley in the courts and newspapers.

In 1923 the mother balked at the fifty dollar a month payment from Paramount, and demanded double the amount. Hart was shocked when he discovered that the studio's legal department had taken steps to avoid publicity by paying hush money. His protests in court that he knew nothing of the clandestine arrangement were ignored by the judge, who found in favor of MacCulley.

Complicating Hart's emotional and financial turmoil was another woman, Winifred Westover, his leading lady in *John Petticoats* (1919). Hart was known for his sometime habit of continuing screen love relationships off the set. He actually proposed to a number of his leading ladies, and surprised Hollywood when he and Winifred married on December 7, 1921. In his autobiography, *My Life East and West* (Benjamin Blom), Hart barely mentions the union, which lasted legally until February 11, 1927, but was really over when the couple separated on May 10, 1922, five months before the birth of their son, William S. Hart, Jr. Their marriage was apparently shaky from the beginning and later produced painful memories for the star.

In 1950, when Hart's estate was being divided among his heirs, Winifred Westover Hart told the newspapers why her marriage didn't work out. She claimed Hart felt that Winifred was trying to force his sister Mary out of their lives. According to the former Mrs. Hart, he said, "What do you think you're doing, taking Mary's place? If that's the kind of stuff you're going to pull, you can get out of here as fast as you can get your things out."

Still suffering from the pangs of separation, Hart starred in *Wild Bill Hickok,* which was released in 1923. The film conformed to the traditional Hart style, with realistic trappings and old-fashioned melodrama supplanting slick action and showmanship. Famous Players-Lasky thought *Wild Bill Hickok* to be inferior to the latest Tom Mix films (eight in 1923) and insisted that Hart throw out his formula and integrate daredevil stunts and comedy into his Westerns. Hart rebelled and produced *Singer Jim McKee* (1923), a heart-rending tale of redemption in the old West. As the title character who robs a bank to support a friend's motherless daughter, Hart didn't alter his cinema ways one bit. Frustrated at the attempts to reason with the star, Adolph Zukor told Hart he would have to submit each story idea to Paramount for approval, or no more films would be made. Hart refused and retired a second time.

J. Gordon Russell, William S. Hart, and Jack Murphy in a publicity shot

For the next two years Western heroics were left to Tom Mix, Buck Jones, Hoot Gibson, and numerous other movie cowboys whose vehicles usually bore little resemblance to Hart's own. Gone was the realism of Hart's West, the sentimentality of Hart's characters. Although some stars, such as Hoot Gibson, varied Mix's formula a bit (in Gibson's case by his ingratiating, almost comic screen character), the glitter and gunplay of the Tom Mix Westerns for Fox became the standard more or less until John Ford broke the mold with *Stagecoach* in 1939.

By 1925, Hart was eager to get back into the cinema saddle. United Artists enthusiastically publicized the fifty-five-year-old actor's return to the land of sage and saloons in an epic about the Cherokee Land Rush entitled *Tumbleweeds.* "What a joy to go to work!" Hart exclaimed in his autobiography about the comeback.

Despite his previous trouble with Famous Players-Lasky, Hart had no problems financing *Tumbleweeds.* He had a contract for two films with United Artists in his pocket when he arrived at the bank requesting $100,000 to produce the Western. To his amazement, the bank lent him the money at the unusually low interest rate

Barbara Bedford and William S. Hart in a publicity shot

of five percent. Upon wiring for the cash, Hart was notified that since money was then "cheaper," the bank could let him have his loan at an interest rate of four and a half percent instead.

Since the founders of United Artists, Mary Pickford, Douglas Fairbanks, Charles Chaplin, and D. W. Griffith, were immersed in conflict, Joseph Schenck, brother of Nicholas Schenck, president of Loew's Inc., was made head of production. It was Schenck with whom Hart had to deal during the making of *Tumbleweeds.*

Pre-production went smoothly. Hart was granted his request to have C. Gardner Sullivan write the screenplay of the Western from a *Saturday Evening Post* story by Hal G. Evarts. Sullivan had scripted many of Hart's by then old-fashioned Triangle films. Barbara Bedford, the star of *Last of the Mohicans* (Associated Producers, 1922), among others, was signed to play Molly Lassiter, with Hart as her paramour, Don Carver. Schenck and Hart set the budget of *Tumbleweeds* at $312,000, a sizable figure for the time. Instead of Lambert Hillyer, who directed many of Hart's films for Artcraft, such as *The Toll Gate, The Testing Block* (both 1920), and

Three Word Brand (1921), the studio insisted that King Baggott helm *Tumbleweeds.* Baggott had been a star in Hollywood even before Hart set foot in front of a movie camera. The tall, handsome Baggott had played leads in dozens of early films, distinguishing himself in versions of *Ivanhoe* (1912), *Dr. Jekyll and Mr. Hyde* (1913), and *The Corsican Brothers* (1915). *Tumbleweeds* was Baggott's first Western after directing nineteen other films. But he was a rugged man, who survived numerous accidents on the set of some wild adventures, and impressed Hart with his professionalism.

King Baggott decided the first scenes would be shot at 5:30 A.M. Hart was fully made-up and ready by 5:00. With his confidence restored, he awaited the roll of the cameras.

"While we waited for the rising sun," Hart wrote in his autobiography, "the morning air was like a long, cool drink—the elixir of happiness. I love acting. I love the art of making motion pictures. It is the breath of life to me!"

Hart was able to bounce back from all his troubles, and his optimistic, naive, sentimental view of life showed in his writing about *Tumbleweeds.* He was going to make an epic comeback in an epic Western in the style of the films of the old William S. Hart, with realism, a moral lesson, and, above all else, no compromises!

For the most part Hart's vision was filmed intact. The only element doubtlessly included solely to satisfy the studio's view of the public's taste was the character of Hart's sidekick, Kentucky Rose, humorously played by Lucien Littlefield.

It is obvious from the film that Hart was not fond of stunt work. In the land rush sequence there is a wagon crash which neither Hart nor Baggott could handle correctly. They used two shots and a cutaway image. A stunt man wasn't even needed. Another scene featured a runaway wagon heading for a gully. It was a trick glass shot. No stunt man needed. Despite his distaste for these effects, Hart pole-vaulted over a fence onto the back of his horse Fritz, in order to enter the race.

Reviewers sometimes enjoyed *Tumbleweeds,* but they did not confuse it with a classic:

New York Times:

The film is more or less an episodic version of the covered wagon epic. . . .

Los Angeles Times:

Down at the Strand it seemed as though all the little boys in town were struggling to get in to see William S. Hart in *Tumbleweeds. . . .* Of the week's pictures, *Tumbleweeds* is by all odds the most thrilling. One scene, the mad race of the homesteaders to claim the land in the Cherokee Strip, is one of the most exciting I have ever seen. . . .

United Artists and Bill Hart have every reason to be proud of this picture, for it pleases his old fans and lives up to the present demand for something of epic sweep in all but strictly modern pictures. . . .

In New York, *Variety* reported that *Tumbleweeds* did well. The Western made $36,300 in one week, the journal stated, second only to the hit *His Secretary,* which pulled in $64,600. It seemed *Tumbleweeds* found favor with the public wherever it went.

Yet United Artists had apparently lost faith in the film by the time it was completed. Perhaps the studio didn't like the idea of Hart taking a share of the box-office receipts as well as a salary. *Tumbleweeds* wasn't given the normal publicity build-up for a production of its size and expense. And the oater rarely played in first-run theatres. Hart was extremely distraught over the mishandling of his epic. He expected to lose $50,000 of his own money because of it.

The star took United Artists to court, refusing to give up in his fight to recoup the losses. It took years to settle the case. In 1936, the Newark *Evening News* reported that Hart collected damages of $80,000. Other sources claim the New York Court of Appeals awarded him $278,000 out of a $500,000 settlement in 1940. But by then it was all academic. William S. Hart had been permanently retired from the screen since 1925. He spent time caring for his 200-acre ranch, "Hills of the Wind," and wrote Western novels, such as the quite favorably received *Hoofbeats,* published by Dial Press in 1933. The former star acted as a technical advisor for MGM's big Johnny Mack Brown Western, *Billy the Kid* (1930), and even lent the studio the real gunfighter's six-shooters.

But that was his closest association to making films until 1939. Astor Pictures Corporation re-released *Tumbleweeds,* and William S. Hart recorded a moving eight-minute prologue to the Western, recounting a personal history of the frontier, as well as his love for the movies. He spoke as an expert on the West, in that cheerful and sentimental way he penned his autobiography. The former Shakespearean actor's strong, steady tones would have made him a natural in the sound Western, had he been a little younger.

William S. Hart has his place as a bulwark of the Western movie. *Tumbleweeds* was his last hurrah, a final burst of heroism from an individual who became a living legend before the Hollywood system swallowed up his frontier and his career.

Max Terhune,
Bob Livingston,
Rita Hayworth,
and
Ray Corrigan

Max Terhune,
Bob Livingston,
and
Ray Corrigan

CHAPTER TWO

Hit the Saddle

Year Released: 1937
Studio: Republic
Producer: Nat Levine
Director: Mack V. Wright
Story: Oliver Drake, Maurice Geraghty, based on characters created by William Colt MacDonald
Screenplay: Oliver Drake
Cinematography: Jack Marta
Music: Alberto Colombo
Art Director: John Victor Mackay
Editor: Lester Orleback
57 minutes

Cast:

Stony Brooke	ROBERT LIVINGSTON
Tuscon Smith	RAY CORRIGAN
Lullaby Joslin	MAX TERHUNE
Rita	RITA CANSINO
Rance McGowan	J. P. McGOWAN
Sheriff Miller	EDWARD CASSIDY
Tim Miller	SAMMY McKIM
Buck	YAKIMA CANUTT
Joe Harvey	HARRY TENBROKE
Hank	ROBERT SMITH
Pete	ED BOLAND

Henchman	GEORGE PLUES
Ranchers	JACK KIRK
	RUSS POWELL
	BOB BURNS
Judge	ALLAN CAVAN
Patrons	GEORGE MORRELL
	WALLY WEST
Drunk	BUDD BUSTER
Bartender	KERNAN CRIPPS

In many ways, *Hit the Saddle* typifies the 1930s "B" Western. Its tightly constructed plot, in which good guys bring bad guys to traditional justice, had plenty of action, a customary dose of comic relief, picturesque outdoor locations, and sparsely furnished sets. But the oater also possesses a dancing chanteuse named Rita (then Cansino) Hayworth, who remains a charming personality even though she attempts to break up the friendship of three men. Most low-budget actioners wouldn't have been as kind to her. This unusual maturity, strongest in the singer, is also evident in other portions of the Western and makes *Hit the Saddle* an endearing, yet actionful entry in Republic's profitable "Three Mesquiteers" series.

By the time *Hit the Saddle* was produced, the "Three Mesquiteers" had settled into the forms of Bob Livingston (Stony), Ray Corrigan (Tuscon), and Max Terhune (Lullaby), who handled the comedy with his dummy Elmer. The trio formed one of the best hero units in the "B" Western genre, which spawned many groups of two and three protagonists who subdued villains, including the "Trailblazers" (Bob Steele, Ken Maynard, and Hoot Gibson), and Buster Crabbe and Fuzzy Knight, along with variations on the Mesquiteers and many others.

Livingston and Corrigan share a relationship similar to the one later fused by Tyrone Power and Henry Fonda as Jesse and Frank in *Jesse James.* Livingston is the matinee idol, high spirited and prone to following his whims. In *Hit the Saddle,* Stony falls in love with a dance-hall singer, and plans to leave the ranch and marry her. Corrigan is the more sensible of the two men. As Smith, he always counsels Stony to stay away from troublesome situations, believing more in the things he can see with his eyes and calculate with his brains than elements in the universe undreamt of in most philosophies in the Mesquiteer productions, save the idealism of Stony Brooke. Terhune is a sharp and snappy foil, whipping out banter with other characters and his dummy Elmer in the best tradition of broad 1930s rat-tat-tat comedy.

The plot of *Hit the Saddle* revolves around the efforts of a villain to capture and sell a bunch of wild horses who live in a deep valley. When the local sheriff investigates, the baddies trample him and blame it on the leader of the horses. The steed is lassoed and brought into town. Most people, including Tuscon Smith, want to exterminate the animal, but Stony refuses to believe the horse is guilty. The absurdity of putting a horse on trial is offset by the interplay between Livingston and Corrigan about how to treat the animal. The townspeople believe Stony is tilting at windmills in his effort to prove the innocence of the stallion. The relationship between Stony and Tuscon has already been severed because Tuscon has bribed the chanteuse into taking the next stage back East.

Yet sympathy is balanced between the two men. It is obvious that Stony can be woefully naive in worldly matters. This is never so evident as when Stony joins the singer in song on the makeshift barroom stage. Stony tries to hold back a grimace and sings as if he were a naughty child being punished and trying to hold back tears. Tuscon emerges as the vestige of sanity in the trio, with Brooke going off on his flights of fancy and Lullaby communing with a dummy.

In the end, of course, Stony is proved right. His faith was justified. And the Three Mesquiteers triumph.

The charm of *Hit the Saddle* is created in part by the sheer joy of watching the actors lend some credibility to the outlandish focus on the horse as an innocent victim of circumstances.* The charisma of Rita Hayworth rubs off in every scene, even at the end when her eyes light up as Tuscon mentions a nice fee for leaving town. She is realistic in her thinking that the money is worth more to her than Stony's affections. Tuscon stands rock cold against the batting of her eyes and her inviting smile. Their opposing dynamics make the scene work, although Rita never takes the material too seriously. Her best lines come early. A co-worker tells Rita about Stony and Tuscon. "Those boys are closer than Siamese twins." Rita retorts, "Oh yeah? Take a look at the baby who's going to perform the operation."

Director Mack V. Wright acts in stride with the other "B" filmmakers of the era by keeping the plot moving. An occasional awkward piece of dialogue explains a relationship or circumstance to avoid slowing down the story. Like many other low-budget Westerns, *Hit the Saddle* benefits from the bare sets, the crudity of which enhances the tale's realism, and from the use of mountains, rocks, trees, and trails which didn't cost a cent to rent.

Hit the Saddle is a fun Western, as were many of the "poverty

*The horse Trigger would later be used as a pivotal character in many Roy Rogers films.

row" oaters that could hide their economy and the fact that they were shot in a week or less. Ironically, *Hit the Saddle,* upon release, was considered one of the weaker Three Mesquiteer films. But time and Rita Hayworth have made it a tantalizing piece of memorabilia.

The Making of *Hit the Saddle*

It appeared that Republic found the actors to play the trio of cowboys in their "Three Mesquiteers" series. *The Three Mesquiteers, Ghost Town Gold* (both 1936), *Gunsmoke Ranch,* and *Riders of the Whistling Skull* (both 1937) were produced with only one casting change. Leading men Bob Livingston and Ray "Crash" Corrigan starred in fifteen of the Westerns, while Syd Saylor was replaced by Max Terhune as the comic sidekick in *Ghost Town Gold.*

The faces weren't always the same. William Colt MacDonald, who worked in Columbia's story department, wrote the first of a series of Three Mesquiteers novels in 1933. Titled *Law of the .45's,* it established MacDonald's formula for rather complex plots featuring one-dimensional characters. Essentially the writer recreated Dumas' Three Musketeers in the American West, a perfect setting for their reincarnation.

Law of the .45's was filmed by a small company and released by Grand National. In this version, Tuscon Smith was played by character performer Guinn "Big Boy" Williams, while Al St. John turned the leading-man role of Stony Brooke into a funny foil. Lullaby Joslin was eliminated. The roles were shuffled again in *Too Much Beef* (1936). Rex Bell starred as a character called Jack Argyle, who assumes the name Tuscon Smith while under cover. Rock Hawkey's script was based on a story by MacDonald, and it can be assumed the studio wanted to get some use out of the names to which they purchased screen rights.

RKO did more justice to MacDonald's creation. *Powdersmoke Range* (1935) starred old-time favorite Harry Carey as Tuscon, Hoot Gibson as Stony, and Guinn Williams who reappeared more appropriately as Lullaby. Also featured in this expansive "B" Western were Tom Tyler, Bob Steele, and cowboy veterans William Farnum, William Desmond, Buddy Roosevelt, Wally Wales, and Franklyn Farnum. In fact, there were so many characters in the tale, there was little room for the plot to breathe.

The Three Mesquiteers really came into being shortly after Herbert J. Yates, a one-time tobacco executive who built a film laboratory, opened up Republic Pictures in 1935. Republic would be a production and distribution house, and Yates would run a virtually one-man operation, exercising the control of a Goldwyn or Harry Cohn.

Along with Republic, most of the minor studios were located on or near Gower Street and Santa Monica Boulevard, which was just south of Sunset. There, on "poverty row," Republic, Monogram, Allied, Liberty, Tiffany-Stahl, World Wide, Majestic, Progressive, Peerless, and others operated hand-to-mouth organizations which could just scrounge up enough capital to pay their actors, writers, and technicians, with little left over for sets, props, and costumes. The "offices" of such "studios" were often in the chief's briefcase. One day the maker of cheap Westerns might be in business, but barely, and the next the company might be broke, leaving creditors dangling.

Republic was different. It was a smooth operation run by Yates which made films in anywhere from three days to two weeks for perhaps $10,000, then rented them out for something like $50,000 in profits. If a small studio could stay in business and keep the productions flowing, it could make out. That's exactly what Republic and Yates did for twenty years until television cut deeply into the finances once obtainable for "B" films.

Of course, Yates needed producers, and Nat Levine was one of his best. Levine had produced a Western similar to MacDonald's creation called *The Three Musketeers* (1933) at Mascot, a sidewalk business which merged with Republic. In 1936, Levine bought screen rights to a MacDonald novel, along with all of its characters.

Levine lured promising actor Robert Livingston away from MGM to star in the Republic serial *The Vigilantes Are Coming* (1936). The performer would fit well into Levine's plans. The son of a couple in the newspaper business, Livingston had started out as a reporter for the Los Angeles *Daily News,* but by the late 1920s he was acting at the Pasadena Playhouse. In 1929 he began his film career at Universal. A dashing actor with jet black hair, Livingston became a contract actor at MGM in 1933, but had appeared in small parts in Metro productions in his three years at Culver City. He eagerly accepted a starring role in a serial for Levine, even though by doing so he marked himself forever as a "B" regular. Few performers who achieved any status in low-budget pictures went on to fame in major vehicles. John Wayne was one exception. And since Livingston had spent some time on a ranch, he wasn't totally unfamiliar with the ways of the West.

Ray "Crash" Corrigan built a reputation as a rugged stuntman, but some say his nickname was in reality a reference to his failure to execute several arduous stunts. Corrigan wanted to be a star. He appeared in a small role in *The Vigilantes Are Coming* and a number of other films before landing the part of Tuscon Smith in the Mesquiteer Westerns.

In the series, the characters of Stony Brooke and Smith were always at odds. Although Livingston was top-billed over Corrigan, Brooke frequently went off on flights of fancy, acted irresponsibly, and had to be rescued by Smith and Lullaby Joslin, the latter having been shaped into a more comical character than MacDonald had ever intended.

The screen friction between Livingston and Corrigan was a reflection of their off-the-set relationship. Both ambitious men apparently could not compete professionally and stay friends. Reportedly one of the reasons for their inability to get along was that Corrigan, the second lead in the series, received more fan mail than Livingston. In any case, perhaps the actors used their dislike for one another to lend more credibility to the squabbles between Brooke and Smith.

But Livingston was being given the star build-up by Republic, and Corrigan wanted the same. Ray Corrigan was a strong-willed man, and a wise businessman determined to achieve his goals. "The man who is completely master of his own body can master almost all of life's problems and difficulties," he once said. "The old saying about a 'healthy mind in a healthy body being able to accomplish miracles' may be aged but nonetheless true." Even while vying for stardom at Republic, Corrigan was also busy building a huge California ranch which would be called "Corriganville."

So Corrigan and Livingston made a good duo. Livingston had the impetuousness and matinee idol features, and Corrigan promoted a very real sense of control onscreen.

Syd Saylor was long gone by the time the cameras rolled on *Hit the Saddle.* Max Terhune played the comic sidekick Lullaby Joslin in many of the series entries, acting as a buffer between Brooke and Smith, and making jokes with Elmer the dummy. Terhune's Republic contract was typical of those of stars at "B" studios, the organizations that lasted long enough to let the ink dry on a legal document, that is. He began a seven-year deal at $100 a week, with yearly studio options. For the first several years, Terhune was a valued property, and as such received annual raises. But the money could never compete with the salaries of even a tightly budgeted major studio such as Warner Brothers.

The cast was rounded out by Western veterans Ed Cassidy, J. P. McGowan, Yakima Canutt (also a stuntman), and Ed Boland. Salaries for performers like these who supported stars in low-budget oaters usually ranged from $10 to $25 a film, but it must be remembered that they could appear in literally dozens of little pictures annually.

An alluring nineteen-year-old named Rita Cansino portrayed a saloon songstress who almost leads Stony Brooke away from the Mesquiteers. Although *Hit the Saddle* was her first and only film at

Ray Corrigan, Bob Livingston, and Rita Hayworth

Republic, Rita had had small roles in about a half dozen movies at Fox and a few other studios. In this Mesquiteers entry she got to perform an original song called "Winding the Trail," with Livingston giving her some rather unenthusiastic back-up. The number, composed by Sammy Stept, had lyrics by Oliver Drake, who was co-author of the film's original story and wrote the screenplay. Republic press people announced that "Rita Cansino, glamorous actress and member of the famous 'Flying Cansinos' dance family, has the romantic feminine role opposite Livingston."

Contract director Mack V. Wright, who had made *The Vigilantes Are Coming* with Ray Taylor, was assigned to shoot *Hit the Saddle.* Wright's first feature was Warner Bros.' *Haunted Gold* in 1932, starring a youthful John Wayne. From there, the director went on to make eleven more "B" properties, including eight Westerns and two serials.

Since economy and speed were the main factors in the making of the "B" Westerns, as many locations as possible were employed. Sparely furnished interiors and two-dimensional exteriors were used over and over again by Republic, as well as by all the small studios that produced short, to-the-point actioners in the 1930s and 40s.

The studio sent a second-unit crew to Montana to get footage of herds of horses roaming the mountain range. The cameramen got too close to their subject at one point and two men were nearly trampled in a horse stampede, according to Republic's publicity corps. Some sources say this Mesquiteer Western utilized stock footage from Mascot's 1926 *The Devil's Horse* instead of new material.

Needless to say, the production crew of *Hit the Saddle* didn't have the research resources available at the major studios. The big companies often sent representatives around the world on searches for unique historical artifacts which could be used in their productions and held out as bait by eager publicists. At Republic, the prop man was forced to use an encyclopedia to verify the accuracy of the costumes, sets, and Western regalia the studio felt should be faithfully depicted. Of course, many of the outfits worn by the good guys and bad guys of the "B" Westerns were more like circus cowboy clothes, with their trim fit and gaudy design, featuring flowing scarves, fringe, and guns which resembled fancy cigarette lighters rather than six-shooters.

Some problems that arose during the making of *Hit the Saddle* could be corrected easily. For instance, the crew had to create their own rainfall, since the real thing moved too fast for film of the 1930s to show well. Making artificial rain, dropped by a spray device erected above the windows of the relevant sets, was, of course, more convenient than waiting for nature.

Shooting was frequently halted when one extra kept getting nosebleeds as a result of firing his gun.

Although *Hit the Saddle* includes footage shot in Montana or culled from another Western, horses had to be brought to the location at Red Rock Canyon for some scenes. Ray Corrigan and Max Terhune found it difficult to control the pinto, leader of the wild stallions. After a few tries, the moment when they grab the horse was lensed with more authority, as the two actors really groped with the rebellious animal. The Western highlights a fight between the pinto, and Volcano, a trained stallion, who became rambunctious when the pinto was being filmed alone. During the shooting of the screen struggle between the pair, the horses started getting serious about mauling one another and a violent battle raged until the two were separated by their trainers.

Bob Livingston barely escaped serious injury while strapped to the pinto. The script called for the villains to capture Stony Brooke and tie him to a horse. After the scene was shot and Brooke was hoisted to the saddle, all the actors rode off. They forgot Livingston was bound across the horse's back, unable to move. The men were riding so fast the actor's screams weren't heard, until one of the horsemen turned around to talk to him. The man grabbed the pinto's bridle and slowed the animal to a halt, then removed the aching, but relieved Livingston.

Such occurrences weren't rare during the making of the "B" Westerns. In the 1930s and 40s, many of the stars were required to do their own stunts if possible, and more than one actor was injured doing things which would have been unthinkable at the major studios. One time in the mid-1930s John Wayne was asked to approach a well and ladle himself some cold water. A sharpshooter would then shoot the ladle out of his hand. Certainly a star wouldn't have been risked like that at Metro or Paramount!

Although many of the early entries in the Mesquiteers series and other low-budget Westerns were made in ten days or two weeks, *Hit the Saddle* was finished in five days. The studio had used Mother Nature, barren sets, and its new camera car to film the chases, and everything was done swiftly, as dictated by Herbert J. Yates. The studio's publicity department gave the fifth entry in the "Three Mesquiteers" series a good build-up:

> FIGHTING THRILLS!
>
> As the Cavaliers of the Cactus Battle Odds to Rescue a Killer Horse!
>
> Two Horses, nostrils distended, eyes aflame . . . battling with deadly flashing hoofs, for the life of a man!
>
> Riders of the range . . . heroes in chaps and leather . . . Vigilantes of the Old West . . . The Three Mesquiteers!

Variety's review typified subsequent critical reaction to *Hit the Saddle:* "Lacking a femme angle, this hayseed drama is nil from the emotional standpoint. It is funny in spots and lively. Musically, it's not so hot. . . . Picture offers some nice outdoor scenics and the Mesquiteers themselves are a likeable trio, despite their varied accents."

About Rita Cansino, the critic wrote, "The girl is highly deficient in terps and as an actress."

Several more entries were made in the Mesquiteer series starring Livingston, Corrigan, and Terhune. But that same year the screen's Stony Brooke decided to take a swim offscreen while on location. He dove off a bridge and smashed his head against the shallow bottom of a river. Athletic Ray Corrigan jumped in to rescue him, and after doctors examined Livingston, it was revealed that he had sustained a fractured skull when the top of his head was peeled back in the accident. Ralph Byrd replaced Livingston in *Trigger Trio* (1937). Years later, Corrigan was still upset over Livingston's alleged failure to thank him for possibly saving his life.

Ultimately, the conflict between the two men grew to the point where they could no longer work together. Livingston left the series and John Wayne took over his role. After Wayne's success as the Ringo Kid in *Stagecoach,* four more of his Mesquiteer films were released, but then he too rode off the Mesquiteer range. Max Terhune's seven-year contract wasn't renewed after the studio realized it had been paying him what was considered an excessive salary. Raymond Hatton became Lullaby Joslin. Bob Livingston returned as Stony Brooke, and Corrigan then decided to leave. Corrigan and his pal Terhune subsequently teamed up for the popular "Range Buster" series at Monogram.

In the midst of all the Mesquiteer changes, *Hit the Saddle*'s female star, Rita Cansino, continued in "B" films, but not at Republic, where her talents weren't appreciated. As Rita Hayworth, she became a star in 1941 on the strength of her performance in Warner Bros.' *Strawberry Blonde,* in a part similar to her character in *Hit the Saddle.*

Bob Livingston and Ray "Crash" Corrigan never rose above the "B" stardom they achieved in the Mesquiteer series. In the 1940s Livingston moved to supporting roles, sometimes the good guy, often the villain. His career ended later in the decade, when the low-budget production started to fall from the public's favor. Bob Livingston went back to the writing he gave up when he joined Universal Pictures twenty years earlier, but made an unexpected comeback of sorts acting in soft-core sex films in the mid-1970s for Independent-International. Corrigan continued as a hero in the "Range Busters" series and in other cheapie Westerns, did stunt work, and organized his ranch "Corriganville" into a profitable spread which he rented out as a movie location. His interest in science enabled him to acquire two-dozen patents for the invention of electrical equipment. Corrigan and Terhune made guest appearances together throughout the country in the 1950s. Max Terhune died in 1972, and Ray Corrigan passed on in 1976.

Hit the Saddle is one of the more ingratiating "B" Westerns made between the two World Wars. Such movies gave audiences illusions and heroes in whose light they could bask as escapist entertainment. Movies such as *Hit the Saddle* showed what could be done with a little film know-how, and gave marginally talented actors such as Bob Livingston and Ray Corrigan a chance to entertain and thrill Saturday matinee addicts everywhere.

Claire Trevor and John Wayne

CHAPTER THREE

Stagecoach

Year Released: 1939
Studio: United Artists release of a Walter Wanger Production
Producer: Walter Wanger
Director: John Ford
Screenplay: Dudley Nichols, based on the story "The Stage to Lordsburg" by Ernest Haycox
Cinematography: Bert Glennon
Music: Richard Hageman, W. Franke Harling, John Leipold, Leo Shuken, Louis Gruenberg
Art Director: Alexander Toluboff
Editors: Dorothy Spencer, Walter Reynolds
Editorial Supervisor: Otho Lovering
Assistant Director: Wingate Smith
Second Unit Director: Yakima Canutt
Set Decorator: Wiard B. Ihnen
Wardrobe: Walter Plunkett
Special Effects: Ray Binger
97 minutes

Cast:

Dallas	CLAIRE TREVOR
The Ringo Kid	JOHN WAYNE
Doc Boone	THOMAS MITCHELL
Hatfield	JOHN CARRADINE
Gatewood	BERTON CHURCHILL
Peacock	DONALD MEEK
Curly Wilcox	GEORGE BANCROFT

Buck	ANDY DEVINE
Lucy Mallory	LOUISE PLATT
Lieutenant Blanchard	TIM HOLT
Luke Plummer	TOM TYLER
Chris	CHRIS PIN MARTIN
Yakima	ELVIRA RIOS
Billy Pickett	FRANCIS FORD
Mrs. Pickett	MARGA DAIGHTON
Captain Whitney	CORNELIUS KEEFE
Billy Pickett, Jr.	KENT ODELL
Captain Sickels	WALTER McGRAIL
Indian Scout	CHIEF BIG TREE
Mrs. Gatewood	BRENDA FOWLER
Sheriff	LOUIS MASON
Mrs. Nancy Whitney	FLORENCE LAKE
Ike Plummer	JOSEPH RICKSON
Hank Plummer	VESTER PEGG
Cavalry Scout	YAKIMA CANUTT
Telegraph Operator	HARRY TENBROOK
Express Agent	PAUL McVEY
Jerry, the Bartender	JACK PENNICK
Sergeant	WILLIAM HOPPER
Captain Simmons	BRYANT WASHBURN
Housekeeper	NORA CECIL
Dancing Girls	HELEN GIBSON
	DOROTHY APPELBY
Cowboys	BUDDY ROOSEVELT
	BILL CODY
Indian Chief	CHIEF WHITE HORSE
Sheriff of Lordsburg	DUKE LEE
Lucy's Baby	MARY KATHLEEN WALKER
Saloon Keeper	ED BRADY
Editor	ROBERT HOMANS
Deputy	FRANKLYN FARNUM
Jim	JIM MASON
Ogler	MERRILL McCORMICK
Barfly	ARTIE ORTEGA

Stagecoach is one of the great Westerns. It has been called the first "adult" Western. Perhaps it was. *Stagecoach* was released at a time when Hollywood showed signs of growing up by producing a number of films with richer content than in previous years. The arrival of such intelligent film fare as *Mr. Smith Goes to Washington, Ninotchka,* and *Juarez* in 1939, in addition to John Ford's sagebrush saga, signified tinsel town's willingness to deal with mature issues such as personal and political corruption, the imperfection of law, revolution, and Communism with deep concern *and* humor. On the surface, these films and others seem more important than *Stagecoach,* a simple story of people riding across the plains. Yet the classic Western resurrected William S. Hart's "good-badman," cutting away much of the mold in favor of the humanity of the Ringo Kid, brilliantly essayed by John Wayne, and set standards of acting, directing, and theme the genre still follows. Above all, *Stagecoach* is concerned with people, not good guys versus bad guys, but real flesh and blood human beings, playing out their lives against the beautiful backdrop of Ford's natural vistas. It's about the Ringo Kid, a man framed for murder, out to avenge himself. It's about Dallas, a prostitute fleeing a town's intolerance. It's about alcoholic Doc Boone, running away from himself. It's about Gatewood, a banker, an embezzler. It's about Hatfield, a gambler masquerading as a gentleman while searching for suckers. It's about Buck, the gregarious driver, Curley Wilcox, the fair-minded lawman, Peacock, the gutsy salesman, and Lucy Mallory, the pregnant woman journeying to meet her husband.

After the six passengers, the driver, and sheriff are introduced, the journey is begun. The first indication of Ringo is an offscreen shot fired from his Winchester to stop the coach. Ford cuts from the coach to the outlaw, standing with feet apart, flipping his rifle, then tracks in rapidly until losing focus, before regaining clarity in a close-up of the kid's face.

Ringo surrenders himself to Sheriff Wilcox, "until Lordsburg," and sits on the floor of the coach at the feet of the other passengers. Wayne's first words in the role which made him a star are, "The Ringo Kid. That's what my friends call me. But my right name's Henry." The simplicity of dialogue is evident throughout. From then on Wayne speaks with economy, in that clipped intonation imitated worldwide.

The stage is set. The film undoubtedly contains a mature viewpoint quite different from the typical pre-1939 Western. Not since the days of William S. Hart could a cowboy expect to take the law into his own hands and emerge as sympathetic as Ringo. In a way, *Stagecoach* embodies cliches, then dashes them. One expects to find a prostitute as good as gold, but not the cynical yet vibrant

Claire Trevor and John Wayne

Donald Meek, John Wayne, Andy Devine, Claire Trevor, George Bancroft, Louise Platt, Tim Holt, John Carradine, Berton Churchill, Francis Ford, and Thomas Mitchell

Dallas portrayed by Claire Trevor. When Wayne tells her of his ranch across the border—"A man could live there . . . and a woman . . . will you go?" it is entirely convincing. He's relaying basic emotion, and the look in her eyes indicates she understands. Doc Boone is the typical drunken doctor alienated from the Hippocratic Oath and the community. Yet he becomes a sure-handed, witty man of courage in the person of Thomas Mitchell. The gambler Hatfield is lithe and appropriately unctuous, but John Carradine's dark, round tones and courtly manner do much to give a convincing portrayal of an alternately gallant and sinister man. His veneer of Southern charm masks his rather elitist, negative view of humanity. The banker looks honest, like a pillar of the community, rather than the thief he is. The salesman looks mousey, and only shows strength of character later. He's not afraid to spiritually embrace Dallas after the prostitute sees Lucy Mallory through childbirth. Sheriff Wilcox sticks to the letter of the law, but evokes its spirit by letting the innocent Ringo ride off with Dallas to the ranch in Mexico.

John Ford's direction is masterful, from the handling of the players to the manipulation of camera, lighting, and editing. His photography of Monument Valley (a locale he would frequently use) set cinema standards rarely matched. Scenes of the coach rumbling through the plains, swirling dust, passing sharply defined sky and clouds, rocks and crags virtually ooze atmosphere, evincing the choked, arid, yet picturesque, somehow noble settings of the West. It's a grandeur fully capable of holding legendary figures enacting mythic tales. Yet Ford's story and people are so real.

The director brings the characters together in the cramped coach. They are so close, it is hard not to reveal a personality, subtly or not. In the small, temporary dwellings, the group splits apart for meals and socializing—Ringo and Dallas in one area, Mrs. Mallory, the banker, and Hatfield in another, making it obvious they don't wish to break bread with "outcasts." Doc Boone spins in his own alcoholic world. Yet complete separation is impossible.

Ford's use of roofed sets implies a claustrophobia eminent in the film and stimulates interaction and conflict. The sunlight driving through primitive windows seems to cleanse the group as a whole when dominating the frame. It appears after the birth of the child. Dallas helps Mrs. Mallory, Doc Boone restores his confidence, and everyone wakes up to a new unification, a new world. That group strength has to be used to fight warring Indians.

The final section of *Stagecoach* reaffirms Ringo's dominance. He still seeks revenge for the murder of his father and brother.

Ignoring Dallas' warning, he goes after them in Lordsburg. Ford asserts Ringo's primacy in a low-angle shot of the outlaw diving to the ground and firing at his enemies. The outdoor scenes here are noticeably darker than normal night shots of the era (perhaps due to the poor conditions of a given point) and therefore lend a more ominous tone to the final showdown in which the Ringo Kid triumphs. In *Stagecoach,* the victory belongs to John Ford, scenarist Dudley Nichols, John Wayne, and the rest of the cast.

The Making of *Stagecoach*

It had been two years since John Ford won an Oscar and the New York Film Critics award as best director of 1935 for *The Informer,* a classic tale of revolution and betrayal. He followed with *Mary of Scotland* (RKO, 1936) and *The Hurricane* (Goldwyn, 1937), two more acclaimed productions. He also directed a fine pair of little films, *Steamboat 'Round the Bend* (Fox, 1935) and *The Prisoner of Shark Island* (Fox, 1936), the former among his personal favorites. Yet he wasn't making the kind of film he liked most. Ford hadn't directed a Western since Fox's *Three Bad Men* in 1926.

On a sunny day in 1937 while yachting off Catalina, Ford read a story in *Collier's* magazine called "The Stage to Lordsburg," by Ernest Haycox. The director became intrigued by the author's main character, an outlaw named Malpais Bill. He thought the oater had the makings of a great Western.

Ford purchased the rights to the material for $4,000, then asked co-worker and friend Dudley Nichols to fashion a script from it. The pair's most distinguished collaboration thus far had been for the award-winning *The Informer,* which also netted Nichols an Oscar for best screenplay. In creating a 123-page script for Ford, Nichols changed the title of the tale to *Stagecoach* and altered the names of the main characters. Malpais Bill became the Ringo Kid, and the prostitute Henriette was dubbed Dallas.

The director immediately faced two big problems with *Stagecoach.* First, he had to convince a studio that it wouldn't lose money financing a Western, when that genre had been primarily the property of low-budget organizations such as Republic and Monogram for the last decade. Then, it was necessary to get a mogul to commit a major star to the production, someone whose reputation wasn't made in the saddle. A Buck Jones, Bob Steele, or John Wayne couldn't be expected to fill the boots of a Gable-size role, could he?

Ford thought otherwise. He had known and liked John Wayne for ten years. The Duke had started in Hollywood as a prop boy, during his days as a student at USC. The two had become drinking and gambling buddies, but Ford hadn't directed Wayne in anything better than bit roles. He thought the time was ripe for a professional reunion.

One night Ford and Ward Bond invited themselves over to Wayne's house for poker. Throughout the years the director often mentioned productions in which he was involved, but only as conversation. Their relationship was essentially social. Ford sometimes walked right by Wayne on a studio lot.

He waited for the right time, then spoke of the project. Ford asked Wayne to read the script, and probed the actor's mind for someone to play the Ringo Kid.

Later Wayne responded with the name Lloyd Nolan. But Ford had his man. He was just testing the Duke's reactions. John Wayne had failed the first time Ford gave him a break. The director had allegedly suggested the twenty-three-year-old Marion Michael Morrison (Wayne's real name) for the starring role in a two-million-dollar Western called *The Big Trail.* The 1930 picture, lensed by Ford's friend Raoul Walsh, was less than successful. Wayne had since gained experience in approximately sixty films, mostly "B" Westerns which kept his career on a secure if mediocre plateau. Maybe the actor's reticence to ask for the role meant he was afraid of blundering, of perhaps destroying his reputation. Ford knew that wasn't the case. A mutual respect for each other's tough, courageous character had started their friendship.

They first met on the set of Ford's *Mother Macree* (Fox, 1928). Wayne gained employment as a prop man, but Ford kept him on in a tiny role. The director decided to test the student's mettle, to see if the forces which propel a personality onscreen could be marshalled in the lanky youth. They discussed football. Wayne was a guard on USC's football team. Ford scoffed, and challenged the Duke to knock him down. The guard bent into position and charged the filmmaker, sending him spiraling to the floor. Ford was impressed.

John Wayne credited the director for being responsible for lifting him out of "B" productions and into major stardom. The actor realized that without *Stagecoach,* he might have stayed in the sphere of low-budgets and seven-day shooting schedules forever.

Their friendship grew in 1930 on the set of Fox's *Men Without Women.* Ford, Wayne, the crew, and several actors were on the boat, about to shoot a diving scene. Heavy swells scared the other performers so that they refused to jump into the water. The cameras rolled and Ford was anxious. He turned to Wayne, and the budding actor dove into the torrent. Ford never forgot that.

In 1937 he really showed his appreciation by offering Wayne the role of the Ringo Kid in *Stagecoach.* As usual, the irascible director's manner was less than impeccable. After pretending to mull over Duke's mention of Lloyd Nolan for the part, he yelled that Wayne should do it.

Duke accepted. Ford had a script, a star, but no producer. Since he was under contract to David O. Selznick, the material was offered to Selznick International. The mogul liked the story and suggested a teaming of Gary Cooper and Marlene Dietrich. Ford vetoed the idea, insisting Wayne was the only man to play Ringo. After some heated negotiations, communications broke down, and Ford went to other studios.

In the summer of 1937 David Selznick expressed concern over the difficulties with Ford. The filmmaker supposedly wanted to terminate his contract due to a stipulation in small print. Selznick believed it was because the producer turned down the *Stagecoach* project. While realizing John Ford's large talents, the mogul didn't want anyone under contract who didn't want to be there, and was inclined to release Ford from any agreement in such a case.

Although Ford submitted the proposal to other studios, they all rejected it with Wayne in the lead. They had a point. Wayne had ignited few sparks in *The Big Trail* and hadn't starred in an important production since. Anyone willing to feature him in a major movie would be taking a risk. Historically, "B" actors, even enormously popular ones such as Tom Mix, Buck Jones, or Tim McCoy, rarely ventured into the area of big budgets after the silent days.

Finally, the director approached independent producer Walter Wanger. Wanger had guided a number of off-beat vehicles in past years, including *Mary Burns, Fugitive* (Paramount, 1935), a moody gangster yarn, *The Trail of the Lonesome Pine* (Paramount, 1936), the first outdoor film in total Technicolor, and *Blockade* (UA, 1938), about the controversial Spanish Civil War. The mogul was intrigued by the notion of casting top stars in a "lowly" Western elevated by dollars and first-rate talent. He too wanted Cooper for the lead.

Ford talked him out of it. Claire Trevor was signed to play the prostitute, Dallas, and Wanger made sure the Duke was supported by a solid company of character players. Other cast members included Thomas Mitchell, John Carradine, George Bancroft, Andy Devine, Donald Meek, Louise Platt, Berton Churchill, and Tim Holt. In small roles were silent film actors Franklyn Farnum and Bryant Washburn, along with stuntman Yakima Canutt, the director's brother Francis, and many others.

Wanger allotted approximately $250,000 for *Stagecoach,* little more than one-tenth of the cost of *The Big Trail* in 1930. Ford decided to shoot what was ostensibly the comeback of the Western primarily in Monument Valley, located in northeastern Arizona.

The director, his cast, and a crew of eighty-five trekked hundreds of miles to the location, which was 180 miles from the nearest railroad. Monument Valley is 4000 feet above sea level, with buttes rising from 500 to 1500 feet above the plains. The site was once the bed of the Triassic Ocean, and as such contained a large number of marine fossils, along with turquoise and dry coral. Over the years 1876-1889 stagecoaches actually traversed the area. So Ford and company were in an historic if primitive part of America.

They set up headquarters in Kayenta, Arizona. Their days were extremely hot, and the nights just as cold. Everyone had to adapt to the rugged conditions. During the ten-week shooting schedule, star Wayne didn't exactly learn how the better half lived in "A" productions. He shared a snake cabin with Yakima Canutt on Harry Goulding's Trading Post. But modern conveniences weren't on Duke's mind as he paced the floor nightly rehearsing his lines and movements.

Ford could be a brutal taskmaster. Yet his anger had a motivation. It went back to 1928 when he cursed young Marion Morrison and dared the young man to knock him down. The director knew his star was at times unsure of his ability, that taking the lead in a production filled with experienced performers made him nervous. Wayne's emotions had to be gathered and shaken free from self-consciousness. The way was to yell and curse at him. And that Jack Ford did.

By the end of a typical day, Wayne would be emotionally drained, and sometimes livid, although eventually he caught on to the director's tactics. Ford even allowed Wayne to perform some of his own stunts, in order to let him feel the courage of the Ringo Kid.

Legend has it that John Ford could be an evil man. He was sometimes accused of being egocentric, selfish, and insensitive. There are several theories regarding the filmmaker's treatment of his upcoming star during the making of *Stagecoach.* One notion has it that Ford liked to see Wayne in the throes of anxiety. The actor had a different idea. It was based on the premise that Wayne already worried about performing with the likes of a Thomas Mitchell or a Claire Trevor. The "B" movie actor's background bothered him. But it apparently didn't affect anyone else. Ford made Duke concentrate on the here and now rather than on who was an established, respected star, and who was a newcomer. The latter proposal seems more accurate. In most cases, lifelong friendships aren't maintained by one friend psychologically torturing another.

Heated discussions on location weren't limited to Ford and Wayne. The director had to keep a solid relationship with other cast members as well. Berating Wayne publicly assured the more experienced co-stars that his casting wasn't merely an act of friendship,

John Wayne

that Duke was going to work like everyone else. With the feelings of the supporting players soothed, Ford had to contend with irate Navajos who rebelled at the inclusion of Apaches in the battle scenes. The tribes had been fighting each other since the last century, and weren't about to merge for an attack on the white man, fake or otherwise. Since the Apaches were needed to outline the typical features of fellow tribesman Geronimo and his warriors, they couldn't be dismissed. Battling Jack Ford solved the problem by upping the Navajos' wages.

Three hundred Indians, mostly Navajos from the Arizona reservation, were employed to attack the stagecoach, an original model used to make the run through Monument Valley in the last part of the 19th century. The staging of the raids was furious, both on film and in reality. With the Indian hordes attacking, raising mountains of dust, the old coach probably received rougher treatment than in the old days. The horses pulling the passengers to safety often attained speeds of up to 46 miles per hour. A grand total of fourteen spectacular horse falls added excitement to the charge, but the Indian army seemed to multiply, not dwindle. The flat plains of Monument Valley were so uncluttered by rock formations at some points, the speeding stagecoach could be seen from distances of 40 miles away.

While representatives of the ASPCA made sure the horses weren't treated with undue cruelty, director Ford kept an eye on the development of John Wayne. Except for the star's ego, nothing else took a serious bruising. As the director later put it, "The only creature that got hurt making our picture was a press agent who got in the way of a posse. Fortunately, there's no society for the prevention of cruelty to press agents."

After the third week of shooting, Ford changed his manner with the progressing Duke. He surprised the cowboy actor with invitations to view the day's rushes, and often complimented him on a fine performance. Continuing to let Wayne get the feel of the important role, Ford allowed him to practice firing real bullets, then substituted blanks during filming.

Producer Walter Wanger kept himself informed on the progress of *Stagecoach,* and became very unhappy when told that the star was doing his own stunts. One day Wanger journeyed to Arizona to visit the set. He saw Wayne on top of a roof about to take life, limb, and the production schedule in his hands. Wanger objected rather loudly, but Ford just smiled when Wayne looked to him for guidance. The man on the roof repeated what his director taught him.

"I'm not an actor. I don't act. I react." He added, "I'm just a stuntman." (He had been a stuntman.)

The lesson was learned and has provided the framework for Wayne's success to this day. He discovered the secret of rendering believable screen portrayals, for him, was to listen to the other actors, to let the words and actions of fellow performers serve as guidelines.

Before filming ended, the cast and crew of *Stagecoach* moved from Monument Valley to Kernville, Victorville, and Oceanside, Arizona, to Chatsworth and Calabassas, California, and then returned to Hollywood. Art director Alexander Toluboff reproduced the Central Station of Lordsburg, and Ford ordered that all interior scenes be shot on sets with ceilings.

Although the shooting stretched to ten weeks, it took an additional three months to edit and score *Stagecoach.* Since the film was lensed largely on the natural ground of Monument Valley, and Toluboff's sets designed with a kitchen-sink realism, it was obvious that the music for *Stagecoach* would have to be true to the 1880s. Musical director Boris Morros chose thirteen old American songs which fit the pattern. The tunes were of a wide variety, encompassing most of the simple types of the time. The love songs included, "Lily Dale" and "Rosa Lee," the ballads "Joe Bowers" and "Joe the Wrangler," and the saloon sob-ballads "She's More to Be Pitied Than Censured" and "She May Have Seen Better Days," along with the blues number "Careless Love," the hymn "Shall We Gather at the River?" and others.

Stagecoach reportedly cost $250,000 to produce, a modest figure at the time.* "In Hollywood, that's considered the price of a good cigar," director Ford quipped to the press.

He was more serious in most other public discussions. In describing his favorite type of story, the feisty Irishman said, "Westerns are typically American. People like them. American audiences like to get out of doors and see scenery."

Stagecoach contains an abundance of plains, mountains, and sky. More significantly, it follows the director's idea of a memorable film. Writing in the *New York Times* in 1928, he declared, "The pictures that people remember for years are not the spectacularly sensational films, but the heart-interest stories of plain people interpreting vital emotions."

New York Times film critic Bosley Crowther wrote about *Stagecoach* before its release. "It will be a fast-action picture, with an unusual economy of dialogue."

Ford and scenarist Dudley Nichols did much to promote that image. They did so in a conversation printed in the *New York Post.*

"We're particularly attached to this one," said Ford, "because it violates all the censorial canons."

"The leading woman is a prostitute," Nichols added.

"There's a banker who robs his own bank," Ford commented.

The pair elaborated on the merits of *Stagecoach* all over the nation.

*It has been thought that more than $500,000 was needed to complete the picture.

"It's a simple, intimate little thing," described Ford. "It isn't even colossal in a small way. It's completely devoid of what the reviewers call 'great directorial touches.' "

"You needn't look for any great writing, either," Nichols advised. "I wrote the plainest kind of dialogue—just the way those guys and gals talk without those sudden inexplicable flights of poetry in conversation."

John Ford

Walter Wanger was also naturally eager to publicize his new production. Although the producer followed Ford's lead on important matters of the project, he began making sounds as if *he* were the boy wonder of *Stagecoach.* However, the following remarks uphold the notion that John Wayne wasn't just another Hollywood pretty boy, which was a theme of the publicity.

"The leading man is not some matinee idol who is already too familiar on the nation's screens, but John Wayne, whom I recruited from Westerns and 'program pictures.' . . . There is, as a matter of fact, not one established star in the cast."

Ford became enraged at Wanger's progressively larger claims regarding responsibility for *Stagecoach.* The conflict erupted soon after the film's premiere at the Fox Westwood Theater in Los Angeles, on February 2, 1939. That night all concerned had to temporarily patch their differences. Wayne invited a number of his old bosses who produced the "B" Westerns to see how a big-budget oater fared. Most of the Duke's guests—Sol Siegel of Republic among them—were unimpressed with *Stagecoach.* Just about everyone else who saw the film reacted favorably. The following is a sample of the reviews.

Cue:

A gripping drama, superbly told, embellished by excellent writing, with splendid performance and direction.

Daily Worker, Howard Rushmore:

You'll comb the Hollywood hills many a day to find a more brilliant team than Walter Wanger and John Ford. . . . Ford has done wonders with the material in the script.

New York Daily News, Kate Cameron, three and one-half stars:

The picture is beautifully photographed and every part admirably acted. . . . John Wayne is so good in the role of the outlaw that one wonders why he had had to wait all this time since *The Big Trail* for such another opportunity.

New York Journal-American, Rose Pelswick:

A super-Western, *Stagecoach* is a great entertainment, a thriller of American frontier that's packed with bang-up scenes of riding, shooting, and fighting with blood-curdling Indian raids and with the U.S. Cavalry coming to the rescue when there's not a moment to spare. . . . Each of the players contributes excellent work, outstanding, however, being Mr. Mitchell who makes the drunken doctor one of the most genuinely likable screen characters in months.

Variety:

Sweeping and powerful drama of the American frontier, *Stagecoach* displays potentialities that can easily drive it through as one of the surprise big grossers of the year.

Ironically, with its uniformly excellent notices, *Stagecoach* created a gulf-like rift between Wanger and Ford. The director threatened to sue the mogul and Lynn Farnol, his advertising and publicity director, for false claims. Wanger ended the friction by admitting publicly that John Ford was the prime force behind *Stagecoach.* He addressed a letter to Farnol, which was reprinted in the film's souvenir brochures.

Dear Lynn:

I think the book on *Stagecoach* is interesting and attractive. It fails, however, to indicate the full measure of credit that is due John Ford for his part in the making of the picture.

I read the story—but after Ford had purchased it and brought it to me. Again, it was Ford who worked with Dudley Nichols creating a fine script, and John Wayne as the Ringo Kid was also Ford's idea.

While I am proud to be the producer of *Stagecoach,* will you please do everything in your power to see that the picture is known as John Ford's achievement.

Sincerely,
Walter Wanger (signed)

Posters advertised *Stagecoach* as "A Powerful Story of 9 Strange People!" The credits read as follows: "A Walter Wanger Production—Directed by John Ford—With Claire Trevor, John Wayne, (in smaller print) Andy Devine, John Carradine, Thomas Mitchell, Louise Platt, George Bancroft, Donald Meek, Berton Churchill, Tim Holt."

Note the placement of Claire Trevor's name before Wayne's. It indicated her status as a rising star, whose credits included *Dead End* (Goldwyn, 1937) and *The Amazing Dr. Clitterhouse* (Warner Bros., 1938). Wayne, of course, had only the string of second features behind him. The other credit arrangement which stands out is the positioning of Andy Devine before Thomas Mitchell. Prior to *Stagecoach,* Mitchell had large roles in such significant films as *Theodora Goes Wild* (UA, 1936), *Lost Horizon* (Columbia, 1937), and *The Hurricane* (Goldwyn, 1937). Conversely, Devine was only a minor actor in many productions.

Soon Hollywood took notice of everyone connected with *Stagecoach.* Ford and Nichols continued already successful careers and collaborated together with Wayne and Wanger on *The Long Voyage Home* (UA, 1940). Republic had a number of John Wayne Westerns still unreleased at the time *Stagecoach* was acclaimed and wasted little time in exploiting the new star's reputation by distributing *The Night Riders, Three Texas Steers, Wyoming Outlaw,* and *The New Frontier* in rapid order. Of course, Wayne went on to become one of the biggest stars in screen history. His image as a Western hero was consolidated in Ford's great cavalry trilogy, *Fort Apache* (RKO, 1948), *She Wore a Yellow Ribbon* (RKO, 1949), and *Rio Grande* (Republic, 1950), as well as in Ford's *Three Godfathers* (MGM, 1948), Hawks' *Rio Bravo* (Warner Bros., 1959) and *El Dorado* (Paramount, 1967), and numerous others. But he would also play a Swedish seaman in *The Long Voyage Home,* a disturbed sea captain in *Wake of the Red Witch* (Republic, 1948), a crotchety ex-lawman in *True Grit* (Paramount, 1969), and other offbeat roles. Claire Trevor, who trained at New York City's American Academy of Dramatic Arts, received a number of offers to star in Broadway plays. John Carradine won solid parts in *The Grapes of Wrath* (20th, 1940) and *Brigham Young* (20th, 1940). Thomas Mitchell's credits immediately following his colorful portrayal of Doc Boone are most impressive: *Mr. Smith Goes to Washington* (Columbia, 1939), *The Hunchback of Notre Dame* (RKO, 1939), *Our Town* (US, 1940), *The Long Voyage Home.*

In a year when *Gone with the Wind* swept the Academy Awards, *Stagecoach* came away with a supporting Oscar for Thomas Mitchell (who also appeared that year in *Gone with the Wind*), and shared the Oscar for Best Score (Richard Hageman, Frank Harling, John Leipold, Leo Shuken, Louis Gruenberg) with *The Wizard of Oz.* And Ford won the New York Film Critics Award as Best Director for the second time.

After World War II *Stagecoach* was reissued on a double bill with *The Long Voyage Home.* The publicity for the Western differed considerably from the original blurbs. "LAST FRONTIER OF WICKEDNESS! . . . Women! Their Souls Stripped Bare! In a West corrupted by violence and gun-fire!" "LOVE in a hail of bullets—PASSION in a blaze of VIOLENCE!" Certainly all those elements are to some extent present in *Stagecoach,* but it is the way such things are subtly presented which makes the film as vital today as in 1939.

Ironically, if John Wayne hadn't come to the rescue, *Stagecoach* might have become just another lost classic. The first negative of the film was chopped to bits by independent distributors for use as trailers, then completely lost due to nitrate decomposition. In 1970, the Duke loaned his personal print of the Western to the American Film Institute, to be copied for its Library.

Despite the kudos, it took years for *Stagecoach* to be truly recognized as a classic in America, a status not diminished by the inferior remake of the movie by Fox in 1966, with Alex Cord and Ann-Margret in the Wayne and Trevor roles, which will probably be remembered only as the last theatrical feature made by Bing Crosby (in Thomas Mitchell's original part). Perhaps Claire Trevor made the most telling remark on the subject. "Yes, the critics liked it and so did the public, but I don't think the public ever dug the film for its true value."

Henry Fonda

Tyrone Power and Nancy Kelly

CHAPTER FOUR

Jesse James

Year Released: 1939
Studio: Twentieth Century-Fox
Producer: Nunnally Johnson
Director: Henry King
Screenplay: Nunnally Johnson
Cinematography: W. Howard Greene, George Barnes
Music: Louis Silvers
Art Director: William Darling, George Dudley
Editor: Barbara McLean
Assistant Directors: Robert Webb, Otto Brower
Production Manager: Sidney Bowen
Property Master: Joseph Behm
Color, 105 minutes

Cast:

Jesse James	TYRONE POWER
Frank James	HENRY FONDA
Zee	NANCY KELLY
Will Wright	RANDOLPH SCOTT
Major Cobb	HENRY HULL
Barshee	BRIAN DONLEVY
Bob Ford	JOHN CARRADINE
Mrs. James	JANE DARWELL
McCoy	DONALD MEEK
Jailer	SLIM SUMMERVILLE
George Runyon	J. EDWARD BROMBERG

Doctor	CHARLES MIDDLETON
Farmer's Boy	GEORGE BREAKSTON
Outlaw	LON CHANEY, JR.
Jesse James, Jr.	JOHN RUSSELL
Roy	GEORGE CHANDLER
Charles Ford	CHARLES TANNEN
Mrs. Ford	CLAIRE DU BREY
Lynch	WILLARD ROBERTSON
Bill	HAROLD GOODWIN
Preacher	SPENCER CHARTERS
Pinky	ERNEST WHITMAN
Deputy	EDDY WALLER
Hank	PAUL BURNS
Tom	ARTHUR AYLESWORTH
Heywood	CHARLES HALTON
Farmer	HARRY TYLER
Farmer's Wife	VIRGINIA BRISSE
Judge Rankin	EDWARD LE SAINT
Old Marshal	ERVILLE ALDERSON
Judge Mathews	JOHN ELLIOTT
Cavalry Officer	JAMES FLAVIN
Boy	LEONARD KIBRICK
Tiller	GEORGE O'HARA
Infantry Captain	DON DOUGLAS
Barshee's Cohorts	WYLIE GRANT
	ETHAN LAIDLAW

Nineteenth-century folk ballads reflect the mythology surrounding bank robber Jesse James with which America has grown up. He was forced to do it, any child or adult will likely respond if asked why Jesse, with his brother Frank, took to a life of crime. And Bob Ford was a snivelling coward who shot his own kin in the back for the reward money.

Jesse James echoes these sentiments. Like its Western neighbor *Stagecoach,* it was released in 1939, a year which featured a decided upswing in the sophistication of Hollywood films. For all its now cliched elements, *Stagecoach* is a Western with real people—people with real problems—who band together in times of crisis. Not since the oaters of William S. Hart had the genre benefited from such a realistic outlook. The makers of *Jesse James* utilized the more liberal attitude of Hollywood. Corruption in business and government had been a key topic in American productions since the gangster cycle began with *Little Caesar* in 1930. Films with social awareness cropped up in every type of production from topical drama to comedy to swashbuckler to Western.

While *Jesse James* certainly wasn't the first film in the sound era to deal with a legendary criminal in an exceedingly pure light (Wellman's *Robin Hood of El Dorado* in 1936, for one, whitewashed the exploits of bandit Joaquin Murietta), it is certainly one of the best. *Jesse James* leisurely unfolds the story of the James brothers as they return home from the Civil War, and accept Union pardons for riding with the notorious Quantrill Raiders. The brothers try to settle down to a peaceful life on the farm, but are disrupted by big business in the form of the railroad that needs the James property. When they refuse to sell their land to corrupt officials at an unfair price, as all their neighbors are forced to, the boys are swindled out of their spread. Their mother is killed in a battle with railroad men, and Jesse and Frank turn to banditry.

Jesse James begins as a rip-roaring adventure, but winds down to show two brothers whose past simply will not let them lead quiet lives.

In the meantime, director Henry King's talent for making films which reflect the essence of rural American life flourishes beautifully. From *Tol'able David* in 1921 through *State Fair* in 1933, *Jesse James,* and onto *I'd Climb the Highest Mountain* in 1951, and beyond, King illustrates the everyday existence of the average American. Such a depiction necessarily slows down his narratives, and in *Jesse James,* this makes for an expansive yet detailed telling of the life and legend of the James boys. The working of the farms, the plotting of the land-grabbing railroad agents, and the unification of the community behind the bandits is illustrated with precision and attention to minute elements.

King's use of the then new three-color process gives the Western a rich look which might have been absent if black and white stock had been substituted. The greens and browns of the rolling hills, the light wheatfields, and the solid, natural feel of the town are eye-filling, and lend importance to the environment in which the story takes place.

Not that *Jesse James* doesn't have its share of spectacular stunts. As Clive Denton notes in his chapter on Henry King in *The Hollywood Professionals: Volume 2* (Tantivy/Barnes), the Western employs horses as an integral part of the bombastic physical actions of Jesse and Frank. At one point, a mounted Jesse crashes through a plate glass window in town during an escape. As Jesse rides over the bumpy terrain, he and his horse take a sudden diving leap off a cliff. That was one of the most exciting stunts executed in Hollywood up to that time.

Yet nothing takes away from the performances of Tyrone Power as Jesse and Henry Fonda as Frank. The pair complement each other well, with Power the symbol of industrial oppression who lashes out at his tormenters, and Fonda portraying the simple farm boy caught up in a web not exactly of his making, but one which he comes to comprehend too well. Power is the stuff of idols, Fonda the down-to-earth performer whose work provides a more rewarding viewing experience with each passing year.

Tyrone and Henry, or Jesse and Frank, are just two good ol' country boys who cross the law, but can never muster the aggressive violence of other outlaws. They rob banks as casually as if making a deposit or legal withdrawal from an account which is years old. When the jealous, beady-eyed, sweaty-palmed Robert Ford shoots Jesse in the back, he murders a simple family man named Mr. Howard, collects the reward, and is vilified for his deed.

At the end of *Jesse James,* Major Cobb unveils a statue of the outlaw in the center of town. He says of the bandit, "His times produced him." And 1939 produced *Jesse James,* a mature Western with a social conscience.

The Making of *Jesse James*

Henry King signed a long-term contract with Fox Studios in 1930, after fifteen years as a distinguished director of such films as *Tol'able David* (First National, 1921), *The White Sister* (Metro, 1924), and *Stella Dallas* (Goldwyn, 1925). He proceeded to helm eleven productions at Fox through 1935, honing his talent for evoking American culture in such easygoing pictures as *Lightnin'* (1930) and *State Fair* (1933).

In 1935 former Warner Brothers executive Darryl F. Zanuck merged his own Twentieth Century Productions (founded in 1933) with Fox and took over as Vice President in Charge of Production at the new Twentieth Century-Fox. Believing it was the era of the fast-action movie, whether crime melodrama, comedy, or romantic yarn, Zanuck decided that Fox would issue a product which had all the zip of the Warner productions being shot in another part of town. And there would be no more cinema tales of country bumpkins of rural life without this added ingredient. The legendary *Variety* headline, "Stix Nix Hix Pix," served as a warning to the freshly incorporated studio.

Henry King was one of the first directors signed by the recently created organization and for the next few years he made stories often set in that placid atmosphere of earlier Fox properties. But there was a large dose of the always appealing comedy in *The Country Doctor* (1936), and the tearful romance of *Ramona* (also 1936) was a built-in audience grabber. From there, director King switched to historical vehicles. He guided Tyrone Power, one of the studio's most highly touted fresh personalities, in *Lloyds of London* (1936), revolving around the development of the famous insurance company, *Alexander's Ragtime Band* (1938), depicting the creation of the title ensemble, and *In Old Chicago* (1938), telling of the city's tragic 1871 fire. (King and Power ultimately made eleven films together.)

In spite of his knack for depicting rural American life, Henry King hadn't directed a Western in almost twenty years. That genre was in need of an alternative treatment beyond the escapist fare being cranked out by low-budget studios such as Republic and Monogram.

Like King, screenwriter Nunnally Johnson was interested in the legendary outlaw Jesse James. As a boy in Florida, Johnson had dreamt of the day when he would write about the colorful 19th-century bandit. So far his most distinguished credits were his scripts for historical spectacles, *House of Rothschild* (Fox, 1934) and *Cardinal Richelieu* (Fox, 1935). He decided to put his desire of decades into action. He spoke with Darryl F. Zanuck about the notion, then travelled through Missouri, the James boys' home state, in search of the truth. A series of half-century-old editorials in a Sedalia newspaper called *The Gazette* gave the writer the concept he'd been searching for. Then and there Nunnally Johnson decided to treat Jesse and Frank as men who were virtually forced outside the law by unscrupulous railroad officials and corrupt lawmen.

Zanuck approved of Johnson's approach, and assigned Frances Richardson and a team of researchers including Rosalind Shaffer and later Jo Francis James (Jesse's granddaughter) to do an in-depth job of assembling a chronicle of the life and times of Jesse Woodson James.

After hearing about the novel approach to the legend, Henry King developed a strong interest in directing the property. Two years of research went into *Jesse James.* Both Johnson (who also produced the biopic) and King contributed to the large accumulation of material. While Johnson stayed in Hollywood to pen the screenplay, the director decided to do some legwork of his own. King recently told me, "I was just as enthusiastic about this script as Mr. Johnson was. We found that he had told a different story than what had been previously told by others. To confirm many of his ideas, I flew to Kansas City and drove out to Carney, Missouri, to the James farm, where I met the son of Frank James—a retired attorney from Kansas City. We sat near the Jesse James gravestone in the backyard where he was buried. He gave me many inside ideas and happenings of the James family. All these I conveyed to Mr. Johnson."

Twentieth Century-Fox announced in July 1938 that it would produce a Technicolor version of the life of Jesse James. The film would correspond to a number of divergent ideas about the cinema. Zanuck wanted action, and he would get it with the numerous gunfights, romantic interludes, bank robberies, and daring escapes. At the same time, Henry King would lens a panoramic view of the post-Civil War West. He could pick out and show artifacts of their existence, the daily life, the things which made them part of American culture. And Nunnally Johnson would get a little closer to a figure he'd been thinking about for years.

Tyrone Power quickly signed for the title role and Henry Fonda was given the part of Frank. The studio borrowed Walter Brennan from Samuel Goldwyn for the role of Major Cobb, but he was replaced by Henry Hull. Fox starlet Nancy Kelly was added to the cast as Power's love interest Zee, along with studio players Randolph Scott, Brian Donlevy, Donald Meek, J. Edward Bromberg, and Slim Summerville. Fonda reportedly had some reservations about accepting the part and sought counsel from, among others, director Henry Hathaway, who urged him to take the role.

Since *Jesse James* was to be a lavish, realistic Technicolor spectacle, it had to be shot on location. "I had learned of a town in Missouri, called Pineville, that had dirt streets, a red brick courthouse, board sidewalks, and was still much the same period as Carney during the time of Jesse James," director King remembered. "I went to Florida and put in a session of preparing the script for production, making no structural changes, but only preparing for the transition from paper to film. From there I met my assistant at Pineville, Missouri, [and] selected all the locations. . . ."

While searching for the proper sites, the director and his assistant heard from many area residents firsthand stories and legends about Jesse which still persist. In the Ozarks, the filmmaking pair reportedly stopped at a cabin to ask a mountaineer if there was a clear patch of land with a stream running through it in the vicinity. There must have been a communication breakdown, for when King told the mountain man why they needed such a spot, the resident supposedly replied, "Mean to say you fellers don't know Jesse's been shot?"

Whether the response was sincere, a joke, or figment of a publicist's imagination, it did reflect the communal atmosphere of the

Tyrone Power and Nancy Kelly

Tyrone Power and Henry Fonda

Ozarks, a land where an outlaw could be called by his first name, as almost one of the family, even though many admitted James was not the hero mythmakers have created. Yet most understood that there were extenuating circumstances surrounding Jesse's conversion to banditry.

With the cast and crew assembled, and locations set, King flew his own plane 1700 miles from Hollywood to Pineville, two days ahead of everyone else. Nine railroad cars were needed to move the equipment, production personnel, and two hundred actors to the town in southwest Missouri. They arrived at the local train stop of Noel to receive the greetings of the entire town who welcomed them, cheering as stars Power and Fonda waved from high atop a platform built for the purpose. Banners, with such greetings as "Hi Ty," blew in the warm Missouri breeze. Many cast members stayed in nearby Pineville and happily participated in the rounds of publicity functions created by Fox, as well as some of Pineville's own gatherings. The crew stayed in Noel, population 461 before the influx of moviemakers and curious tourists. Area residents generously opened their homes to the people from Hollywood.

And Hollywood gave them a good show, even before a foot of film was shot! King asked property master Joseph Behm and a number of others to accompany him on some pre-dawn preproduction work. Even at that early hour there were hundreds of onlookers watching the crew's every move. The director was determined to entertain his audience as well as get the job done.

Joe Behm recalled that morning for me. "I never had so many visitors in my life. There were hundreds. Bob (assistant director Robert Webb) had rehearsed the scene. Now we were waiting for the Great Messiah (King). He arrived an hour late. . . ."

"Who are these men, Bob?" he asked his assistant.

"They're doubles for Ty and Hank," Webb responded.

"Get me the wardrobe man," King ordered.

The gentleman arrived quickly. "Can I help you, Mr. King?"

"No, you can help yourself by doing what I told you. They [the actors] look like they just came from Western costume. Who approved this wardrobe?'

"You did, Mr. King."

The director considered the outfits. "Mmmm, not as bad as I thought." He then studied the horses to be used. King wanted to see head wrangler Sid Jorden. "What glue factory did you rescue these nags from?" bellowed the filmmaker.

"I brought them from Hollywood," answered Jorden.

"You what? Do you mean to stand there and tell me you brought these nags from Hollywood? Look at the company's money you've squandered bringing these horses here! My God, man.

Don't you realize you're in the great state of Missouri? They breed the finest horse flesh in the world here." The director examined the saddle bags on the mounts. "What are these?"

"They're saddle bags, sir."

King couldn't believe it. "I'm making a picture of that famous Robin Hood of Missouri, not a Laurel and Hardy comedy." Someone handed King a cup of coffee. "I'm here to work, not drink that slop," he shouted and flung the cup to the ground. "Bob, let's get this show on the road."

It must be remembered that Henry King began in Hollywood as an actor and was well aware of how to stimulate an audience. But as a director he could also get the job done. It was the way he did it for a crowd that made working with him a memorable experience, among other things. "The larger the crowd, the meaner he'll get," Joe Behm recalled.

For Henry King had standards. His work vibrates with the color of small details, so he necessarily paid strict attention to little things during pre-production. Before arriving in Missouri, he checked out some props in Hollywood.

As Joe Behm remembered, "He came to the prop room, to see the props I'd selected. He viewed them like General Patton viewing his troops. He picked up a saddle bag. 'What's this?' 'It's a saddle bag, sir.' 'Glad you told me, I never would have guessed it. The grain in the leather is not coarse enough, [and is] running the wrong way.' He picked up the holster with two .45 revolvers. 'Where are you going to use these?' 'They're for *Jesse James,* Mr. King.' 'You're not going to use them in my picture if I have anything to say about it, and I assure you, I do. Don't you ever do any research? These are .45 Colts. Jesse James used Smith and Wessons.' I pulled out a picture of the outlaw and pointed out that Jesse was carrying Colts. King yanked the item out of my hands and glared at it. 'That's not a photograph, that's an artist's conception of Jesse. Looks to me like you did your research at the Fox Hills bar.' "

Despite the tough talk, King and Behm are friends to this day and play golf together.

Henry King reminisced about the making of *Jesse James.* "I received full cooperation from all the residents of Pineville—in fact, all of McDonald County, of which Pineville is the county seat. The weather was warm but not uncomfortable. Making a motion picture in Pineville became quite a curiosity to other states to the degree that the railroad and bus lines ran excursions to Noel, Missouri, the nearest railroad station to Pineville. The average number of spectators each day would exceed 3,000."

Before shooting started, the crew had to do some refurbishing to push Pineville back into the 19th century. Any paved streets were covered with six inches of dirt. Wood awnings were erected over the sidewalk, and several improper modern artifacts were removed or covered up. As if to make the heroic tales of Jesse James fresh in the minds of area residents, Fox stepped into the outlaw's savior role and leased the home and lands of Mrs. Florence Crowder as a set. With the generous rental fee, Mrs. Crowder and her children could afford to pay off the mortgage on her property.

Throughout the production of *Jesse James,* Fox was besieged by people offering technical advice for the film. Two men claimed they rode with Jesse James, another insisted he was the farmer who buried the outlaw, and many reputed neighbors of the legendary outlaw wrote reams of stories about the subject.

Director King wasn't untouched by a myriad of "experts" on James. One man actually claimed to be the bank robber. "As a matter of fact, he bore a striking resemblance to the famous outlaw," King said at the time. "And he was familiar with every detail of James' life. He said that Bob Ford hadn't killed him at all, that he escaped. Later he claimed to have found Ford and killed him." Soon after, it was discovered this "Jesse," who would have been close to ninety in 1938, was actually a local resident. "But he sure scared me for a minute," the filmmaker admitted. "It would be embarrassing no end to find after making *Jesse James* that the outlaw himself was sitting in the balcony watching it!"

The cast and crew adapted well to their circumstances, with the help of friendly townspeople and local businessmen, who enjoyed a boon due to the thousands of tourists who travelled from miles around to watch the production. But, of course, there was no film laboratory in the area, especially one equipped to handle the new Technicolor stock being used to photograph the Western. A messenger was dispatched to Nesho, Missouri, at regular intervals. From there a chartered plane took the undeveloped stock to Kansas City, where it was rushed to Hollywood by Air Express. And not wanting to be completely isolated from the production, Zanuck had a teletype installed between Hollywood and Pineville.

Although Henry Fonda's mid-Western drawl was perfect for the role of Frank James, Tyrone Power had to alter his stage-trained speech to accommodate the accent of his character. Power felt that playing a person who really lived helps an actor bring added sincerity to the role, and was happy to enhance the believability of his performance with a different inflection.

Helping Power to get into character were a number of actual possessions of Jesse James. Aided by James' granddaughter Jo Frances, who served as technical advisor, Henry King obtained the boots Jesse died in. He also found the gun Robert Ford used to shoot the outlaw in the back—a Winchester percussion cap firearm,

Tyrone Power

loaned by the Ford family, who at the time were living quietly in St. Joseph, Missouri.

The director insisted on using only area natives who looked the part as extras. Among many were Jo Frances James, who worked in the escrow department of the Bank of America in Los Angeles, and lived with her sixty-two-year-old father, Jesse James II. A distant cousin of the James boys, Harold Goodwin, was also in several crowd scenes. Fortunately the wardrobe and prop departments were able to outfit the extras, chosen from the thousands who applied, because many either still owned or wore appropriate garb like that donned by their grandparents. A minimum of crape hair was needed for beards, as a crop of elders from the Ozarks had been growing their own for years.

While locals came by bus, car, train, or foot to the scene of *Jesse James,* actress Claire Du Brey did quite a lot more for a small part in the film. She flew almost 2000 miles to the set from Hollywood one morning, acted a segment with John Carradine, drove to Kansas City, then flew back to tinsel town that night. Fortunately the actress wasn't called back for retakes!

Claire Du Brey emerged from Pineville unscathed, but the performers who spent the entire six weeks on location couldn't say the same thing. There were numerous small accidents during the production, nothing to cause interminable delays but nuisances just the same. The most harrowing experience suffered during the shooting may have involved Brian Donlevy, who plays Barshee, the villainous railroad agent. After the land is obtained from the farmers, Barshee rides into the small town of Sedalia in a horse-drawn buggy like a conquering warrior surveying his territory. While director King was shooting a large scene, with thousands of onlookers, the horses pulling the actor became nervous. Even a quiet crowd can be an annoying presence and the noise of a marching band unnerved the animals. Suddenly the creatures bolted, knocked down a trumpet player, and galloped at the hordes of extras. People scattered everywhere. Serious injuries were miraculously avoided when quick thinking Donlevy grabbed the reins and gave them several strong yanks. The horses calmed down and order was restored. From this point on, screen villain Donlevy was a hero to the people of Pineville, and he couldn't walk down the street without being besieged by autograph seekers. Later the actor learned the white sailor cap he wore constantly could be spotted and identified from blocks away. So Brian Donlevy discarded the head gear and became as anonymous as star Henry Fonda was when the cinema's Frank James walked around town.

Other accidents occurred. It seemed something happened to just about every major cast member. When not on the set, Nancy Kelly often practiced riding a horse sidesaddle. On one occasion a stirrup broke and she was thrown into a barbed wire fence. Her dress and two petticoats were torn to pieces by the sharp wire, but the clothing was heavy enough to prevent the actress from sustaining any major cuts or bruises. With a little iodine from the company doctor, she made a quick recovery. Luckily experienced wardrobe people had learned long ago to bring at least two of every costume on location.

Next was Tyrone Power's turn. He received a gash on the foot by stepping on broken glass while surfing on the Elk River.

Lon Chaney, Jr., sprained his ankle in a fall. Then the next day as King was filming a scene the cinch snapped on the saddle of the horse Chaney was riding and the actor fell to the ground, unconscious. The husky Chaney was heard to crack after the second incident, "With my luck, I'll probably break my leg tomorrow." He didn't, but director King probably made him wish he had.

Apparently some of the cast and crew did a little too much celebrating at the end of certain days' shooting to suit the filmmaker. He let it all out on Chaney. "Where did you learn to ride? At a bar on Hollywood and Vine! If you'd stay out of Shadow Lake at night and not get loaded on that rot gut whisky you'd be a lot better off. I'm going to put everyone on curfew. Shadow Lake closes at nine o'clock from now on. Get his horse ready; we'll try it again."

Chaney made a fatal mistake. "I'm through for the day, Mr. King. [I] can't mount a horse," Joe Behm remembered him saying.

"You're through in the picture as far as I'm concerned," declared King. "Send him home, Bob!"

That night some of the company was having a drink at Shadow Lake. Came nine o'clock and the lights started blinking on and off. Time to retire. It turned out that the director let people stay up as long as they wanted unless it affected their work. Poor Chaney was King's example. But the point was made.

Despite the accidents, there was at least one man who made life better for all concerned. Henry Fonda was, according to Joseph Behm, "just one of the boys." He had fun with the crew. "He'd come on the set in the morning, 'What are we shooting today, boys?,' look the scene over for a minute, then say 'Let's get the show on the road.' " Fonda's easygoing, thoroughly professional manner was a help off the set as well. The weather was characteristically hot during the summer of 1938 in Missouri, and Fonda managed to rig up a makeshift air conditioner to cool things off. He gathered an electric fan and a quantity of dry ice and made it work. The gallant Fonda also found time to fix Nancy Kelly's camera (even the stars sometimes like to take pictures on location!) and aided studio electricians. Yet even Fonda couldn't avoid physical difficulties. He accidentally shot himself in the leg with a pistol. The blank cartridge left severe powder burns on his flesh. The actor was rushed to a Kansas City hospital where anti-tetanus treatment was administered.

Except for the various minor accidents, the six weeks of location shooting proceeded relatively undisturbed by the enormous crowds which gathered to watch the action. This was accomplished due to the cooperation of the townspeople of Pineville, helped by a tough security man hired by King who lived in the area. Nevertheless, there were a few incidents. In one scene featuring the James boys' getaway following a bank robbery, they toss some of the stolen loot in the air to distract the posse. In order to add realism to the moment, the director instructed that certain bills be marked as worth a dollar each. The first time King shot the action dozens of extras trampled the ground in search of the prized bills. Realizing he couldn't get the scene shot with so many interested parties, King closed the set and the shooting progressed.

"I don't blame them. I almost jumped in there myself," King said later.

Another time the locals presented the problem of quantity over quality. The director recalled for me a day in which he must have felt he was guiding a cast of thousands. "On Labor Day I did encounter some difficulty, attempting to make a scene with the camera on the top of the new railroad train on its maiden trip. There were 1,000 people swarming over the hills from all directions. Of course, this would have been wonderful except that they were in the wrong costumes."

But mostly it was a cooperative crowd getting a good show from the film company. A minor problem occurred during the shooting of the scene where Barshee firebombs the James farm. Director King had sent Joe Behm to find buckets which could be used by a bucket brigade to douse the fire. The prop master was, as usual, successful in his efforts to obtain the right material. The big day came. As Joe Behm remembered it, his friend Henry King came strutting on the set, already entertaining the audience. He called for Behm to bring him a megaphone (King had sent Behm on a wild chase earlier to locate that necessary directorial showpiece). The filmmaker tipped his hat to the women, and announced through the megaphone, "My name is Henry King." This brought applause. The director smiled. "The director of this great picture, *Jesse James,* the Robin Hood of this great state of Missouri." The reception to that "sounded like thunder." "What you see," King continued, "on the screen is my work. Without your patronage at the theatre I'd be out of a job." That drew a laugh. Joe Behm put the buckets near the well. "There's only one request I have. When I call for quiet, I want to hear a pin drop." King tipped his hat and headed for the well, then stopped suddenly. He started screaming through the megaphone, "What idiot put these buckets here?" Behm hurried to the scene. "Do you mean you came all the way to this great state of Missouri without cedar buckets? Answer me! You're a disgrace to my profession," the director bellowed, still playing to the crowd, but getting his point across. "Bob Webb, send this man home by the next train! No, make him bum his way! He isn't worth the train fare! Well, don't stand there like a dummy. I want twenty cedar buckets for this scene—won't shoot until I get them." It took two hours for Joe Behm to find a cedar bucket. But he did, King had his authenticity, and the onlookers got a good show.

Perhaps the most frustrating experience for Joe Behm came when King decided to shoot the opening scene of *Jesse James.* Jesse would be shown at work on the farm. For this, the director wanted a "hillside plow with a hickory shank." Off went Behm and an assistant knocking on doors throughout the area in the middle of the night, with hopes of getting the prop for the next morning's set-up. After a long search, they arrived at a small farm. An old man wearing a flannel nightgown and cap answered the door. He pointed a shotgun at the duo from Hollywood. People just didn't come calling there at 2 A.M. When informed of their needs, the farmer sold them a plow for fifteen dollars. In the morning King saw the plow and changed his mind. He now desired a "scythe with a wheat cradle." Behm went back to the same farmer, who sold him the scythe for $27.50. By the time the property master got back with the new item, the filmmaker had decided to stick with the first plow.

"Don't know how I survived this picture," Behm recalled. "At the time it was a tragedy. After all these years it's one big laugh."

After the shooting was completed, King donated the props used in making *Jesse James* to the people of Pineville. Most of the material was auctioned off, but the town decided to keep the wood awnings erected over the sidewalk. It has been estimated Jesse James stole over $200,000 during his crime spree which ran from 1866 to his death in 1882, the longest record in American history. But the profits derived from the moviemakers and thousands of tourists more than made up for it. So Missourians were finally paid back, in a way, and the name James could stand for good, bad, and big bucks! Jesse's 20th-century value had whitewashed his 19th-century deeds, to a certain extent. But the legend lives on.

King and Power flew back to Hollywood together in the director's private plane. The filmmaker spent about a month in the editing room preparing the production for release. He left behind a second unit in Pineville, under the guidance of assistant director Otto Brower, to lens a spectacular cliff jump. The scene depicts Jesse's escape from the bungled Northfield, Minnesota, raid. A stunt man was flown in from Hollywood and the group journeyed to a corner of the Lake of the Ozarks for the shooting.

At the site, all agreed the jump couldn't be made. The cliff was just too steep. And horses don't voluntarily leap off cliffs. A slide was constructed and covered with vegetation. A crew member hung a blanket in front of the horse, which was snapped away at the moment before the plunge. Brower and the camera crew waited down below on a barge. Before an assistant had a chance to push the horse on to the slide, the animal slipped and toppled into the lake. The horse injured itself and drowned before it could be rescued. The stunt man swam to shore, shaken but unhurt. A second horse was obtained and the shot set up once more. With the cameras rolling, the slide broke before the horse could leap. The stunt man was ripped from the saddle, and crashed against the cliff. The horse plunged into the water. Somehow the man swam underwater to the horse and emerged in the saddle. The take was later described as one of the most exciting stunts of the year by enthralled critics and moviegoers.

Despite the kudos for assistant director Brower, his crew, and the stunt man, the A.S.P.C.A. reacted strongly to the death of the first horse.

S. R. Kent, president of Twentieth Century-Fox, wrote a letter of protest to Sydney H. Coleman, president of the American Humane Association. It read in part, "This organization is not in the habit of inflicting cruelty on dumb animals. All of this type of work is carefully watched, and while in the filming of *Jesse James* we used over 300 horses at various times and while it was necessary to secure exciting scenes, there was only one accident. This is unusual and a very good record for a picture of this type."

There was some confusion over whether the horse was actually drowned. Whatever the case, Fox was very cautious in the future about any recurrences.

The studio knew it had a potential box-office champ on its hands and naturally did not want adverse publicity to besmirch the idealistic quality of the Western.

When Major Cobb unveils a statue to Jesse at the film's end, the construction stands as an epitaph to the man and a symbol of the theme of *Jesse James.* The plaque says:

In loving remembrance
Jesse W. James
died April 3, 1882
aged 34 years, 6 months, 28 days
murdered by a traitor and coward
whose name is not worthy to appear here

Director King restated the film's treatment of the outlaw. "Those who knew him or heard about him as youngsters believe that Jesse James was driven to a life of crime by the hounding of enemies who persecuted him, that the efforts of unscrupulous railroad owners to steal his mother's farm at Sedalia, Missouri, for the right of way for the first Iron Horse, started him on his bloody trail of banditry.

"In the film we do not glorify him. Neither do we picture him as all bad. We attempt, instead, to trace the psychological causes that led him into train and bank robbery, and to depict with historical accuracy the most famous of his exploits. We have tried to respect the judgment of historians and at the same time keep in mind what those people who were his sworn friends thought of him."

Writer/producer Nunnally Johnson wanted to add a dime novel tone to the script, despite the more complex aspects described by King. "Why not put it that way? Hadn't we two chases in it, and a baby-mother scene, and shootings galore?"

Johnson, King, and Zanuck wanted that tense excitement which comes from thoroughly sympathizing with the lead character. "When Jesse put down that gun and turned around, we used to scream at him, 'Look out, Jesse, don't put down that gun.' It was a terrific moment. We all knew what was coming. I tried to get some of that in the picture. I wanted to get the feeling of that last scene."

Reviewers had widely differing opinions of *Jesse James:*

Daily Worker, Howard Rushmore:

The James Boys were not bandits of their own choosing; rather they were victims of a social system which forced them to take up six guns instead of plows. And for that reason alone we can thank Twentieth Century-Fox for a film of unusually high calibre and social significance.

London Observer:

Jesse James is too long, too Technicolored and too fragmentary. I admit the virtues of its style of story-telling. It is a restrained style; it never shouts or exaggerates; it tries quite deliberately to catch the human qualities of these people, but at the expense of what might be called their "front page value."

New York *Daily News,* Kate Cameron, four stars:

The Johnson dialogue glitters with bright lines and his story is full of . . . breathless suspense.

New York *Sun,* Eileen Creelman:

It is a good Western, told with astonishing sympathy for the brutal outlaws. For some unexplained reason the picture ends with an extraordinary eulogy of Jesse James over his grave, with Henry Hull, as the newspaper publisher, having to state in so many words that his country is proud of Jesse James. It would be interesting to know if Hollywood is just as proud of John Dillinger and Al Capone.

New York *World Telegram,* William Boehnel:

The whole thing moves with great gusto and abandon under Henry King's vigorous direction, and it is acted to perfection by a notable cast, and in particular by Mr. Power as Jesse, Henry Fonda as Frank James, Nancy Kelly as Zee, Henry Hull as Major Rufus Cobb and Randolph Scott as Will Wright.

Jo Frances James, granddaughter of Jesse, was unenthusiastic over the Western. "I don't know what happened to the history part of it," she told the newspapers. "It seemed to me the story was fiction from beginning to end. About the only connection it had with fact was that there once was a man named James and he did ride a horse."

Nevertheless, Twentieth Century-Fox set up a lavish publicity campaign for *Jesse James:*

The Biggest Money-Maker This Industry Has Ever Had!

The Most Exciting Entertainment Ever Brought to the Screen!

The Epic of a Lawless Era and the Most Famous Outlaw Who Ever Lived!

The Greatest of That Kind of Picture Which Has Made This Business of Ours!

And finally, a poster's eye view of the legend of Jesse James:

To the simple folk who knew him . . . a victim of injustice! To the girl who married him . . . a brave and gentle lover! But to the world . . . *an outlaw, a killer, a wolf!*

Contests were devised to spur the public's already large interest in the life and times of the James boys. One gimmick offered a prize to the person who best fit the lines of a ballad about the outlaw to a series of illustrations. Another promised a fifty dollar "reward" for the man who shot Jesse James. The plan was to have an actor dressed as the bandit walk a pre-arranged route, probably ending at a local theatre where the film headlined, and attract locals to lie in waiting.

The next year Fox made a sequel to *Jesse James,* called *The Return of Frank James,* starring Henry Fonda again as Frank, with

Henry Hull, John Carradine, J. Edward Bromberg, and Donald Meek repeating their roles in the fine Western, directed by Fritz Lang.

After the success of *Jesse James* and *The Return of Frank James,* Hollywood attempted numerous versions of the careers of the brothers (a number had been done before as well). The most distinguished titles are *I Shot Jesse James* (Screen Guild, 1949), *The True Story of Jesse James* (20th, 1957), the official remake of the Power/Fonda version, and *The Great Northfield, Minnesota Raid* (Universal, 1972). But there are also bizarre entries such as *Jesse James Meets Frankenstein's Daughter* (Embassy, 1966), in addition to a short-lived television series, featuring Christopher Jones as Jesse.

Henry Fonda

CHAPTER FIVE

Drums Along the Mohawk

Year Released: 1939
Studio: Twentieth Century-Fox
Executive Producer: Darryl F. Zanuck
Producer: Raymond Griffith
Director: John Ford
Screenplay: Lamar Trotti, Sonya Levien, based on the novel by Walter D. Edmonds
Cinematography: Bert Glennon
Music: Alfred Newman
Art Directors: Richard Day, Mark Lee
Editor: Robert Simpson
Assistant Director: Eddie O'Ferna
Production Manager: Duke Goux
Set Decorator: Thomas Little
Wardrobe: Gwen Wakeling
Sound Effects Editor: Robert Parrish
Property Master: Joseph C. Behm
Color Consultants: Natalie Kalmus, Henry Jaffa
Color, 103 minutes

Cast:

Lana Borst Martin	CLAUDETTE COLBERT
Gilbert Martin	HENRY FONDA
Mrs. McKlennan	EDNA MAE OLIVER
Christian Reall	EDDIE COLLINS
Caldwell	JOHN CARRADINE

Mary Reall	DORRIS BOWDON
Mrs. Weaver	JESSIE RALPH
Father Rosenkranz	ARTHUR SHIELDS
John Weaver	ROBERT LOWERY
General Nicholas Herkimer	ROGER IMHOF
Joe Boleo	FRANCIS FORD
Adam Hartman	WARD BOND
Mrs. Denooth	KAY LINAKER
Dr. Petry	RUSSELL SIMPSON
Blue Back	CHIEF BIG TREE
Innkeeper	SPENCER CHARTERS
George	ARTHUR AYLESWORTH
Jacobs	SI JENKS
Amos	JACK PENNICK
Robert Johnson	CHARLES TANNEN
Captain Mark Dencoth	PAUL McVEY
Mrs. Reall	ELIZABETH JONES
General	LIONEL POPE
Paymaster	CLARENCE WILSON
Pastor	EDWIN MAXWELL
Mrs. Borst	CLARA BANDICK
Daisy	BEULAH HALL JONES
Mr. Borst	ROBERT GREIG

As in John Ford's cavalry epics of the 1940s, *Drums Along the Mohawk* is a classic blend of American history and culture, reflected in the themes of loyalty, honor, courage, and independence which forged the director's great career. Eighteenth-century America is a subject filmmakers have approached infrequently, and productions set in colonial times were not generally successful at the box office. But, along with D. W. Griffith's *America,* Ford's Revolutionary War saga stands as an epic about a nation in the throes of birth, a chronicle of personal struggle as well as historical events.

Farmer Gilbert Martin marries Lana Borst, daughter of well-to-do parents. Some of the bride's family express reservations about the couple's plans to live and work Martin's farm in the wilderness of the Mohawk Valley. At first Lana Martin finds life difficult on the farm, where the community is minus the polished gentility she is used to. All is peaceful, however, until the British drive the Iroquois Indians into the valley. The Martins and other farmers are forced to take refuge in a nearby fort, looking on helplessly as the Indians destroy their homes. After losing everything, the Martins are hired by Mrs. McKlennan to work on her land. The Indians strike again. But this time the settlers are ready and ultimately repel the attack. With the valley once more at peace, the farmers set about rebuilding their lives.

Although the conflict in *Drums Along the Mohawk* revolves around the Indians, the British, and the settlers in general, and between the whites and renegade Caldwell in particular, the real struggle exists in the confrontation of prim, proper Lana Borst Martin with the harsh realities of farm life, as personified by Gil Martin. It is that chafing of wilderness and civilization which propels scenarists Lamar Trotti and Sonya Levien's action in the early stages, and makes possible the establishing of the bond of the community, and the equality of all men. Americans live and die together in the films of John Ford, and those who leave the fold, as Caldwell does, are the very incarnations of evil.

As Lana Martin, Claudette Colbert can whine like a little girl or genteelly perform the social rituals of the properly trained 18th-century lady and be utterly convincing in both roles. Henry Fonda's Gil Martin is a simple man of the soil who doesn't really change much in the course of the film. And that's what makes the pair such a magnetic team: Colbert's tranformation from spoiled rich lady to warm, beautiful pioneer woman, and Fonda's steadiness of character, evenness of tone. They grow together to become one with their neighbors in the fight against the warring Indians.

The epic status of *Drums Along the Mohawk* is only possible because of the flesh-and-blood believability of the men and women in this colonial Western. They aren't just actors. They are Lana Martin, Gil Martin, Mrs. McKlennan, Christian Reall, Mary Reall, Mrs. Weaver, John Weaver, Father Rosenkranz, Joe Boleo, Adam Hartman, and the rest of the frontier people who built America. That is the secret of Ford and scriptwriters. By 1939 cowboys and Indians was old white hat and old black hat, to say the least. The makers of *Drums Along the Mohawk* and other Westerns that year made the genre seem new again. With caring about the characters comes attention and reaction.

That's why the Indian attacks in the production are truly horrifying. The painted red men are as frightening to a viewer as they are to the settler staring at a tomahawk about to split his skull. Ford was a decade away from a sympathetic treatment of Indians in *Fort Apache.* Here they are the unknown enemy—not necessarily bad, just dreaded opponents. The antagonist is really Caldwell. John

Carradine's traitorous schemer is slick in ways his gambler in *Stagecoach* never could be. Caldwell is a renegade for his own personal gain, nothing more! He has turned his back on his neighbors, and that John Ford cannot abide. It is so easy to hiss when the tall, intense actor comes onscreen one might recall picturing Carradine as the mustached meanie who tied so many little Nells to the train tracks in turn-of-the-century pulp stories and two reelers.

When the tired, makeshift army comes back from battle in the rain, it is a tragic and suspenseful turn of events. Families wait to see in what condition fathers will return, if at all. It is here that Lana Martin becomes truly imbued with the hearty spirit of the land. While waiting for Gil to come back, she cares for the sick and wounded. Such scenes recall King Vidor's depiction of tired soldiers moving down the road in *The Big Parade.*

Although the crops are burned, the farmers will reseed, row by row. Although the farms are ashes, the families will rebuild, board by board. The affirmation of pioneer existence comes with Ford's beautifully filmed harvest scenes. The clear blue skies, the mountains, the waving wheatfields are forces which cannot be defeated. If one farmer dies in battle, another will take his place. The spirit of the people is unbreakable.

Drums Along the Mohawk is a powerful and inspiring cultural history of the American colonial pioneers. It is one of the building blocks of John Ford's monumental chronicle of the frontier.

The Making of *Drums Along the Mohawk*

When the Will Hays Code of 1934 decreed that sex and violence in the movies would have to be toned down considerably, and that the gangster could no longer be treated like a hero in wolf's clothing, Hollywood was in a quandry. What to do next? Seemingly the studios were stripped of the successful crime film format exemplified by *Little Caesar, Public Enemy, Scarface,* and others. Sophisticated romantic comedies a la Lubitsch would have to restrict the verbal foreplay and sexual innuendo. The presentation of modern times in cinema was to be purified. That notion didn't seem to guarantee a box-office bonanza.

The only thing to do was go into the past. Romance would replace realism (such as it was). Something new was shoved aside for something old, but that aged commodity channeled into lush romanticism, adventure, and spectacle hadn't been popular in Hollywood since the 1920s. So, in a way, such escapism was fresh.

In the mid-1930s, epic romance and adventure novels captivated a public eager to get away from the realities of the Depression. As it did a decade earlier with the work of romantic author Elinor Glyn, Hollywood eagerly purchased screen rights to many popular bestsellers which could be turned into escapist entertainment. Warners produced *Anthony Adverse,* based on the gargantuan novel by Hervey Allen, and began the Errol Flynn cycle of adventures with a filmization of Rafael Sabatini's *Captain Blood.* Other period productions, not necessarily based on bestsellers, followed. Paramount did *The Scarlet Empress.* Metro made *Treasure Island* and *The Merry Widow.* Cecil B. DeMille continued his epic mold with *The Crusades.* Universal produced those entertainingly unreal horror tales. The cycle proceeded until America's entry into World War II dictated a shift to patriotic tales of war and the homefront.

Even though the productions were set in the past or in remote locales, it didn't stop the realism which imbued Hollywood filmmaking via gangster and social dramas from seeping in. *Captain Blood* has tirades against slavery. *The Scarlet Empress* contains an almost dream-like yet very real depiction of political corruption. Goldwyn's *The Hurricane* revolves around a native's struggle for justice in a white-dominated world.

So it was with that delicate balance that Fox produced *Drums Along the Mohawk,* released in 1939, a year in which Hollywood productions started to become more sophisticated. The makers of the screen version of Walter Edmonds' novel which sold close to 250,000 copies, a phenomenal amount for the time, would have to be people experienced in period production, but who could create an adult film about America's colonial days.

Director John Ford had lensed the spectacular *The Hurricane* two years earlier, and had just finished *Young Mr. Lincoln* for Fox. So Darryl F. Zanuck knew Ford was more than able to strike the equilibrium necessary for the success of *Drums Along the Mohawk*—spectacle, maturity, and, in this case, a grasp of Americana.

The script was written by Lamar Trotti and Sonya Levien. Trotti had already penned the screenplays for *Judge Priest* (1934), *Steamboat 'Round the Bend* (1935), and *Young Mr. Lincoln* (1939), all produced by Fox and directed by Ford. So the pair worked well together. And the writer's scenarios for *Slave Ship* (1937) and *In Old Chicago* (1938) proved he could animate period America as well as epic grandeur.

In adapting the material for the cinema, Trotti and Levien sensibly eliminated or diminished much of the historical sidelighting, concentrating instead on the story of Lana and Gil Martin's efforts to make a life for themselves in the wild Mohawk Valley. Nevertheless, the script finely illustrates American colonial culture. And the character of Lana was made more sophisticated and mature than she appeared in the novel, facilitating a smoother transition from the dainty girl Gil marries into the hearty and loving pioneer woman she becomes.

Henry Fonda was chosen to play farmer Gil Martin. The actor had made his debut in *The Farmer Takes a Wife* (Fox, 1935), and for the next few years essayed many country characters in rural or period settings. His previous role to portraying Martin was as the young President-to-be in Ford's classic *Young Mr. Lincoln.* In order to play Honest Abe as a thirtyish lawyer, Fonda was requested to refrain from getting a haircut so that his appearance might be more in keeping with the character. Fonda's last trim in fact was in December 1938, and he was just about to get a clipping for the first time in months when he received word to let the hair grow for *Drums Along the Mohawk.* Unlike many stars who might have balked at maintaining a head of what was then considered unfashionable long hair, Fonda gracefully complied. Since the actor's ancestors were from New York's Mohawk Valley, perhaps he was in some way trying to be true to their memory. In any case, such selfless devotion to his art is one of many reasons Henry Fonda was presented with the American Film Institute's special life award in March 1978.

Claudette Colbert signed to portray Lana Borst Martin. Unlike Fonda, her career had veered almost totally away from rustic productions, especially Westerns. Her only appearance dressed in calico had come a decade earlier. *Drums Along the Mohawk* would be her first major action tale. She long had been used to scripts laced with comedy and light drama, often set in regal or rich locales, such as the ones in *Tovarich, Bluebeard's Eighth Wife,* and *Midnight.* Yet the actress was able to convey upper class charm and sophisticated behavior in any role, a talent she applied as Lana. And her part in the 18th-century Western was not completely dissimilar from the spoiled heiress of *It Happened One Night,* a portrayal for which she won a well-deserved Oscar.

While the stars were being signed and the script prepared, it was the large responsibility of Fox's technical departments to design the film's sets, create the costumes, and find or build artifacts of colonial American culture. The last duty proved to be something of a problem. Twentieth Century-Fox was a relatively new studio, only coming into being in 1933 when co-founder Darryl F. Zanuck left Warners to form Twentieth Century Productions, which merged with Fox Studios in 1935. Although Fox pictures began in the nickelodeon days, the studio hadn't dealt much with projects set in 18th-century America and had to manufacture most of the props used in *Drums Along the Mohawk.*

Claudette Colbert

"This picture was the most physical and technical one I'd been assigned to," prop man Joseph Behm told me recently. Before Behm and the property department could create the necessary artifacts, they spent several weeks in research. The studio assigned Behm a sketch artist to rough out and blueprint the items he wished to reproduce.

The first time he met with director John Ford to show him an armful of designs, the filmmaker, as usual, left no doubt as to who was in charge. But he also illustrated his ability to delegate responsibility.

Joe Behm recalled the conversation. After he produced the material for Ford's scrutiny, the director said, "Fine! What do you want me to do? Prop the show for you?

"No, sir, but I have orders from Mr. Little (set decorator Thomas Little) to have you initial all plans before I put them to work," replied the surprised prop man.

Ford studied the material. "Your work shows imagination Joe. That's half the battle. I okay everything. Don't bother to show me any more sketches. You've got a blanket approval for everything you think we need."

As Behm started to leave, Ford told him that if any trouble was forthcoming from "that tall drink of water" (Little), he should let him know, and he'd settle the matter with Darryl Zanuck.

Like the other major studios, Fox had its representatives sometimes scour the world in search of unique props for productions. Ironically, one of the studio's men found a number of artifacts of 18th-century warfare on a 20th-century battlefield! The man in Africa located 100 flintlock muskets like the ones used in the Revolutionary War which had previously been in the hands of Ethiopian soldiers futilely trying to repel Mussolini's aggression. The muskets appear in *Drums Along the Mohawk.*

Ford did several weeks of pre-production work himself, then took his cast and crew of 300 to the mountains of South Utah, 11,000 feet above sea level, an area where the nearest town was forty miles away.

Fox had to cut roads through dense forest and marsh lands in order to gain access to the location. Many of the trees felled in the building of the paths were used in the construction of sets such as a huge fort, a church, and individual homes. Approximately 200,000 feet of lumber were transported to Cedar Breaks, Utah.

The studio built a tent city capable of housing and feeding the 300-member company. Water was piped from streams and a pair of 2,500-gallon water tanks and heating equipment were installed. Cabins were electrically equipped by engine-driven generators.

The prop department had its own tent. The floors were wooden, as was the three-foot wainscot which served as the walls. As usual, toilets and showers were in separate quarters. "The women were put in a special section," said Behm, "with a six-foot wire fence to separate them from the men. Had a night watchman, Stubby

Muselman, patrolling the area." With a company on location for a month, director Ford evidently didn't want to take a chance on off-the-set interplay between the sexes or the curiosity of area residents somehow bogging down the production. Additionally, Fox hired approximately 1,000 native extras.

The studio purchased crops of wheat and corn from surrounding farms for the film's harvest scenes. Prop man Behm had no complaints about the food. "Reminded me of the food we ate on the farm during 'Trashing Season'—steak, ham, pork chops, sausage, eggs, hot cakes." Production companies were usually treated as well as possible.

Being essentially cooped-up in the mountains made it necessary for the cast and crew to seek their own diversions. Claudette Colbert went fishing. Henry Fonda chummed around with the crew. And Joe Behm was kept hopping by John Ford, and was one day called to the director's tent.

"Joe, get me a baby grand piano, [and] put it in the recreation tent." Behm was willing to please, and knew that part of his job was anticipating the needs of his director, but, he thought to himself, "Where am I going to find a baby grand in this God-forsaken country?"

Behm and co-worker Jack Stubbs took the trip down a long, winding dirt road to Cedar City, going door to door, until one resident agreed to rent the pair his piano. Behm and Stubbs proudly brought the prize to Ford, who was then setting up the first shot for the next morning.

The director instructed his cast and crew. "Glen (cameraman Bert Glennon), [I] want a long shot from here with a 25 mm lens. [The] stockade gates are closed. Jack Pennick, you'll be drilling your men here. Just the normal background action—very placid. Joe will give you the props. He knows what I want. Then suddenly we hear the shouts of the Indians. Jack, take your men to the parspits, start shooting, then on cue I'll yell 'Jack.' You give the order to open the gate. [I] want Hank and Claudette to make their entrance in a Model-T Ford touring car steaming and chugging. [It] comes to a stop here," said the filmmaker, indicating the position of the auto.

Prop man Behm was somewhat mystified why Ford should want the stars to enter the picture riding in a car which wasn't invented until 150 years after the story took place! He couldn't figure it out. After consulting with assistant director Eddie O'Ferna, Behm went off to get Ford the car he wanted. "Once again the same day, [I] was on my way down the hill to Cedar City," Behm reminisced. "[It] was a long drive at night. The most important thought in my mind: 'Where am I going to find a Model-T in this small town?' "

Although the Cedar City stores were closed, Behm found a garage open. Fortunately, the owner was a member of a "Horseless Carriage Club," and knew a man who had a Model-T. On the condition that the car owner accompany Behm, the men towed the old auto up to the location site.

The next day Behm moved the necessary props from Gil Martin's wagon to the car. The shooting was about to commence. Some men were making adobe bricks, other crew members placed the cannon, Jack Pennick drilled the soldiers, oxen pulled logs, children scurried about. Ford appeared and told Behm to ready Fonda and Colbert. After the stars arrived, Behm took them outside the gate. As soon as the actors saw the Model-T, they burst into laughter.

"What the hell is this, Joe?" asked Fonda.

Behm explained as best he could. He also instructed Hank Fonda to pull a wire just as the car came to a stop inside the gates of the fort, which would let off a puff of steam from under the hood. With everything set, people got into their places. The cameras rolled. The scene went from morning calm to the frenzy of an Indian attack. The gates opened and in chugged Fonda and Colbert. Fonda pulled the wire and the engine seemed to explode. Ford yelled "cut," ran over to make sure the actors were unhurt, then said simply, "Fine—okay, print it. That one was for Mr. Zanuck. Load the props into the wagon. Let's shoot it again."

Director John Ford's way of wiling away the hours on location was to play practical jokes!

And the filmmaker had his share of problems which assuredly built a tension which found release in such comical actions. For one thing, Ford had a difficult time rounding up the necessary 300 Indians needed as extras. The call was for red men belonging to the Five Nations of the Iroquois Confederation, namely the Mohawks, Oneidas, Onandagas, Cayugas, and Senacas. Only two Iroquois presented themselves, and one was too short to appear in the production. Ultimately, Ford had to settle for Indians from any tribe.

Another time there was a conflict over the Model-T and the grand piano the director requested. One day while Joe Behm and others lunched on the set, Duke Goux, the film's production manager, questioned the prop man. "Who do you think you are? Who authorized you to rent that piano?"

Behm started to answer but was cut off. "Wait'll I finish talking," barked Goux. "I've sent the damn things back. Another thing, you made a [fool] of yourself using that Model-T in a period picture."

The listeners remained quiet while Goux talked on.

"I'm running this company, no one else. The sooner you guys get that in your stupid heads, the better off you'll all be," concluded the production manager.

After the day's work ended, Jack Pennick came to Behm's tent and said that Ford wanted to see him immediately.

"Joe, why did you send that piano back?" asked the confused director. "I had it so we could entertain the crew."

Behm didn't respond. But the filmmaker had to have an answer. Jack Pennick spoke up.

"Joe didn't have anything to do with it skipper," explained Pennick. He relayed Goux's earlier comments, including, "he told us, he was running the company—no one else."

Ford said, "Get Mr. Goux, Jack."

Goux arrived quickly. "Did you want to see me, sir?"

"Yes, Mr. Goux," replied Ford. "I've been enlightened of the facts. This is your company, you're the boss, no one countermands your orders. You've questioned my integrity, you sent the piano back, you criticized Mr. Behm for following my orders. . . ."

"But, Skipper. . . ."

"Don't Skipper me. I'm Mr. Ford to you. [I] want to clarify this whole situation; I'm running the company. When I give an order it's followed out, regardless of its authenticity. Bring back that piano—now!"

Goux motioned to Joe Behm. "Okay Joe, get the piano back."
"[I] don't think you heard me straight. *You* bring back the piano. Mr. Behm is through for the day."

"Yes, sir. Right away," said a chastised Goux.

"And another thing, Mr. Goux! You're barred from my set," instructed the director.

"Yes, sir. Is that all, sir?"

"That's enough, don't you think?"

As always, John Ford knew what he wanted and knew how to get it. He rewarded loyal co-workers, and replaced those who went against him. He was always in control. When a company member could help bring an idea to fruition, as did Joe Behm, that was especially pleasing to Ford.

Before the cameras rolled, the director created a segment of the battle between the Indians and settlers which he thought would be more exciting if the audience could see the arrows penetrating the white men. He asked Joe Behm to devise a mechanism which could make this possible. Originally the director was going to use the man who performed Errol Flynn's archery, but the archer's fee was excessive, and Ford didn't like the man anyway. So Behm willingly accepted a most difficult assignment.

After considerable work, the prop man created a hollow arrow

Claudette Colbert and Henry Fonda

Henry Fonda and Claudette Colbert

in which a wire could be passed through and attached to the target. Behm made a breast plate six inches by eight inches for the intended victim, with a three-quarter inch cork backed by a one-eighth-inch steel plate. A piano wire was placed in the center, and the plate buckled under the actor's clothes. A flange was attached to the arrow. Behm's assistant Jack Stubbs would hold the wire off-camera, while the prop man fired the arrow. Ford liked the idea, and brought Fox executive Bill Koenig around to witness a demonstration. With a flair for the dramatic, Behm decided to use a flaming arrow. He wrapped oakum around the arrow head and soaked it in gasoline. Stubbs hid behind a rock. Behm gave the cue, Stubbs stood up, and Behm shot the arrow into its target. Koenig was happy with the money-saving invention. Such ingenuity is why Joseph Behm spent so many years at Fox.

With creative people at his side, it's little wonder Ford had a relatively easy time making *Drums Along the Mohawk.* Even nature, that old enemy of location filming, helped out considerably. Since the Cedar Mountains were 11,000 feet above sea level, the weather was constantly dry and the skies clear. This condition was perfect for Technicolor shooting. The panoramic long shots in the production would come out sharp. If Ford had made the colonial Western in black and white, the good weather would have hindered the physical quality of the work, because the contrast between light and dark areas would have been too high.

Early in the Utah morning the sky was a distinct, consistent, cloudless blue. By eleven in the morning, tiny clouds formed high in the sky. At one or two in the afternoon beautiful formations shaped, and 3:30 saw the accumulations blossom completely, sometimes hiding the sun. Taking advantage of the weather, Ford scheduled his closer shots for the first thing in the morning. The longer set-ups were saved for the afternoon. Since nature performed as if on Fox's pay roster, the director was able to shoot as many as twenty-three scenes per day. Only an occasional reflector was needed to erase small shadows. Mother Nature did the rest.

When the location work was completed, the studio was obligated to dismantle all the sets, including the huge fort, since everything was on government property. Crew members tried in vain to tear the fort down, but found they had done the job of building too well. It would be necessary to dynamite the structure. That gave Ford an idea. Why waste a spectacular stunt like that? So he penciled in a section of the Indian attack in which the fort is blown up. When the company left, they just carried away the debris.

Drums Along the Mohawk was released in the fall of 1939. "When torch and tomahawk spread their terror . . . and frontier women fought beside their men . . . these two [Fonda and Colbert] braved the wilderness together," shouted one poster advertising the production.

Part of the Fox publicity campaign was an appeal to patriot and civic groups since *Drums Along the Mohawk* was not only American history but an affirmation of American ideals at a time when the world crisis divided the nation. The studio urged schools to run essay contests on the subject of colonial times and marketed the usual paraphernalia of artifacts usually promoted for period pictures.

Reviews were generally favorable:

New Republic, Otis Ferguson:

Since John Ford directed it, it is well above the average historical picture.

New York Herald Tribune:

Drums Along the Mohawk has consummate staging; it has also splendid acting. Henry Fonda is perfectly cast as Gil Martin. . . . Claudette Colbert brings warmth and depth to the character of Martin's wife. *Drums Along the Mohawk* lacks unity, but thanks to its director and its playing, it is a genuinely distinguished historical film.

New York Times, Frank S. Nugent:

Drums Along the Mohawk was tailored for Mr. Ford's measure. It deals with a colorful period. It is romantic enough for any adventure-story lover. It has its humor, its sentiment, its full complement of blood and thunder. About the only Ford staple we miss is a fog scene. Rain, gun smoke and stockade burnings have had to compensate. The fusion of all has made a first-rate historical film, as rich atmospherically as it is in action.

Claudette Colbert stayed away from Westerns until the 1950s, when she starred in *Texas Lady* (RKO, 1955). Henry Fonda continued to make distinguished appearances in a wide variety of sagebrush sagas, from *The Ox-Bow Incident* (Fox, 1943) and *My Darling Clementine* (Fox, 1946) to unsympathetic roles in *Fort Apache* (RKO, 1948) and beyond to Leone's *Once Upon a Time in the West* (Paramount, 1968).

The 1940s and 50s were John Ford's greatest years as a director of Westerns: *My Darling Clementine, Fort Apache, Three Godfathers* (MGM, 1948), *She Wore a Yellow Ribbon* (RKO, 1949), *Wagon Master* (RKO), *Rio Grande* (Republic, both 1950), *The Searchers* (Warner Bros., 1956), *The Horse Soldiers* (UA, 1959), and, wrapping up his great career in the 1960s, *Sergeant Rutledge* (Warner Bros., 1960), *Two Rode Together* (Columbia, 1961), *The Man Who Shot Liberty Valance* (Paramount), a segment of *How the West Was Won* (MGM, both 1962), and, finally, *Cheyenne Autumn* (Warner Bros., 1964).

Lamar Trotti penned the scripts for two Westerns by William Wellman—*The Ox Bow Incident* and *Yellow Sky* (Fox, 1948).

And for his imagination and flair behind the camera, Joseph Behm went on to become an assistant director at Twentieth Century-Fox and worked on dozens of Westerns over the years.

Drums Along the Mohawk is a fine example of a production made largely on location. It showed how moviemakers often lived by their wits when away from the studio, and took advantage of their environment to enrich a film in ways which could never be duplicated on a sound stage.

Gary Cooper and Doris Davenport

Gary Cooper (with hands behind back)

CHAPTER SIX

The Westerner

Year Released: 1940
Studio: United Artists
Producer: Samuel Goldwyn
Director: William Wyler
Screenplay: Niven Busch, Jo Swerling
Cinematography: Gregg Toland
Music: Dmitri Tiomkin
Art Director: James Basevi
Editor: Daniell Mandell
Assistant Director: Walter Mayo
Set Director: Julie Heron
Wardrobe: Irene Saltern
Sound: Fred Lau
100 minutes

Cast:

Cole Hardin	GARY COOPER
Judge Roy Bean	WALTER BRENNAN
Jane-Ellen Mathews	DORIS DAVENPORT
Caliphet Mathews	FRED STONE
Chickenfoot	PAUL HURST
Southeast	CHILL WILLS
Mort Borrow	CHARLES HALTON
Wade Harper	FORREST TUCKER
King Evans	TOM TYLER

Mr. Dixon	ARTHUR AYLESWORTH
Teresita	LUPITA TOVAR
Juan Gomez	JULIAN RIVERO
Lily Langtry	LILLIAN BOND
Bart Cobble	DANA ANDREWS
Eph Stringer	ROGER GRAY
Bantry	JACK PENNICK
Shad Wilkins	TREVOR BARDETTE
Tex Cole	BILL STEELE
Buck Harrigan	BLACKJACK WARD
Lee Webb	JAMES "JIM" COREY
Charles Evans	BUCK MOULTON
Joe Lawrence	TED WELLS
Mex	JOE DE LA CRUZ
Man	FRANK CORDELL
John Yancy	PHILIP CONNOR
Hezekiah Willever	CAPTAIN C. E. ANDERSON
Seth Tucker	ART MIX
Leon Beauregard	WILLIAM GILLIS
Abraham Wilson	BUCK CONNOR
Joe Yates	DAN BORZAGE
Walt McGary	SPEED HANSON
Abigail	GERTRUDE BENNETT
Martha	MIRIAM SHERWIN
Elizabeth	ANNABELLE ROUSSEAU
Janice	HELEN FOSTER
Langtry's Maid	CONNIE LEON
Langtry's Manager	CHARLES COLEMAN
Ticket Man	LEW KELLY
Man at Window	HEINIE CONKLIN
Stranger	LUCIEN LITTLEFIELD
Orchestra Leader	CORBET MORRIS
Sheriff	STANLEY ANDREWS
Prisoner	PHIL TEAD
Stage Manager	HENRY ROQUEMORE
Man Getting Haircut	BILL BAUMAN
Deputy	HANK BELL

The notion that character actors did not essay top parts in pre-World War II Hollywood productions has held up well. While Humphrey Bogart and Edward G. Robinson shattered the myth that a star had to be good looking to play cinema heroes, the general rule that handsome is as handsome does dominated. The Gables, Flynns, and Coopers headlined while normally supporting players such as Edward Arnold, Alan Hale, and Walter Brennan stayed in the colorful background. This was especially true of Westerns, where the formula stuck very strongly.

That's what Samuel Goldwyn and William Wyler changed in *The Westerner*. This movie is about a cowboy named Cole Hardin who rides into Langtry, Texas, and is accused of horse-stealing. Judge Roy Bean has every intention of hanging Hardin. But the cowboy knows of the jurist's obsession with meeting celebrated stage star Lily Langtry, and Hardin saves his hide by claiming to know the performer. Hardin offers to introduce Bean to Lily. While the two men develop a healthy respect for one another, Hardin is disenchanted with Bean's ruthless endeavors to keep homesteaders from settling the open range.

Although Gary Cooper is top-billed as Cole Hardin in *The Westerner* and can even be said to portray the title role, it is Walter Brennan's acting as Judge Bean which stands out in the production. Brennan is an ornery, mealy-mouthed, ill-clothed, unshaven frontier fascist who loves from afar. His yearning reaches such unreasonable heights that his normally sharp mind is a virtual slave to anyone claiming to know Lily. Cole Hardin, cowboy everyman, exploits Bean's fantasies.

William Wyler was an excellent choice to direct this unlikely Western. He began his career lensing "B" sagebrush sagas at Universal in the late 1920s. These are all formula stories but they contain a flowing sense of plot and pace. In *The Westerner,* Wyler throws out some cliches of the genre, molds others, and explores little-used frontier territory.

As Hardin, Gary Cooper is not the focal point of the story, unlike his presence in *The Virginian* (Paramount, 1929), *The Spoilers* (Universal, 1930), or *The Plainsman* (Paramount, 1936). Any stock leading man could have adequately essayed the part, say, a Jon Hall or Ronald Reagan. But only an actor of Cooper's caliber, and one so identified with Westerns,* could have taken a bland character and competed with salty Walter Brennan's memorable portrayal of Judge Roy Bean as a crude man who loved like a boy. Wyler made sure Cooper had opportunities to employ his ability to create memorable moments or perhaps define a personality by a

*Before John Wayne appeared in *Stagecoach,* Cooper was the premier cowboy star of the 1930s, even though his range extended far beyond the genre.

slight facial movement or hand gesture. When Cooper stares in the window of Doris Davenport's ranch, Wyler's image frames a man alone, forever on the outside looking in.

Single images which summarize a relationship, emotion, or the feel of a moment occur frequently in the films of William Wyler. Perhaps Wyler's significant, beautifully arranged shots stem from the influence of all the Germanic horror films made at Universal (or the German productions themselves), while he was on staff at the studio. The haunting imagery in such works as *Frankenstein* (1931), *The Mummy* (1932), and *The Bride of Frankenstein* (1935) isn't so far removed from Cooper's face in the window or the frame of the wheels of the mortician's wagon rolling slowly in front of a corpse. The latter shot serves to punctuate a death scene. Of course cameraman Gregg Toland, with his brilliant sense of depth and lighting, must share in the credit for the physical quality of *The Westerner.*

When the moment that Bean will look upon his dream girl arrives, Wyler packs the scene with danger. The friction between Bean and Hardin has come to a head because the jurist has burned down the fields of a rancher. There has to be a showdown. When Bean dies in the gun battle with the cowboy, he can go to his grave with the satisfaction of having met Lily Langtry. Hardin introduces him after the fight. Bean can hardly stand, as life slowly wrenches itself from his body due to the bullet wounds inflicted by Hardin. Lily doesn't say a word. She is still the image Wyler has created. She is a star, something to be worshipped. You wouldn't have a cup of coffee with her. That is the source of the power to the climax of *The Westerner.* Bean dies to meet Lily, and she remains as remote as ever.

The Westerner too is detached, separated from its genre by glorious imagery, the focus on Judge Roy Bean, and the ethereal painting of Lily Langtry.

The Making of *The Westerner*

Samuel Goldwyn wanted to make a Western. But not "just" a Western. He wanted to produce something different. A Goldwyn film had an identity all its own. The movie mogul who began his career in 1913 as co-producer of *The Squaw Man,* often erroneously credited as being the first production shot in Hollywood, maintained a reputation for releasing distinguished family fare with solid story values and giving unknowns the star build-up in major productions.

United Artists' *Stagecoach,* Fox's *Jesse James,* Warner Brothers' *Dodge City,* and Universal's *Destry Rides Again* arrived in 1939 to show Hollywood that Westerns could be big box office and not merely economically budgeted, quickly shot vehicles which turned small profits with small-time stars. Goldwyn didn't want to compete with the action-filled, epic grandeur of the first three, or the out-and-out comedy of the fourth. Combining those styles might create a fresh Western, replete with characterizations rather unique to the genre, a wide scope, and a climactic clash.

Director Wyler worked almost exclusively for Goldwyn in the late 1930s. The filmmaker made *These Three, Come and Get It* (replaced Howard Hawks), *Dodsworth* (all 1936), *Dead End* (1937), and *Wuthering Heights* (1939). Wyler too wanted to make a Western.

For a man born and raised in Alsace, on the border of France and Germany, it was extremely ironic that Wyler's first films should be Westerns. In the mid 1920s he happened to meet Universal head Carl Laemmle in Paris, and the mogul offered to send the young man to Hollywood to learn the craft of moviemaking. Wyler eagerly accepted and worked his way up from menial jobs to filming the first of seven Westerns for the studio starting in 1926. By the time the talkies came to stay, the director had filmed such low-budget titles as *Lazy Lightning, The Stolen Ranch* (both 1926), *Hard Fists, Straight Shootin', Blazing Days, The Border Cavalier* (all 1927), and *Thunder Riders* (1928), as well as the independent production *Shooting Straight* (1927). The director shot these low-budget properties in one week each. He spent three days in production, took a day off, returned to the studio on Friday to read over the next script, and on Saturday rehearsed the cast. By Monday the cameras rolled.

Although these hoss-operas were by no means comparable to his later work, Wyler did learn basic elements such as story construction and editing by making one film per week. And they gave him a general frame of reference which he attempted to use a dozen years later for *The Westerner.*

When the director signed to lens *The Westerner,* he sent over to Universal for prints of his early sagebrush sagas. Although Wyler found nothing could be learned from screening the films, he discovered to his dismay that one of the Westerns was embarrassingly bad. But since the production hadn't been seen for a decade (and wasn't likely to ever be re-released), Wyler and his editor reportedly cut over 800 feet out of the hour-long vehicle, then returned the carefully edited print to Universal. Known as "Ninety-Nine Take" Wyler, one who would shoot scenes over and over again in the quest for perfection, the director also spent weeks in the editing room polishing a work. And, to him, there were at least 800 reasons why it should be that way.

Goldwyn liked a perfectionist, for he was one himself. Both producer and director were men who would fight for what they wanted, take chances, stick with an element until it was right.*

In 1940, Wyler put *The Westerner* into perspective. "People may get the idea that this is a regular Western, a go-after 'em, hard-riding, action Western. Well, in a way, it's a Western. There is plenty of melodrama at times, and riding too. But really it's a comedy. And the funniest scene in it is a chase—one man chasing another. You'd think it was melodrama. But it's a comedy. Walter Brennan chases Gary Cooper, and knocks him off the horse too. There isn't a thing at stake, not even the heroine's life or the father's mortgage. But it's funny and maybe exciting too."

Although the director couldn't find anything useful in his early Westerns, his own summary of their worth provides a link between them and *The Westerner.* "They were just like an episode in a TV show. They were all very elementary, very corny stories of a cowboy and a girl, a villain and a chase, plus a fight."

In *The Westerner,* the cowboy is played by Gary Cooper, the girl is Doris Davenport, the villain Walter Brennan, the chase already described, and the fight comes at the end. But it is the relatively unimportant status of the cowboy, the alternately ruthless and touching character of the bad guy, Judge Roy Bean, the nature of the chase, and the circumstances and positioning of the fight which make the difference.

But it wasn't always that clear. Niven Busch recently related to me something of the odyssey of *The Westerner.* "Sam Goldwyn was in trouble with *The Westerner* when I joined the drill. Jo Swerling was halfway through a screenplay which nobody liked. Goldwyn had bought a ten-page original based on the life of Judge Roy Bean. There was really only a slim tracing of story and no character for Cooper at all. I came in to trouble shoot and wrote a new screenplay, making Cooper a saddle bum passing through the Pecos county. The love-hate relationship between Coop and Brennan was pretty much my work."

Busch has always been fascinated by the special relationships he believes were shared by men and women in the 19th-century American West. And that interest provided a strong influence on the growth of the movie Western. "I don't personally claim credit for pushing Western pictures into the stylized drama they took on in

---

*Author Niven Busch rendered a concise picture of the mogul. "Samuel Goldwyn was a genius showman with fantastic taste as an entrepreneur. He could tell little from the written page—his wife Frances read scripts to him—but once he had committed himself to a creative idea he knew exactly how it should look on film and spared no expense or trouble in making his visions come true. Certainly he had some trouble with the English language but he could be pretty damned articulate when the need arose."

the 50s and 60s," Busch informed me, "but I do feel I was ahead of my time in presenting obsessive relationships as I have seen them develop between lonely people and as I feel intuitively that they must have been in the early West. The father-daughter fixation of the Huston and Stanwyck characters in *The Furies* (Paramount, 1950) is a good example of this, also the mutual sex obsession of Pearl and Lewt in *Duel in the Sun* (Selznick Releasing Corporation, 1946). This same fierce concentration of emotion also surfaces in *Pursued* (Warner Bros., 1947), when the Teresa Wright character marries Robert Mitchum so as to kill him on their wedding night.

"I believe that the single-mindedness of lonely people was a basic motivating power among the Western frontier cultures. This is what I was trying to get over in my Western films. I know both from intuition and from observation that the characterization is true."

Sam Goldwyn wanted archetypal Western man Gary Cooper to essay the role of Cole Hardin. In between the descent of William S. Hart and the solidifying of John Wayne as a giant of Hollywood's West, Cooper was the biggest star making oaters. Such productions provided him with strong, dominant parts. Things revolved around these screen cowboys. In *The Westerner,* Cole Hardin serves as a buffer for the activity of Judge Roy Bean, from the unlawful magistrate's dictatorial reign to his unrequited love for Lily Langtry.

Cooper realized the relative insignificance of his character and couldn't understand why Goldwyn wanted him for the role. Why would the mogul pay Cooper the highest salary in Hollywood at the time for a character who could be portrayed by any number of lesser leading men, or one of Goldwyn's hopeful unknowns? The names Doris Davenport, Walter Brennan, Lillian Bond, and Fred Stone provide the answer. Who would go to see a big-budget production featuring the aforementioned and only a moderately well-known leading man, or, worse, a new player? Goldwyn realized that he needed Cooper for star quality. The actor could attract an audience. And the part required a performer who could bring out the sympathy Cole Hardin feels for Bean, despite the jurist's corrupt nature, and play comic scenes with conviction.

Wyler was very happy Cooper signed to play Hardin. The director respected the star's intuitive ability to recognize the essence of a scene or bit of dialogue and do the right thing without being asked. Since Wyler liked to do many takes, he needed actors who could be fresh and inventive after a dozen recitations of a single line. "I don't know any other actor who can do what he does with a scene," Wyler said. "I couldn't even tell another actor how to do it. If you tell Gary that here, after this line, is a chance for a funny look, he'll get the idea. I couldn't explain what kind of a look, but he'll get the idea. He'll do something with that look no one else could do."

Other directors such as Victor Fleming and Henry Hathaway were impressed by Cooper's sixth sense about a character. It made their jobs easier. Perhaps part of the star's knack for illuminating movements or line readings came from his extremely relaxed general attitude as the highest paid star in Hollywood. "Things are what they are because they are that way," Cooper once said. "If I get into something, I let it carry me along until I get tired of it and then I do something else. If you do that you won't have to worry. I won't."

Walter Brennan appeared so nonchalant about his role that he could get into the character without anyone realizing it. Niven Busch said, "I met Walter coming back from lunch one day on the Goldwyn lot and as soon as he saw me he twisted his neck to one side and stood there with his chin cocked around at a strange angle. He was in costume for the role, but I never connected this with the cramped attitude he'd assumed, and when he continued his awkward attitude I inquired, 'Did you do something to your neck, Walter?' 'Well, no,' he said, 'not *my* neck. You know the story about Bean. He was hanged one time but they cut him down and saved him. That would have given him a crick in the neck, wouldn't it?' He was just showing us how Bean's must have looked. I had never read anything about this—but Brennan had—and his research gave us the running gag of the dislocated neck which afflicts Brennan throughout the film: his adversary-buddy Cooper has to repair it by poking him in the jaw."

Director Wyler originally wanted his wife, Margaret Tallichet, for the female lead, but Goldwyn vetoed the idea, insisting instead on contractee Doris Davenport. She was one of his aspiring performers, who had actually been overlooked by the executive the first time she worked for him as a Goldwyn Girl in *Kid Millions* and suddenly elevated to the female lead in mid-production. After that the movie career of then Doris Jordan seemed to fizzle out, so she went to New York to find modelling jobs. Four years later Doris came back to Hollywood, changed her name to Davenport, and was one of the hundreds tested for the role of Scarlett O'Hara in *Gone with the Wind.* Reportedly Wyler objected to Davenport, but Goldwyn insisted the actress be used.

The mogul also imported British musical star Lillian Bond to portray Lily Langtry. *The Westerner* gave Bond her first important cinema role after appearing in a number of London revues and plays such as *The Scandals, Stepping Out, Follow Through, The Wife's Away,* and *Springtime for Henry,* along with a New York stint in *Accent on Youth*.

Twenty-one-year-old Forrest Tucker signed a Goldwyn contract to make his debut in *The Westerner*, which was also the first movie for Dana Andrews, under contract to Goldwyn since 1938. Goldwyn wanted Andrews brought along slowly, so after first signing the actor, he insisted the performer hone his skills onstage before appearing in a film. Andrews' first screen role consisted of twelve words in *The Westerner*, for which he trained by appearing in two dozen Pasadena Playhouse presentations. He also followed Goldwyn's order to wear a dental brace and asked for a received permission from the boss to marry.

Although *The Westerner* purports to tell the truth about Judge Roy Bean in 1880s Texas, Goldwyn, along with scenarists Niven Busch and Jo Swerling, stretched the truth as per Hollywood's way with history. The film asserts Bean took over the judgeship of a town without being appointed and that he actually met Lily Langtry before dying of gunshot wounds inflicted by fictional Cole Hardin. A college professor named Dr. C. L. Sorricheshan attempted to correct false impressions he felt were created in *The Westerner.*

"Bean was appointed peace justice August 2, 1882," he told newspapers in 1940. "But the country between Pecos and Langtry was tough. It needed a justice of the peace badly and the Rangers couldn't wait until Bean's appointment." Apparently the Texas Rangers gave Bean permission to set up a court in the town of Vinegarroon, which the judge renamed Langtry. He was lawfully elected to his post in 1885 and remained in that position almost steadily until his death by natural causes in 1902. Some of the elections were honest, but at least one was rigged. In 1896, for instance, Bean received 100 more votes for the position of judge than there were people in the district. So Bean was a rascal. And he never did get to meet Lily Langtry, although the celebrated actress did journey by train to Langtry, Texas, in 1904 to pay posthumous homage to one of her most ardent fans.

The making of a film about a real person tends to unearth individuals who claim to have known the subject. When Fox shot *Jesse James,* the studio found several relatives of the famous outlaw, one of whom served as a technical consultant. Of course, the chance for publicity caused some old-timers to conjure fantasies about a Jesse James or Billy the Kid which were beyond the imagination of the brightest screenwriter. However, hard evidence in 1940 reportedly showed that two individuals who claimed to have known Bean and Langtry were telling the truth, although Niven Busch didn't recall any such people appearing in the Western.

Marie Lawton had been a chorus girl in "Jersey Lily's" musical company. "Nothing can be written that can exaggerate her charm

Fred Stone, Gary Cooper, and Forrest Tucker

Walter Brennan and Forrest Tucker (center)

and beauty," she said of Lily Langtry. "Everyone who saw her seemed to fall in love with her." Eighty-two-year-old Cal Cohen, a retired clown, appeared on the set one day clutching documented evidence that he had known Bean. As a bartender in the judge's saloon, he remembered seeing the prime authority west of the Pecos shoot down at least a dozen men. Cohen described Bean as an illiterate who so loved Lily Langtry that he wanted his men to hold up a train she was to ride and bring her to him. Gary Cooper was impressed with the man and asked that Cohen be given a small part in *The Westerner.* To add a touch of authenticity, Cal Cohen played the bartender in Bean's saloon.

Although liberties were apparently taken with Bean's life, the Texas frontier of the 1880s was researched thoroughly for *The Westerner.* Art director James Basevi meticulously reconstructed the Grand Opera House in Fort Davis, Texas, where Lily Langtry had performed. Set decorator Julia Herron found it difficult to find furniture authentic enough to resemble the plain style of the late 19th-century West tables and chairs. Gary Cooper's outfit was more in keeping with the style of the "B" movie cowboy heroes than their real counterparts, but co-star Doris Davenport had only three changes of costume—all simple calico—throughout the entire film—a rare occurrence in Hollywood at a time when most female performers seemed to wear entire wardrobes in the course of one picture.

Goldwyn instructed that the Western be accurate to the smallest detail, so researchers sifted through library and archive files searching for defunct 19th-century magazines such as *The New York Clipper, The Volcano, The National Stage and Sport, The New Woman,* and *Art and Artists.* They knew that Lily Langtry's picture appeared on the cover of each of the journals at least once, but didn't know what the publications looked like.

Eight and a half miles of roadway was cut through Goldwyn City, located near Tucson, Arizona. The path wound through mountain ranges and forests of cholla and saguaro cacti. The 250-member production company of *The Westerner* traversed the land around Goldwyn City for four weeks. Weather problems and other delays caused Sam Goldwyn great worry. And his battle to get the most out of his production in every way wouldn't be done with the completion of the film.

Many real-life cowboys were employed by the studio. Feeling that they were on their own turf, the modern Westerners figured they could outsmart the Hollywood characters at horse trading, gambling, or in any other traditional aspect of Western life. But they didn't take into account the fact that Gary Cooper grew up on a Montana ranch and knew as much about horseflesh as they did.

Coop was offered two ponies for $150, but the quick-witted star talked the price down to $125 for the pair. Special effects cameraman Archie Stout showed the ranch hands they weren't the only ones who could handle a deck of cards. Stout was a friend of John Ford's, and to be in that great director's circle, one had to be tough, a man's man, and a dedicated cardplayer.

As with most action films shot on location, the making of *The Westerner* expended a lot of real sweat, blood, and energy in the creation of the make-believe violence. Keeping control of a herd of 7000 cattle, the largest ever assembled for a movie until then, was the job of the professional horsemen hired by Goldwyn. They had to drive the herd across the Mexican border into Arizona. It might just as well have been an actual journey, with a payoff at the end. Early in the shooting Cooper injured his leg and had to be lifted onto his horse before the cameras rolled on each take. With Wyler at the helm, Cooper must have gotten on and off the saddle many times. Walter Brennan found out what it was like to die in a William Wyler film. The actor had to do his death scene nine times before the director found one he was satisfied with. Since Brennan had been expiring on the screen for over ten years (the first time was in 1928s *Smilin' Guns*), he was used to it.

When the day's filming was done, the cast and crew couldn't go into Bean's saloon and order shots of red-eye. They would have had to settle for the water spiked with amber-colored vegetable dye which filled the whiskey bottles. Sometimes a wall of a cinema bar might be lined with the real thing for the sake of authenticity. But to avoid any trouble from anti-liquor groups, the shelves of the saloon were filled with near-beer, a drink which contained only ½ of 1% alcohol and was a favorite during Prohibition.

Dmitri Tiomkin's musical score for *The Westerner* was built about songs of the era. A sixty-man orchestra, including members of the Los Angeles Philharmonic, along with a guitarist and chorus, integrated ditties such as "Portland Fancies," "Varsorienne," "My Beautiful Creole Belle," "Tenting Tonight," "While Strolling in the Park One Day," "Come Home, Father," and "Are You Going to the Ball This Evening?" into the compositions.

It can't be said that United Artists didn't give *The Westerner* an all-out promotional campaign. An ad for the production pictured a stern-looking Gary Cooper on horseback, with an insert on the right featuring Cooper and Doris Davenport. This large sketch of Coop set the tone for the publicity.

The pressbook to theatre owners read:

> Goldwyn showmanship . . . the hallmark of superior entertainment that speaks the language of box-office . . . shines

through every reel, every sequence, every shot of *The Westerner.*

It's a picture that challenges your exploitation showmanship to come up to the measure of the producing showmanship which Goldwyn has lavished on the production.

Gear your selling campaign to the lusty, gusty, rough-and-tumble epic of kangaroo court days in West Texas that the story tells . . . sell the spectacle of the roaring prairie fire, thundering cattle stampede, pioneer border warfare, and desperate fighting for land and love of women, with your most spectacular exploitation and publicity efforts.

The campaign is all here—and it's all yours! Use the checklist given in the table of contents . . . examine this pressbook page by page for the materials and ideas with which to sell *The Westerner* to your town . . . AND THEN GET THEM WORKING FOR YOU!

UA also called for a "fashion tie-up," which would sell hats, gloves, and jewelry styled after those in *The Westerner.* A new dance, "The Westerner," was created. Local groups would be encouraged to discuss kangaroo courts. There would be a "Westerner" menu contest. And every town would have its own very special "Westerner," a man who fit the rugged description of Cole Hardin.

The Westerner had a gala premiere in Fort Worth, Texas. A huge crowd met a group from Hollywood which included Gary Cooper, Walter Brennan, Doris Davenport, and Lillian Bond. Amon Carter, publisher of the Fort Worth *Star Telegram,* galloped around on a fawn-colored pony, decorated with silver spangles, to welcome the stars. Other made-up cowboys milled around, some on horse, some on foot. They were kept from shooting off their weapons for fear of stampeding the horses.

The performers put on a show at the Fort Worth Coliseum to benefit 10,000 orphans. Just about anything they did was fine with area residents. A huge crowd of 300,000 turned out for the premiere of *The Westerner.* Master of ceremonies Bob Hope had a playful wrestling match on stage for the possession of the microphone.

Despite the valiant publicity efforts of United Artists, *The Westerner* received a mixed critical reception:

New York *Daily News,* Kate Cameron, three stars:

Except for the character of the self-styled judge, the story of *The Westerner* follows the usual pattern of the horse opera.

New York Herald Tribune, Howard Barnes:

It is probably the fault of the narrative that *The Westerner* is only sporadically entertaining. At the same time, William Wyler hasn't helped matters appreciably in his staging.

New York *Morning Telegraph,* Leo Mishkin:

All of these recognized artists of the cinema, Cooper, Wyler, Goldwyn, et al., apparently believed that they could put some very artistic stuff into what is nothing more nor less than a good old-fashioned hoss opera, and it's a debatable question as to whether artistic stuff really belongs in such a work.

New York *Post,* Archer Winsten:

It is fortunate that *The Westerner* was produced by Samuel "The Touch" Goldwyn, directed by the perfectionist William Wyler, improved by the noblest of lanky cowboys, Gary Cooper, assisted by Walter Brennan's best performance, and is having its premiere at Radio City Music Hall. . . . Because if it weren't for all those things you would realize it's all the same story that shows every other week at the Central Theatre in the guise of a common, bang-bang Western.

New York Times, Bosley Crowther:

This strangely ambiguous situation, which finds Mr. Cooper as the star and Mr. Brennan as the leading player, seems to be the fatal weakness in this frequently fascinating picture. . . . If someone could just have decided who should carry the ball, instead of letting it pass from one to the other, *The Westerner* might have been a bang-up, dandy film. And that, we are sorry to say, it isn't.

The Westerner was William Wyler's last oater until *The Big Country* (UA, 1958), an epic melodrama with sporadic power but little of the fine quality of *The Westerner.*

Gary Cooper went on to many more distinguished roles, some in Westerns, including his Oscar-winning performance as the lawman in *High Noon* (UA, 1952).

Screenwriter Niven Busch penned Western novels and scripts. His work on *Pursued* (Warner Bros., 1947) and *The Furies* (Paramount, 1950) resulted in a pair of unique, compelling "psychological" Westerns. But he is probably best known for fighting a losing battle with David Selznick over *Duel in the Sun.*

The Westerner was Doris Davenport's only major feature film. After roles in "B" productions, she drifted out of the business.

Lillian Bond did little else in the cinema.

Walter Brennan won the Best Supporting Actor Oscar for the third time for *The Westerner* in what was clearly a leading role. He went on to appear in more Westerns and was a prominent character in Howard Hawks' *Red River* (UA, 1948) and *Rio Bravo* (Warner Bros., 1959).

Dana Andrews fared better with Twentieth Century-Fox which shared his contract with Goldwyn and subsequently achieved stardom in Fox's *The Ox-Bow Incident* and in Goldwyn's *The North Star,* both 1943.

Forrest Tucker spent years as a leading man in "B" films and as villains in prestige productions. One of his more recent parts was the chief bad guy in *Chisum* (Warner Bros., 1970).

After *The Westerner,* considered by many one of the screen's finest depictions of frontier Americana, Sam Goldwyn stayed away from the sagebrush saga.

The Westerner showed that the American frontier could be more than just the fodder for a familiar grind of cowboy movies. It broke some old rules about plot and character, and in doing so helped expand the borders of the genre enough to let in the psychological Western, the anti-Western, the satirical Western (like John Huston's look at the Bean legend in *The Life and Times of Judge Roy Bean* in 1972), and all the other variations which have come and gone in the last forty years.

Errol Flynn and Charley Grapewin

Gene Lockhart, Olivia de Havilland, and Errol Flynn

CHAPTER SEVEN

They Died with Their Boots On

Year Released: 1941
Studio: Warner Brothers
Executive Producer: Hal B. Wallis
Associate Producer: Robert Fellows
Director: Raoul Walsh
Screenplay: Wally Kine, Aeneas MacKenzie
Cinematography: Bert Glennon
Music: Max Steiner
Art Director: John Hughes
Editor: William Holmes
Assistant Director: Russell Saunders
Dialog Director: Edward A. Blatt
Technical Adviser: Lieutenant Colonel J. G. Taylor, U.S. Army, Retired
Makeup: Perc Westmore
Gowns: Milo Anderson
Sound: Dolph Thomas
138 minutes

Cast:

George Armstrong Custer	ERROL FLYNN
Elizabeth Bacon Custer	OLIVIA DE HAVILLAND
Ned Sharp, Jr.	ARTHUR KENNEDY
California Joe	CHARLEY GRAPEWIN
Samuel Bacon	GENE LOCKHART
Crazy Horse	ANTHONY QUINN

Major Romulus Taipe	STANLEY RIDGES
General Philip Sheridan	JOHN LITEL
Senator Sharp	WALTER HAMPDEN
General Winfield Scott	SYDNEY GREENSTREET
Fitzhugh Lee	REGIS TOOMEY
Callie	HATTIE McDANIEL
Lieutenant Butler	G. P. HUNTLEY, JR.
Captain Webb	FRANK WILCOX
Sergeant Doolittle	JOSEPH SAWYER
Senator Smith	MINOR WATSON
Lieutenant Roberts	GIG YOUNG
Second Lieutenant Davis	JOHN RIDGELY
President Grant	JOSEPH CREHAN
Mrs. Sharp	AILEEN PRINGLE
Mrs. Taipe	ANNA Q. NILSSON
Youth	HARRY LEWIS
Cadet Brown	TOD ANDREWS
Rosser	WALTER BROOKE
Captain McCook	SELMER JACKSON
Frazier	WILLIAM HOPPER
Corporal Smith	EDDIE ACUFF
Waiter	SAM McDANIELL
Charles	GEORGE REED
Jones	PAT McVEY
Adjutant	WILLIAM FORREST
Lieutenant Walsh	JAMES SEAY
Captain Riley	GEORGE ELDREDGE
Colonel	JOHN HAMILTON
Nurses	RENIE RIANO
	EDNA HOLLAND
	MINERVA URECAL
	VIRGINIA SALE
Head Nurse	VERA LEWIS
Station Master	SPENCER CHARTERS
Men in Bar	FRANK ORTH
	RAY TEAL
Clergyman	HOBART BOSWORTH

Staff Sergeant Brown	DICK WESSELL
Staff Officer	WELDON HEYBURN
Orderlies	HARRY STRANG
	MAX HOFFMAN, JR.
	FRANK MAYO
Salesman	IRVING BACON
Officers	GARLAND SMITH
	ROY BARCROFT
	DICK FRENCH
	MARTY FAUST
	BOB PERRY
	PAUL KRUGER
	STEVE DARRELL
Colonel of First Michigan	RUSSELL HICKS
Colonel of Fifth Michigan	VICTOR ZIMMERMAN
Soldier	IAN MacDONALD
Sentries	LANE CHANDLER
	ED PARKER
Adjutants	SOL GORSS
	ADDISON RICHARDS
Telegrapher	JACK MOWER
Jane	ALBERTA GARY
Maid	ANNABELLE JONES
Major Smith	HUGH SOTHERN
Tillaman	ARTHUR LOFT
Sergeant	CARL HARBAUGH
Corporal	G. PAT COLLINS
Woman	VIRGINIA BRISSAC
Settler	WALTER BALDWIN
Bartenders	WADE CROSBY
	JOE DEVLIN
	FRED KELSEY
Newsman	HERBERT HEYWOOD
Chairman	JOSEPH KING
Congressman	ED KEANE
Veteran	FRANCIS FORD
Grant's Secretary	FRANK FERGUSON

A brash spectacle if there ever was one, *They Died with Their Boots On* combines the enthusiasm of the typical Warner action tale with the epic scope of such Westerns as *Tumbleweeds* and *The Iron Horse.* The performances of Errol Flynn and Olivia de Havilland (together on their eighth movie) have a depth absent in their previous teamings, and the sympathy with which director Raoul Walsh guides this whitewashed biography of General George Armstrong Custer makes for a truly powerful statement on America's mistreatment of the Indians.

The film opens as Custer enters West Point in 1857. Although the eighteen-year-old is at the bottom of his class, he is an expert fighter who gets into numerous skirmishes with classmates. The growing friction between the North and South divides the student body. A group spearheaded by Ned Sharp, Jr. tries to persuade others to support the violent, criminal activities of John Brown. Custer, Sharp, and others brawl over the question, resulting in Sharp's dismissal from the academy. The enmity which has erupted between Custer and Sharp will last until the final moment of their lives. Just before the start of the Civil War, Custer meets and weds Libby Bacon. When the fighting begins, Custer joins the Second Cavalry and, through a clerical error, is commissioned a colonel. He distinguishes himself in battle and rises to the rank of general. After the war he settles down to the life of a country squire with Libby. Civilian life bores him, so he returns to the Army as a colonel and is assigned to Fort Lincoln in the perilous Dakota Territory as the commander of the Seventh Cavalry. Here Custer and Sharp meet again. As before, they are on opposite sides: Custer wants to make peace with the Indians while Sharp and his father are part of a secret organization which seeks to drive a railroad through sacred Sioux burial ground. To arouse interest in the Black Hills territory, the conspirators fabricate stories of a gold strike, and people flock to the area. Custer attempts to stop the Sharps in Washington but is thwarted by a political machine. The Colonel convinces President Grant of the plot, and the chief executive allows Custer to return to his regiment. Realizing an Indian war is about to break out, Custer sacrifices himself and the Seventh Cavalry until reinforcements can arrive to defeat the red men. After Custer's death, Libby compiles enough evidence against the conspirators to smash the group, and in doing so clears her husband's name.

They Died with Their Boots On covers much American history. In 138 minutes Walsh goes through the Civil War, the Indian struggles, the corruption in Washington, and the exploits of General Custer. The momentum of this sprawling Western is spurred by tightly packed but strongly developed narrative threads, and the

Errol Flynn (right)

Olivia de Havilland and Errol Flynn

energetic performance of Errol Flynn, who is perfect for the sanitized Custer Warners presents.

Each epic event in the film benefits from finely executed mass action scenes, as well as power from the human conflicts which propel them. The lifelong conflict between Custer and Sharp is illustrated early and their personalities are defined. From the image of Flynn on horseback, in a highly decorated uniform which is often laughed at by fellow officers, blond hair daintily touching his shoulders, he could be a memorial statue, all bronze and little humanity. But when Flynn speaks, all the arrogance incumbent in an egotist like Custer bursts through, despite the purification of his character and deeds by scriptwriters Wally Kine and Aeneas MacKenzie. Yet the celluloid commandant is also an idealist, a man willing to surrender his life for the common good. Battling Custer is the scheming Ned Sharp, played by Arthur Kennedy with a sense of obsession that appears to be on the verge of the psychotic. As such, the two actors exchange power for power in their tangles, Flynn with his aggressive nobility, Kennedy employing an aura of illness which is suggested physically by his sneering stares and pinched together countenance.

The war between the Army and the Indians is taken to a human level by Custer and Chief Crazy Horse. Anthony Quinn lends dignity to an already well-written character with his impressive figure, steady facial expressions, and deep voice. In presenting the two men as equal, Walsh's Western offers something more realistic than had been Hollywood's tendencies until *Broken Arrow* shattered Indian stereotyping in 1950.

The romance of Custer and Libby reaches a depth of emotions other screen relationships shared by Flynn and de Havilland never attain. The characters come to share a commitment to be fair to the Indians, and stymie Sharp's plans to put a railroad through the Black Hills. The complexities of this dramatic situation gives the actors a real chance to show their histrionic abilities. When the Seventh Cavalry must ride off to face a huge, multi-tribe war party, it sets up the most touching scene in *They Died with Their Boots On.* Mr. and Mrs. Custer share a final moment together in their cabin.

"You can't go. You'll be killed. I won't let you go," Libby pleads.

"I must go," says Custer. "It's my duty. I'm an officer in the United States Army."

If these lines sound mawkish, the strength of the readings by the actors provides a poignancy which must be heard, not read. She has accepted his decision. Knowing that he will die in battle, Custer breaks the chain off his watch, and gives it to Libby to have repaired. She has seen the action, but says nothing. They part. With Libby alone in the room, the camera pulls back, and she collapses. The quiet intensity of this moment makes for one of the most memorable scenes in the work of Raoul Walsh.

If Warners' study of Custer provides faulty history, the depiction of the battle of the Little Big Horn is tragically accurate. Hopelessly outnumbered, the men of the Seventh form a circle, attempting to thwart the Indian attack which gains momentum with each fallen soldier. In the end, Custer is left alone. The image is of the General with sword in hand, hatless, blond hair waving in the wind with the fringe of his buckskin jacket, and the American flag speared to the ground. Crazy Horse strikes him down, as both men knew it had to be.

They Died with Their Boots On is a lavish spectacle which chronicles the life of George Armstrong Custer and depicts the growing pains, the tragedies, and the triumphs of the American West.

The Making of *They Died with Their Boots On*

Errol Flynn would no longer work with director Michael Curtiz. After a half-dozen years as one of the most successful star-director teams at Warner Bros., after *Captain Blood* (1935), *Charge of the Light Brigade* (1936), *The Perfect Specimen* (1937), *The Adventures of Robin Hood* (1938), *The Private Lives of Elizabeth and Essex, Dodge City* (both 1939), *Virginia City, The Sea Hawk, The Santa Fe Trail* (all 1940), and *Dive Bomber* (1941), Flynn had had enough of Curtiz.

Curtiz claimed to have discovered Flynn by casting him as a corpse in *The Case of the Curious Bride* in 1935. When Robert Donat fell ill before the start of *Captain Blood,* Curtiz remembered the likable quality of the twenty-five-year-old Australian who portrayed the dead man. Even during the making of that classic swashbuckler, the relationship between Curtiz and Flynn began to falter. It was said the director took the safety tips off the swords used by Flynn and Basil Rathbone during a climactic dueling scene. Another story has it that Curtiz ordered real spears flung at Flynn during the production of *The Adventures of Robin Hood,* in order to make the actor's reaction more believable.

Whether or not these are myths, there is no doubt Michael Curtiz was an exacting taskmaster on the movie set. He wasn't averse to castigating an actor or technician in public if that person failed to perform. Some of his actresses even complained to the Joseph Breen Office because of the Hungarian's abusive language.

Conversely, Errol Flynn was an easy-going devil-may-care man who remained puzzled by his screen image. He could accept his stardom, but the feeling persists that he never understood why he was a star. Although Flynn had almost as many amorous adventures offscreen as on, he was, in his own way, a hard and diligent worker. The actor needed an understanding director, one who could spot talent hidden beneath all that studio gloss, and develop a more relaxed attitude toward the star.

Both Curtiz and Flynn were strong willed and could be very stubborn, so a breakup was probably inevitable. Hard-nosed actors rarely function up to their capabilities for equally tough-hided directors. Armed with his own sometimes absolutely correct ideas about how a scene should be played, the argumentative actor will not compromise, and an equally determined director with an aggressive personality is faced with a stand-off. Result, no victory, no defeat, no quality film. Bette Davis is an excellent example of a knowledgeable performer who found it very difficult to work with a man like Curtiz, although they were able to make several good pictures together. Yet she functioned brilliantly with mild-mannered but talented director Edmund Goulding in *Dark Victory* (1939).

Despite the battle of egos, Curtiz and Flynn together spelled box office, until the filmmaker's penchant for going over budget began to reflect in the profit margin. The costs of *The Sea Hawk,* their final swashbuckler as a team, rose to $1,700,000 due to production delays and the construction of expensive devices such as a hydraulic lift to make the studio boat rock.

Jack Warner wanted to spend about $2,000,000 on a lavish, semi-factual biography of General George Armstrong Custer. *They Died with Their Boots On* would feature the star-director partnership of Flynn and Curtiz. No thanks, said the actor. The combination of Flynn's animosity for Curtiz and the Hungarian's production extravagance forced the studio to remove the filmmaker from the project.

It was decided that Raoul Walsh should replace Curtiz. Warner liked Walsh, a director who made a reputation with war films and adventures in the 1920s, but was mired in mediocre properties throughout the 1930s until the mogul signed him to a seven year contract in 1939. Walsh's Warner films had so far found favor with the public and many of the critics. *The Roaring Twenties* (1939), *They Drive by Night* (1940), *High Sierra* (1941), and *Manpower* (1941) are all hard-hitting productions about taut tough guys (Cagney, Raft, Bogart, Robinson) who spout sizzling dialogue.

They Died with Their Boots On gave Walsh his biggest budget to that time. Previously his Warners actioners cost about

$1,000,000 each. However, he was used to handling expensive productions. *The Thief of Bagdad* (UA, 1924) was a costly venture, as were several more of his silent epics.

Most important, Raoul Walsh believed he could work with Errol Flynn. The actor welcomed the change of directors. Walsh's ability to live a rugged life off the set matched Flynn's own love of adventure. The filmmaker provided an excellent contrast to all work and little fun Curtiz. Walsh would treat Flynn gently and, at the proper times, guide that actor both on and off the set. Later when Jack Warner wanted to terminate Flynn's contract, Walsh talked both parties out of actions which they might later regret. Errol Flynn was brought along as a talent to be nurtured, a diamond which had to be cut, so when he tapped the jewel, a handful of glittering offsprings were produced. The treatment worked. Flynn gave one of his best performances in *They Died with Their Boots On.* Olivia de Havilland has often said that the star was a better actor than even he suspected.

But Walsh wanted something more than a top performance from Flynn. As long as the biopic wasn't going to tell the true story of the egocentric, aggressive general who led his troops into a massacre, the director wanted to make a statement about America's treatment of the Indian. Although most Westerns until then treated the red man as an ignoble savage, Walsh attempted to show that the Indians only turned violent when treaties signed in good faith were violated by the white man.

They Died with Their Boots On was filmed on location forty miles north of Hollywood. On the first day of shooting Walsh ran afoul of the Screen Actors Guild. The first scenes he wanted to lens were the spectacular battles between the Indians and the Army. The director needed at least 300 soldiers and 400 red men. Previously a filmmaker was permitted to use anybody who could ride a horse as an extra. But the Guild passed a rule saying only the union had the privilege of selecting such players. So Walsh had to take whatever was offered. That mandate led to tragedy.

The studio had a difficult time getting Sioux Indians for the production. Although they wired a reservation at Fort Yates, North Dakota, and received sixteen braves, Walsh employed anyone who vaguely resembled an Indian. Many of these reasonable facsimiles included Filipinos. Some of the other "red men" had facial hair which didn't allow them to be shot in close up. One Indian had a full beard, another wore a blond handle-bar mustache. The director decided to film only the real Sioux in the closer shots, and leave the rest to fill out the panoramic frames. Before every chase sequence, Walsh made the extras who would appear on horseback walk their mounts across the set. Anyone who didn't feel capable of doing the hard riding was excused from participation without a loss in pay. During the production a number of extras spent entire days drinking coffee and playing cards while the others rode across the plains.

To shoot the action, Walsh and the crew stood on top of scaffolds seven stories high, in order to obtain a sweeping view. While there, the men behind the camera watched as a number of the extras tramped through the takes like buffoons. Many couldn't even ride a horse. One steed stepped in a hole, toppled over, and before long a half-dozen other horses and riders collided with the downed mount. Even though stunt men were used who charged

Errol Flynn in a later action pose

$35 a fall, by the end of the day more than eighty soldiers and Indians were unceremoniously knocked from their horses. Some three dozen braves were sent to the ground as they charged toward the river to rally with a camp full of Sioux. Two dozen extras sustained injuries serious enough to warrant hospital treatment. Stunt expert Al Delamore was sent to Cedars of Lebanon Hospital with a fractured jaw and a mouth missing three teeth. Curly Gibson broke an elbow. Tony Alvoraco received a pair of broken ribs. Cecil Kellog finished one day's shooting with a deeply cut chin. And more were bruised and burned from being dragged along straw-covered earth by their horses.

At one point Russ Saunders, Walsh's assistant, called the studio and requested sixty additional extras to replace the injured ones. The studio panicked at the alarming statistics Saunders reeled off and sent a hospital on wheels, including two tents, bedding, doctors, and nurses to the location site. When the buses left the studio the next morning at six to carry the extras to the set, an ambulance followed close behind.

By the finish of any day's work, the hospital tents were filled with the "war wounded." Walsh, angered at the woefully inadequate bunch of extras supplied by the Guild, finally convinced the union of the error of its ways. He quickly replaced the inexperienced players with those who could ride, and the picture progressed more evenly.

Anthony Quinn saw the absurdity of the situation. One morning the buses and ambulance pulled out on schedule, but the train of cars had an addition. Quinn rented a hearse to follow the ambulance—which amused even Walsh, who was especially grateful to the actor when a number of extras who couldn't stay on horseback jumped off the bus at the sight of the long black car.

There were three tragic accidents on the set. One extra fell from a horse and broke his neck. Another died of a heart attack. The third was the most macabre. Walsh was filming a scene of the Union cavalry riding across a bridge rigged to explode on both sides. Jack Budlong, playing a young lieutenant, led the charge. As the explosives went off, the actor was thrown straight up in the air. His sword ripped through his hand and lodged point up in the bridge. Budlong was run through as he hit the ground. Usually performers seen in long shot receive fake swords, but Budlong had insisted on using the real thing. The property man argued with him for some time, but the actor was insistent.

The tragedy on the cinema battlefield was offset somewhat by the rapport which developed between Walsh and Flynn. The actor gave a fine performance as the brash but heroic Custer. The final scene between Flynn and Olivia de Havilland is one of the most touching in Raoul Walsh's oeuvre. Both players handled the difficult moment with remarkable understatement. Possibly de Havilland's reported crush on the popular leading man aided their sensitive, passionate love scenes. The actress definitely had fond memories of her director. "I was perfectly delighted when Raoul Walsh was assigned . . . and I told Errol that I was sure he would be pleased with the choice. I had already worked with Walsh on *The Strawberry Blonde* and I knew what I was talking about." She remembered the filmmaker as a "sensitive man" with "great tact" and "a fine insight into character." Such qualities made him a master director of Errol Flynn.

Jack Warner heaped praise on everyone connected with *They Died with Their Boots On* and especially applauded Errol Flynn. In the future their relationship would be anything but cordial, but for the moment Warner was Flynn's champion.

Reviews were mixed:

Dallas Morning News, John Rosenfeld:

The picture takes so many liberties with history that we feared, until the last reel, that Warner Brothers was going to give Custer the victory of the Little Big Horn on June 25, 1876. . . . The skullduggery of the Grant regime was too complicated for the movie writers. The picture loses continuity and meaning in these sequences. Only the vigorously staged last stand with hundreds of mounted horses and with great expertness from the camera crew flying over the battleground rescues the picture.

New York *Daily News,* Kate Cameron, three and one half stars:

Proper editing would have made this one of the most popular pictures of the year as it is filled with exciting action and tells an absorbing story of one of America's most colorful heroes.

New York Post:

To come right down to it, all the performances in *They Died with Their Boots On* are splendid for action melodrama, which is what this is with bells on. Director Raoul Walsh has been particularly successful in saddle scenes.

New York Sun:

Maybe *They Died with Their Boots On* is the proper title to put on the whole business after all. They certainly died all right: Flynn and the other players, and the script and story, and the dialogue and direction. That's a massacre that even compares with the Little Big Horn. . . .

Raoul Walsh

Raoul Walsh directed eleven more Westerns before retiring after *A Distant Trumpet* (Warner Bros.) in 1964. The best of these are *Pursued* (Warner Bros., 1947), *Silver River* (Warner Bros., 1948), *Colorado Territory* (Warner Bros., 1949) (a virtual remake of *High Sierra), The Lawless Breed* (Universal, 1952), *Gun Fury* (Columbia, 1953), and *The King and Four Queens* (UA, 1956).

Errol Flynn made six more movies with Walsh and starred in several Westerns in the late 1940s and early 50s, but none came close to *They Died with Their Boots On.* And he never worked with Olivia de Havilland again, although both later appeared (separately) in *Thank Your Lucky Stars* (1943).

They Died with Their Boots On is an action-packed depiction of one of the most tragic events in American history. Here Warners distorts the truth about Custer and presents him as he should have been—strong, bold, sensitive, and honorable. In this Western, the Hollywood dream factory has made the world go away. But the writers and director Raoul Walsh have created a powerful illustration of the shameless manner in which the white man treated the Indian, which makes *They Died with Their Boots On* both a fantasy and a very real document, a factually inaccurate story which has the sting of truth.

Henry "Harry" Morgan, and Henry Fonda

CHAPTER EIGHT

The Ox-Bow Incident

Year Released: 1943
Studio: Twentieth Century-Fox
Producer: Lamar Trotti
Director: William Wellman
Screenplay: Lamar Trotti, based on the novel by Walter Van Tilburg Clark
Cinematography: Arthur Miller
Music: Cyril J. Mockridge
Art Directors: Richard Day, James Basevi
Editor: Allen McNeil
Assistant Director: Ad Schaumer
Property Master: Joseph Behm
Set Decorators: Thomas Little, Frank Hughes
Sound: Alfred Bruzlin, Roger Heman
77 minutes

Cast

Gil Carter	HENRY FONDA
Donald Martin	DANA ANDREWS
Rose Mapen	MARY BETH HUGHES
Mexican	ANTHONY QUINN
Gerald	WILLIAM EYTHE
Art Croft	HENRY MORGAN
Ma Grier	JANE DARWELL
Judge Daniel Tyler	MATT BRIGGS

Arthur Davies	HARRY DAVENPORT
Major Tetley	FRANK CONROY
Farnley	MARC LAWRENCE
Monty Smith	PAUL HURST
Darby	VICTOR KILIAN
Pancho	CHRIS-PIN MARTIN
Joyce	TED NORTH
Mr. Swanson	GEORGE MEEKER
Mrs. Swanson	ALMIRA SESSIONS
Mrs. Larch	MARGARET HAMILTON
Mapes	DICK RICH
Old Man	FRANCIS FORD
Bartlett	STANLEY ANDREWS
Greene	BILLY BENEDICT
Winder	PAUL E. BURNS
Sparks	LEIGH WHIPPER
Jimmy Carnes	GEORGE CHANDLER
Moore	GEORGE LLOYD
Sheriff	WILLARD ROBERTSON
Deputy	TOM LONDON

The forces which drive men to violence are brilliantly explored in *The Ox-Bow Incident.* The lust for blood to quell inner torment infects the judgment of average people in a Western which may very well be the most grim production released in the United States during World War II.

Cowboys Gil Carter and Art Croft ride into Bridger's Wells, Nevada. It is discovered that a local rancher named Kincaid has been reportedly murdered by cattle thieves. Since the sheriff is out of town, Major Tetley, a former Confederate officer who has kept his title, organizes a vigilante group to hunt the criminals. After a hard ride, the men cross paths with three strangers—Donald Martin, a Mexican, and an old man, who claim to have purchased cattle from Kincaid. When they cannot produce a bill of sale, Tetley puts them on trial as rustlers. Outsiders Carter and Croft try to persuade the vigilantes to bring the trio back to town, but their words are lost on a crowd bent for revenge. The three cowboys are sentenced to die. Martin is allowed to write a final letter to his wife. Then, one by one, the men are hanged. The next morning the sheriff returns and tells the stunned vigilantes that Kincaid is alive and did indeed sell

Martin the cattle. Back in town, all is quiet. Carter reads an excerpt from Martin's letter in the saloon. Carter and Croft then ride out of town.

The Ox-Bow Incident is a classic study of the roots of violence. It is perhaps the first of what has been called "anti-Westerns," or oaters which illustrate modern themes and do not necessarily embody all the structural components of the genre. Although there is clearly a conflict between good people (the accused) and bad (the vigilantes), Lamar Trotti's script examines both the positive and negative qualities of each group. Tetley's need to command, to always be right, is examined. It is explained that Ma Grier comes from a time when the only law was a common understanding among Westerners and violation of the faith meant swift punishment. Trotti commiserates with the plight of Tetley's weak-willed son, Gerald, forced to choose between what he feels is right and the desire to please his father. Such soul-searching took hold in many Westerns after World War II, just as the *film noir* introduced a deep perversion into the mentality of the average cinema urban criminal. In *The Ox-Bow Incident,* the mind's violence replaces hard riding, chase sequences, and gun fights. Even the lynching is relatively quiet. That is the source of its power. The contradiction between the life-ending action and the physically subdued manner in which it is accomplished is positively eerie.

The alternating of real exteriors and painted sets gives the Western a nightmare quality, a vagueness of time and place which makes *The Ox-Bow Incident* a moral tale relevant to every era. This quality highlights the difference between the film and most other sagebrush sagas of the era. The images begin in the simple reality of a crude Western town, then descend to a mad sphere where gnarled, make-believe trees and dim studio skies heighten the horror of a kangaroo court glazed in an insanity which leads to the murder of three men.

The reading of Martin's letter out loud has been roundly criticized in many quarters. At one point, director William Wellman closes in on Carter as he recites Martin's final words, the brim of the cowboy's hat jutting out on top of the frame, allowing the presence of remorseful others to be barely pictured. If Wellman had built the Western to a fever pitch with pulsating music, fast cutting, and an explosive ending, like the knock-out punch in a prize fight, revealing the moral of the story in the contents of the letter, the story would have been tonally, as well as verbally, redundant. But everything is done with the hush of enveloping death. Wellman keeps the tone of the Western as if it were a timid man acting out violent or heroic fantasies through the characters, then returning to his modest life.

The Ox-Bow Incident says that anyone could be mistaken for a criminal if punishment is meted out on impulse. The performances of Henry Fonda as Carter and Dana Andrews as Martin are incredibly similar. While in different positions, both men are essentially non-violent, confused by the spiralling hate and madness around them. They know what's right, but nobody else wants to know. Fonda and Andrews are so alike here, they could have switched roles. Donald Martin is everyman. He might have been Gil Carter.

When Carter and Croft drift out of Bridger's Wells to deliver the letter to Martin's wife, Carter knows he himself could have written it. *The Ox-Bow Incident* bases its case against mob violence on those words which could have been written by us all.

The Making of *The Ox-Bow Incident*

William Wellman had a conversation with producer Harold Hurley in 1940 about a film version of a novel called *The Ox-Bow Incident* by Walter Van Tilburg Clark. Hurley wanted to star Mae West in the picture. Wellman couldn't understand where she was going to fit into a narrative where the roles went to men. The producer planned to have the scene-stealing performer act as sort of a hostess to the cowboys, entertaining them and feeding them after they ride into town. The director loved the basic story, but couldn't see butchering it into a vehicle for a glamorous star. So he dropped out of the project.

Hurley had recently been dismissed by Paramount for differences of opinion with studio heads. The producer took an option on Clark's book for $6,000, then looked for a screenwriter, director, and cast.

Six months later Wellman and his wife, Dotty, ran into Hurley at Arrowhead Hot Springs. The producer related his frustration at not being able to get a package assembled to make *The Ox-Bow Incident.* Bill was still quite taken by the story and offered Hurley $6,500 for the screen rights. The ex-Paramount executive accepted without hesitation. The director known as "Wild Bill" planned how to excite producers about a grim story set in 1885 Nevada which Hurley felt would never be filmed.

Wellman sat up all night reading the novel to his wife. She was equally enthusiastic. Wellman contacted author Clark, and both men worked hard to sell the project to a studio. The director called on all the executives he'd worked for. He talked to Selznick and people at MGM, Warners, and other studios. Everyone told him that since America was involved in a war, nobody would want to see such a morbid, depressing screen tale. It was reasoned that audi-

William Wellman

Dana Andrews, Paul E. Burns, and Henry Fonda

ences needed fantasy and patriotic war dramas with optimistic endings.

Neither Wellman nor Clark wanted to alter the concept of the material in order to sell it. Clark was familiar with the structural components of the Western and always found that they got in the way of his themes. Yet the author believed it to be important to have contact with and understand the past before dealing with the present. So he had decided to write a Western novel using the basic material, characters, situations, etc., and try to bring them to life again in a way which would be relevant to a world in crisis.

Although Ford's *Stagecoach,* King's *Jesse James,* and others had liberated the Hollywood Western, in a way, from the Tom Mix escapist formula which promoted sagebrush theatrics such as gunplay, horsemanship, and fancy costumes, producers believed Americans didn't need an anti-Fascist parable with an unhappy, downbeat ending. Perhaps if Wellman had taken the property around Hollywood even a year or two earlier, he could have sold it with more ease. In the early and mid 1930s, Warners and other studios made many popular actioners which smacked of social criticism. Wellman himself lensed *Public Enemy* (1931), *Heroes for Sale,* and *Wild Boys of the Road* (both 1933) there, three films which make important points about 20th-century America. In 1936 he helmed *Robin Hood of El Dorado,* a gangster melodrama set in Western garb for MGM, depicting how societal corruption forces a young man into a life of crime.

The leading citizens of the Nevada town in *The Ox-Bow Incident* take the law by the scruff of the neck when they lynch three men believed to be guilty of murder. They are proved wrong, and the novel ends on a downbeat note. Hollywood had dealt with lynch law in *Fury* (Paramount, 1936) and *They Won't Forget* (Warner Bros., 1937), so the subject itself wasn't taboo. Bad timing was the major reason why it took Wellman and Clark so long to film the Western tale.

But Clark wrote the book in 1937-38, years in which the aggression of Nazi Germany unsettled Europe and the world. He was happy that critics saw a parallel between the crazed brutality of the vigilantes and the ruthless Nazis, but worried that reviewers failed to mention that the unlawful executions which occur in 1885 Nevada could happen anywhere at any time. Clark was writing about those forces of mankind which foster mob violence when all the right stimuli are present.

After being turned down by virtually every other studio in town, Bill Wellman contacted Darryl F. Zanuck, Vice President in Charge of Production at Twentieth Century-Fox. Wellman and Zanuck, colleagues at Warners, had a friendship which began during the production of *Public Enemy* and ended with the making of *Call of the Wild* (Fox) in 1935. Both men were hot-tempered and demanding. Both understood what was right for a film and didn't care who knew it. In 1937, Wellman had to return to Fox to film some scenes for his classic *A Star Is Born* (UA). To let Zanuck know he was on the lot, Wild Bill heaved a brick through the mogul's office window.

With this in mind, Wellman called up Zanuck. Yet he also knew that the cigar-chomping producer was largely responsible for bringing a new vitality to Warners a decade earlier, through socially relevant crime films, dramas, and even musicals. Then Zanuck was interested in the day's headlines as the next day's box-office attractions. Perhaps he would see the modern theme of *The Ox-Bow Incident.* Zanuck's secretary didn't think the mogul would even speak to Wellman. But the director had brought her an occasional belt of liquor in the past, and she returned the favor by connecting him with her boss.

Zanuck's willingness to forget the past and deal with the present impressed Wellman. The director came to his office and told him about his project. Zanuck was intrigued and asked to read the novel. Several days later Wellman got the go ahead. There was only one stipulation. Wellman had to film any two projects Zanuck handed him, no questions asked. However, the director was to receive the salary he requested. It must be remembered that by 1942, when *Ox-Bow* went into production, Bill Wellman was one of the most respected directors in Hollywood. His temper and on-set antics were tolerated because he made good box-office movies fast. Wellman had shot the classic *Wings* (Paramount, 1928), the first film to win the best picture Oscar, *Public Enemy, A Star Is Born,* a brilliant inside look at Hollywood, and *Nothing Sacred* (UA, 1937), a riotous, crowd-pleasing satire on everything from reporters to rural America. Wellman wanted to make *The Ox-Box Incident* as much as he had desired to direct those productions. So he consented to Zanuck's terms.

Wellman and Clark agreed to let screenwriter Lamar Trotti author the script and produce the Western. Trotti had penned a number of excellent period scripts for Fox, including *In Old Chicago* (1938), *Young Mr. Lincoln,* and *Drums Along the Mohawk* (both 1939), so the director knew he was getting someone who understood the pleasures and problems of writing about the past. Like Clark, Trotti also wanted to make a statement about the times. Wellman was primarily interested in story values. As many filmmakers of his era believed, Wellman felt the first ingredient of an excellent picture had to be fine writing, without which it was impossible to do anything of quality.

With the dedication of Wellman, Clark, and Trotti, the pre-production of *The Ox-Bow Incident* went smoothly. Then Zanuck, who was serving in the armed forces, made lengthy trips to New York and London. The mogul hadn't seen the proposed budget for the Western, but when other Fox executives realized what the film would cost, they attempted to scrap the property. William Goetz, Bill Koenig, and Lew Schrieber tried to persuade Zanuck to terminate production and sent him a telegram detailing their objections to producing *The Ox-Bow Incident.* Goetz was fair enough to allow Wellman to defend his position. The director put this simple post-script on a telegram to the mogul. "May I ask you to remember our handshake? Yours ever, Bill." Zanuck wired back his support of Wellman, and the filmmaker never forgot it.

Although Zanuck felt the film would lose money, he believed the prestige of having such a non-commercial picture on Fox's credentials would add to the studio's prestige. Zanuck would feel the same way about Henry King's *The Gunfighter* a half-dozen years later. The quality which made Darryl F. Zanuck an outstanding studio head was that despite a brash, aggressive, and undeniably egotistical nature, he was a man who recognized talent and believed his people needed freedom to grow, to create without interference from the front office. But he also felt that each man in a movie unit was a separate entity and shouldn't be allowed to mix. Zanuck would only let a writer talk to a director through the script. The benefits of giving the artist enough room for personal expression had been reaped by Zanuck in *Public Enemy,* Busby Berkeley's musicals, and many more.

Trotti's screenplay retained Clark's characters and followed the plot structure closely. The major deviation came in the form of the letter written by Donald Martin to his wife. In the novel, Clark doesn't disclose the contents of the last statement. In the film, the letter is read by Gil Carter, after the mob has lynched the innocent trio.

The casting of the film was much less controversial than other pre-production arrangements. Henry Fonda agreed to do the leading role of Carter as soon as it was offered, but he had to agree to star in a minor comedy called *The Magnificent Dope* (1942) as well. Dana Andrews wanted desperately to play the victim, Martin, but found it difficult to convince others. The actor realized he needed a breakthrough role to escape the handful of small parts and second leads he had essayed in Fox and Goldwyn productions for the past few years. Andrews had to play Donald Martin if his career was ever to become meaningful. The actor's sad eyes, sincere face, and slightly Southern accent made him as well-suited to the role as the unshaven, soft-granite countenance of Henry Fonda flecked with

Henry Fonda in an action pose

innocent eyes was to Gil Carter. Contract players Anthony Quinn and Francis Ford (director John's brother) rounded out the trio accused of killing rancher Larry Kincaid. William Eythe and Frank Conroy were to play the meek son and sadistic father, respectively, along with the studio's old reliable Jane Darwell in the uncharacteristically unsympathetic role of Ma Grier. Mary Beth Hughes, Harry Morgan, Harry Davenport, and Marc Lawrence had significant supporting parts.

Wellman decided to go against the practice of shooting Westerns on location. Some scenes at the beginning and end of *The Ox-Bow Incident* were lensed outdoors, but the bulk of the tale, which occurs at night, was filmed on sets with painted backdrops. Cinematographer Authur Miller advised Wellman that photographing night for night might not lend the realism one might expect. The cameras were not able to pick up objects in the distance visible to the naked eye with the film stock of the time. So sets were substituted.

For a director who had built an early reputation as a proponent of "documentary realism," or making a fiction film as if the events were taking place naturally before the camera, with a minimum of artificial effects, that decision must have been difficult. But Bill Wellman was also known as one of the fastest workers in Hollywood. He could direct three films in the time it would take others to finish one. Part of the reason for Bill's label as a super-efficient filmmaker stemmed from the clever ways he covered up his perplexity.

Wellman and character player George Chandler worked out a system to delay a production any time Wellman had a problem. When he got stuck on something, the filmmaker signalled Chandler, and the actor would drop a line, miss his cue, or slip out of sight, so that Wild Bill could lose his temper and call a break. Then he'd close the door to his office and stay there until the solution revealed itself. Chandler was in thirty-six Wellman pictures, including *Ox-Bow,* and it can be assumed many lines were muffed so that the director received breathing room to solve a problem regarding those artificial sets.

There was nothing Wellman liked better than to lighten up a heavy moment during the making of a film with a funny story or practical joke. Dana Andrews broke up the cast and crew one day with a tale about his early days as a movie projectionist in Huntsville, Texas. The nineteen-year-old student was showing Wellman's *Wings* and, since the theatre wasn't yet equipped to handle the production's musical soundtrack, Andrews created his own system with a phonograph and several well-placed speakers. In his enthusiasm, however, Dana synchronized lilting violin music to the battle scenes and heavy drum rolls to the romantic moments.

Despite the joke on Wellman, the director and the actor got along fine. Andrews was pleased by Wellman's tough standards, and Bill wasn't averse to changing a scene he thought to be out of place or accommodating a member of the cast when necessary.

Wild Bill earned Andrews' admiration when he re-arranged the shooting plan for the actor. Dana's daughter Kathy was born during the production, and the morning after the event, which kept the actor up all night, Wellman shot out of schedule a sequence in which Andrews is sleeping. Here the director temporarily returned to his documentary realism, as when Andrews was ordered to go to sleep once the cameras rolled, he did just that!

Yet the movemaker could be as commanding as any who ever lensed a foot of Hollywood film. Joseph Behm, the property master on *The Ox Bow Incident,* remembers a time when his boss wouldn't take "no" for an answer. "Besides being a great and colorful director, Bill was also a two-fisted drinker. The word 'fear' was not in his vocabulary. I remember on one occasion, I told one of my assistants to give one of the stars a call with the second unit. Bill and I were having dinner that night. The actor came to me. 'Joe, I refuse to work with a second unit director.' Bill said, 'You'll go with the second unit.' 'Now wait a minute, Bill (said the actor), this is none of your business.' 'I'm making it my business.' He got up, hit the man on the chin, knocking him over a table, then he started kicking him in the face. The actor got up, ran out of the dining room, Bill after him. There was never a dull moment working with him."

Henry Fonda, Mary Beth Hughes, and George Chandler

Just about everyone got along fine throughout the production, although of course some were more popular with co-workers than others. Fonda, Andrews, and Francis Ford were greatly respected and liked by everyone. Anthony Quinn, as Joe Behm put it, "was on the set to work, therefore he didn't make many friends," but remained a gentleman at all times. William Eythe, who played Gerald Tetley, did not seem to take to his character very well. His role in the Western was his first major part in Hollywood, after being noticed as a psychotic Nazi officer in John Steinbeck's *The Moon Is Down* on Broadway. "I'm a normal human being and I prefer not to make a career of hysteria," Eythe said at the time. He did go on to less-intense roles in a number of Fox productions, but a love of the theatre prevented Eythe from fulfilling the promise of his early films.

When *The Ox-Bow Incident* was released in May 1943, America was deeply involved in World War II. Critical reception was mixed, but few reviewers denied the Western's power:

> *The Nation,* James Agee:
>
> *Ox-Bow* is one of the best and most interesting pictures I have seen for a long time, and it disappointed me. . . . It seems to me that in *Ox-Bow* artifice and nature got jammed in such a way as to give a sort of double focus, like off-printing in a comic strip. Here was a remarkably controlled and intelligent film; and in steady nimbus, on every detail, was the stiff over-consciousness of those who made it of the excellence of each effect, to such a degree that the whole thing seemed a mosaic of over-appreciated effects which continually robbed nature of its own warmth and energy.
>
> *New York Herald Tribune,* Otis L. Gurnsey, Jr.:
>
> It is a depressing arrival in days that are depressing enough already.
>
> *New York Times,* Bosley Crowther:
>
> . . . an ugly study in mob violence, unrelieved by any human grace save the futile reproach of a minority and some wild post-lynching remorse. . . . William Wellman has directed the picture with a realism that is as sharp and cold as a knife. . . . A heartwringing performance by Dana Andrews as the stunned and helpless leader of the doomed trio does much to make the picture a profoundly distressing tragedy.

The Ox-Bow Incident did not make money at first, but added a touch of class to Fox's lineup. The studio tried to generate some interest in the production:

It's Tough—It's True—It's Terrifying—It's Terrific.

It will chill your blood with terror . . . and make it boil with fury.

Merciless as the lash of a whip across your face!

Publicists produced material suggesting that law schools hold mock trials in *The Ox-Bow Incident* tradition, and endeavor to determine a more legal fate for the three men. But nothing could induce the wartime moviegoer to sit through anything that didn't make him laugh, give the thrills and chills of chases, or at least affirm American unity in times of crisis.

In later years, William Wellman could happily report about the fate of his Western. He wrote in his autobiography, *A Short Time for Insanity* (Hawthorn), "They released it abroad (as *Strange Incident*), and it was over there that it became popular. So much so that they re-released it here; and on the second time around, it got some acclaim and incidentally a little money. Whatever it got, I was proud of it, and so was Zanuck; if it hadn't been for him, I would never have been able to make the picture."

But Wellman never forgot one reviewer who said the stark production had less value than the least of the "B" Westerns being cranked out at rapid rate by poverty-row studios. The director kept a copy of the critical piece in a bank vault.

Today *The Ox-Bow Incident* is viewed by film historians with various levels of applause. Some say it is an out and out classic; others assert the film had potential but is hurt by those artificial sets, and the unnecessary reading of Martin's letter. In fact, the divulgence of the contents of the last statement by the doomed rancher is the most argued about facet of the Western today. It is a philosophical piece of writing which rings false to many, in that a man making a final contact with his wife would be infinitely more personal. It has also been said that the letter unnecessarily emphasizes the story's theme. Following is an extract from the last will and testament of Donald Martin.

A man just naturally can't take the law into his own hands and hang people without hurting everybody in the world, because then he's not just breaking one law but all laws. Law is a lot more than words you put in a book, or judges or lawyers or sheriffs you hire to carry it out. It's everything people have ever found out about justice and what's right and what's wrong. It's the very conscience of humanity.

There can't be any such thing as civilization unless people have got a conscience, because if people touch God anywhere,

where is it except through their conscience? And what is anybody's conscience except a little piece of the conscience of all men that ever lived?

This lengthy but poignant statement on man's condition was written by Lamar Trotti. It doesn't appear in Walter Van Tilburg Clark's novel, but the feelings are echoed by another character. Wellman defended the reading of the letter until his dying day. He insisted that both he and author Clark favored its inclusion in the script.

Henry Fonda felt the role of Gil Carter was one of the best in his career. It has been alleged that *The Ox-Bow Incident* was the only Fox film he did with which he was totally satisfied.

Dana Andrews asserted: "My most satisfying experience was in the role of Martin. . . . It gave me a chance to try to do something I'd always wondered whether I could manage—playing a character who was sensitive without making him seem weak."

The Ox-Bow Incident made the *New York Times'* Top Ten list for 1943. Wellman won a best director award from the National Board of Review, and Henry Morgan was also honored for his portrayal of Art Croft, sidekick of Carter.

Fox made a forty-five-minute "Pocket Edition" of the classic for TV in 1955, starring Cameron Mitchell as Donald Martin, under Gerd Oswald's direction. The new version was released theatrically only in Great Britain.

After lensing *The Ox-Bow Incident,* Bill Wellman was obliged to direct two films of Zanuck's choosing. The first was a competent war story called *Thunderbirds* (1942), the second a more elaborate, occasionally effective, semi-factual biography of Bill Cody, labelled *Buffalo Bill* (1944).

Darryl F. Zanuck had kept his word to Wellman, so Wild Bill reciprocated. *The Ox-Bow Incident* is a rare example of a film made with the total cooperation and dedication of everyone involved, from novelist to scenarist to director to producer to actors to technicians. And the Western is a testament to the fact that quality does sell. It sometimes just takes a little longer.

Gregory Peck, Jennifer Jones, and Joseph Cotten

Jennifer Jones and Gregory Peck

CHAPTER NINE

Duel in the Sun

Year Released: 1946
Studio: Selznick Releasing Organization
Producer: David O. Selznick
Director: King Vidor
Screenplay: Adapted by Oliver H. P. Garrett, David O. Selznick, from the novel and script by Niven Busch
Cinematography: Lee Garmes, Hal Rosson, Ray Renahan, Charles P. Boyle, Allen Davey
Music/Music Director: Dmitri Tiomkin
Art Directors: James Basevi, John Ewing
Editors: Hal C. Kern, William Ziegler, John D. Faure, Charles Freeman
Second Unit Directors: Otto Brower, B. Reeves Eason
Assistant Directors: Lowell Farrell, Harvey Dwight
Production Designer: J. McMillan Johnson
Set Decorator: Emil Kuri
Sound: James Stewart, Richard De Weese
Special Camera Effects: Clarence Slifer, Jack Cosgrove
Color, 138 minutes

Cast:

Pearl Chavez	JENNIFER JONES
Jesse McCanles	JOSEPH COTTEN
Lewt McCanles	GREGORY PECK
Senator McCanles	LIONEL BARRYMORE

Laura Belle McCanles	LILLIAN GISH
The Sin Killer	WALTER HUSTON
Scott Chavez	HERBERT MARSHALL
Sam Pierce	CHARLES BICKFORD
Helen Langford	JOAN TETZEL
Lem Smoot	HARRY CAREY
Mr. Langford	OTTO KRUGER
The Lover	SIDNEY BLACKMER
Mrs. Chavez	TILLY LOSCH
Sid	SCOTT McKAY
Vashti	BUTTERFLY McQUEEN
Gamblers	FRANCIS McDONALD
	VICTOR KILIAN
The Jailer	GRIFF BARNETT
Frank	FRANK CORDELL
Ed	DAN WHITE
Jake	STEVE DUNHILL
Cavalry Captain	LANE CHANDLER
Barbecue Caller	LLOYD SHAW
Eater	BERT ROACH
Dancers	SI JENKS
	HANK WORDEN
	ROSE PLUMMER
Man at Bar	GUY WILKERSON
Engineer	LEE PHELPS
Man at Barbecue	AL TAYLOR
Narrator	ORSON WELLES

Duel in the Sun is a film on fire. Brimming with passion and melodrama, the story examines the distintegration of a powerful frontier family in the wake of encroaching civilization. Like its characters, the Western gives in to earthy appetites. That makes for its destruction. Yet out of the ashes and burning embers comes a smoldering fury which is as compelling as it is repulsive.

Gambler Scott Chavez is executed for murdering his faithless wife, and his half-breed daughter, Pearl, is hired to work at the ranch of powerful Senator McCanles. She becomes romantically embroiled with the young McCanles brothers: Lewt, an egotistical cowboy who becomes an outlaw, and Jesse, a soft-spoken man trying to arrange a peaceful settlement between ranchers and railroad officials who wish to run train tracks through the prairie. Jesse, who has a bitter fight with his father over the railroad, rejects Pearl, and she has sexual tangles with Lewt. When Lewt refuses to marry her, she gets engaged to Sam Pierce. Lewt kills Pierce and is sought by the authorities, but Senator McCanles hides his son. Lewt's violent ways continue and he shoots his unarmed brother, causing Pearl to track Lewt into the desert, seeking revenge for Jesse's murder. They engage in a gun battle. Both are killed.

At 138 minutes in glorious color, *Duel in the Sun* is far too bloated for its own good. Somewhere beneath the thumping passions of Lewt and Pearl, which symbolically extend to all points of the film, from lighting to camera angles to music, there is a harrowing plot about Westerners facing the reality that the wilderness must become part of a modernizing America. Ranchers, farmers, railroad men, and townspeople will have to learn to live together.

The Western might have ranked with *Tumbleweeds* and *The Gunfighter* as a chronicle of the men and women of the earth who are displaced by the roots of 20th-century civilization. Instead, *Duel in the Sun* counts on the power of love and lust, and the anxiety and violence which springs from such feelings to unify and propel the narrative. Since Joseph Cotten's Jesse is basically a gentle, reasonable man, it is up to Jennifer Jones' Pearl and Gregory Peck's Lewt to carry the story. Jones is miscast in the role of an earth vixen, a woman who makes men's blood boil even as she moves about her daily chores. David Selznick, the film's producer (and the actress' husband), and the myriad screenwriters employed to bring Niven Busch's tightly plotted novel to life would have been wiser to have tailored the role of Pearl to fit her extremely quiet, almost timid yet enchanting screen personality. In her best roles (one is the peasant girl in *The Song of Bernadette),* Jones rests slightly above the earth, almost in the heavens compared to the surrounding characters. She is a spirit-like presence in the cinema, like a butterfly one can admire but never quite touch. If those qualities had been promoted, a presence might have emerged similar to Leni Riefenstahl's mysterious nymph in *The Blue Light* (1932), a woman/child who flits through the mountains and villages, her suspicious eyes darting back and forth, communing with nature as one of its offspring. In *Duel in the Sun,* the very real magnetism possessed by Jennifer Jones is projected into a high-powered atmosphere that it gets lost in. She is almost swallowed up by the size of the production.

As one of the most manly post-World War II stars on the screen, Gregory Peck is capable of reshaping his strong, commanding figure to suit a particular role or the scope of a story. His sharp, deep, rounded tones make it seem as if a voice is coming from the heavens when he speaks. As Lewt, Peck easily adjusts from good guy to (a rarity for him) villain. Those same qualities transform him into a devil incarnate lurking in the shadows for his prey (Pearl, Jesse). The evil McCanles' soul is in keeping with the trend of the time to etch bad guys whose actions constantly reach harrowing levels of psychosis. Lewt is one of the meanest leading characters in the American cinema and certainly the vilest role Peck has yet portrayed—with the exception of Dr. Josef Mengele in *The Boys from Brazil.* The son of willful Senator McCanles confirms his darkest implications when he blows up an entire railroad, then calmly rides away whistling, "I've Been Working on the Railroad."

Despite its pomposity, *Duel in the Sun* is a visually exciting film. It blends the talents of David Selznick, an important influence on the physical look of *Gone with the Wind,* and the more down-to-earth imagery of director King Vidor, whose pictures like *The Crowd* (MGM, 1928) and *Our Daily Bread* (UA, 1934) brilliantly illustrate an acute eye for realistic cinematography. Along with the help of Lee Garmes and other cinematographers and directors, the Selznick/Vidor team demonstrates an extreme care with lighting, camera angle, and composition. From the moments where Lewt and Pearl interact in the dim lighting of the McCanles ranch at night to the breathtaking gathering of the ranchers to combat the railroad and cavalry to the final scene of Pearl trekking the arid desert with sunspots shining on the lens, the photography in *Duel in the Sun* is hypnotically effective.

Duel in the Sun is nevertheless a failed epic. Its beauty has the quality of being an accident of nature, a fascinating freak confused at its own creation and purpose, floating about looking for someone to give it meaning.

The Making of *Duel in the Sun*

It all started innocently enough. Arthur Niven Busch wanted to produce and write a film starring his new wife, Teresa Wright. So he decided to adapt his recent novel, *Duel in the Sun,* for the screen. Not that the new Mrs. Busch was in great need of a career boost from her husband. Since making her screen debut in *The Little Foxes* (Goldwyn) in 1941, Teresa Wright Busch had co-starred in such fine features as *Mrs. Miniver* (MGM, 1942), for which she won a Best Supporting Actress Oscar, *Pride of the Yankees* (Goldwyn, 1942), and Hitchcock's *Shadow of a Doubt* (Universal, 1943).

Busch wanted to put her in a strong story revolving around the love triangle of a half-breed Indian girl and two brothers, set against the backdrop of a conflict between cattlemen and the railroad. The role of Pearl Chavez would provide Teresa Wright with a thick, earthy stream of sharp dialogue and movements, something she hadn't yet attempted in the cinema.

In 1943, RKO gave the producer/writer a $1,000,000 budget for *Duel in the Sun.* It was quickly agreed that John Wayne should play the bad boy Lewt McCanles. Before the cameras were ready to roll, Teresa Wright became pregnant. A search was initiated for a replacement. Hedy Lamarr took the part. But she too, as the legend goes, was waiting for a blessed event.

Jennifer Jones was approached to portray Pearl. At the time, David O. Selznick was guiding her career and would only let the actress accept the assignment if certain stipulations were met. Niven Busch remembered the situation. "He liked the story and so did she but he made so many conditions to her playing the role that negotiations became impossible. He specified we had to use one of five directors, naming several who were unobtainable—William Wyler, George Stevens. Also he was to have approval of the sets, costumes, and locations and the right to make the final editing—really insane stipulations. My studio boss at RKO, Charles Koerner, got the message. Selznick wanted to buy the story so Koerner sold it to him—at what he thought was a large profit (maybe one percent of what he would have made had he produced the picture at RKO)." Obviously, Selznick wanted to make a star vehicle for his wife, to consolidate the stardom she had achieved in *The Song of Bernadette* and *Since You Went Away* (UA, 1944).

The mogul was known as a man who didn't just sit in the background of a production, issuing memos and demanding reports of a film's progress, although he did volumes of the former and much of the latter. The man acknowledged as the guiding genius behind *Gone with the Wind,* rather than its writers or directors, was habitually involved in every aspect of a project. Selznick's first step was to hire Oliver H. P. Garrett to rewrite Busch's lean, tight script. The original version was a short, very probably powerful tale of the old West, if it was anything like the novel. But Selznick desired something more grandiose, on the order of *Gone with the Wind,* only better! David O. Selznick wanted to catapult Jennifer Jones to screen heights on the basis of what he promised would be the most spectacular Western ever made. When Garrett produced a retouched version of Busch's novel, it was submitted to the Joseph Breen Office for censorship clearance, as per the practice of the day. With a few suggested changes, Breen okayed the material.

The director of *Duel in the Sun* had to be someone who could handle human interest material as well as lavish, epic productions.

Jennifer Jones and David O. Selznick

Joseph Cotten, Lillian Gish, and Lionel Barrymore

Selznick wanted King Vidor, who had just terminated a twenty-year association with MGM, because of conflicts regarding *An American Romance* (1944). Vidor liked the idea of working for an independent producer, even one as omnipresent as Selznick. And he was drawn by Busch's script, material which he later compared to *High Noon* in scope and impact.

King Vidor was an able director of spectacle as well as kitchen-sink drama. *The Big Parade* (MGM, 1925) set standards for the war film which have never been superseded. Vidor's brilliant interweaving of battle horror and the camaraderie of three soldiers proved that he was a master filmmaker.

Although Oliver Garrett altered Niven Busch's story, Selznick did more work. And the producer required researchers to check and re-check the accuracy of the scenario's depiction of 19th-century Western life. Men and women familiar with Western folklore, dancing, and customs made sure that Selznick's epic was historically accurate.

Money flowed continuously to insure the success of *Duel in the Sun* from every conceivable angle. With Vidor as director, Selznick cast another new star, Gregory Peck (Wayne had since dropped out), as Lewt McCanles, Joseph Cotten as Jesse McCanles, Lionel Barrymore and Lillian Gish as Senator and Mrs. McCanles, with such fine players as Walter Huston, Herbert Marshall, Charles Bickford, Harry Carey, Otto Kruger, and Butterfly McQueen offering solid backup.

If Selznick envisioned a certain actor for a role, the performer would be signed, no matter what. Walter Huston's character, the "Sin Killer," was only scheduled to take four days to shoot. Huston's agent insisted the actor be paid his usual fee of $40,000 per assignment, especially since his client normally would not accept such a small part. Selznick agreed to the sum, providing Huston would be available for ten weeks. In the end, long production delays forced Selznick to pay Huston overtime. But the producer got what he went after.

King Vidor began filming *Duel in the Sun* in the fall of 1944. The cast and crew of the Western would travel 200,000 miles to six different locations before the project was completed. Selznick had one entire railroad and the McCanles Ranch transplanted to a site in the midst of a desert and mountains near Tucson, Arizona. There were 57 speaking parts in the production, backed by 6,526 extras. It took a tractor and twelve pack mules to transport the people and equipment to the impenetrable location in the Arizona mountains.

The production company was large enough to look like a wagon train, which moved from makeshift homes to locations daily. There was a grip truck, a water truck, a loading truck, a vehicle carrying a generator, transport buses, prop tents, wardrobe tents, makeup tents, recreation tents, dressing rooms, and a wooden structure which broke the wind when the cameras rolled. Three vans were needed to transport the electrical supplies. Men drove 400 horses and 400 head of cattle to the McCanles spread, known as the "Spanish Bit." Twenty tons of props included 107 revolvers and 100 packs of poker chips. Artifacts were examined for authenticity and the entire load checked for comprehensiveness. A forty-man crew had worked two months restructuring the land around Tucson to fit Selznick's specifications. In sixty days and sixty nights the crew levelled a hill and built the sprawling two-story "Spanish Bit," two barns, and windmill. Real trees were stripped down, rebuilt and painted, then placed on platforms and moved around the sets when needed. The platforms were then buried in earth. The McCanles ranch itself took five weeks to construct. Tarpaulins had to be stretched over the incomplete structure every evening to prevent vicious winds from tearing it down.

From the beginning of the production, David Selznick was everywhere, into every aspect of its creation. He constantly rewrote dialogue and whole scenes, eliminating some, adding others. Niven Busch felt that the script used to make *Duel in the Sun* was not his in any way. That much had been altered. And Selznick wasn't through changing words and actions once the shooting began. While King Vidor was filming in Hollywood, Selznick would come down to the lot late in the afternoon with material he'd revamped and request that the director lens it the new way. This irked Vidor, as he had often just finished with a sequence that the mogul wanted taken again. When the company journeyed to the Arizona location, Selznick took a room in a Tucson hotel and sent an avalance of telegrams to Vidor on the mountain. If Selznick was the West Coast god who created the celluloid *Duel in the Sun,* than Vidor was his Noah, desperately trying to keep what he considered an overblown production from dying under its own weight. "When King was half through Selznick started fighting with him," Busch recalled recently. "Nothing King could do was right. King also got the message—Selznick wanted to take over direction himself—but King hung in there for a long time."

Production problems and conflicts were expensive and time consuming. It would cost Selznick $15,000 a day when weather halted the filming, excluding the stars' salaries.

Early in 1945 Selznick sent memos to Vidor and his assistants about the value of arriving to work on time and quickly making the first take. The mogul thought it was good for the company morale to waste as little time as possible. Vidor rightly complained that just reading the voluminous memos bogged down the schedule.

After a while, Selznick decided nothing should be done without his approval. While Vidor shot in the studio, the mogul had to be consulted before every shot was taken, to check the lighting, camera angle, positioning of players, anything that might affect the scenes—all of this historically the director's job. Vidor put up with the suggestions, trying to accommodate himself to the man who not only bankrolled the production, but who changed the character of Niven Busch's novel to fit his own vision.

Although Vidor and Selznick had a twenty-year friendship, their personal bond did not ease the constant friction. The director asserted the producer ordered retakes when the originals were fine, and more than once found the camera crew missing at a crucial point, as they had been sent elsewhere on Selznick's order. This particularly annoyed Vidor, and the men had terrible rows over the lack of communication, or perhaps simply because *Duel in the Sun* had in reality at least two directors working on it from start to finish.

At one time or another, Sydney Franklin, William Cameron Menzies, Josef Von Sternberg, and William Dieterle were employed to co-direct with Vidor. Thus the cast and crew were often so spread out it proved impossible to keep track of them.

Josef Von Sternberg was hired as a "special visual consultant." Both Vidor and Selznick knew and liked the filmmaker and appreciated Sternberg's talent for creating dazzling cinematography. By the mid 1940s, however, the man who had made a star of Marlene Dietrich was at a career low. He hadn't shot a feature since the strange and fascinating *The Shanghai Gesture* for United Artists in 1941. The filmmaker's penchant for florid narratives imbued with cynicism and sensuality were not in favor with wartime audiences.

At first Sternberg was helpful with suggestions about imagery, costumes, and hairstyles. He may also have influenced the fine use of color in the Western, although Selznick and cameraman Ray Renahan were also major influences on this aspect of the production. When Sternberg started creating camera set-ups which would take four or five hours to complete, Selznick removed him from the project.

Three major cameramen shot *Duel in the Sun,* with assistance from numerous others. Hal Rosson began the filming, but a general strike in Hollywood which closed down the production forced him to honor his next commitment. Lee Garmes replaced Rosson. Renahan came later to reshoot many scenes and add new ones.

Aside from the constant bickering of Vidor and Selznick, undoubtedly putting a strain on star Jennifer Jones, the weather and the Joseph Breen Office surely made acting in *Duel in the Sun* one of the most arduous experiences of her career. It was extremely hot in the Arizona mountains on the day when her famous ride into the desert was done. Lights bounced off the camera lens to give the scene a steaming look straight out of an inferno. The rocks, sand, and mountainous background had to reflect the arid desert, and heighten an already melodramatic sequence. The actress crawled all over the rocks in her gun duel with Gregory Peck, and received many wounds and bruises from doing this florid finale. She also trained hard to perform the dance routines. All in all she learned three different taxing dances. One had to be scrapped because Peck's other commitments forced him to be elsewhere when the routine was to be shot. The second dance died in the censor's office. These heartbreaking revisions came after months of rehearsal. The third dance was filmed, but the star worked fifteen-hour days doing that segment and just about every other in the year-long production of *Duel in the Sun.* And each day she had to spend several morning hours applying the makeup which transformed her into a half-breed and more time at the end of the day removing it.

If nothing else, the stresses on Jennifer Jones proved that Selznick wanted to make a great picture at all costs. He spared nothing and no one to achieve his artistic end, including himself. He would confer with King Vidor about details as minute as the positioning of Gregory Peck's hat on his head and order assistant Otto Brower to reshoot a massive scene the mogul already liked, just to include more horses. With all the money spent to make the Western, it was obvious he didn't mind stretching the budget in the quest of perfection. Nor was he timid about looking for bold new effects or suggesting that the director(s) search for fresh ways of filming. One such instance occurred when Selznick asked cameramen to take more chances with the light of day. Lensing scenes at dawn or dusk rather than waiting for perfect lighting might create dazzling cinematography, he thought. Some striking imagery in *Gone with the Wind* reflects this leaning.*

The producer also felt there were too many close-ups in the film. This is a particularly unusual position for a mogul, as historically top executives liked to showcase stars, create larger than life moving busts of top actors and actresses which were supposed to hypnotize movie audiences. Even more ironic is the fact that he included his "Trilby," Jennifer Jones, in the criticism as well.

The struggle between Selznick and Vidor finally came to an end two days before the director was slated to finish *Duel in the Sun,* about a year after production began. Selznick became angered at Vidor for allegedly holding up filming. Vidor, it turned out, couldn't work because one of the assistants had taken the crew

---

*Victor Fleming, the spectacle's main director, was also adept at creating sparkling visuals.

King Vidor

elsewhere. He felt this had occurred once too often. King Vidor told David O. Selznick to direct the rest of the property himself. Noah was forced off the ark before the flood ended. Efforts at a reconciliation by Selznick were futile. William Dieterle, the maker of great biographical pictures at Warners during the 1930s, supervised production for a while.

In typical fashion, Selznick ordered Dieterle to reshoot a number of Vidor's scenes. Years later Vidor alleged Dieterle's versions were so like his own it was impossible to tell them apart. Vidor thought Selznick might have done this to create confusion about who deserved directorial credit. "He tried to get a co-director's credit," said Niven Busch of Selznick, "but the directors guild, stronger at that time than the writers guild, refused to allow it."

After *Duel in the Sun* was completed, Vidor, Selznick, and an editor sat in a projection room at the Directors Guild with an arbitration board. Before editing, the Western consisted of 1,490,000 feet of film, enough for 137 two-hour movies. Selznick insisted Vidor shot only 6,280 feet of stock, leaving the rest to others, and further asserted that the latter figure would grow with the inclusion of many retakes and additional scenes. According to Vidor, the board ultimately decided that he did indeed lens about ninety percent of the finished production.

Although there were many cameramen on *Duel in the Sun,* Lee Garmes claimed to have shot about seventy percent of the work. He took all the interiors and some of the most memorable segments including the climactic moment when the barbed wire fence is cut and the meeting of the carriages, photographed with gelatins to provide a glowing red intensity.

The last shot of *Duel in the Sun* was made in late summer, 1945. They were redoing the barbecue picnic section when Selznick arrived and announced that World War II was over. One might have wondered at that point whether he was referring to America's fight against the Axis powers or the homefront squabbles between the makers of *Duel in the Sun.*

Even the musical score was a source of conflict. Dmitri Tiomkin composed some beautiful melodies, namely "Rio Grande," "Orizaba," "On the Trail to Spanish Bit," "Rendezvous," "Prairie Sky," "Trek to the Sun," "Passional," "Love Eternal," and the title tune, "Duel." Tiomkin had written the music for such romantic pictures as *Lost Horizon* (Columbia, 1937) and *The Great Waltz* (MGM, 1938), so he was used to employing large orchestras, a Hollywood tradition at the time. The image-breaking Selznick rightly determined that a large and expensive orchestra was often wasted playing music which had to be recorded very low to prevent it from disturbing the dialogue of, say, a romantic interlude. Therefore the mogul requested that Tiomkin try to utilize a smaller orchestra, thus effecting a small savings. Perhaps this situation somewhat aggravated the dubbing of the music onto the soundtrack. The orchestra had particular trouble recording "Orizaba," used for the dance of Tilly Losch, because Selznick, Vidor, or somebody made too many cuts in the scene for the musicians to follow its rhythm. It got to the point where Tiomkin had to play an album of music for *Duel in the Sun,* recorded by Arthur Fiedler and the Boston Pops, to show his people how the music should be rendered.

Censorship problems began as early as fall 1945. One of the most vociferous attacks came on January 1947 by the Catholic Church of Los Angeles. Reverend John J. Cantwell spearheaded the drive to persuade Selznick to change certain aspects of the finished film.

Duel in the Sun was slated for a mid-1946 release, but the extensive revisions forced Selznick to push back the opening until December of that year. In order to qualify for Oscar consideration the following spring, a film had to show commercially in Los Angeles for one week by December 31 of the preceding year. So, as the story goes, Selznick decided to withhold the epic in his endless search for perfection.

One of the changes made in response to pressure from the church was the addition of a prologue explaining that the "Sin Killer," who called himself a priest, was not an ordained minister. Just two of at least forty scenes cut or totally eliminated included the "degradation scene," in which Gregory Peck forces Jennifer Jones to submit to his sexual advances, along with her aforementioned dance. The torrid choreography became the largest of the revisions. It was estimated that the alterations cost $200,000. The furor was heightened by the fact that due to a delay at the Technicolor laboratory, the Western had to be shown on December 31 without first being approved by the Legion of Decency. Reverend Cantwell of Los Angeles then recommended that all Catholics refrain from viewing the production until it could be classified.

"It tends to throw audiences on the side of sin," reported *Tidings,* the official journal of the Los Angeles Catholic Archdiocese. "It includes brutal killing and rape is more than suggested. It ignores good taste and proper regard for audience sensibilities in the treatment of a low subject. It shows Jennifer Jones as unduly, if not indecently, exposed, and it shows a character, acting as a minister of religion, who parodies prayer and thus becomes a comical figure."

Senator Everett Dirksen also went on record as criticizing *Duel in the Sun.* Paul MacNamara, Selznick's publicist, sent the politician a long, detailed letter about the production, showing how much the Selznick Organization had cooperated with the Joseph Breen Office and the Legion of Decency. MacNamara estimated there were approximately twenty-five separate contacts with the Breen Office during the making of the Western.

Duel in the Sun was given a "B" rating by the National Office of the Legion of Decency and that seemed to satisfy everyone. Yet

Selznick's troubles were far from over. Oliver Garrett, who adapted Niven Busch's novel for Selznick, was so unhappy about the fate of his script that he once demanded his name be removed from the credits. Selznick also had to deal with Niven Busch. "I took him before an arbitration board of the Screenwriters Guild," Busch informed me recently. "He was trying to get a screenwriter's credit on *Duel in the Sun.* In the end he got the credit. He didn't deserve it. He had mashed together excerpts from a number of scripts written by professional writers. I was not one of these. I was defending the rights of my fellow writers. After the Selznick vs. Busch case the Screenwriters Guild changed its rules. Now a producer cannot get a writing credit unless he writes the entire script without aid from anyone else." Although Niven Busch did not see immediate victory three decades ago, time has proven that his action was justified.

Paul MacNamara did not have much faith in the box-office potential. He counselled Selznick to distribute the Western quickly, on a multiple-run plan in which it would show in many theatres in a given city, instead of just a single high-yield house. This "saturation booking" would follow an expansive media blitz. An unprecedented $2,000,000 was set aside for advertising. Allegedly MacNamara wanted to release the epic to coincide with an eclipse of the sun. The notion, if it ever truly was conjured, did not sit well with the mogul. More earthly strategies included distributing 100,000 labels containing the name of the film, along with 5,000 packs of sunflower seeds and 7,000 tiny parachutes. Selznick disapproved of many of the publicity gimmicks. He was particularly distressed to learn of plans to drop a thousand balloons containing gifts on Times Square in New York City, and running what amounted to a "Miss Duel in the Sun" contest. He scrapped the ideas quickly. The mogul was concerned that the Western would appear ridiculous, and the Selznick Releasing Corporation, newly formed, would lose stature. MacNamara then drew up some more dignified ad campaigns.

Repairs were made on *Duel in the Sun* up to the minute of its release. Selznick wanted moviegoers to perceive Lewt McCanles as a totally unsympathetic and evil man, yet somehow compelling. He and King Vidor had argued about how far they could go in a negative depiction of Lewt before the audience lost sympathy with him. The producer decided to have Lewt confirm his devil personality by blowing up a train, killing the engineer and a fireman, and then riding away singing "I've Been Working on the Railroad." At a preview, some members of the audience were audibly revolted by the scene, but did not become unattracted to him because of it.

Duel in the Sun cost $5,255,000, plus the extra expense of prints and publicity. It was estimated that the Western would have to gross $7,000,000 to break even. *Gone with the Wind* was made for $4,000,000 the decade before and went on to become the biggest moneymaker of its time. So Selznick had some confidence, but admitted if it had been produced by a major studio the price might have been $1,000,000 less.

Duel in the Sun opened for general release in May 1947. Paul MacNamara's prediction of the critical reaction proved correct:

> *Cue,* Jesse Zunser:
>
> . . . absurdly overblown emotional steam bath . . . frequently and comically reminiscent of the 1890 school of panting passion and asthmatic melodrama.
>
> *New York Herald Tribune,* Howard Barnes:
>
> Vidor's toil is evident in more than one scene, but it is fumbling in the over-all staging of the production. For every passage of comparatively convincing period reconstruction, love-making or violence, that comes up on the screen, there are a half-dozen exaggerated sequences to match.
>
> *New York Times,* Bosley Crowther:
>
> He [David Selznick] and his director King Vidor have also whipped up some eye-dazzling scenes of wide-open ranching and frontiering, all in color of the very best, of course. Indeed, some of the compositions, achieved with color and musical background, evoke sudden and singular sensations that are conspicuously superior to the whole. Oh brother—if only the dramatics were up to the technical style!
>
> *New Yorker,* John McCarten:
>
> Many of the Hollywood stereotypes are here—the mean old cattle baron, his long-suffering wife, his bad son, his good son, and the hostile railroad men who want to put a line across the property. The picture is full of stars, and all of them are leaden, particularly Miss Jones and Mr. Peck who conduct their incessant wrestling match with a hopeless gravity and a dismal persistence. I should like to be able to report that the film is worth going to just for the unintended laughs, but I'm afraid its faults will annoy rather than amuse you.

Although the picture was publicized as "The Picture of a Thousand Memorable Moments," the public preferred to call it "Lust in the Dust."

Yet all the suffering and lavish spending made *Duel in the Sun* the largest grossing Western of its period. To date, including a 1959 reissue, the epic has made $11,300,000 in distributors' domestic rentals. Of the genre, only *Butch Cassidy and the Sundance Kid* (Fox, 1969), at $46,000,000, *Blazing Saddles* (Warner Bros., 1974), at $35,200,000, *Jeremiah Johnson* (Warner Bros., 1972), at $21,500,000, *Little Big Man* (National General, 1970), at $15,000,000, *Paint Your Wagon* (Paramount, 1969), at $14,500,000, *True Grit* (Paramount, 1969), at $14,250,000, and *How the West Was Won* (MGM, 1962), at $12,100,000, have outgrossed Selznick's opus. And, since all those films, with the exception of the last, were released approximately a quarter-century or more after *Duel in the Sun,* one can imagine the actual number of customers the costly work attracted.

Of course, everyone in the Selznick organization was ecstatic at the financial success of *Duel in the Sun.* Despite the odds, it became a box-office winner.

But the film failed to turn Jennifer Jones into the archetypal sex goddess or movie queen of the 1940s. Betty Grable and Rita Hayworth shared that position. With the 1950s, Marilyn Monroe ushered in the stark, nubile, lightheaded cinema sexuality which was prominent for a decade and is still popular today. Jennifer Jones could never fit that mold. She was an actress so delicate that sound men often had trouble recording her weak voice.

King Vidor followed *Duel in the Sun* with several episodes of a mediocre multi-starred project called *On Our Merry Way* (UA, 1948). Then he lensed a screen version of Ayn Rand's *The Fountainhead* for Warners in 1949. He made two more spectacles, *War and Peace* (Paramount, 1956) and *Solomon and Sheba* (UA, 1959), before his career ended. Vidor never worked for Selznick again.

Peck and Cotten did. Peck starred in Selznick's 1948 *The Paradine Case.* Cotten acted again with Jennifer Jones in Selznick's *Portrait of Jennie* (1948) and played the lead in one of the mogul's co-productions, *The Third Man,* in 1950.

Teresa Wright, the actress originally slated to portray Pearl Chavez, acted in *Pursued* (Warner Bros., 1947), a memorably moody Western which her husband Niven Busch had scripted from his own novel.

Although *Duel in the Sun* made money, some historians have written that this problem production broke David O. Selznick's great faith in himself. He never again approached the heights of *Gone with the Wind,* the quality of *Since You Went Away,* or the epic scale of *Duel in the Sun.*

Yet this Western stands as a historically significant example of the censor's reign on old Hollywood, as well as a warning to those moviemakers who wish to exercise complete control over a production.

The quality of *Duel in the Sun* may be best described in the opening narration tacked on to the Western after it was finished. In terms of scope, the words recall two of Pare Lorentz's great documentaries of the 1930s, *The Plow That Broke the Plains* and *The River.* But the passions are all Selznick's.

As the theatre darkened on that May day in 1947, the curtains opened and images began flickering from the screen. Orson Welles spoke authoritatively. "For more than half a century, over the great and rolling plains of the cattle country . . . a legend has lingered, like dust particles in sunlight, up-flung by long-vanished herds of Texas longhorns . . . a strange story of a young outlaw and a half-breed Indian girl, a tale told on nights when there's a heavy ground mist and the moon's behind a distant ridge, for it is there, some say, you can glimpse the shadowy figure of Pearl Chavez on a horse, still following her lover; Pearl, who came from down along the border, and who was like a wildflower sprung from the hard clay, quick to blossom, early to die."

Montgomery Clift

CHAPTER TEN

Red River

Year Released: 1948
Studio: United Artists release of a United Artists-Monterey Production
Producer: Howard Hawks
Director: Howard Hawks
Screenplay: Borden Chase, Charles Schnee, based on the story "The Chisholm Trail" by Chase
Cinematography: Russell Harlan
Music: Dmitri Tiomkin
Art Director: John Datu Aresma
Editor: Christian Nyby
Second Unit Director: Arthur Rosson
125 minutes

Cast:

Tom Dunson	JOHN WAYNE
Matthew Garth	MONTGOMERY CLIFT
Tess Millay	JOANNE DRU
Nadine Groot	WALTER BRENNAN
Fen	COLEEN GRAY
Cherry Valance	JOHN IRELAND
Buster McGee	NOAH BEERY, JR.
Quo	CHIEF YOWLACHIE
Melville	HARRY CAREY, SR.
Dan Latimer	HARRY CAREY, JR.

Matthew as a Boy	MICKEY KUHN
Teeler Yacey	PAUL FIX
Sims	HANK WORDEN
Bunk Kenneally	IVAN PARRY
Old Leather	HAL TALIAFERRO
Fernandez	PAUL FIERO
Wounded Wrangler	BILLY SELF
Walt Jergens	RAY HYKE
Maylor	GLENN STRANGE
Wrangler	TOM TYLER
Laredo	DAN WHITE
Colonel	LANE CHANDLER
Gamblers	LEE PHELPS
	GEORGE LLOYD
Dancehall Girl	SHELLEY WINTERS

Red River is an epic Western about the lives of trail drivers and their role in the expanding of the frontier to civilization. The film's richness of character, narrative, and realistic details make it among the most balanced spectacles in the genre.

Tom Dunson is an embittered cattle rancher whose fiancée recently has been killed by Indians in a wagon train massacre. Dunson shelters the lone survivor in the attack, a youngster named Matt whom he adopts. Over the years Tom Dunson is revealed as a strong man with a rigid code of ethics. He lives by the law and he expects his drovers to do the same. As Matt grows up and apprentices in Dunson's profession, he becomes alienated by his foster father's dictatorial ways. They fight over the final destination of a herd of cattle. While Matt wants to drive them on a less arduous trail to Kansas City, Dunson insists the herd be taken the hazardous route to Abilene. The final split occurs when Dunson kills one of the hands. Matt and the other drovers commandeer the herd and head for Kansas City. On the way to town, Matt falls in love. Dunson catches Matt at the Kansas City railhead, where they engage in a vicious brawl. But Matt's girl brings both men to their senses using reason and a rifle.

Rancher Tom Dunson has seen his loved one brutally murdered and his ranch on the edge of destruction. The one chance he's got for survival is to drive the herd along a dangerous trail. Although a rugged existence has toughened his spirit, life has slowly dried Dunson's sense of fair play into a cold set of rules.

John Wayne and Joanne Dru

John Wayne and Walter Brennan

Necessity has made him a dictator. As Dunson, John Wayne is always tough, the image of a Westerner weaned on hard times. But in the beginning there is a gentleness of character. The star crosses this treacherous ground slowly, following scenarists Chase and Schnee's intentions, and Wayne's anger toward his foster son extends beyond rage into a growling psychosis. The role of Tom Dunson was Wayne's most complex assignment until that time.

Montgomery Clift's Matt stands up to Dunson because the younger performer makes no attempt to match the other's massive screen presence. As he did so brilliantly with roles throughout his subsequent regrettably short career, Clift in essence becomes Matt. The character's rage is inside him and reveals itself in a natural way. Wayne's thunder and Clift's rain may be of different material and timbre, but both are evident, like the sound separation in a stereo system. Wayne is the bass and Clift the treble.

The way men do their jobs was of interest to director Howard Hawks throughout his fifty-year career in Hollywood. In *Red River,* the sun and the wind and the driving of cattle and the sleeping under the stars summer and winter are unsparingly recreated. The drovers handle the herd as if holding a baby. The work requires extreme dedication. A sneeze can start a cattle stampede. The only requirement for the job is the ability to follow orders. Formal education is irrevelant. "Sign your name or make your mark," Matt tells the drovers. Yet some things should be learned quickly. "Watch his eyes," Dunson tells Matt about a prospective opponent in a gunfight. The eyes tell all. Stare a man down. Get command, watch his movement. Do it to him before he does it to you. Yet Dunson can still insist that someone who has violated the rules have a decent burial. The rancher will even read the Bible over the grave.

Red River is able to maintain a balance between the spectacle of a great cattle drive and the personal conflict of Dunson and Matt because the script is broken into two separate blocks of time—one fifteen years after the other. No space is wasted bridging the gaps of one or two years with short scenes or montage effects. In this way, *Red River* stays neat and strong and characters can grow as the struggle of Dunson and the drovers develops.

Red River documents the opening of the Chisholm Trail. It is a personal history of the West through the eyes of Tom and Matt Dunson, as filmed by Howard Hawks, Borden Chase, John Wayne, Montgomery Clift, and the others.

The Making of *Red River*

Despite a rugged personality and love of adventure, Howard Hawks had never directed a Western before. He began two projects in the genre, but had been replaced or simply departed long before they were completed. Individualistic Hawks committed the unpardonable sin of shoving Louis B. Mayer on the set of *Viva Villa* (MGM, 1934) and walking off the production. Mayer assigned Jack Conway to finish the semi-factual biopic about Mexican revolutionary/bandit Pancho Villa. A half-dozen years later Hawks went against producer Howard Hughes during the making of *The Outlaw* (RKO, 1940), and the eccentric millionaire took over direction himself.

Hawks started in Hollywood shortly after World War I making short films and occasionally took the dual role of producer and director, as with *Scarface* in 1932. He decided to do both jobs in lensing his first Western, and thus guarantee himself a better chance of being around when the production was finished. Hawks' company, Monterey Productions, worked out a deal to co-produce *Red River* with United Artists. The director and Charles K. Feldman bought rights to a five-part serial by Borden Chase called *The Chisholm Trail,* which appeared in the *Saturday Evening Post* and concerned the first cattle drive from Laredo, Texas, to Abilene, Kansas.

For a while, at the studio's request, Hawks considered doing a Western about the legendary King Ranch. But then the knowledgeable filmmaker described some objectionable historical occurrences about the ranch, and United Artists withdrew the request. Hawks instead would simply film a tale about people who drove cattle.

Borden Chase agreed to fashion a screenplay from his serial. *Red River* was to be the writer's first distinguished screen credit. But he had to make some changes in his original concept. Hawks always contributed to his screenplays, whether at the beginning or right on the set, and often could be seen rewriting dialogue, then shooting the fresh material moments later. The most significant deviation from the original story occurs in the climactic fight between gunfighter Cherry Valance, Tom Dunson, and Matt. In Chase's tale, Valance wounds Dunson, who is about to shoot down Matt. Dunson is carried off to Texas to die. Instead, Dunson and Matt engage in a tough brawl ended by a woman firing a rifle at the men. Motivating the conflict is Matt's usurping of power from his foster father, as Dunson's obsession to finish the cattle drive his way has tragic consequences.

Gary Cooper was the first actor approached to play tough-skinned, hard-living Tom Dunson. But Cooper didn't like the ruthless nature of the character and turned it down. Hawks admired Cary Grant very much from their screwball comedies together and approached him to portray Cherry Valance. Grant rejected the offer not because he didn't like the moral fiber of the man, but because the part was too small and Hawks refused to enlarge it. It's a great pity Grant never appeared here, as his slick good looks, impeccable manners, and soft, sometimes calculating eyes would have provided a fine contrast to Cooper, or even better, to tough John Wayne, who finally was signed to play Dunson.

Charles Feldman, Wayne's agent, interested the star in what was to be the most offbeat role of his career until then. For several years the actor sought more demanding parts, like the one he was to have had in *Duel in the Sun.* Now, in 1946, he was ready to vary the image of the eternal American good guy. Wayne had been in and out of the saddle for almost twenty years. He'd just won World War II on the movie screen. And he wisely picked a rather unsympathetic part to mark his latest adventure in the celluloid West. The variation put him on the trail of Rooster Cogburn in *True Grit,* his Oscar-winning performance.

Hawks wanted Montgomery Clift to act the role of Matt after having admired the young performer's triumphant portrayal several years earlier in Lillian Hellman's *The Searching Wind* on Broadway. Hollywood also had sought him for several years, but Clift wanted his cinema debut to be at the right time. He wasn't swayed by promises of fame and fortune. The correct property and an opportunity to act with John Wayne persuaded him to make his first screen appearance in *Red River.* Monty Clift reportedly signed a five-picture contract with Hawks, but the Western was the only film they ever did together. Although Clift actually made his screen debut in this film, his second effort, *The Search* (MGM, 1948), was released before *Red River*.

Clift was both enthusiastic and apprehensive about appearing in the sagebrush saga. Advance publicity linked it with *Cimarron* and *The Covered Wagon,* two acknowledged classics. Yet Clift knew nothing about the West and couldn't ride a horse. John Wayne had trepidations about acting with Clift, and also felt that Hawks needed some lessons in making Westerns. The star was certainly one of the experts in the genre by then. Between making *Stagecoach* in 1938 and *Red River* a decade later, the actor had learned much about the production end of filmmaking and had begun to take an active part in a property from its conception to release. The Duke had come a long way from the quiet, insecure actor who felt ill at ease in the company of such professionals as

Montgomery Clift and John Wayne

Montgomery Clift and Joanne Dru

Thomas Mitchell and John Carradine in *Stagecoach,* to the take-charge man of *Red River.* And the actor let Hawks and co-producer Feldman know they needed help in making Westerns.

One afternoon, he spotted the pair sitting around a swimming pool. From their conversation Wayne concluded they could benefit from his assistance. Perhaps Hawks and Wayne initially had different ideas about filming a hoss opera, but the two worked well together and became close friends. Yet Hawks' method of working is well-known for being concise. He would talk to his production crew, including the writers, instruct them, then wait at the golf course or in the sun by a swimming pool for them to do their jobs.

He'd already sent out scouts to five states and Mexico in search of locations for *Red River.* Terrain resembling Texas badlands, rivers, and Kansas plains was needed.

With Wayne and Clift signed for major roles, Hawks gave the part of Cherry Valance to newcomer John Ireland. The female lead fell to Margaret Sheridan, another new face. Sheridan was only one of the many actresses discovered by Hawks, including Lauren Bacall, Joanne Dru, and, later on, Charlene Holt and Laura Devon. The director's old friend Walter Brennan played the veteran cowhand.

Hawks had wanted Brennan to play the cook Groot, but the performer needed some convincing. Hawks wanted the character to lose his false teeth in a poker game, and before every meal to have to borrow them back. Brennan recoiled at the notion, but Hawks convinced him that it was right. And Brennan trusted Hawks. Their relationship had developed on the set of Goldwyn's *Come and Get It* in 1936 (Hawks was replaced by William Wyler). The then forty-two-year-old actor had asked Hawks if he wanted a reading with or without the teeth. That attracted the filmmaker's attention. When he heard Brennan's delivery and saw that toothless face, it was enough. Originally slated for several days' work on the Goldwyn property, Hawks made the role last six weeks. Brennan had received a supporting Oscar for his performance, and credited the director for his success.

While casting and searching for locations, Hawks worked on the budget with Feldman and United Artists and set it at $1,500,000, with $150,000 of that going to Wayne as base salary, plus a percentage of the profits. The actor also wanted Hawks to hire professional Westerners and a group of experienced stuntmen. Perhaps Wayne knew of director Raoul Walsh's problems with amateur riders while filming *They Died with Their Boots On.* And maybe Hawks had too, because he hired seventy experienced horsemen.

Shortly before production commenced, Margaret Sheridan informed Hawks she was five months pregnant. Obviously a replacement was needed. The director suggested Joanne Dru, a twenty-two-year-old actress he had put under contract in 1945. Dru's five-and-a-half-foot body, highlighted by flowing brown hair, green eyes, and a striking face which murmured of self-confidence, seemed well-suited to the role of the woman who makes Matt and Dunson settle their differences. Despite the filmmaker's approval of the leading lady, he felt the script needed rewriting to accommodate her special talents. Scenes showing the woman doing card tricks, for example, were changed. Twenty years later, Howard still had the character in mind. In *El Dorado* (Paramount, 1967), he cast Charlene Holt as a female card-sharp.

It took Hawks' scouts almost three months to find the right locations for *Red River.* They traveled 15,000 miles by plane, over Texas, Oklahoma, New Mexico, and Sonora and Chihuahau in Mexico. Elgin, Arizona, near the Mexican border, population seven, became the anchor town for the *Red River* production company. The tiny village rested on the edge of an expansive plain 5,000 feet high. Hawks spent $1,000,000 for the two months' location work there.

While Hawks set up the site for filming, art director John Aresma supervised the construction of four sound stages in Hollywood. A huge set, 110 x 120 feet, simulated a desert exterior. Twenty tons of sand and fourteen feet of mesquite were imported from Arizona, along with a selection of rocks—at a cost of $20,000. For clouds, the studio substituted a glass-painted background, highlighted by sun arc lights. The interior of the ranch house duplicated the 1840 Empire Ranch house. Among the scenes shot on these sets were close-ups of the wagon train, the Indian fight, the wranglers' camp before the stampede, the banks of Red River, and more.

The Arizona mountain served beautifully for *Red River.* Close to the Whetstone Mountains and Apache Peak, the area boasted, within a fifteen-mile range, land which resembled the Texas badlands and the plains of Kansas. Within a thirty-mile radius ran the San Pedro River. Monterey Productions rented part of the Rain Valley needed for shooting, as well as a ranch built in 1860.

Eighty thousand gallons of water were required for the *Red River* company. Thirty-five thousand alone went to the more than 9000 head of cattle Hawks needed plus 25,000 gallons for settling dust which kicked up constantly. Another 20,000 were used by the cast and crew, which included 500 actors, 10 assistants, and numerous technical people. It took eight cattle trucks five days to transport all the steers to the location. The Anderson

Boarding and Supply Company provided seventy-five portable tent-cabins wired for electricity and running water. Four hundred people lived in the cabins during the month-long shoot at a cost of $150,000. An additional $20,000 supplied hay for the horses and cattle.

Wardrobe man Jack Miller needed $150,000 to outfit the 500 actors. Six costumes for Joanne Dru cost $20,000.* Each member of the cast received two to four pairs of boots, sometimes worth as much as $100 a pair. The budget grew steadily, but resourceful Howard Hawks had just about everything under control.

During the filming, the director, of course, found it impossible to turn the weather on and off at will. Rainstorms caused John Wayne to catch a cold and gave Joanne Dru influenza. Hawks himself was bitten by a centipede and had to be hospitalized. But these are just a few of the dangers of location production faced by most movie outfits spending any degree of time in the wilds of America. Indeed, Hawks and company were like temporary pioneers, working their way into the frontier, as if to see what it was like and report back to moviegoers via the cinema screen.

Sound effects man Richard De Weese contended with the stomping of cattle hooves and the humming of a swarm of locusts which plagued the crew by the thousands.

Under the pressure of nature and an expanding budget, plus having to deal with actors inexperienced in location filming, director Hawks nevertheless felt confident enough to sometimes give orders to his people from as far as three miles away, communicating with his company via walkie talkie. Nine units and a radio truck moved all around the Arizona mountains. Some scenes were so expansive, traffic managers helped control the masses of man and beast.

The shooting of the cattle stampede took ten days. Six of the fifteen cameramen employed maneuvered to capture one of the largest collection of animals in cinema history. Mechanical means were used to frighten the animals. Second unit director Arthur Rosson worked with the steers, strategically deploying twenty-five Arizona wranglers and ten from Hollywood. Seven men were hurt during the filmed ruckus.

Earlier Hawks discovered the name Rain Valley was an ironic one. The valley which held the San Pedro River was dry until storms came during production. However, five dams had to be constructed to divert enough water into the San Pedro.

Even though the water was something of a curse to the *Red River* company, at least once rainfall lent a new dimension to a

*At least two of every costume were brought on location as insurance against ripping, tearing, or total destruction of the original garment.

John Wayne

competent, if ordinary, scene. Dunson is reading the Bible over the graves of two cowhands. The moment shows the boss' reverence for life and lends insight into the ways of the cowboys. Clouds formed while Hawks set up the shot, which was planned to include a clear sky. Hawks decided to wait for the rain, and his hunch that the blasting drops would add to the somber mood proved right.

It was expected that Wayne and Montgomery Clift would have their own ideas about their characters and wouldn't be reluctant to discuss them with Hawks. Wayne had a problem projecting old age and, in fact, the director felt his star was pressing too hard. Hawks asked Walter Brennan, who at the ripe age of fifty-four had been essaying older roles for a decade, to help the actor ease into the extra years. But John Wayne didn't care for Brennan's approach—to have Tom Dunson shuffle along. Wayne felt this weakened the image of the cattle boss as a hard man. He recalled the cattle drovers he'd known as a boy, and all of them walked the land proudly. None was stoop-shouldered or bow-legged. Hawks and Wayne argued about this but eventually worked out the disagreement. As the production progressed, Howard Hawks became increasingly impressed with Wayne's ability and altered the script to include more strenuous scenes for the performer.

On another occasion, the director and the star disagreed about the humor of a comic moment. Hawks told Wayne of a bit where Dunson's finger gets caught between the saddle horn and a rope. Some cowboys get drunk, heat up an iron in the fire, and cut off the digit. The Duke failed to see the comedic possibilities, so the moment was shelved. Howard brought the scene back with Kirk Douglas' finger in *The Big Sky* (RKO, 1952). Wayne thought it was hilarious and realized he had made a mistake.

Hawks realized Wayne was a powerful presence even in the 1940s. Knowing this, he mentally prepared for some problems between Wayne and Clift, two highly individualistic artists. The director believed the two would make a great team, but Wayne wasn't as sure. After production began, the veteran Western star began to like working with Clift. But he didn't think Hawks could stage a realistic fight involving Dunson and Matt. Yet Clift tried hard to adapt himself to the rugged life of lensing an action tale. He had gone to riding school to learn how to handle a horse. By showing himself a willing student of the genre, Monty Clift earned the respect of his co-workers. When *Red River* was released, Walter Brennan told the press how much he admired Clift's talents.

Since novice Clift had no idea how to defend himself in a screen battle, Hawks took the time to teach the young actor to maneuver and throw a punch. Three days later the director had a scrappy, dust-kicking brawl on celluloid. Perhaps Clift's ignorance of the subject aided the true-to-life look of the fisticuffs. The best fights in cinema history tended to leave the actors with very real cuts and bruises, and sometimes more serious injuries. Ironically, the more realistic bouts look little like most of the staged fight scenes in Westerns. For the most part, they are much slower. As the showmanship is toned down, so is the speed. The conflict of Alan Ladd and Ben Johnson in *Shane* (Paramount, 1953) is a good example of this. The knockdown battle of John Wayne and Randolph Scott in *The Spoilers* (Universal, 1942) is both speedy and lengthy.

As expected, Clift and Wayne had to adapt to each other's acting style, especially Clift. A New York actor, Montgomery Clift needed to relate deeply to anyone with whom he was performing. At first excited about shooting a particular scene with Wayne, the young performer's enthusiasm slowly diminished. The section of the script revolves around Matt's taking over of the cattle drive from Dunson. Clift was disturbed by Wayne's technique. The Duke learned from John Ford not to act for the camera, but to react to what was going on around him. Therefore Wayne's need to physically relate to Clift was not great. Monty complained to Hawks that Wayne didn't even look at him once. The director explained to his young star to be that many have tried to best John Wayne on-camera, but few have succeeded. In the final analysis, the teaming of the two was inspired, as each played off the other's differences—age, height, voice, face, and screen personality.

On a lighter note, Hawks even had trouble with a temperamental cow. Child performer Mickey Kuhn played Clift's part of Matt as a boy. In one scene, Mickey was to lead the cow out of the woods. The cow simply wouldn't budge. The director placed filled water buckets just out of camera range to entice the animal. It didn't work. He even instructed cowhands to fire blanks in an attempt to get the cow's attention. Finally, after nineteen takes, the four-legged creature decided to let Mickey lead him away.

Well aware that good relations with area residents was an absolute necessity for any film company, Howard showed rushes of the day's work to people who filled the small theatre near the location site. Hawks even brought in features for the movie-hungry audience.

After two months of location work, and extra time polishing the production in Hollywood, the final cost of *Red River* was more than $3,000,000, double the original budget. As if that wasn't enough, Hawks' old nemesis Howard Hughes decided to sue United Artists for allegedly lifting that final battle between Dunson and Matt from his (Hughes') production entitled *The Outlaw* (on which Hawks had originally worked in 1940).

Little doubt existed that the *Red River* scene was very similar to the climax of *The Outlaw,* and UA became extremely concerned over the possibility of a lengthy court battle. Hawks couldn't go to Hughes and ask the millionaire to withdraw his claim on the basis of past friendship, as their relationship long had been strained. Finally John Wayne talked to Hughes. The star agreed that the scene in *Red River* resembled the one in *The Outlaw,* and he said that Hawks had tried to cut *Red River* to accommodate Hughes' objections, but found the lack of the big moment to be harmful to the Western. Since Wayne and Hughes were friends, the star requested that the producer drop his suit on that basis. Howard Hughes decided not to go to court, and *Red River* went on to become a classic.

Even with the ending which shows Tom Dunson as an honorable man, Howard Hawks wondered if the audience would accept Wayne's atypical characterization. Since Dunson made a horrible mistake and lost the girl he loved, he felt an obsessive need to fulfill every one of his other goals. Dunson will not admit failure to himself and cannot own up to error. Yet his empire is on the verge of destruction. He can't let the cowboys walk out. Could the audience still sympathize with Wayne, Hawks thought to himself. That ending about which Hughes dropped his lawsuit turned Dunson's eroding nature around and won the public's love.

Movie posters spread in cinema lobbies across the land proclaimed:

> In 25 years, only three!
> *The Covered Wagon, Cimarron,* and now Howard Hawks' great production—
> RED RIVER

Reviewers generally applauded the film, its director, and its stars:

New York Sun, Eileen Creelman:

> It's a big, smashing Western, with good, tough direction, good, tough acting. The film is long, five minutes over two hours; and that's too long, even for a top notch action film. . . . The characters are sound ones, from John Wayne's portrayal of the terrible old Dunson and Montgomery Clift's quietly confident Matt to Walter Brennan's comic Groot.

Time:

> When people discuss the real artists of picture-making, they seldom get around to mentioning Howard Hawks. Yet Hawks is one of the most individual and independent directors in the business. Even when he has a routine chore to do, he gives it character; when a picture really interests him, he gives it enough character to blast you out of your seat. *Red River,* which Hawks produced and directed, clearly interested him a lot.

Variety:

> *Red River* will take its place among the other big, box-office-important Western epics that have come from Hollywood

over the years. It's a spectacle of sweeping grandeur, as rugged and hard as the men and the times with which it deals.

Although *Red River* flowed way over budget, the classic Western ultimately grossed approximately $10,000,000. In the year of *The Treasure of the Sierra Madre* (Warner Bros.), *Red River* failed to win a single major Academy Award and was ignored by other cinema-related organizations such as the National Board of Review and the New York Film Critics. Yet it remains respected as the first completed Western of director Howard Hawks, featuring one of John Wayne's best performances. When John Ford saw how well Wayne had played Tom Dunson, he went on to make that great series of cavalry Westerns with the star. Most important, however, *Red River* proved that Wayne could really act and that Hawks knew how to make a Western.

George O'Brien and John Wayne

CHAPTER ELEVEN

Fort Apache

Year Released: 1948
Studio: Argosy Pictures/RKO
Producer: John Ford
Director: John Ford
Screenplay: Frank Nugent, from the story *Massacre* by James Warren Bellah
Cinematography: Archie Stout
Music: Richard Hageman
Conductor: Lucien Cailliet
Art Director: James Basevi
Editor: Jack Murray
Assistant Directors: Lowell Farrell, Jack Pennick
Production Manager: Bernard McEveety
Set Director: Joe Kish
Makeup: Emile La Vigne
Costumes: Michael Meyers (men's), Ann Peck (women's)
Second Unit Director: Cliff Lyons
Sound: Joseph Kane, Frank Webster
Special Effects: Dave Koehler
127 minutes

Cast:

Captain Kirby York	JOHN WAYNE
Lieutenant Colonel Owen Thursday	HENRY FONDA
Philadelphia Thursday	SHIRLEY TEMPLE

Lieutenant Mickey O'Rourke	JOHN AGAR
Sergeant Mulcahy	VICTOR McLAGLEN
Captain Sam Collingwood	GEORGE O'BRIEN
Emily Collingwood	ANNA LEE
Sergeant Beaufort	PEDRO ARMENDARIZ
Quincannon	DICK FORAN
Major Michael O'Rourke	WARD BOND
Silas Meacham	GRANT WITHERS
Mrs. Gates	MAE MARSH
Cochise	MIGUEL INCLAN
Sergeant Shattuck	JACK PENNICK
Newspaperman	FRANK FERGUSON
Stage Guard	FRANCIS FORD
Mrs. Mary O'Rourke	IRENE RICH
Dr. Wilkens	GUY KIBBEE
Guadalupe	MOVITA CASTENADA
Officer at Dance	MICKEY SIMPSON
Recruit	RAY HYKE
Ma	MARY GORDON
Hick Recruit	HANK WORDEN
Reporters	ARCHIE TWITCHELL
	WILLIAM FORREST
Cavalrymen	FRED GRAHAM
	PHILIP KEIFFER
Stage Driver	CLIFF CLARK

Fort Apache embodies the dignity, grandeur, and romance of the best John Ford Westerns. This epic of the Indian wars upholds the nobility of white and red men who must engage in combat and illustrates unity among the cavalry ranks even though one of them is a glory seeker whose aggression is a by-product of his ambition. Here, as in all Ford films, the honor of the group is paramount.

Colonel Owen Thursday believes in the manifest destiny of the white man to rule the frontier. The struggle between the Indians and the Army is aggravated by Silas Meacham, a renegade who sells rifles and whiskey to the tribes. Thursday stands on his egotism, refusing to reason with the chiefs. Captain Kirby York has a more realistic view of the troubles, but is constantly overruled by

Thursday. When York refuses to carry out an order, Thursday threatens to court-martial him. When words no longer suffice, Thursday attacks the Indians, and his troops are slaughtered. In order to maintain the integrity of the service, York covers up his superior's tragic order which led to the massacre.

Despite the odds, the virtues of right over wrong, or personalities, men stick together in *Fort Apache,* even if the alliance is sometimes uneasy. The conflict at the post is acted out by Wayne and Fonda. Wayne represents the true frontiersman, who shares a mutual respect with the Indians born of a common understanding of the demands of the wilderness. Fonda is the upstart from the East, the martinet with the Machiavellian strategies who values rigid notions of racial interrelationship. Such ideas are rooted in an ignorance of the West which has come to mask his grandiose personal goals. With Fonda as the swaggering, self-righteous Custer-like leader who alienates the enlisted personnel, Wayne is the officer who has the same kinship with the men as with the Indians. Loyalty is developed when soldiers face anxiety-filled situations as part of their daily existence, when a man sometimes has to look to his buddy on the field for both physical and mental reinforcement of the common values of army life.

The balance of Wayne and Fonda exemplifies the structural harmony of *Fort Apache.* For every character there is an antagonist of equal strength. For every thread moving in one direction, there is another heading the opposite way.

Fort Apache has a larger scope than Ford's later two films in his cavalry trilogy *(She Wore a Yellow Ribbon* and *Rio Grande).* In most genre productions until then, including Ford's, the Indians were traditionally represented as mean-looking braves in war parties, zooming arrows through the air, and making savage wagon train or homestead attacks. They are visible only in the basest form, stripped of their culture and their humanity. In *Fort Apache,* the landscape is enlarged to include a reasonably accurate, if brief, depiction of the Indians as a force which met the cavalry head-on, man for man, not white hero to red devil. Ford has respect for the tribes. The affirmation of their individuality and honesty gives the Western a unique vibrance, which in turn stimulates the strife between Wayne and Fonda.

In this film, although he broadens the sphere to provide a portrait of the West relative to the personal struggle, the director never gets carried away with the "significance" of the story. Like Wayne, Ford is down there with the enlisted men, looking not at the pages of history but at the people who populated the frontier. The drama is beautifully relieved, and thus heightened, by the antics of the director's renowned stock company: Victor McLaglen, Ward

Bond, Dick Foran, George O'Brien, Jack Pennick, Pedro Armendariz, among others. Fordian humor is always broad, to be sure, but it is so naturally engrained into his predominantly Irish players that laughs come fast and free.

While Ford's view of the West is romantic, as of course were most pre-World War II cinema concepts of the frontier, the filmmaker's misty eyes don't quite convey a rose-colored view of the love relationship shared by John Agar and Shirley Temple. The two young people swoon in the background. Neither can create the power of Wayne, Fonda, or the enlisted personnel. The lovers properly exist on the periphery of the tale, descending for a touch of sweetness, giving that sense of equilibrium to Ford's harsh look at Fonda's Western politics. Yet even the director gives in to sentiment, as beautifully exemplified by Dick Foran's tender serenade at the outpost party.

The cast of *Fort Apache* is fine from top to bottom. Along with the might of Wayne and Fonda, added steadiness is achieved by Wayne's restraint and Fonda's ability to give even the most unsympathetic characters a sense of reality which makes it impossible to hate them. McLaglen, Bond, Foran, Pennick, and the others are

George O'Brien, Anna Lee, Shirley Temple, John Wayne, and Henry Fonda

complete professionals. Newcomer John Agar and newly mature Shirley Temple provide the zesty youthful excitement necessary to counteract the others' crusty experience, while veterans Mae Marsh and Anna Lee add able female support.

Fort Apache lovingly chronicles the glories rather than the gore of the frontier, yet never gets bogged down in spectacle or sentiment. John Ford's first cavalry film is a beautifully cut diamond broken into precision pieces of action and drama.

The Making of *Fort Apache*

One day John Ford was directing one of the dozens of films he made at Fox when the head man dropped by the set with a guest, Darryl F. Zanuck. As soon as Ford spotted the pair, he stopped the cameras, and told everyone to take a break. He introduced the visitors to his company, and urged his cast and crew to get a good look at the men, as it was the first and last time the duo would be seen on the set.

It wasn't an unusual day. Every time producers or moguls were visible within an eye-view radius of a John Ford production, the director invariably stopped shooting. This was his way of telling studio heads they weren't welcome on his set. And since his films made money, few argued.

A man with that sense of command makes a natural producer, a decision-maker. So it wasn't surprising when long-time colleagues Ford and Merian C. Cooper formed the independent Argosy Pictures, to make movies and sell them to major studios for distribution. The first Argosy property was *The Fugitive,* released by RKO in 1947. Taken from Graham Greene's *The Power and the Glory,* it starred Henry Fonda as a radical priest betrayed by a man he once helped. The tale, a mood piece which found little favor with anybody, had an atmosphere similar to the doom-ridden tone of *The Informer,* the movie which solidified Ford's reputation in the 1930s. Curiously, *The Fugitive* didn't find favor with a public then eager for films with greater psychological realism, a trait certainly evident in this complex story.

Ford got to thinking about Westerns, a genre which he helped lift out of the doldrums of the "poverty row" range of the early and mid-1930s into a new surge of artistic expression in 1939. The director's last Western was *My Darling Clementine,* released by Fox in 1946, a leisurely moving richly detailed rendition of events leading up to the famed gunfight at the O.K. Corral, which was a favorite of his children.

The director asked reporter and former *New York Times* film critic Frank Nugent to adapt a story by James Warren Bellah called *Massacre* into a scenario. Nugent called his script *War Party.*

Ford changed the title to *Fort Apache,* thus emphasizing the army outpost as the center of the action. The film would be about life at the fort, the conflicts between men and women. The struggle with the Indians was merely the climax of a romantic, rugged, and, above all, dignified narrative of the white man and the red man.

John Wayne signed for the role of Captain Kirby York, a veteran soldier who knew and respected the ways of the Indians. Henry Fonda, a Ford favorite in both *My Darling Clementine* and *The Fugitive* as well as in *The Grapes of Wrath,* took the part of Lieutenant Colonel Owen Thursday, an officer who believed the only good Indian was the proverbial dead one, and that the conquest of the red man was the way to glory.

John Agar made his film debut as a young officer who has just graduated from military school. Agar had very little previous acting experience at the time, being the scion of a rich Chicago meat packer, so he suited his role well. Despite his lack of talent, Agar had one big advantage over the hundreds of young men who invaded Hollywood after World War II in search of stardom: he was married to Shirley Temple, the darling of the screen. This helped the twenty-six-year-old man who wanted a shot at stardom and a chance to be seen by producers.

Ironically, Agar's presence during the pre-production planning of the Western allowed Ford to spot his wife. Shirley Temple was trying hard to erase the little girl image which made her the darling of Depression audiences. Such froth as *Honeymoon* (RKO), *The Bachelor and the Bobby Soxer* (RKO), and *That Hagen Girl* (Warner Bros., all 1947) kept her working but failed to advance her career. She had yet to convince the producers of her ability to essay parts meant for mature young women. Ford decided to give her that chance in *Fort Apache,* and signed her to play Philadelphia Thursday, Agar's romantic interest. So the Agars had another thing in their favor: they could make love onscreen, then go home and practice! John Ford's job was made easier by the round-the-clock admiration shared by the newlyweds.

Much of the rest of the cast were men with whom Ford had had personal and professional relationships for years. Veteran actor George O'Brien came out of retirement to play the commandant of Fort Apache. (O'Brien had starred in *The Iron Horse* [Fox] for Ford back in 1924.) Victor McLaglen, who played the rowdy Sergeant Mulcahy, had won an Oscar under Ford's direction for *The Informer* (RKO) thirteen years earlier. Ward Bond, Dick Foran, Grant Withers, and Jack Pennick each had essayed many characterizations, both big and small, in the films of John Ford. Mexican

Shirley Temple and John Agar

star Pedro Armendariz and old reliables Paul Fix, Anna Lee, and Mae Marsh—who had made her first film in 1912 and had important roles in *Birth of a Nation* (Mutual, 1915) and *Intolerance* (Triangle, 1916)—rounded out the list of players.

John Wayne was extremely concerned over his role in *Fort Apache.* It was his most complex part in years, aside from his portrayal of Tom Dunson in *Red River.* In fact, Ford gave Wayne the York character on the strength of his performance in Hawks' classic Western. Since *Stagecoach* in 1939, Wayne had busied himself with more than a dozen productions which rarely tested his acting mettle. While shooting *Fort Apache,* the actor also maintained an office at Republic Studios, where he made several actioners for his own production company. Apparently a series of mishaps, including a particularly nagging leak in his office, didn't help his concentration.

In order to find a non-Ford opinion about his performance, Wayne asked supporting player Paul Fix to watch while he read the lines and help him over any rough spots in the script. Fix stood out of camera range (and, presumably, away from director Ford) during the takes, giving hand and face signals like those a third-base coach would flash to a batter when the next pitch could mean victory or defeat in a baseball game. Ford wasn't one to miss much and became aware of the clandestine arrangement. Without saying a word to either man, the filmmaker decided to push Fix even harder than he drove most of his other actors. At one point, Fix's character had to fall on some broken rocks. Ford required the actor to repeat the painful action so many times that Fix finally refused to continue. His director loudly stated that such a refusal meant that Fix would never work for Ford again. So Fix walked off the set.

John Ford, the director, knew what he wanted. He didn't compromise on the set, nor did he change scripts or camera angles radically once they were created. In fact, he generally allowed the cameramen to work out the details of the movements and only mapped out specifics when necessary. Ford had faith in his crew. And the beautiful look of the director's films proves not only that he was a true cinema artist, but that he possessed the ability to choose quality co-workers.

Yet Ford knew that location shooting posed problems which sometimes had to be solved by altering the schedule. Like most of his other classic Westerns, *Fort Apache* was lensed at Monument Valley, on the border of Utah and Arizona. Ford knew the flat plains and mountains of the area well. This allowed him a key vantage point not always held by other directors who make movies outdoors. He thus was able to better position himself to photograph a rainfall or windstorm and give his work an extra touch of authenticity along with the fresh air of improvisation without spending days revising the script.

John Agar felt the effects of Ford's directorial personality more than once. Ford followed his usual habit of rigorously initiating a cinema rookie into the ways of moviemaking. Nothing Agar did was good enough. His delivery was bad. He didn't know how to move. The boy from Chicago had no idea how to ride a horse. Agar took the harsh treatment hard. He had no way of knowing Ford only did this to get a better performance and to make the veteran players more secure. To make matters worse, Ford also reportedly picked on Shirley Temple, a move which doubtlessly improved the

Poster for
Fort Apache

The men and women of Fort Apache minus John Wayne

couple's ensemble performance. Yet George O'Brien remembered the actress as being such a knowledgeable professional that even the great Ford could not win the upper hand with her.

John Wayne remembered the feeling of being a new actor in a Ford production. He explained why Ford behaved as if he had a mean streak the size of Route 66 in him. Agar understood. The young performer admired and respected Wayne, and the star encouraged Agar while reading over the script with him and even giving him riding lessons.

That attitude was typical of John Wayne. Despite the fact that he was the star of *Fort Apache* (or perhaps because of it), Wayne got into costume and makeup each morning before anyone else showed for work. The star's cooperative nature and sense of duty certainly helped director Ford trim a slated seventy-seven-day shooting schedule into forty-four and cut the budget from $2,800,000 to $2,100,000. Ford was also able to do this because he might spend as much as six months preparing a project. And of course he was particularly concerned with the budget of *Fort Apache* because he was co-producing the venture for Argosy Productions.

RKO gave *Fort Apache* a nice publicity build-up. The studio suggested that local theatres showing the Western distribute cardboard arrowheads and advertise sales on Indian goods in town stores. They also asked exhibitors to search for people who lived during the frontier days and interview them about the West. Advertising headlines read:

> Masterpiece of the frontier . . . it's got scope and sweep, human scenes straight from the shoulder! . . . A story of brave women . . . long, lean cavalrymen . . . their fighting . . . humor!
>
> Epic in sweep! . . . Intimate in heart power! Lusty in the humor of reckless cavalrymen! Warm with the love of loyal women! The screen's supreme adventure in action!

Reviews varied:

Cue:

> The film swings like a pendulum between the monotone of dull barracks life and the screaming high pitch of the Indian wars; but unfortunately for *Fort Apache,* the action on screen doesn't get under way until too late to wake a lethargic audience. The large cast does a competent if not distinguished job.

New York Herald Tribune, Howard Barnes:

> When he [John Ford] is dealing with fighting men, horses

and vivid pageantry, the film has pulse and dramatic power. Unfortunately he has lingered too long over a conventional narrative to make his latest offering measure up to so distinguished a Western predecessor as *Stagecoach.*

New York Times, Bosley Crowther:

. . . for the standard movie audience, *Fort Apache* will chiefly provide a handsome and thrilling outdoor drama of "war" on the American frontier—a salty, sizzling visualization of regimental life at a desert fort, of strong masculine personality and of raging battles beneath the withering sun. For, of course, Mr. Ford is a genius at directing this sort of thing and Frank S. Nugent has ably supplied him with a tangy and workable script.

Variety:

Fort Apache undoubtedly will cause considerable critical pro and con because of the openly commercial approach John Ford has used on the subject. He has aimed the picture directly at the average theatregoer, bypassing non-profitable art effects. As a consequence, the film has mass appeal, great excitement and a potent box office outlook. . . . [The] cast is as tremendous as the scope achieved by Ford's direction . . . some of the roles are very short but all are effective.

John Wayne's performance as Captain York helped elevate him from a star into someone who possessed both a cinema magic and a true ability to emote on screen. *Fort Apache* solidified Ford's stock company of actors which has deservedly come to be given the respect one would accord any repertory group of actors performing in small towns all over America. Shirley Temple had finally co-starred in an adult role. John Agar's career temporarily profited from *Fort Apache.* Sadly, the actor's penchant for drinking slowly ruined his marriage as well as a promising life in the cinema. By the mid-1950s Agar was acting in "B" productions. Frank Nugent would continue his association with Ford on such productions as *She Wore a Yellow Ribbon, The Quiet Man* (Republic, 1952), *The Searchers* (Warner Bros., 1956), *The Last Hurrah* (Columbia, 1958), and *Donovan's Reef* (Paramount, 1963). Cameraman Archie Stout went on to win an Oscar for his color photography of *The Quiet Man.*

Fort Apache offers a tough but positive illustration of Western frontier existence, portraying both Indians and whites with dignity. This John Ford film was a bridge between the epic oaters of the later 1930s and the 1950s productions fraught with the anxieties and doubts of an atomic age.

Debra Paget and James Stewart

Jeff Chandler, James Stewart, and Jay Silverheels

CHAPTER TWELVE

Broken Arrow

Year Released: 1950
Studio: Twentieth Century-Fox
Producer: Julian Blaustein
Director: Delmer Daves
Screenplay: Michael Blankfort, based on the novel *Blood Brothers* by Elliott Arnold
Cinematography: Ernest Palmer
Music: Alfred Newman
Art Directors: Lyle Wheeler, Arthur Hogsett
Editor: J. Watson Webb, Jr.
Color, 93 minutes

Cast:

Tom Jeffords	JAMES STEWART
Cochise	JEFF CHANDLER
Sonseeahray	DEBRA PAGET
General Howard	BASIL RUYSDAEL
Ben Slade	WILL GEER
Terry	JOYCE MacKENZIE
Duffield	ARTHUR HUNNICUTT
Colonel Bernall	RAYMOND BRAMLEY
Goklia	JAY SILVERHEELS
Nalikadeya	ARGENTINA BRUNETTI
Boucher	JACK LEE
Lonergan	ROBERT ADLER

Miner	HARRY CARTER
Lowrie	ROBERT GRIFFIN
Juan	BILL WILKERSON
Chip Slade	MICKEY KUHN
Nochalo	CHRIS WILLOW BIRD

Broken Arrow was *not* the first Western to depict Indians sympathetically. Films such as *The Vanishing American* (Paramount, 1925) and *They Died with Their Boots On,* along with a number of "B" Westerns, portrayed Indian figures as human beings, not just mounds of muscles with painted faces who scalped innocent settlers. In fact, the Indian-as-protagonist theme goes all the way back to the one- and two-reelers of D. W. Griffith and Thomas Ince before World War I. *Broken Arrow* is a classic production which happened at the right time. Its plea for racial tolerance is interwoven with a realistic depiction of Indian culture, enhanced by the cinematic sense of director Delmer Daves.

The film begins with Tom Jeffords telling how he became a friend to the Apaches after volunteering to help negotiate a peace treaty between their chief, Cochise, and the U.S. Army. While in the Indian camp, Jeffords learns much about Apache life and falls in love with Sonseeahray, a beautiful young squaw. The fragile cease-fire Jeffords had arranged is broken when a wagon train is attacked. While he tries to put together a new settlement, the Indians hold a war counsel. A group of renegades headed by Geronimo leaves Cochise to wage battle against the Army. With a second uneasy peace arrangement established, Jeffords weds Sonseeahray. The couple is ambushed by a group of Indian-hating whites, and she is killed. Cochise persuades hate-filled Jeffords that they must now work harder than ever to find peace.

By the time *Broken Arrow* was lensed in 1949, Hollywood productions had dealt with such complex issues as racial and religious bigotry and the after-effects of war, as well as the psychology of the criminal mind. The Western was already changed by the post-war realist trend, as witnessed by *Red River*.

The beauty of *Broken Arrow* is the strength with which it carries out the theme of understanding. Instead of merely making pious statements, the script examines Indian ways, showing how they differ from white culture. "You try to understand our ways," says Cochise. "It is good to understand the ways of others," replies the frontiersman. Jeffords learns a unique way of communicating. He watches a ritual, featuring Indians wearing spots and streaks of colorful paint, and with feathers symbolizing the spirit of good and evil. "Without words it tells you things," Jeffords decides.

Delmer Daves uses the artifacts of white and Indian existence, along with the Arizona landscape, to portray his story. In the camp, Jeffords shaves with a straight razor. Daves' image is a medium-close shot of Stewart; then Debra Paget is seen in a reflection of the round mirror. "I thought you were skinning yourself," blurts the astounded squaw.

The most striking scene in *Broken Arrow* is neither violent nor moralistic. The wedding of Tom and Sonseeahray employs the natural colors of man and nature in the creation of a human experience. The squaw wears a blue and white fringed outfit, with white beads and a bracelet. Her hair is tied with white bands. The blue sky, brown teepee, and white horse in the background make for a pure and simple elegance. The couple's hands are tied together, and each has a wrist cut. They kneel down on the earth and blend their blood as one. On white horses, they ride through the hills to their wickiup.

The sad moments are equally powerful. Daves uses the wordless way of communication by detailing the tragedy of the injustices against the red man in one image. A dead Indian lies on the ground. Only the face and part of the torso are visible in the lower part of the frame. There is a vaguely defined frenzy of fighting behind him. His loincloth flaps and his hair moves gently against the battle-created wind.

As Tom Jeffords, James Stewart began a rejuvenated career as a star of tough, colorful Westerns. His characteristic abilities to play a comic scene and engage sympathy with those innocent eyes are augmented here with a razor-sharp passion, exhibited in full force with the death of his wife. Relative newcomer Jeff Chandler's Cochise is stoic and reasonable, similar to Tom Dunson in the early stages of *Red River,* and he is surprisingly literate.

It is Cochise who supports Jeffords after the white man's wife has been killed. "As I bear the murder of my people, so you will bear the murder of your wife," he tells Jeffords in a steady tone. That strength of simplicity, that truth, that nobility is what *Broken Arrow* is all about.

The Making of *Broken Arrow*

Delmar Daves began his career in Hollywood Westerns with a letter of introduction to James Cruze. The nineteen-year-old law student was hired as a property assistant on Cruze's *The Covered Wagon* (Paramount, 1923), regarded early as a classic, but now thought of as an awkward antique. Daves was writing scripts by the end of the decade. He directed his first film, *Destination Tokyo* (Warner Bros., 1943), because as the screenwriter of the submarine tale, he knew more about the subject than anyone on the Warners lot.

The director established himself as a message-bearer with the liberal *Pride of the Marines* (Warner Bros., 1945). And since Daves had been born in San Francisco and had spent much time on movie locations in Arizona and California before World War I, he had had ample opportunity to cultivate an interest in the heritage of the West.

The Covered Wagon was Delmer Daves' first and last experience with the Western until *Broken Arrow.*

Stagecoach had heralded the "comeback" of the Western in 1939, but the war slowed down further development. By 1949 Daves had lensed seven films. He read a novel called *Blood Brothers* by Elliott Arnold, which had just been optioned to Twentieth Century-Fox. The book contained something of the moral and psychological dilemmas then popular in the *film noir,* along with a social commentary to fit the times.

Actor Jeff Chandler was aware that his agent Julian Blaustein had originally bought the property and tried to sell it to Columbia. At the time Chandler busied himself making his film debut in *Sword in the Desert* (Universal, 1949) after a career in radio. But that didn't stop the aggressive performer from attempting to win the role of Apache Chief Cochise in the production. When Blaustein sold the rights to Fox, he also secured the part of Cochise for Chandler. When the promising deep-voiced performer found out that he was to co-star with James Stewart, it was almost too good to be true.

Blaustein eyed Stewart to play Tom Jeffords from the start. The star liked the character as well, but balked at signing a long-term contract with Fox. Stewart was one of the very few major actors of the 1930s and 1940s who survived without being bound to one studio for a lengthy period. Since post-war Hollywood saw the development of a number of "free-lance" leads, his bargaining position was good. Yet Stewart wanted to make the Western. His last foray into the genre had been Universal's humorous, action-packed *Destry Rides Again* in 1939.* Few opportunities surfaced for the performer to do another oater, and he needed a change from comedy pictures. Stewart thought so highly of the story that he wanted to co-produce the vehicle with Blaustein, but eventually signed a single-picture contract to appear as Jeffords, with no production chores.

As usual, the Fox research department thoroughly assembled information on the people and the period of *Broken Arrow.* Then

*Although Stewart starred in *Broken Arrow* before *Winchester '73,* the latter film was released first.

Michael Blankfort sat down to write a story of bigotry and brotherhood.

Delmer Daves wanted *Broken Arrow* to reflect the Indian way of life, their quiet dignity and moral standards. While different in many ways from the whites, the Apaches desired peace with the encroaching civilization. Everyone concerned felt the film had to promote the notion of equality among the races.

To give the Western a realistic background, Daves brought his cast and crew of almost 200 to the site where the events to be filmed actually occurred eighty years earlier. With the help of 400 Apaches and 100 area residents, the *Broken Arrow* company settled into the isolated Coconino Mountains, part of the National Forest of Arizona.

One of the problems of location shooting was arranging to have the day's rushes processed. Since there were of course no film laboratories in the Arizona mountains, an Indian runner rushed the undeveloped stock on foot to the nearest automobile, thirty miles away. From there it went to a distant lab, to be returned as quickly as the runner could carry it.

As expected, the Hollywood people found something of a communication gap between themselves and Indian associates. Some crewmen constructed an Apache home called a "wickiup," then went to work elsewhere. When Daves and company returned to the site, they found Indians occupying the tent-like shelter, assuming it had been abandoned.

Although the researchers for *Broken Arrow* provided a meticulous investigation into the lifestyle of the Apaches, one Indian was forced to break with tradition to achieve proper dramatic effect. Nineteenth-century Apaches never wore any sort of chest covering, but one of their ancestors, Jim Red Finger, had to wear a buckskin shirt. Jim's torso contained a large tattoo which read, "Remember Pearl Harbor." Some of the authentic Apaches who served as extras in the Western were Chief Ba-ha, who was an advisor to the White River Apaches, and Lambert Stone, a 104-year-old Indian who had broken with his brothers in the last century to follow Geronimo.

The construction crew built air-conditioned housing quarters for many of the Indians, but the red men refused to live in them. They quite correctly insisted that going quickly from the 110-degree Arizona summer heat to artificially cooled environments was unhealthy. Most preferred to sit on the dusty ground wrapped in blankets, absorbing the powerful sun rays.

Director Daves instructed two Indians to make food coolers, fire grates, and a bough bed in the traditional Apache manner. Since the men didn't know where to begin, they consulted "The Boy Scouts' Handicraft Book," much to the stunned filmmaker's surprise. And as if there weren't already enough misconceptions, an archery expert had to teach many Apaches how to use a bow and arrow!

During the filming Debra Paget, Stewart's seventeen-year-old co-star, was involved in a number of mishaps. The young actress had been recently signed by a Fox talent scout and had made appearances in the studio's *Cry of the City* and *House of Strangers* (both 1948) on the back lot. As such, she had no experience facing the hazards of rural location work. Her first encounter could have been most serious, but she escaped uninjured. Since Debra's blue-green eyes were inconsistent with her Indian role, she had to be fitted with brown lenses. When Daves shot a close-up, one of the fake lenses exploded under the heat of the huge incandescent lamps the director employed. Later she was bitten by a tarantula. Her closest brush with death happened during an offscreen swim in a creek. The starlet developed stomach cramps and was reportedly on the verge of drowning when she was rescued by an area resident.

Delmer Daves also had difficulty framing Stewart and Paget in close-ups, due to the tremendous difference in their heights. During the love scenes, the 5′2″ actress almost appears to be a little girl leaning on the chest of 6′3½″ star Stewart.

With Paget adapting to the rigors of 19th-century Arizona mountain living, Stewart felt the need to spurn the use of a double as much as possible. During one take Indian arrows were shot at his feet, and the actor's very real fear of this and other occasions doubtlessly helped his performance.

Chandler meanwhile found he already possessed something of the makings of Cochise. A 1946 auto accident had provided him with scars which the makeup man simply accentuated. As such, Cochise's battle injuries were quite authentic. And the actor impressed everyone with his enthusiasm, as Chandler constantly flew back and forth between the location and Hollywood to do radio work. (He was a regular on "Lux Radio Theater.")

There were few big battle scenes to lens in *Broken Arrow,* so the six-week shooting schedule proceeded without major tie-ups. James Stewart even decided to wait until filming was over to marry Gloria McLean.

Twentieth Century-Fox created an expansive publicity campaign to promote what they felt was a socially important production as well as a box-office draw:

> Twentieth Century-Fox, with special pride, presents a widely heralded motion picture . . . the powerful and unusual story of a white man's love for an Indian girl, that shattered the barriers of color and hate.

James Stewart

James Stewart and Debra Paget

It took 80 years to tell this story. And 80 years from now it will be remembered.

The advertisements were somewhat subdued in comparison to posters for more action-filled, violent, and melodramatic Westerns. But the change was quite appropriate.

Broken Arrow was applauded by the Association of Indian Affairs. Following is an excerpt from the organization's statement to Fox:

> *Broken Arrow* is one of the first movies since *The Vanishing American* to attempt a serious portrayal of the Indian side of American history. For years the films have shown all Indian wars as a contest between murdering red savages and heroic white men. Now, at last, 20th Century-Fox's *Broken Arrow* shows honestly what happened on both sides in the great Apache war. In the Technicolor picture Jimmy Stewart and a convincing cast led by Debra Paget and Jeff Chandler prove that the American Indian must be considered a first class citizen. Perhaps this presages a new screen literature of the West in which the Indians will be depicted as they really were, and are. *Broken Arrow* also points out to Hollywood that stereotypes can be discarded and that both Indians and whites emerge as human beings: cruel, frightened, courageous, kindly. . . .

Despite the tremendous advance publicity, *Broken Arrow* received a mixed reception:

> *Cue:*
>
> Elliott Arnold's novel, as brought to the Technicolor screen, is an intelligent, literate, spectacular and superbly photographed Western drama. . . . The action is swift, the film picturesque and colorful.
>
> *New York Times,* Bosley Crowther:
>
> We cannot accept this picture as either an exciting or reasonable account of the attitudes and ways of American Indians.
>
> *Saturday Review,* Robert Gessner:
>
> . . . if you like action and are sentimental about Noble Savages who do not scalp, you'll enjoy *Broken Arrow.* Although it's old Indians in a new bottle, it's the best vintage in many a moon.
>
> *Variety:*
>
> Essentially it's an appealing, sentimental Indian romance, with plenty of action to offset the more placid moments. Beauti-

fully photographed in Technicolor, against a lush Arizona background, and with James Stewart heading an accomplished set of performers, pic looks set for good returns.

Broken Arrow failed to win any major Academy Awards, although Jeff Chandler came within three votes of receiving the best supporting Oscar for his sincere portrayal of Cochise. The trend-setting Western did not win any recognition from the National Board of Review or the New York Film Critics. *Film Daily* gave no award that year.

Despite the less than triumphant reception accorded *Broken Arrow,* the film did open new vistas for many of Hollywood's leading men. Since rugged Jeff Chandler won acclaim as an Indian, and subsequently played Cochise in Universal's *The Battle at Apache Pass* (1952), producers felt safe in later casting such diverse male talent as Robert Taylor, Burt Lancaster, Rock Hudson, and Elvis Presley as Indians in Westerns.

Indian regalia became marketable after *Broken Arrow,* just as millions of coonskin caps lined sales counters following Walt Disney's *Davy Crockett* later in the decade. Department stores were stocked with fancy headdresses, buckskins, tomahawks, knives, bow and arrow sets, and more flashy paraphernalia of 19th-century Indian existence.

From *Broken Arrow,* James Stewart went on to act in a handful of fine Westerns throughout the 1950s. He successfully bent his image away from the light dramatic and comic leads he etched so well for Frank Capra, adding a welcome touch of leather in his performances. Delmer Daves continued to direct top Westerns during the next decade, most of which were more violent than *Broken Arrow.* Yet they had the same respect for location, color, and character. *The Last Wagon* (Fox, 1956), *Jubal* (Columbia, 1956), *3:10 to Yuma* (Columbia, 1957), and *Cowboy* (Columbia, 1958) stand out among Daves' eight other Westerns. Fox's own "pocket edition" of *Broken Arrow* for TV in 1956 starred Ricardo Montalban, Rita Moreno, and John Lupton. The subsequent TV series based on the film also had Lupton playing Tom Jeffords, with Michael Ansara as Cochise.

Broken Arrow added a new dimension to the Hollywood Western—the human Indian. The film is also a classic example of the use of color in the Hollywood cinema—one of the few of its kind.

Gregory Peck

CHAPTER THIRTEEN

The Gunfighter

Year Released: 1950
Studio: Twentieth Century-Fox
Producer: Nunnally Johnson
Director: Henry King
Screenplay: William Bowers, William Sellers, based on a story by Bowers and Andre De Toth
Cinematography: Arthur Miller
Music: Alfred Newman
Art Director: Lyle Wheeler
Editor: Barbara McLean
Production Manager: Joseph Behm
Assistant Director: Johnny Joghson
84 minutes

Cast:

Jimmy Ringo	GREGORY PECK
Peggy Walsh	HELEN WESTCOTT
Sheriff Mark Strett	MILLARD MITCHELL
Molly	JEAN PARKER
Mac	KARL MALDEN
Hunt Bromley	SKIP HOMEIER
Eddie	RICHARD JAECKEL
Alice Marlowe	JEAN INNESS
Mrs. O'Brien	MAE MARSH
Mrs. Pennyfeather	VERNA FELTON
Charlie	ANTHONY ROSS

Mrs. Devlin	ELLEN CORBY
First Brother	ALAN HALE, JR.
Second Brother	DAVID CLARKE
Third Brother	JOHN PICKARD
Jimmie	D. G. NORMAN
Mac's Wife	ANGELA CLARKE
Jerry Marlowe	CLIFF CLARK
Archie	EDDIE EHRHART
Pablo	ALBERTO MORIN

The Gunfighter is the story of a man whose time has passed . . . a film about the death of the West, and one which prophesizes the chameleon-like rebirth of the frontier as modern civilization. The land will use those it needs to survive.

Gunslinger Jimmy Ringo rides into town. Tired, saddle-worn, he seeks solace from Sheriff Mark Strett, an old friend. Ringo simply wants to hang up the guns and also hopes to rekindle a relationship with his former wife, who teaches school under the name Peggy Walsh, and to see his little boy. The frightened townspeople try to get rid of Ringo, but he will not leave. It seems as though the gunfighter is waiting for something. One day, a young punk, out to make a name for himself by gunning down "the top gun in the West," kills Ringo in a duel. The cocky survivor is told that it is just a matter of time before he meets someone faster on the draw.

The Gunfighter is a slow, talky, very deliberately paced Western which moves inexorably toward it climax when Ringo is killed. The prevailing atmosphere of doom is hinted at in the dialogue. It is a feeling which has followed Ringo since he achieved a reputation as a fast gun. But the glory has to give way to the gore. Ringo learns there is always somebody else waiting to best him with a pistol, lurking in the shadows, or in a bar, or on the trail. There is no escape. The legend has outlived its usefulness, and now it will consume the man that is Jimmy Ringo.

No one but Sheriff Strett will have anything to do with the real Ringo. However, the ladies of the town seem to enjoy being terrified by his presence. A brilliant comic scene exemplifies the difference between myth and reality in *The Gunfighter.* Ringo is in the sheriff's office, talking to some women who want to hang the gunslinger. They don't even know what he looks like. It is one of the rare moments of humor in this downbeat production.

Scenarists William Bowers and William Sellers, along with director Henry King, replace the typical action of a Western script with a pulsating re-creation of a frontier town and its people. Since the genre had been freed from the need to always employ the structural mechanics of violence and hard riding, the filmmakers could give the town the drab look of the last century, clothe the characters in the bland and sometimes ill-fitting attire of the West, and concentrate on the interaction of the people in the story.

For over thirty years, director Henry King had made rural and period American characters in their settings breathe a life which wasn't consistently matched by anyone other than John Ford. Therefore the talks between Ringo and Strett, and the scenes with Ringo and his ex-wife get down to the kitchen sink reality of everyday emotions. The glamour is ripped from Ringo and the only thing left is a man in pain, engaging in what he knows in his gut to be a futile attempt to find a place in a more civilized West of calm sheriffs, schoolteachers, and town meetings. There is no retirement home for gunfighters but the grave.

Gregory Peck plays Ringo on a level of intensity far removed from the passion he put into the role of Captain Ahab in *Moby Dick* (Warner Bros., 1956), but the quest for peace, for cessation of anxiety is the same. Peck's drooping mustache, period haircut, and beaten-up hat distances the actor from his star image, thus shifting the emphasis almost completely to the character.

Such dramatic changeovers aren't needed for the other performers. Millard Mitchell, Jean Parker, Helen Westcott, and, at the time, Karl Malden had no set image in the Hollywood of 1950. That Mitchell, with his thick mustache, and a stare which looks to be permanently engrained on his face, bears a resemblance to George K. Barnes, the actor who fired the final shot at the camera in 1903's *The Great Train Robbery,* further ensconced him into the real past. As the punk who shoots Ringo, Richard Jaeckel was and is still a familiar face whose name is always just a breath away from memory. Yet it is that haunting degree of recognition that lifts Jaeckel from the ranks of the gunman who wishes to make a reputation by shooting down Ringo into a symbol of all the misguided young men who blast themselves into a slow death when they become a legend.

The Gunfighter is a powerful tale of woe, a story that had to be in the evolution of the West and the Western film.

Gregory Peck and Jean Parker

Millard Mitchell, Helene Westcott, and Gregory Peck

The Making of *The Gunfighter*

Harry Cohn had a script and a major star to play the lead. He wanted neither. So the Columbia mogul dropped plans to lens *The Gunfighter,* starring John Wayne in the title role. The Duke wanted very much to essay the complex part of the aging Westerner who is weary of his violent ways. Director Andre De Toth, who had penned the story with William Bowers, was going to helm the production but he went on instead to film Columbia's *Man in the Saddle* (1951).

Darryl Zanuck of Fox liked the story, but had reservations about the script. Zanuck spoke of his vision for *The Gunfighter* to producer/scenarist Nunnally Johnson. He had always wanted to make a Western which would stand with *Stagecoach* as a classic in its field. Although Zanuck applauded Wellman's *The Ox-Bow Incident,* he longed for an oater which combined high quality art and magnificent box-office returns. The mogul felt *The Gunfighter* could be transformed into such a work.

Johnson agreed to produce the property and redo the script. He changed the material to make it resemble the dogged realism of the films of William S. Hart. A somber tone was reflected in the relatively bare scenes, bland clothes, and ramshackle buildings. Zanuck approved of the change.

The studio wanted to cast Gregory Peck in the role of Jimmy Ringo. Peck had just finished *Twelve O'Clock High,* an excellent Fox war drama directed by Henry King. The star brought King a copy of the script to *The Gunfighter.* The director was equally enthusiastic about its possibilities and immediately decided that Peck should be molded to fit into the shabby, dull environs of the story. King wanted the actor to cut his hair, shave the back of his neck to resemble a "soup bowl" cut, and grow a mustache.

Zanuck was out of town during the filming of *The Gunfighter* and wasn't aware of Peck's mustache until he screened the film shortly before its release. The growth caused much trouble later on.

Before the mogul left, he and King cast *The Gunfighter.* The director told me recently the pair had no preference about using established players or relative unknowns. "We, meaning Mr. Zanuck and I, tried to get the best people for each role."

What a history in some of those faces! For instance, Mae Marsh made her 175th movie appearance in *The Gunfighter,* as Mrs. O'Brien. She had started in films at the turn of the century, working with D. W. Griffith while the master was perfecting his craft. Helen Westcott, female lead, became news as soon as she was born . . . as Hollywood's New Year's baby in 1928. Her picture appeared in all the Los Angeles newspapers. And Jean Parker starred in a number of fine productions in the 1930s, including *Little Women* (MGM, 1933) and *The Ghost Goes West* (Paramount, 1936), before returning to the theatre. Parker hadn't been in a major film for almost fifteen years.

Production began on *The Gunfighter* in fall 1949, on the Fox back lot. Much strenuous research went into the set design for the Western, and Gregory Peck did his best to make Jimmy Ringo a real gunfighter, apart from the rest. The star accomplished this in several ways. He drew his gun with the left hand, and used a crossover move. Peck learned that most gunfighters were geniuses at bluffing opponents and employed the mythology surrounding them to get out of as many battles as they fought.

Fox hired historian Sylvester Vigilante, head librarian of the History Room of the New York Public Library, to make sure *The Gunfighter* was accurate. Vigilante let Peck know that a sheriff like Wild Bill Hickok always had an advantage over a sought gunslinger. Hickok decided before he found the man that he was going to kill him. Knowing this made him deadlier than even those who were quicker on the draw. Peck wanted to get used to wearing guns, so he had them strapped around his waist every evening. The six-shooters had last been donned by George O'Brien for Fox's 1931 *Riders of the Purple Sage.*

The studio even found an 1870 slot machine. In one scene, Peck takes a gamble and wins three rare, period coins, placed there for added realism. This type of thing is an intangible ingredient in the effort to accurately depict an era, yet even when the objects are hidden from the camera, they can greatly enhance an actor's development of a character. The technique has been used from the silent era to the present, from Erich Von Stroheim's order that officers in *The Merry-Go-Round* (Universal, 1923) wear a particular type of underwear, to Robert Altman's insistence that drawers on the set of *McCabe and Mrs. Miller* (Warner Bros., 1971) be filled with artifacts of turn of the century Northwestern life.

Helping director King greatly in the matters of props, locations, and plain logistics was his old friend Joseph Behm. They had worked together in a number of pictures, including Fox's 1939 *Jesse James.* "Most directors followed a pattern," prop man Behm said in comparing King to his peers recently. "He was always ready to listen to any suggestion, always advocated that the money spent on a picture should be on film, not behind the camera."

The filmmaker wanted to shoot for one day on location at Lone Pine, California, but the production's budget made such a venture doubtful. At the time such a journey indicated two days' travel for the cast and crew of 100, plus housing and food. But Joe Behm had

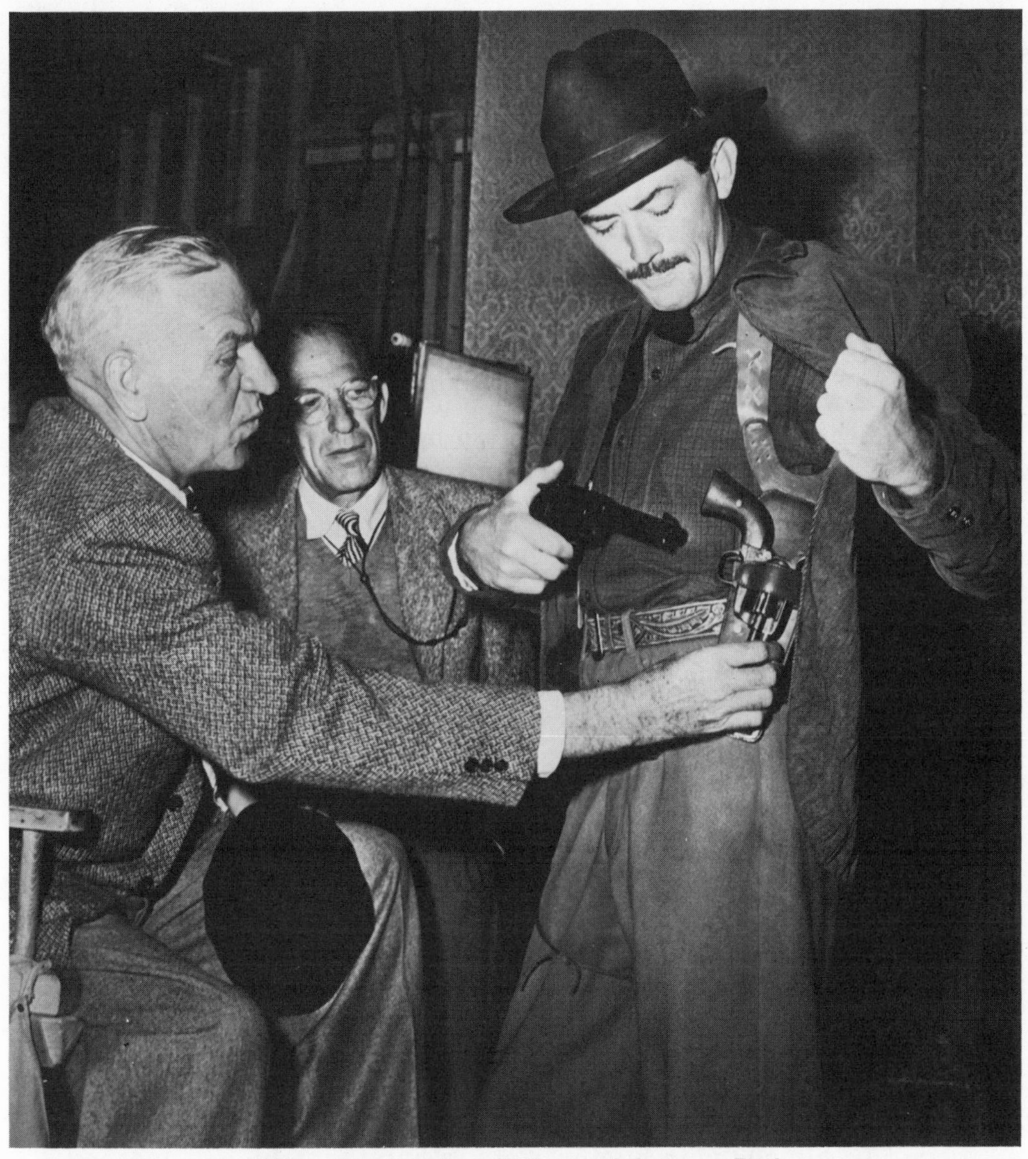

Henry King, Arthur Miller, and Gregory Peck

an idea. He made sure King could indeed do the filming desired in a single day, then suggested that they transport the company via plane, an unusual thought for the period. Since the director was a pilot, he approved of the plan. Behm chartered a DC-6, and told the crew to report at 6:30 A.M., in their working garb, the actors in costume, to the airport. They were given breakfast on the plane, and dinner on the flight back. The day before Behm sent up a truck full of equipment and hired local transportation. The camera equipment was taken on the plane. The prop manager's brainstorm saved director King two days on the production schedule.

So the making of *The Gunfighter* proceeded without any large conflicts or production delays. Director King did however have a slight problem with co-star Jean Parker. The actress hadn't appeared onscreen for five years, and for the past fifteen had shuttled back and forth between the stage and "B" movies, and she was nervous at the prospect of returning in such an important Western. One day King quietly took her aside, sat her down in a projection room, and screened *The Ghost Goes West.* He told her that she could be as good in *The Gunfighter* as she was in Rene Clair's charming fantasy. Joseph Behm recently called her "a vivacious lady off stage, always joking, but when she was called on for a scene, it was like turning off a faucet."

But the filmmaker couldn't help her with the extremely tight, 19th-century corset the player had to wear. The enslaving device was loosened periodically to give Jean Parker a chance to breathe freely.

The only difference between the director's image during *The Gunfighter* and the way he had appeared on countless projects before was the beret he learned to wear while filming *Prince of Foxes* (Fox, 1949) in Rome to combat drafty sound stages. And the beret didn't prove to be an obstacle when he looked through the viewfinder of the camera.

Henry King got along well with cameraman Arthur Miller. They had worked together on *The Song of Bernadette* (Fox, 1943). Miller respected directors who knew their business and understood the principles of cinematography and lighting, a comprehension surprisingly not shared by some of King's peers. King and Miller were of one mind regarding the physical look of *The Gunfighter.* Neither wanted their production to be a glamorous Western. There are no process shots, no cinema fakery in the film.

Things went so well that Gregory Peck conducted a press meeting on the set to announce a financial plan for a budding organization called the Actors Company Project. Not that Peck usually occupied himself with business other than that which concerned a production at hand. "The pro of all pros," Joe Behm reminisced about Peck. "This artist knew his script and the character he was playing, was a professional, was on the set to work, didn't want to win any popularity contest."

Although Darryl F. Zanuck hadn't seen any of the rushes for *The Gunfighter,* written reports informed him the picture was excellent. Producer/writer Nunnally Johnson praised King for his work. He especially liked the consistent tone of the film. That proved to be the trouble—that and Peck's mustache. Spyros Skouras, president of Twentieth Century-Fox, hated the star's hairy upper lip. When Zanuck returned to Hollywood, he had the same opinion, but still thought highly of the Western. King brought all the finest qualities out of the script, yet Zanuck unhappily considered *The Gunfighter* to be an artistic success with a "no sale" future at the box office.

King remembers Zanuck as being a brilliant producer, and assured me he was under no pressure from the mogul during or after making the Western. The property would rest on its own merit. The director recalled Zanuck as being a great film editor, a man who understood movies in the cutting room as well as on a profit-and-loss sheet.

But everyone still hated the mustache on Peck. Nunnally Johnson seemed to bear the brunt of the blame for the hair. The writer always claimed to be as taken aback as anyone else the first time the star appeared minus his usual clean-shaven countenance. But he liked the touch and saw it as a Remington-type effect, a final brushstroke on the character. Spyros Skouras levelled the accusation at Johnson that he had cost the production $1,000,000 by dreaming up the facial hair. Since anything Skouras said was of questionable content to Nunnally Johnson anyway, such remarks didn't bother him. In fact, he was pleased that someone thought he could do so much damage. Henry King has since claimed credit for the mustache.

Publicity for *The Gunfighter* was superbly tailored to fit the tone of the film. Action was relatively downplayed, in favor of the tragedy of Ringo's character:

> This Was the Gunfighter . . .
> Trapped by the Fame He Killed for . . .
> Reaching out to a Woman
> From His Loneliness.

Critics raved about *The Gunfighter:*

New York Herald-Tribune, Howard Barnes:

It is difficult to pull a screen Western out of rutted paths, but Nunnally Johnson has done quite a job in that direction with *The Gunfighter.* Henry King has done an expert job in staging *The Gunfighter,* keeping a delicate balance between acts of violence and the underlying morality of a changing society. Peck is so good in the chief role that he dominates the film from beginning to end, but he has ample support.

New York Times, Bosley Crowther:

It is good to see it now only for the sheer entertainment it provides in the way of suspenseful melodrama surrounding a haunted and hunted man, but it comes, in this corner's estima-

Gregory Peck in an action pose

> tion, as a caustic and wholesome anodyne to the fever of six-gun heroics that is shot in most Western films. All that we want to tell you is that these happenings take place with rare suspense amid a tingling accumulation of good, pungent Western atmosphere, thanks to Henry King's fine direction of a tangy and crisply written script; that the film gives a poignant demonstration that the lonesomest man in the world is an old, glory-trailing gunfighter—and that this is a Western you should see.

Critical raves didn't silence the anger of hordes of Gregory Peck fans dismayed about the star's mustache. Mail from forty-five of Peck's fan clubs poured into Fox protesting the unwelcome addition to their idol.

Today *The Gunfighter* is considered one of the best Westerns of the 1950s. Director Sam Peckinpah, a master of the genre himself, has much respect for King's sad tale of Jimmy Ringo, and, in fact, wrote the script for the 1957 "pocket edition" of the film Fox made for TV under the title *End of a Gun* with Richard Conte as Ringo and John Barrymore, Jr. as the punk.

Although Henry King's career didn't end until a dozen years later, the director only lensed one more Western. *The Bravados* (Fox, 1958) is a stinging tale of revenge also starring Gregory Peck. King's *Jesse James, The Gunfighter,* and *The Bravados* stand as a top-notch trio of Westerns as good as any three made by any other director, except possibly John Ford and Howard Hawks. Considering they were the only three sound Westerns Henry King ever directed, it is quite an accomplishment.

Gary Cooper and Grace Kelly

CHAPTER FOURTEEN

High Noon

Year Released: 1952
Studio: United Artists
Producer: Stanley Kramer
Director: Fred Zinnemann
Screenplay: Carl Foreman, based on the story "The Tin Star" by John W. Cunningham
Cinematography: Floyd Crosby
Music: Dmitri Tiomkin
Production Design: Rudolph Sternad
Art Director: Ben Hayne
Editors: Elmo Williams, Harry Gerstad
Sound: Jean Speak
Set Decorator: Emmet Emerson
85 minutes

Cast:

Will Kane	GARY COOPER
Amy Kane	GRACE KELLY
Jonas Henderson	THOMAS MITCHELL
Harvey Pell	LLOYD BRIDGES
Helen Ramirez	KATY JURADO
Percy Mettrick	OTTO KRUGER
Martin Howe	LON CHANEY, JR.
William Fuller	HENRY (HARRY) MORGAN
Frank Miller	IAN MacDONALD
Mildred Fuller	EVE McVEAGH

Cooper	HARRY SHANNON
Jack Colby	LEE VAN CLEEF
James Pierce	ROBERT WILKE
Ben Miller	SHEB WOOLLEY
Sam	TOM LONDON
Station Master	TED STANHOPE
Gillis	LARRY J. BLAKE
Barber	WILLIAM "BILL" PHILLIPS
Mrs. Henderson	JEANNE BLACKFORD
Baker	JAMES MILLICAN
Weaver	CLIFF CLARK
Johnny	RALPH REED
Drunk	WILLIAM NEWELL
Bartender	LUCIEN PRIVAL
Fred	GUY BEACH
Hotel Clerk	HOWLAND CHAMBERLIN
Minister	MORGAN FARLEY
Mrs. Simpson	VIRGINIA CHRISTINE
Scott	PAUL DUBOV
Charlie	JACK ELAM
Coy	HARRY HARVEY
Sawyer	TIM GRAHAM
Lewis	NOLAN LEARY
Ezra	TOM GREENWAY
Kibbee	DICK ELLIOTT
Trumbull	JOHN DOUCETTE

High Noon is a classic film about moral responsibility. It is taut, from the Carl Foreman script which reflects eighty-five minutes in the life of a man who takes a courageous stand against great odds, to the flat, grainy cinematography, rhythmic editing, and absence of optics such as fades and dissolves, to the tight as a nail in wood performance of Gary Cooper as the lawman.

Marshal Will Kane weds a Quaker girl opposed to violence and then learns that Frank Miller, a killer he had sent to jail, has been pardoned, and is returning to Hadleyville with three cohorts for revenge. Although his new wife threatens to leave on the noon train with or without him, Kane realizes he must remain to fight the men.

But he has to face them alone. The townspeople will not support him. Even Kane's deputy turns away. At the noon hour, Amy Kane and Helen Ramirez, who is acquainted with all concerned, board the train. The Miller gang arrives. When Amy hears the bullets roar, she runs to her husband's aid. In a slow, painful process, Marshal Kane kills three of his opponents. Mrs. Kane shoots the fourth. With the battle over, Kane throws his badge in the dust, and he and his wife ride out of Hadleyville.

High Noon moves like the ticking of the clock it so often refers to in the story. Although the Western is styled in the new realism embraced by post-war Hollywood, scenarist Foreman, director Fred Zinnemann, and cinematographer Floyd Crosby shape the natural look into a hard, unworldly form. The characters are all quite real, but the negativity which dominates many of the scenes and all of the people except Kane, Amy, and Helen makes for an extraordinary grim portrait that almost, but not quite, becomes a nightmare.

The script is extremely believable, yet its close knit squeezes out the little funny and sad moments which make up a life. The love between the Kanes is barely established at the beginning of the film. Therefore it is easy to accept the fact that she would walk out on him. Each relationship the Marshal has with a member of the town or Frank Miller is already set. The only thing left is the alienation of the lawman from his community. Having such unions formed offscreen lends force to the narrative and suspense to the inevitable showdown. Because the 85-minute movie need not include lengthy explanatory sections, it can concentrate on developing each of those minutes.

The photographic quality features high contrast. In many spots *High Noon* resembles a newsreel. In the journalistic or documentary cinema, from parts of the "March of Time" series to the work of Fred Wiseman, the non-fiction cameraman shoots what he sees, with a sparsity of cinematic effects added later. Consequently, images can look grainy, badly composed, with perhaps occasional inaudibility in the soundtrack. *High Noon* blends the sharp black-and-white diversity of the on-the-spot newsreel footage with a form of editing in the montage tradition of Eisenstein. The result is something of a mutant. The images of the town, Kane walking against a dull sky, and the shoot-out do look tough and gritty, but they are pieced together with a dramatic precision unknown in the old news film. For instance, when the train whistle blares through Hadleyville, each of the main characters is brought into sharp focus, one by one, like the sound detonated in a series of explosions.

Gary Cooper's Will Kane is a body of tension. There is none of the typical Cooper humor in Kane. No funny looks, quizzical cocks of the eyebrow, comical throat clearings. Cooper moves through *High Noon* like a man in pain who wishes to suffer in silence.* But the agony is evident.

In her first major role, Grace Kelly is the bastion of purity: white, blonde, young, beautiful, refined, virtually auditioning for blue blood. Yet it fits perfectly. She is literally Cooper's oasis in a desert of deceit, courtesy of cowardly friends Lon Chaney, Otto Kruger, Lloyd Bridges, and the villains.

High Noon may come across like a subway thundering into Grand Central Station, but it is due to that unrelenting power that each tick of the clock builds to an almost unbearable suspense only broken by the death fight where Cooper is forsaken by everyone save his darling Grace.

The Making of *High Noon*

Between 1948 and 1950 Carl Foreman scripted four acclaimed Stanley Kramer films—*Home of the Brave, Champion* (both UA, 1949), *The Men,* and *Cyrano De Bergerac* (both UA, 1950). The first three are etched in that hard, realist school of cinema popular in Hollywood after World War II. Realism, war, corruption, personal decimation, and faith emerged as themes in Foreman's scripts. He was hailed as a vital member of the American cinema's new wave, a man who set new standards for movie productions which were less compromising yet still box-office.

But Carl Foreman was still striving. With *High Noon,* he wanted to accomplish more daring deeds. And he wanted to direct. The work would be a hundred-minute picture which reflected real time—minute for minute—onscreen. Foreman eschewed opticals of any variety. Then he came up with a story.

The plot began to grow. It would concern a lawman who has just wed a Quaker. The conflict would be with a killer, the town, and the new wife.

Foreman discussed the concept with producer Kramer, who wanted to do the narrative. But after *High Noon* was discussed with others, someone told Foreman the tale sounded like something which had just been published. Researchers found a story in the *Saturday Evening Post* by John W. Cunningham called *The Tin Star.* All concerned felt it necessary to purchase screen rights to the title to avoid a lawsuit. Foreman himself found the resemblance scant. He believed the similarity began and ended with the aging lawman who is stalked by a killer.

---

*He was hurting from an ulcer during production.

Lloyd Bridges, Katy Jurado, Gary Cooper, and Grace Kelly

The credits of *High Noon* would ultimately list Cunningham as the creator of the original story for the Western. Doing so only added to the rift between Foreman and Kramer after the production of the property.

During that time the Communist scare took its toll on Hollywood. In 1947, a group known as the "Hollywood Ten" went to prison for refusing to tell the House Un-American Activities Committee whether or not they were Communists. Foreman engaged in related strife with the Committee, and this put him into conflict with Kramer as well. Shortly after the release of *High Noon,* Foreman was blacklisted in Hollywood and travelled to Great Britain to put his career back together.

Over the years, some have alleged Foreman actually produced *High Noon* as well as wrote its screenplay. It has been said that he was denied credit for the former job because of the blacklist. Stanley Kramer recently described the extent of his own participation in the making of *High Noon.* "It was my production. The film was made simultaneously with my company's commitment to Columbia on *Death of a Salesman* but I supervised the script and casting, selected the director, and controlled the editing and scoring of the production—including the use of the ballad for the theme and bridges.

"The entire film was the product of a creative conclave which began with *So This Is New York* (1949). George Glass, Carl Foreman, Herbert Baker, and Sam Zagon were part of that group as participants and later we went our separate ways."

Kramer and director Fred Zinnemann had worked well together on *The Men*, a sympathetic tale about the rehabilitation of a paraplegic, played by Marlon Brando, who ultimately shows the kind of courage Will Kane develops in *High Noon*. Zinnemann was under contract to Kramer and agreed to lens the Western. Perhaps this was another issue which divided Kramer and Foreman.

Early in the pre-production planning of *High Noon*, Zinnemann was away directing a documentary for the Orthopaedic Foundation of Los Angeles, called *Benji* (1951). So Kramer was largely responsible for casting the Western.

Lee Van Cleef made his cinema debut as one of the dreaded Miller brothers. The role of course led to dozens of similar parts in future cowboy movies. Ironically, Kramer had wanted Van Cleef to play a relatively good guy. After the producer and his brother Earl had spotted him in the play *Mister Roberts*, they offered him the role of deputy sheriff, on the condition that he have his nose fixed. Van Cleef said no, but signed to be one of the four bad men. Lloyd Bridges finally agreed to play the deputy. Van Cleef since has revealed his preference for playing villains onscreen, and in fact considers it natural that the audience should hate him.

There was some disagreement as to who should essay the role of Will Kane. "Gary Cooper was my choice," Stanley Kramer informed me. "There were some other actors under consideration—the reservations mostly due to Cooper's age—but he seemed the logical marshal—tired, drawn, dedicated."

Director Zinnemann had a happy association with Cooper on their only assignment together. Zinnemann considered Cooper a real star, a screen personality, and understood that the actor's magnetism was rooted in his personal charm. Cooper's only problem, in the filmmaker's judgment, was when he tried to get too serious. Then he overacted. As William Wyler said about Cooper when they worked on *The Westerner*, the performer was instinctively brilliant, acting on intuition.

During *High Noon's* production, Zinnemann tried to bring out that instinct through subtle suggestions rather than more obvious directorial instruction. He often asked Cooper why he didn't look tired, when his character had such frustration eliciting the aid of the people of Hadleyville. After the Western was released, a number of critics praised Cooper's acting out of Will Kane's fear, especially the sad look in his eyes. Zinnemann was surprised by this, as he didn't discuss the subject with Cooper and wasn't aware of the actor considering it as a guiding force either.

Many felt *High Noon* was intended as an allegory of the men who stood alone against the Communist hunt in 1940s and 50s America. Will Kane was seen as a symbol of those who defied Committee orders to inform on others, and who even refused to appear at all. The price for their stand was often a break with the community, an alienation from friends and co-workers. Carl Foreman found out all about that. The writer has said it was he walking down that street in Hadleyville, not Kane. A subpoena awaited him while he penned *High Noon*. Foreman felt it might be his final work in Hollywood.

Carl Foreman might have expected a struggle with Gary Cooper over the scenarist's alleged Communist leanings. Cooper was of course known as a staunch Republican and anti-Communist. As soon as he was subpoenaed, Foreman told Cooper that he would not give names or admit or deny affiliation with the Communists. He wouldn't surrender his human dignity to go on working in the motion picture industry. Foreman told Cooper he could leave the cast of *High Noon*, no questions asked. Gary Cooper supported Carl Foreman's position.

On the day Foreman was named in testimony before HUAC, he went to the location site of *High Noon* and explained to his cast and crew the situation he would face, and what he would say. In silence, Foreman's co-workers listened to a man making a statement on his interpretation of human existence and what a man had to do to retain self-respect. It was truly the action of a 20th-century Will Kane. As Foreman left the set to begin the process which ended with his blacklisting, he heard someone call from behind. He turned around and saw Gary Cooper. Cooper was moved by Foreman's words and entreated the writer not to let himself be sent to jail. At least Foreman had supporters in the celluloid Hadleyville.

While Foreman battled with HUAC, Zinnemann and cinematographer Floyd Crosby might have been preparing for a tangle with the front office. Both men wanted the Western to possess a unique cinematic look. Crosby had won an Academy Award for shooting *Tabu* in 1931, and was responsible for the breathtaking cinematography in Pare Lorentz's classic documentary *The River* (1937), produced by the U.S. government. Although in later years he photographed a number of horror entries which were anything but realistic, Crosby had the documentary spirit engrained in his professional being. When it was released by a smart director, the effects could be brilliant. They wanted *High Noon* to have the gritty, hard feel of the Italian neo-realist films made by directors such as

Fred Zinnemann in 1978

Grace Kelly

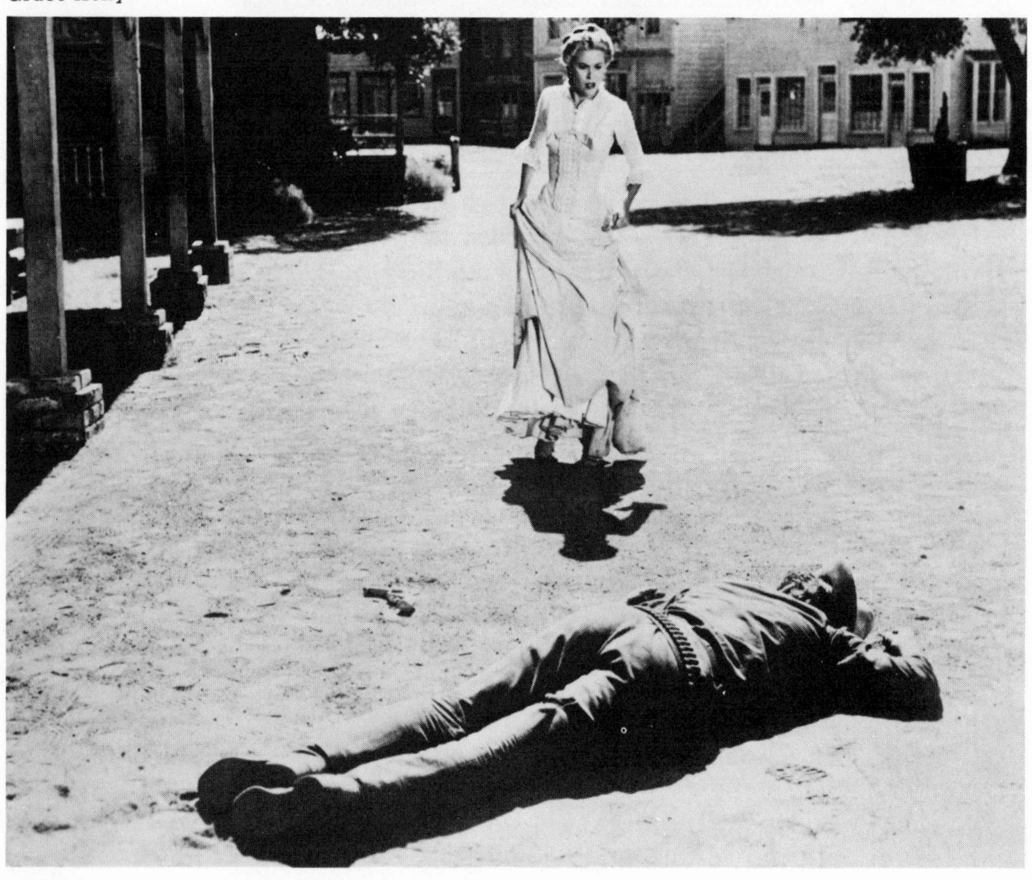

Rossellini and De Sica. They wanted the oater to reflect early Stanley Kramer productions which possessed a sharp, unglamorous edge. The pair saw *High Noon* as a 19th-century newsreel. The Civil War photographs of Matthew Brady were studied. Zinnemann did not want the traditionally beautiful backgrounds prevalent in the Western. So Crosby shot without filters on his camera, and the result was a dull, washed-out sky. He also arranged flat lighting, which enabled him to remove much of the depth in the images. United Artists complained about what was thought to be poor photography, but Zinnemann and Crosby proceeded to do the film their way, somehow convincing nervous executives of the propriety of their approach.

Despite the strong stance of the director and his cameraman, *High Noon* was very much a group effort. For instance, the creation of the famous gun battle which climaxes the film was the result of hard work by many people. Carl Foreman wrote the scene, then Zinnemann, Kramer, and art director Rudolph Sternad discussed its key elements. The art department made a series of sketches which showed every shot in the scene, and how it related to the ones before and after. The sketches turned out to be amazingly accurate depictions of the final images in the film. The team then met with cameraman Crosby and composer Dmitri Tiomkin to finalize the segment from every viewpoint. Zinnemann credits this exacting pre-planning with allowing the crew to shoot the exciting scene so quickly and efficiently.

Among the ideas the director himself had for *High Noon* were the repeated shots of the empty railroad station and tracks, and of Gary Cooper moving watchfully along an empty sky. Zinnemann made it a point to have Crosby lens close-ups of Cooper with shadows under his eyes, to underline the facial anxiety.

Completed in the fall of 1951, *High Noon* ran as Carl Foreman planned it. With the total cooperation of co-workers, the writer made a unique, satisfying film, which said something about the times, and managed to entertain as well.

At a sneak preview, though, *High Noon* failed to engage the audience. Producer Kramer spent hours trying to decide what went wrong, and how he could improve a good picture. Letting moviegoers see more of Cooper's pain and anxiety might win their sympathy, thought Kramer. So extra close-ups of the actor's face were taken. In order to heighten suspense, the producer inserted a number of tight shots of clocks, each building to the tolling noon hour. A final touch came when he asked Tiomkin to compose a ballad. Tiomkin protested that he wasn't a songwriter, but the creator of movie music had previously signed a contract to work on *High Noon* until Stanley Kramer decided it was complete.

Tiomkin composed a catchy, thumping tune, and Ned Washington supplied the words to a song called "Do Not Forsake Me, Oh My Darlin'." Tex Ritter was then called in to sing the theme song for *High Noon.*

With those additions, *High Noon* received strong reaction when released in 1952:

Daily Worker:

The usually tight knit plot carries the usual amount of cynicism and misanthropy. The high-point of the film, with Gary Cooper stalking down the street in intense loneliness, is a classic restatement of the anti-human theme of nearly all cowboy and detective yarns: in this world all you can rely on is yourself and the power in a pair of guns; don't trust your neighbors, people are no damn good.

New York Times, Bosley Crowther:

Mr. Zinnemann has so made his picture that you get the dusty feel of a Western town, the lean and solid nature of its people, the loneliness of the plains, and the terrible tension of waiting for violence and death in the afternoon. This is no storybook Western; this seems a replica of actuality. It is a picture that does honor to the Western and elevates the medium of films.

Pravda:

It is not accidental that the first Oscar in 1953 was awarded to Gary Cooper for his film *High Noon,* in which the idea of the insignificance of the people and masses and the grandeur of the individual found its complete incarnation.

Variety:

A basic Western formula has been combined with good characterization in *High Noon,* making it more of a Western drama than the usual outdoor feature. . . . Zinnemann carefully and deliberately makes the most of the good cast by the threat of impending violence. Script sometimes gets him a bit too involved in the development of side characters and their reactions, but he manages to keep the tension constantly mounting until it is resolved in the highly-satisfactory, guns-blazing climax.

High Noon grossed almost $4,000,000, an impressive figure for a black-and-white production.

The Western received numerous awards and honors, as did many of its participants. Gary Cooper won his second Oscar for his portrayal of Will Kane. Dmitri Tiomkin and Ned Washington

Gary Cooper in an action pose

copped an Academy Award for their trend-setting theme song, and Tiomkin also won for his score. Elmo Williams and Harry Gerstad were honored by the Academy for their brilliant film editing. *Film Daily* chose *High Noon* as one of the ten best pictures of the year, as did the National Board of Review. The New York Film Critics voted the Western the best picture of 1952 and named Fred Zinnemann as best director. The Screenwriters Guild considered Carl Foreman's script to be the top of the year.

As time passed, *High Noon* was attacked as being excessively mannered and for presenting a false image of the West. Howard Hawks stated a number of criticisms of the production and, in fact, claimed to have made *Rio Bravo* (Warner Bros., 1959) to correct the impressions left by *High Noon.* Both Hawks and John Wayne felt the community of Hadleyville would have gone to the aid of the lawman. These 19th-century Americans who fought nature and the Indians together would not have been intimidated by four gunfighters, no matter how blood-thirsty they were.

Fred Zinnemann was surprised anyone would take such an attitude toward *High Noon.* Several years ago he spoke of his overall feeling for the Western. He thought of the film as etching a theme set in the West.

Producer Stanley Kramer expressed his views on *High Noon* to me, along with a reaction to the criticism. "The theme of *High Noon* had to do with the responsibility of citizenship in a community in a democracy. When a man takes a moral stand based upon his objections and principles, it becomes the obligation of the citizenry to express its own responsibilities and morality by supporting him.

"When Gary Cooper dropped his badge in the dust, at the end, and left the town, he challenged the cowardice, immorality, and irresponsibility of the townspeople. It may be that Howard Hawks or John Wayne took a position that this would have been unthinkable in the real West—but what leads them to believe it was limited to a Western in the first place? The same story could easily be transplanted to a mining town, or a factory town."

By the time *High Noon* received all its awards and criticism, Carl Foreman was no longer part of the Stanley Kramer team. Newspapers reported that the two split up in October 1951, with Foreman receiving $285,000 for his share of the production company.

Like Will Kane, Foreman left the town in which he worked and lived. The writer went to Great Britain and had little difficulty obtaining jobs. In 1957, he made an Academy Award winning comeback as the producer of *The Bridge on the River Kwai* (Columbia), directed by David Lean. Foreman has since been involved in writing, producing, and directing a number of Columbia releases, including *The Key* (1958, script), *The Guns of Navarone* (1961, script and producer), *The Victors* (1963, script, producer, director), *Born Free* (1966, producer), *Mackenna's Gold* (1969, script and producer), as well as other productions.

Three years after the release of *High Noon,* Stanley Kramer made his directorial debut with *Not as a Stranger* (UA), which he also produced. In the past twenty years, Kramer has produced and directed about a dozen pictures for which he has achieved a reputation as one of the most social-conscious filmmakers working today. Many of his efforts have been criticized for containing lofty, highly liberal sentiments which often produce a plodding, cliched quality which renders them impotent. Yet there is no denying the power of *The Defiant Ones* (1958), *On the Beach* (1959), *Inherit the Wind* (1960), *Judgment at Nuremberg* (1961), or *Guess Who's Coming to Dinner* (1967).

After several years in unimportant movies, Gary Cooper achieved his proper status once more in *High Noon.* But he never again reached the pinnacle of Will Kane, although *Man of the West* (UA, 1958) shows the star at his toughest.

Lee Van Cleef spent the ten years following *High Noon* playing a villain in Westerns, with little variety in his characters. By the early 1960s, his image was so over-exposed that the actor was virtually unemployable. In 1965 Sergio Leone asked Van Cleef to portray a sympathetic role in *For a Few Dollars More,* with Clint Eastwood. Lee Van Cleef went on to stardom in Europe.

Fred Zinnemann continued his distinguished career with *From Here to Eternity* (Columbia, 1953), *The Sundowners* (Warner Bros., 1960), *A Man for All Seasons* (Columbia, 1967), and *Day of the Jackal* (Universal, 1973), among others.

Perhaps the best story of the making of *High Noon* was the one Carl Foreman lived. He wrote about himself in the character of Will Kane, but unlike the lawman, Foreman was able to return triumphantly to the town that drove him away. Perhaps Kane was a moral champion for his courage, but the quality of the Westerner's victory is uncertain as far as his personal life is concerned. A moviegoer can never be sure what price Kane paid for his stand. Foreman came back, and everybody knew it.

Alan Ladd and Van Heflin

CHAPTER FIFTEEN

Shane

Year Released: 1953
Studio: Paramount
Producer: George Stevens
Associate Producer: Ivan Moffat
Director: George Stevens
Screenplay: A. B. Guthrie, Jr., based on the novel by Jack Schaefer, with additional dialogue by Jack Sher
Cinematography: Loyal Griggs
Music: Victor Young
Art Directors: Hal Pereira, Walter Tyler, Emile Kuri
Editors: William Hornbeck, Tom McAdoo
Costumes: Edith Head
Color, 118 minutes

Cast:

Shane	ALAN LADD
Mrs. Starrett	JEAN ARTHUR
Mr. Starrett	VAN HEFLIN
Joey Starrett	BRANDON DE WILDE
Wilson	JACK PALANCE
Chris	BEN JOHNSON
Lewis	EDGAR BUCHANAN
Ryker	EMILE MEYER
Torrey	ELISHA COOK, JR.
Mr. Shipstead	DOUGLAS SPENCER

Morgan	JOHN DIERKES
Mrs. Torrey	ELLEN CORBY
Grafton	PAUL McVEY
Atkey	JOHN MILLER
Mrs. Shipstead	EDITH EVANSON
Wright	LEONARD STRONG
Johnson	RAY SPIKER
Susan Lewis	JANICE CARROLL
Howells	MARTIN MASON
Mrs. Howells	NANCY KULP
Mrs. Lewis	HELEN BROWN

"Sometimes nothin'll do but your own sweat and muscle," Van Heflin says early in *Shane.* And that's exactly the technique producer/director George Stevens, his cast, and his crew employed in the creation of this classic Western.

The gunfighter Shane rides into the Wyoming territory looking for work as a farm hand. He knows his profession is on the wane in a civilizing West. A farmer named Starrett gives the man a job. Both Mrs. Starrett and their son, Joey, take to Shane quickly. Trouble is stirred up when Starrett refuses to sell his property to Ryker, a rancher looking to control the area. Ryker hires a gunslinger called Wilson to intimidate those who won't sell out. At first, Shane will not resort to violence against Ryker and his taunting subordinates. Little Joey cannot understand the gunfighter's reticence. Ultimately, Starrett must set out to have a showdown with Ryker, but is waylaid by Shane, who, pushed too far, straps on his pistols and shoots down Wilson and goes after Ryker and his men. Realizing he can no longer remain with the Starretts, Shane rides off, despite the tearful pleadings of the adoring Joey. "Shane. Come back, Shane," the boy screams as the gunfighter moves out of his life.

Like Jimmy Ringo in *The Gunfighter* and Pike Bishop in *The Wild Bunch* (Warner Bros., 1969), Shane knows the West is in the throes of change and the transformation will leave no place for his kind of man. At one point Shane warns ruthless cattle-baron Ryker, "Your days are over." "Mine?" replies the surprised man. "What about yours, gunslinger?" A silence acknowledges the question. "The difference is, I know it," laments Shane.

The protagonists in most George Stevens films are outcasts, from the professor in *Talk of the Town* (Columbia, 1942) to George Eastman in *A Place in the Sun* (Paramount, 1951), Jett Rink in *Giant*

(Warner Bros., 1956), and the ultimate stranger, Jesus Christ, in *The Greatest Story Ever Told* (UA, 1965). They are also tarnished romantics, soft cynics who were once idealists but have been turned inside out. Shane is such a man. The life he cherishes is disappearing rapidly. So he looks for a place to settle into anonymity before he is gunned down.

The narrative in *Shane* moves so slowly and meticulously it seems to be grown from the earth. Director Stevens builds his drama tenderly, making much use of color and the dissolve shots which were his trademark. The setting of *Shane* is in one way dreamlike, in another starkly realistic. The land surrounding the Starrett farm and the dwelling itself is a warm, medium brown. A light blue sky tops cobalt mountains which resemble a painting. Yet the town is a shabby construction similar to Altman's Presbyterian Church in *McCabe and Mrs. Miller* (Warner Bros., 1971). Basic brown dominates. The difference between the land and the sets constantly hums in the background, never really calling attention to itself, yet creating a fine balance.

The progression of the story resembles an isometric exercise: there is obviously a tremendous conflict building, but the hand-over-hand development gives the impression of going nowhere at all. It is as if *Shane* is floating in space. Instead of employing massive camera movements or elaborate cutting effects, Stevens dissolves often, from shot to shot, scene to scene, giving the Western an ethereal amosphere. Even the actions of the characters are often agonizingly meticulous. When Shane and Starrett chop wood together, Stevens makes much of their first shared job. Later, as Wilson shoots down Torrey, the hired gun beats the farmer to the draw, but doesn't fire. He makes the sodbuster suffer before blasting him into the muddy street.

The real impact, or counter-impact, of the Western is illustrated in the barroom where Shane fights another of Ryker's cronies. Stevens slowly layers images of their struggle, enlarging the scope with the inclusion of Starrett and more of Ryker's men, until only the farmer and the gunfighter are left standing ten minutes later. The drama of the fisticuffs is heightened considerably by the attention to the minutiae of battle. The violent episode is fully developed, minus elliptical editing to jolt the continuity. Many close and medium shots of the men are employed. As the camera slides around the saloon, bodies walk between the lens and the action, creating tension by obliterating the view. Shane and his opponent circle each other. Offscreen space is used to again expand the area of the scene as voices out of camera range shout encouragement.

Three dissolves capture Shane's exit from the Starretts' life. The first comes when he rides away from the farm. The second ends with

Brandon de Wilde and Alan Ladd

Alan Ladd, Jean Arthur, and Van Heflin

the close-up of Joey's sad face, shifting to a long shot of the gunfighter from the back, astride the horse, moving into a very blue sky and almost icy mountains. Stevens drags out the boy's agony as well as the viewer's by then showing Shane going into town against that sky, with Joey eagerly running after him, only to dash hopes of the gunfighter returning with that last dissolve.

Shane is a romantic lament for the passing of the wilderness. It has the ease and simplicity of a folk song and the artistry of an epic.

The Making of *Shane*

Shane was the second installation of what critics have called George Stevens' American Dream trilogy of films. The director had just finished *A Place in the Sun,* his adaptation of Theodore Dreiser's novel *An American Tragedy,* about a murder which tarnishes the innocence of an entire society. *Giant* (Warner Bros., 1956), a sprawling production chronicling the growth of the oil industry, completed the trio.

Shane was to be Stevens' first Western since *Annie Oakley* (RKO) in 1935. Prior to *A Place in the Sun,* his reputation rested on simple comedies, dramas, and adventures which quietly touched the heart or tickled the funny bone. Themes were homespun. The story was the thing, and it blossomed slowly. In the 1950s and 60s, however, the filmmaker turned out powerful statements about America and mankind against bulging historical backdrops. In *Shane,* Stevens took an uncomplicated, slow-moving tale containing Western archetypes such as the gunfighter, the rancher, and the farmer, mixed into a typical conflict between cattlemen and sod-busters, and turned it all into a penetrating personal vision.

One summer in college, George Stevens, Jr. was poring over potential screen material for his father when he discovered a small novel called *Shane* by Jack Schaefer. He told Stevens the story of the gunfighter who was looking for a place to settle down, and the screen idea was born.

A number of years earlier, George Stevens, Frank Capra, and William Wyler formed Liberty Films, one of the first independent production companies in Hollywood. Later the trio sold their business to Paramount, and each agreed to make a certain number of pictures at the studio. After *A Place in the Sun,* Stevens had one film to go in his agreement. *Shane* became that property.

The setting had to be just right. The director saw *Shane* unfolding in a valley surrounded by jagged mountains which looked as if they had been ripped apart. Streams and hills shaped the terrain. The actors expressed their entire being in what the moviemaker termed "illustrative faces." The Westerners were real. He would have none of that white hat vs. black hat stuff, where good is good and bad is bad, and the twain only met in the final showdown. Stevens wanted to show the men and women who really won the West.

Period photographs and drawings by such artists as William Henry Jackson and the paintings of Charles Russell were of great help to Stevens in determining the look and feel of the West. He discovered that most pioneers wore "homespuns," made from material brought from the East, patched many times over the years. And that suited the director just fine. "My father had a fetish against calling what people wore costumes," George Stevens, Jr. recalled for me. "They were clothes." On the set of *Shane,* the filmmaker kidded Van Heflin about the unrealistic attire he had donned for Universal's *Tomahawk* in 1951. Stevens instructed the wardrobe department to find old clothes, or make new clothes appear worn. None of his actors would look like they had just emerged from a fitting at a fashionable clothier.

After studying volumes of material, Stevens engaged sketch artist Joe De Young to put the physical notions of *Shane* into drawings for Paramount executives. De Young, who was unable to speak, was an old native of the West who contributed much to George Stevens' understanding of the frontier. The director and the artist spent long hours together, as Stevens always worked out his concepts in minute detail, leaving nothing to chance. Yet such thorough preparation didn't prevent him from altering any aspect of the film he thought necessary, or receiving ideas from coworkers. Stevens and De Young developed a great friendship during the course of their professional relationship.

The pair toured the West in search of the perfect location for *Shane*. They finally decided on Jackson Hole, Wyoming, which boasted the geography Stevens had held in his mind for so long. They considered using Teton Range, west of Jackson Hole, but the filmmaker rejected the area because so many other productions used the land as background. George Stevens wanted something unique, untouched by Hollywood hands.

A Place in the Sun went into release in September 1951. In December newspapers announced that Alan Ladd would star in *Shane*, along with Jean Arthur and William Holden. Originally the director wanted Holden and Montgomery Clift to appear as Starrett and Shane, respectively. Since Clift (who had just made *A Place in the Sun* with Stevens) was off on another assignment and reportedly not interested in the Western project, the director looked elsewhere. Then William Holden dropped out. Finally, Stevens asked Paramount just who was available to do *Shane*.

Alan Ladd, Jean Arthur, and Van Heflin were the performers chosen to star in the Western. Rounding out the cast were Brandon de Wilde, Jack Palance, Ben Johnson, Emile Meyer, Edgar Buchanan, Elisha Cook, Jr., and other performers who looked as if they had jumped out of 19th-century daguerreotypes.

The actors were both old and new faces. Some were veterans in search of a role to rehabilitate a worn image. The careers of Alan Ladd and Jean Arthur floated on past glories. They weren't yet anachronisms in a more independent Hollywood, but rather remained in a limbo of sorts. Ladd had been starring in routine actioners, while Arthur had been absent from the screen since *A Foreign Affair* (Paramount, 1948).

Both looked tired. Ladd had achieved fame with his blond hair, a twinkle in the eye, sparkling teeth, and baby face. By the 1950s his countenance strongly hinted of middle age. The actor's voice, always light, sometimes with a cocky lilt, became more resolved, quiet, almost monotoned, as if he had accepted his fate. George Stevens, Jr. remembered Ladd as being very similar to the characters he played in the movies. He was a soft-spoken man who was

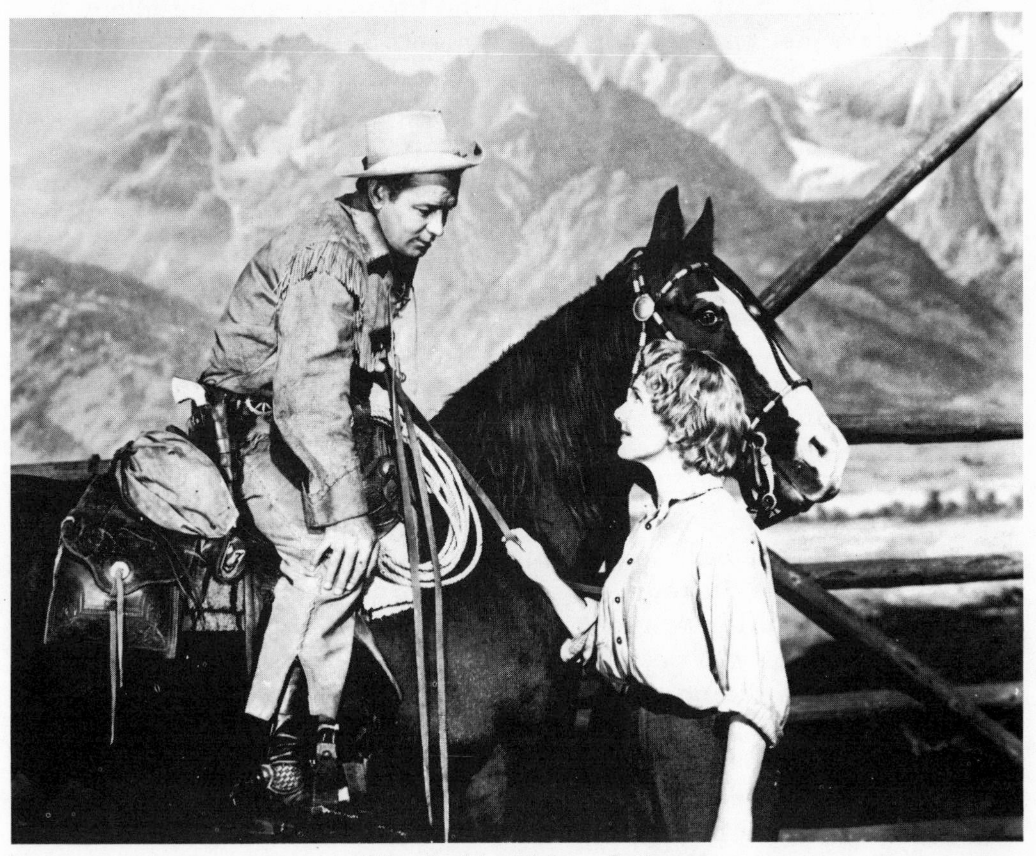

Alan Ladd and Jean Arthur

both qualified and enthused about taking the title role in Stevens' Western.

Jean Arthur appeared forever like a farmer's wife in *Shane*. After fifteen years of enacting tough, independent, often sophisticated women, she was ready for a part which brought out her introspective, sensitive self. "Dad had worked with Jean Arthur on many occasions before," George Stevens, Jr. recalled. "Jean was older than one would normally anticipate for that part. I recall her as a grey-haired lady. She had a blonde hair piece which she wore for the picture. She was not working much then, and she had always been a reticent person. She kept very much to herself, came in and did her job, and did her job well."

Van Heflin's face could have been carved on Mount Rushmore. He personified strength and dignity, although the solid leading man rarely acted charismatic roles. The typical Heflin screen image seemed for all the world like someone who could be passed on the street and hardly noticed. In the mid-1950s William Holden was in-between types. He attempted to change from the handsome youth of the 1940s into the tougher, more complex actor he became in the 1960s. Heflin was there all the time. When he left MGM to free-lance just before *Shane* came along, Heflin found good pictures harder to come by. Stevens' Western changed his luck, at least temporarily.

Jack Palance became an incarnation of evil, while Brandon de Wilde symbolized innocence. Neither actor had been seen on the screen much before *Shane*. Palance's major roles were in *Panic in the Streets* (Fox, 1950) and *Halls of Montezuma* (Fox, 1951). De Wilde's sole appearance was in *Member of the Wedding* (Columbia, 1952), before the Western was released.

It appeared that Palance's features were cut with a knife. The razor sharp angles of his cheekbones, nose, forehead, and jaw were a maze which led to the seemingly coal-black eyes with which Palance hypnotized opponents.

Pudgy young de Wilde was Alan Ladd as a boy.

With a strong cast and a script by A. B. Guthrie, Jr., the noted novelist who specialized in penning realistic tales of the American frontier, George Stevens was set to film *Shane*. Unlike such directors as Howard Hawks and William Wellman, who preferred lensing stories as quickly as possible, Stevens tended to shoot scenes many times, rewrite dialogue, and hold up a production if necessary when something didn't fit. He could often be seen wandering around a set, not saying a word, but thinking about the script, reviewing dialogue in his mind, constantly checking camera angles, to make sure everything was as he wished. And even that wasn't enough. Like most Hollywood directors, Stevens made cover shots of each set-up to give himself a wider choice of material in the editing room. Yet he went further. The filmmaker always took action from different angles as well.

This technique was, of course, hard on the actors. George Stevens, Jr. explained his father's reason for shooting so much stock. "It's always a more demanding experience for actors to work with someone who goes to the extent that my father did to achieve a kind of standard, an effect really. But I think that while the actors might become impatient in terms of the time taken, they have the feeling of being part of something important and they're going to come off better than they normally do because of that. Also by shooting all that film, by getting the raw material, you can make the film in the editing, and gain from the performances what you want."

While in the editing room, the director exercised total control. "In all of his films after the war, and I think some before the war, he had a projection room with controls at his hands where he could run both machines that were in the booth behind him backward and forward. He actually used that room like a movieola," said George Stevens, Jr. "In talking about the control you need to make a picture, he said there are really four elements of the picture: the preparation of the script and casting, the shooting, the editing, and the distribution and publicity. And he said, if I had to give up control of any one of those four, I'd give up control of the shooting.* . . ." He was involved in every frame, every sound effect, every detail of the editing.

When production began on *Shane* in Jackson Hole, local residents were impressed by the accuracy of the Western's "costumes," which the director called "clothes," as well as by the sets built by the construction crew. Starrett's farmhouse, for instance, was notably minus quaint touches. It was squat and weatherbeaten. The same held true for the town. The saloon and general store bore more resemblance to the series of shacks Robert Altman constructed twenty years later for *McCabe and Mrs. Miller* than the many splendored sets of Michael Curtiz's *Dodge City* (Warner Bros., 1939). Stevens' town was laid along a muddy road, where boots and wagon wheels sank and slushed their way from one end of the makeshift hamlet to the other. The wooden walkways looked similarly weatherbeaten.

That's just what George Stevens wanted. He had always wondered why towns in Hollywood Westerns were constructed on *both* sides of a street. Period photographs indicated real frontier communities generally sat on only one side of a thoroughfare. Since

*Alfred Hitchcock might very well agree with this notion.

most sagebrush tales were made in the studio or on backlots, buildings had to be erected to block out a length of Van Nuys Boulevard which would stick out in the background of any shot taken near it.

The director even had special ideas for the street. He wanted it *muddy*. By the time Stevens was ready to shoot the scene in which Torrey is gunned down by Wilson, the production already was behind schedule, and everyone had to work a grinding seven days a week. The gunfight was to take place on a Sunday. On Saturday, the crew spent hours hosing down the street to get the sloppy, muddy look the filmmaker conceived. The goal was to have the street look as it should after a rainstorm. When Torrey walked toward Wilson, his feet sank into the ground, giving the action a foreboding quality.

In order to insure the realism of *Shane,* Stevens made two more significant decisions. One, he would not use Technicolor stock. Two, he would film in all kinds of weather. The director didn't like what he called the "rainbow quality" of Technicolor footage. To his mind, it tended to render a bright, glossy, glamorous image which didn't fit *Shane*. Sunny or cloudy, Stevens and crew would be out there making a movie. He wanted to show the audience exactly what the farmer and the rancher went through on the American frontier.

Stevens insisted on executing a perfect vision, and told the press: "I'm one of those who feels everything—everything that goes into a picture affects the viewer, although he doesn't realize the impact of tiny, minor things that are built up for him. This working upon the subconscious has a great effect, greater than most moviegoers or moviemakers realize."

Little things such as clouds could really change the look of a scene. Stevens of course realized this. Normally, when a cloud passed over a set while the cameras rolled, the cinematographer automatically stopped shooting. Stevens kept the action going. In later years, many people commented on the change of lighting and the shadow cast—subtle effects which added immeasurably to the compelling quality of the moments.

The attempt to lens *Shane* in a true environment especially impressed Secretary of the Interior Oscar Chapman. Chapman, the Supervisor of Grand Teton National Park, along with members of the Rockefeller family, toured the *Shane* set. The group decided to request that Paramount's constructions be moved to the Rockefeller's Ferry Museum site on the Snake River once filming was completed. They felt the buildings accurately represented life in 19th-century Wyoming.

If the town in *Shane* prophesied the Presbyterian Church in *McCabe and Mrs. Miller,* then Stevens' attitude toward violence in the Western anticipates Sam Peckinpah's concern with the reality of bloodletting in *The Wild Bunch* (Warner Bros., 1969). While Stevens' depiction of violence is nowhere near as graphic as Peckinpah's, the director of *Shane* felt that in order to heighten audience attention in the shootings, it was necessary to show the impact of a bullet hitting a man. To do this, a wire was attached to all the performers slated to fall before bullets. Fastened to a leather belt buckle on a given player, the wire was controlled by a pulley on a block. As the bullet roared from a pistol, a crewman jerked the wire and pulled the victim backward.

The long fist fight between Shane and Chris was staged with incredible precision by Stevens. To get Ladd and Ben Johnson to swing their fists, fall, and turn just right, the director went through the motions himself, showing them how to hit the bar, how to land on the floor. Then the filmmaker put an unusual emphasis on the reactions of the people watching the battle. The struggle was often completely covered by onlookers. Of course, all the battles were filmed repeatedly, from a multitude of angles. Stevens wanted to do fights which had a sense of reality often absent in typical screen barroom brawls, yet still retain a mythical touch. The slow, extremely deliberate pacing of the fisticuffs rendered this tone.

Despite being minutely prepared from every conceivable angle, Stevens didn't hesitate to add or drop dialogue, bits of business, or anything that would help improve the film. George Stevens, Jr., who worked as company clerk on the production and kept track of camera angles and set-ups, later recalled that "the script was being rewritten day by day. [There was] constant revision and shaping, particularly when we were on location, where the key scenes were being filmed out of doors." One such scene was the funeral. There was very little dialogue in the burial of Torrey, but the words spoken meant a lot. This section of the Western, as with all the rest, was planned to the most minute detail. Yet when it came time to shoot, Stevens decided to add a child playing a harmonica, dogs running around, and similar backdrop touches. The director travelled the West in search of the hilltop seen in *Shane*. The burial took place above the valley where the town was erected, with farmhouses in the distance. Through the precise placement of the town, houses, and burial grounds, Stevens was able to give this section of the picture a special air of community, as the camera was able to include many elements in a given shot.

Young Brandon de Wilde may have been less than happy with George Stevens' meticulous direction, even though it produced a classic performance from the boy actor. Although George Stevens, Jr. remembers Brandon de Wilde as having a good time on the set of *Shane*, after it was released, de Wilde vowed not to do another

George Stevens

movie unless it was a swashbuckler. Of course, he went on acting in Wellman's *Goodbye, My Lady* (Warner Bros., 1956) and many other productions.

Although Jack Palance spoke only twelve lines in *Shane*, they were enough to win him an Oscar nomination as Best Supporting Actor of 1953. Despite the fact that his role established his reputation as one of the screen's foremost heavies, Palance eventually looked upon villain roles such as Wilson with disdain. "I want to get away from sadistic killers," he told one reporter. "When I go home at night I get the feeling that people are following me."

Paramount executives initially were less than enthusiastic with *Shane*. The Western cost approximately $3,000,000, which was over its budget. As the story goes, when the front office saw Stevens' film, they tried to sell it for its negative costs.

It wasn't until the movie was re-issued that *Shane* received the perfect publicity:

There never was a man like Shane.
There never was a picture like *Shane*.

Reviewers varied in their opinion of *Shane,* but the critical applause, along with a groundswell of public support, made Paramount see what a good piece of cinema they had produced.

The New Leader, Wallace Markfield:

With *Shane*, Stevens has crowded into the Western every shopworn device and mannerism which has been collecting in the virtuoso director's handbook since they came up with William S. Hart.

Newsweek:

Under guidance any less skillful than that of producer-director George Stevens, this new film might have been just another handsome, large-scale Western. As it turned out, *Shane* comes close to being a classic in its field. . . . But when Stevens and his carefully chosen players get through with them, the stock characters have become real and completely believable human beings. (If Shane is on the fabulous side, Ladd gives in his portrayal of him the best performance in his screen career.) Time after time Stevens invests the screenplay with imaginative and realistic details that are little short of brilliant.

Saturday Review, Arthur Knight:

Shane is a big Western, with all the barroom brawls, the riding and the shooting indigenous to the breed. Perhaps because it is a big Western, it has a tendency to talk out its problems a bit too much, to draw out its climaxes a little too far. But few films in this genre, big or little, have so well succeeded in conveying both the substance and the meaning of the eternal Western conflict between the good and the bad.

Variety:

Strong box-office possibilities accrue to this socko drama of the early West, which draws on sound plot and characters, solid directorial interpretation and fine playing to give it both class and mass appeal.

Cinematographer Loyal Griggs won an Oscar for his color photography in *Shane*. *Film Daily* and the National Board of Review named *Shane* as one of the ten best films of 1953. *Photoplay* awarded Alan Ladd a Gold Medallion for his performance in the title role. Stevens was nominated for the Best Director Oscar, and also for the same award presented by the Directors Guild.

Shane proved to be one of Alan Ladd's final quality productions. In 1958 he acted a part similar to Mr. Starrett in Michael Curtiz's *The Proud Rebel* (Buena Vista), with his young son David. His appearance as Nevada Smith in *The Carpetbaggers* (Paramount, 1963) shortly before his death in 1964 indicated that Ladd could have developed into a fine character performer.

Van Heflin went on to more supporting roles and some leads in low-budget pictures. Brandon de Wilde grew to adulthood onscreen and appeared until his death in an auto accident in 1972.

Although some have asserted that *Shane* does not wear well today, the classic Western stands as a unique contribution to a tired genre, an example of personal vision triumphing over familiar content.

Mercedes McCambridge (first rider)

Ben Cooper, Joan Crawford, and Scott Brady (right)

CHAPTER SIXTEEN

Johnny Guitar

Year Released: 1954
Studio: Republic
Producer: Philip Yordan
Associate Producer: Nicholas Ray
Director: Nicholas Ray
Screenplay: Philip Yordan, based on the novel by Roy Chanslor
Cinematography: Harry Stradling
Music: Victor Young
Art Director: James Sullivan
Assistant Director: Herb Mendelson
Set Decorator: John McCarthy, Jr., Edward G. Boyle
Costumes: Sheila O'Brien
Special Effects: Howard and Theodore Lydecker
Makeup: Bob Mark
Hair Stylist: Peggy Gray
Color, 110 minutes

Cast:

Vienna	JOAN CRAWFORD
Johnny Guitar	STERLING HAYDEN
Emma Small	MERCEDES McCAMBRIDGE
Dancin' Kid	SCOTT BRADY
John McIvers	WARD BOND

Turkey Ralston	BEN COOPER
Bart Lonergan	ERNEST BORGNINE
Old Tom	JOHN CARRADINE
Corey	ROYAL DANO
Marshal Williams	FRANK FERGUSON
Eddie	PAUL FIX
Mr. Andrews	RHYS WILLIAMS
Pete	IAN MacDONALD

Johnny Guitar is an examination of the consequences of paranoia and greed. It is one of the most bizarre and compelling Westerns ever made, among the first "psychological Westerns."

A former gunfighter named Johnny Guitar rides into a town divided into two groups: on one side, the followers of power-mad Emma Small, who wishes to buy all surrounding land and sell it to the railroad; on the other, the few supporting saloon-owner Vienna, who refuses to be bought out. With the town marshal and a vigilante group, Emma storms Vienna's place and threatens her. Later in the bar Vienna has a reunion with Johnny, who also enters into a rocky relationship with the Dancin' Kid and his gang. The Dancin' Kid loves Vienna and is in turn desired by Emma. When the Kid and his cohorts rob the town bank, Emma pressures a teller into implicating Vienna in the crime. The vigilantes return to capture the saloon owner and lynch young Turkey Ralston. Johnny saves Vienna from the mob, and the blood-thirsty pack tracks them to the Dancin' Kid's mountain hideout. A gun battle ensues. Emma shoots the Dancin' Kid between the eyes, Vienna kills Emma, then she and Johnny walk through a waterfall and embrace.

Johnny Guitar, as does *The Ox-Bow Incident*, warns of the dangers of mob rule. As one of the rarest of Westerns, *Johnny Guitar* is played out by two women, with Emma representing the theme through her lustful obsession and Vienna reacting in the courageous way all moral people must. Johnny is somewhere in the middle, pretending not to care about the struggle, but in the end coming through, like most anti-heroes do.

The female stars trade power for power. Joan Crawford's Vienna is proud and strong, fiercely independent, but loyal to friends and employees. As Emma, Mercedes McCambridge embodies the then-fashionable psychosis of the antagonist, who through some deep-rooted desire crushes all who go against her. "I'm going to kill you," Emma warns early. "I know," replies Vienna. "If I don't kill you first." Johnny just sits there strumming.

While the women provide the cold stares and taut, angry words, the men engage in wild banter, as if poor-man versions of Robert Benchley and Alexander Woollcott were fighting a duel of verbal one-upsmanship. "What's your name?" snarls the Dancin' Kid. "Johnny Guitar," answers the man. "That ain't no name," the Kid sneers. Soon they go through the same dialogue, but switch roles. Johnny and outlaw Bart Lonergan play a game involving drinking. The gruff criminal keeps plying Johnny with whiskey in an effort to get him drunk, then recoils in mock horror when the guitar player turns down the "friendly" gesture. Vienna is always there to stop the insanity. "Heads, I'm gonna kill you, Mister," warns the Kid. "Tails, you can play her a tune." Vienna grabs the coin. "Play me a tune," she commands.

Along with the word games, *Johnny Guitar* has a stark passion to distinguish itself from other Westerns. The hatred between Vienna and Emma is most intense in the scene where the vigilantes come for the saloon owner. Emma is in black, with a gunbelt wrapped around her. The posse wears black. Vienna is in a flowing

Joan Crawford and Mercedes McCambridge

white dress, sitting up against a flaming red background. Here is Vienna, strikingly beautiful, a woman whose self-determination is the envy of the townspeople. There is Emma, blaring her evil intentions to the world.

Although the men support the women all the way through, the performances of Sterling Hayden and Scott Brady are remarkably vibrant. Hayden adeptly manages a strong image despite the laid-back style of Johnny, whose command of events is just as sure as Vienna's ability to run the saloon independently. Scott Brady displays a surprising ability to keep the Kid a balanced personality. For all the wisecracking dialogue which might have ordinarily been put in the mouth of a streetwise juvenile delinquent, Brady holds the masculine integrity of his immoral bad man, even though Johnny is obviously superior to the Kid.

In *Johnny Guitar*, as in all director Nicholas Ray's films, people define their own worlds. It is when one sphere psychotically overlaps the other that tragedy occurs. "You've got to own everything. You can't stand to see anyone else live!" Vienna screams at Emma. So Emma must die. And that tension gives *Johnny Guitar* a crackling life.

The Making of *Johnny Guitar*

The people who made *Johnny Guitar* are a curious mélange of professionals. In one way or another, by 1954 none of them really fit in the Hollywood mold. Where once there had been a place, perhaps an exalted throne, for some, there was now a grope for cinematic identity—except, of course, for Crawford.

Hollywood of the 1940s saw a breakdown in the studio strongholds. During World War II, Greta Garbo, Norma Shearer, Jeanette MacDonald, and Joan Crawford left MGM. These women, the virtual female bastions of Louis B. Mayer's paradise the previous decade, were vanquished by V-J Day, at least at Metro.

Unions demanded more of the profits. Stars were less eager to sign long-term contracts which guaranteed employment but severely restricted their choice of scripts. Many wanted to follow the lead of James Stewart, a star who was contracted to MGM, but managed to obtain his best parts elsewhere as a free lancer. Of course, when the heavyweights left, the middle-budget leading men and women were either dropped or made to take lesser roles in second-rate vehicles in order to fulfill their contracts—and then they too were out. The studios began paring their rosters and becoming more selective as to whom they put under long contracts.

After years in radio and theatre, director Nicholas Ray shot his first two films for RKO, and followed them with another pair with Bogart for Columbia. Between 1950 and 1952, Ray did work on four back at RKO, then went into a period of inactivity. He didn't like any of the scripts producers offered, and he wasn't one to compromise easily.

The filmmaker always had been outspoken and had achieved a reputation for liberal views, but his work was never thwarted by the House Un-American Activities Committee, nor by the fear of the Red-taint which ended many productive cinema careers. Since Ray had faced investigation by the OSS during the war and was found free of any ties to subversive organizations, anti-Communist groups apparently felt nothing more could be gained by subjecting him to further scrutiny.

After rejecting more than a dozen scripts, Ray received one titled *I Married a Communist*. The property was so ludicrous, Ray decided to turn it into a gangster movie. His liberal friends were aghast at the director's intentions. At that time many less controversial talents found it difficult to obtain any work at all. That Ray should toy with such a tender issue was considered by some to be ill-advised.

Eventually Ray simply refused to make *I Married a Communist*. The numerous turn-downs came to the attention of Howard Hughes, the head of RKO. The director met with the millionaire at Hughes' modest Santa Monica Boulevard office. He explained his failure to make a workable project out of *I Married a Communist*. Hughes must have been impressed with Ray's stance. A year later the producer asked Nicholas Ray to take charge of RKO and was turned down. *I Married a Communist* was helmed later by British director Robert Stevenson and was released as *The Woman on Pier 13*.

By 1954, Nick Ray was ready to work again. He wanted to make an allegorical Western about the McCarthy Committee, and he needed to show up all of Hollywood. Most film people then told him the Western was no longer a viable screen form. Television had taken over the oater. But he would produce and direct an adaptation of Roy Chanslor's novel *Johnny Guitar*, a book which highlighted a battle between two women. When the filmmaker proved the project could both be good and have a big box-office response, Warners gave him a chance to make *Rebel Without a Cause*.

Ray made a deal with Republic, a studio which had ground out hundreds of low-budget actioners since its formation in 1935. The director assured studio head Herbert Yates that *Johnny Guitar* would be done cheaply and well.

Republic itself was something of a misfit among Hollywood studios of the 1950s. According to veteran director Allan Dwan,

Yates wanted desperately to make a star of glamorous Vera Hruba Ralston, a former championship skater with limited acting ability but who happened to be Mrs. Yates. It's a wonder she wasn't in *Johnny Guitar*.

The cast of *Johnny Guitar* is something to behold even minus Vera Hruba Ralston. Joan Crawford accepted the role of Vienna, the hard-loving, gunslinging, basically righteous woman who fires the jealousy of ranch owner Emma Small, played by Mercedes McCambridge. The onscreen conflict of the two women soon went past the cameras during the making of *Johnny Guitar*. Like Nicholas Ray and Republic Studios, Crawford and McCambridge were at odds with the Hollywood of 1954.

Crawford long had been a movie star in every sense of the word, struggling to maintain a level of quality in every one of her productions. But advancing age and a changing studio system were too much for even Crawford to battle successfully, at least for long. Yet her career was dotted with comebacks. She was a fighter all the way. She had brought herself from an impoverished background to fame as a showgirl through hard work. When Hollywood beckoned in 1925 in the form of an MGM contract, the ambitious ex-hoofer fulfilled everything expected of her, and much more. Her role in *Our Dancing Daughters* (1928) caused F. Scott Fitzgerald, who knew of such things, to describe Joan as the archetypal flapper. She made all but two of her first forty-six films at MGM, where she had been labelled "box-office poison" on more than one occasion. She came back in 1938's *Mannequin*, the story of a working girl. She and Louis B. Mayer parted company in 1943, and she signed with Jack Warner. She idled for two years, then made the most spectacular return and copped an Oscar for portraying the title role in *Mildred Pierce*, under the direction of Michael Curtiz. For the next several years Joan Crawford played hard-bitten feminists far removed from the flapper or society woman of her screen past. In 1954, her only film was Republic's *Johnny Guitar* (and her only Western), a production everybody outside the studio thought would surely fail. Crawford once said she'd play Wallace Beery's mother if the role was right, a statement which explains her presence in a film as bizarre as *Johnny Guitar*.

Conversely, Mercedes McCambridge was anything but a movie star. McCambridge was often referred to as "radio's greatest actress" of the 1940s, when she performed in as many as fifteen dramatic shows a week. While Crawford changed her image at Warners, McCambridge won an Academy Award as Best Supporting Actress for her film debut in *All the King's Men* (Columbia, 1949). Although it seems evident that she tried hard to fit into Hollywood's pattern of casting, McCambridge had only appeared in one other major film, *Lightning Strikes Twice* (Warner Bros., 1951), by the time *Johnny Guitar* came along. Cast as an unbalanced woman in *Lightning Strikes Twice*, she gave a fine rendition in a complex part, but in doing so perhaps labelled herself as a player of neurotic females, a type difficult to overcome in any era. Had she started a decade later, Mercedes McCambridge would have found a slightly wider variety of offerings, but by the end of the 1960s her life had changed drastically. She was a middle-aged divorcée, as well as a recovered alcoholic.

Sterling Hayden probably could have been one of the biggest stars of the 1940s and 50s if he had toned down his highly individual personality. Contracted to Paramount in 1941, with a golden boy image and a promising future in films, Hayden soon enlisted in the U.S. Army under a pseudonym to escape the publicity inevitable when a movie star entered the armed forces. The actor was always more interested in the real world of adventure than in celluloid enterprises and, as such, always maintained he acted for money, not art. His best role prior to *Johnny Guitar* was that of a tired, day-dreaming criminal in John Huston's *The Asphalt Jungle* (MGM, 1950). Like director Nicholas Ray, Hayden was also outspoken, and even admitted being a Communist in the 1940s. Since he refuted former Red notions, Hayden could work in Hollywood, although rarely in anything on the level of *The Asphalt Jungle* or *Johnny Guitar*.*

Philip Yordan, producer and scenarist of *Johnny Guitar*, was also something of an individual among screenwriters. A popular concept is that writers who went into films did so purely for money. Admittedly, this has been true in many cases, with such as Fitzgerald, Faulkner, and Nathanael West going to Hollywood and doing little for their literary reputations except perhaps amassing an economic cushion for their work as novelists. Yordan found early success as a playwright and made in excess of $50,000 for some of his post-war screenplays. Yet he lived in a modest apartment and in interviews seemed to worry about possessing too much money. Most film executives would have told him that scripting *Johnny Guitar* was a good way to demean his dollar value.

Johnny's rival for the affections of Vienna is the Dancin' Kid, played by Scott Brady. Brady, brother of actor Lawrence Tierney, made his film debut in 1948 and became a stalwart second lead or occasional villain in major productions and a hero in "B" films throughout the 1950s. His career suffered with the coming of the

---

*In the 1970s, however, Hayden's career has been rejuvenated with co-starring roles in a number of important films, including *The Godfather* (Paramount, 1972), *The Long Goodbye* (UA, 1973), and *King of the Gypsies* (Paramount, 1978). He also has become a successful novelist with several best-sellers.

Joan Crawford and Sterling Hayden

The torching of the saloon

independent actor after World War II. Those who possessed the star power made film-by-film deals. Others, like Scott Brady, found that studio payrolls could no longer support middle- and small-budget leads like himself. Brady was fairly handsome, intense, and able to play both good and bad guys, but he lacked star quality and the range to compete with contemporaries Brando, Clift, Newman, Don Murray, and others. So he found his way to Republic for the most off-beat role of his screen life thus far.

As a final touch, Ray cast Ward Bond as the weak-willed leader of the mob actually run by Emma Small. The director is said to have been amused that Bond, in reality a staunch anti-Communist and a supporter of the McCarthy hearings, was himself a tiny cog in the illegal posse, that allegory that Ray related to McCarthy and the House Un-American Activities Committee.

At the outset, Ray told Philip Yordan to avoid love scenes between Crawford and Hayden. Every time something romantic is about to happen in the film, they are interrupted, either by others or by themselves. Nicholas Ray didn't want the tension to die for a minute.

To shoot *Johnny Guitar,* Ray and company travelled to a mountainous area near Sedona, Arizona, about twenty-five miles north of Flagstaff. Soon after production commenced, Joan Crawford and Ray began to argue. In their hotel, Crawford reportedly told her director in no uncertain terms that she wanted to co-produce the Western and change some of the casting and screenplay. Ray refused. Crawford's conflict with him led to opposition by Sterling Hayden. The actor told newspapermen of his disdain for the star. He felt that she loved friction on the set and would create trouble if there was none. In general, Hayden felt the public should know the truth and was tired of many performers hiding behind glorious images.

Nicholas Ray set up the celluloid animosity between Crawford and McCambridge by correctly leading their characters in totally opposite ways. He told McCambridge to give her performance a real bite, so much so that it contrasted heavily with the comparative sweetness of Crawford's Vienna. Aware that he asked much from his actress, Ray was that much more impressed by her ability to make it work.

Some critics have written about the lesbian relationship implied in the script, but Ray has rejected that notion. The director wanted the women to relate more closely to each other than to any of the men. In doing so, their scenes together were sizzling with tension, escalated, no doubt, by their offscreen feuding.

The reasons why Joan Crawford was so aggressive on the set of *Johnny Guitar* were taken with her to the grave in 1977. She never spoke about them for publication. But Nick Ray felt trouble brewing after production began in Arizona. On the day he was to shoot a scene of Emma speaking to the posse, Ray let Crawford go back to the camp. He did several takes, and when the shooting terminated, everyone on the set applauded McCambridge's fine performance. For some reason, the director turned around and saw Crawford in the distance, sitting on top of the hill viewing the proceedings. That night, as he travelled around making sure nobody was getting too drunk to work the next day or losing too much money gambling, he overheard star Crawford giving orders on the telephone for a limousine to take her back to Hollywood. He also noticed clothes scattered all over the highway. Apparently, Crawford had taken McCambridge's outfits and strewn them in a burst of temper. Somehow the director talked Crawford into finishing her role, but couldn't persuade her to end the conflict with McCambridge.

Reportedly Mercedes McCambridge went to Joan Crawford's cabin several times to make peace, and each time was asked to leave. After a while, there was apparently nothing to do but make the best of a bad situation. When *Johnny Guitar* was released, McCambridge made what some considered a mistake by talking openly about the problems on the set of the Western. Supposedly Crawford had wanted Claire Trevor for the role of Emma, and that may have been the root of the trouble.

In any reported feuds between actors on a movie set, two things must be taken into consideration. One, each performer is, hopefully, there to do the best job possible, to enhance not only the role, but the entire work. Two, players also have an obvious responsibility to their own careers. Therefore, unspoken contests of one-upsmanship are not unusual during the making of a film. It must be understood that *Johnny Guitar* featured two aggressive women trying to make a place for themselves in the cinema. That one was a veteran trying to regain a foothold and the other a relatively fresh personality endeavoring to establish a career might have been the cause of the sparks between the pair.

Even if one wishes to think the worst of Joan Crawford in this situation, the star's business sense cannot be denied. To squelch rumors that she and McCambridge had fought during the making of *Johnny Guitar*, she asked her co-star to attend a gala function for the premiere of another Joan Crawford starrer, *Torch Song* (MGM, 1953). McCambridge obligingly showed up, and the pair were photographed all smiles, and even embraced each other for reporters. One photo shows the two holding each other, smiling, but they are touching each other at arm's length, as if one had asked the other to dance at a grammar school party, and both were uncertain about the steps. McCambridge later revealed that Crawford had asked her to pretend they were friends for the sake of *Johnny Guitar*.

A relatively lackluster publicity campaign (traditional with Republic) was devised for *Johnny Guitar*:

Play Me a Song, Johnny . . . and put a lot of love into it.
one poster read.

Joan Crawford as the woman who loves JOHNNY GUITAR. Starring—Sterling Hayden, Mercedes McCambridge, Scott Brady—with Ward Bond, Ben Cooper, Ernest Borgnine, John Carradine.

Johnny Guitar received varying reviews:

Cue:

. . . this film is a strange, often strikingly artistic, decoratively imaginative, and nearly always absorbing drama. Frequently, however, it reaches so far artistically to make its point, that it stumbles over its own artiness. . . . Nicholas Ray's deft direction has a rhythmic, almost musical pace, as it slips swiftly from amorous to murderous.

New York Herald Tribune, Otis L. Guernsey, Jr.:

. . . Mr. Ray, the director, has aimed high in this impressionistic Western, and his imagination is often strong enough to lift *Johnny Guitar* within full view of his goal. It is an eccentric movie, often laughable by ordinary standards of frontier drama on the screen, but with considerable novelty in its conception and details.

New York Times, Bosley Crowther:

. . . there were possibilities in this stenciled but workable plot and in the lush accumulation of performers that Republic put into the film. However, neither Miss Crawford nor director Nicholas Ray has made it any more than a flat walk-through or occasional ride-through of Western cliches.

Time:

This one is a crossbreed of the Western with a psychoanalytic case history. Somehow, strains of Greek tragedy, Germanic grand opera and just plain better class living have also slipped into the mixture.

Variety:

Guitar is only a fair piece of entertainment, seemingly headed for spotty returns, even with exploitation.

Johnny Guitar made money for Republic and, as Nicholas Ray said, enabled him to direct *Rebel Without a Cause*.

In the following years, *Johnny Guitar* became a cult classic. It is now revered by the French and some American film historians as one of the weirdest Westerns ever filmed. And Europeans understood the symbols of anti-McCarthyism in the film. When Ray journeyed to Barcelona, Spain, to receive an award for the Western, he found the city divided politically over *Johnny Guitar*.

Despite its economic success and later cult interest, *Johnny Guitar* did little to advance the careers of anyone but Nicholas Ray. Joan Crawford went on to a handful of pedestrian vehicles, but made another comeback co-starring with Bette Davis in *Whatever Happened to Baby Jane?* (Warner Bros., 1962). Sterling Hayden continued to go his own way, and later took to writing about his exploits as well as living them. Hayden also has enjoyed the aforementioned rejuvenated cinema life in the 1970s. Scott Brady went into television as "Shotgun Slade," but he too has since made something of a comeback as a supporting character on the small screen, and has had a recurring role on "Police Story." Mercedes McCambridge went on to a curious film career—with occasional films like *Giant* (Warner Bros., 1956), *A Farewell to Arms* (Fox, 1957), *Suddenly Last Summer* (Columbia, 1959), and *Angel Baby* (Allied Artists, 1961). In the last decade, she has overcome tendencies toward suicide and alcoholism, and her most notable recent credit at this writing is the chilling voice she supplied for Linda Blair in the demonic possession scenes of *The Exorcist* (Warner Bros., 1973). Even here she faced problems receiving proper recognition.

Nicholas Ray made *Johnny Guitar* his way and benefited both artistically and financially. During the 1950s and early 60s he made a string of films which form a core more personal than many of his contemporaries. His last Hollywood film was *55 Days at Peking*, released by Allied Artists in 1963. Now financially secure, Ray has been teaching filmmaking to students around America for the past several years. He is always willing to talk to the studios about a project, but will never make what he calls a "deal," turning down hundreds of thousands of dollars in sure profits to make movies with students in eight and sixteen millimeter and videotape.

Like Nicholas Ray, *Johnny Guitar* is an original, something everybody said would fail. But it, and he, keep right on going.

James Stewart

CHAPTER SEVENTEEN

The Man from Laramie

Year Released: 1955
Studio: Columbia
Producer: William Goetz
Director: Anthony Mann
Screenplay: Philip Yordan, Frank Burt, from a *Saturday Evening Post* story by Thomas T. Flynn
Cinematography: Charles Lang
Music: George Duning
Art Director: Cary Odell
Editor: William Lyon
Recording Supervisor: John Livadary
Sound: George Cooper
Color, 101 minutes

Cast:

Will Lockhart	JAMES STEWART
Vic Hansbro	ARTHUR KENNEDY
Alec Waggoman	DONALD CRISP
Barbara Waggoman	CATHY O'DONNELL
Dave Waggoman	ALEX NICOL
Kate Canaday	ALINE MacMAHON
Charley O'Leary	WALLACE FORD
Chris Boldt	JACK ELAM
Frank Darrah	JOHN WAR EAGLE
Tom Quigby	JAMES MILLICAN

The Man from Laramie is about people who push themselves to the limit, out of some inner need: in them is a force they instinctively trust and are helpless to control. Yet in the real world they embrace a hard-line pragmatism which stresses experience over intuition or theory. The Western is one of the finest examples of the psychologically motivated, action-filled genre productions of the 1950s.

Will Lockhart arrives in the New Mexico cattle country masquerading as the operator of a freight line. In reality, he is an army officer trying to discover who sold rifles to the Apaches. Lockhart's brother had been killed in an ambush by Indians using the weapons. On the plains he meets Dave Waggoman, ill-tempered scion of a wealthy rancher. Lockhart has unknowingly wandered onto Waggoman land to use the plentiful salt flats. Vic Hansbro, Waggoman's foreman and foster son, orders Lockhart's mules killed and wagon burned for trespassing. Back in town, Will is befriended by Barbara Waggoman, the rancher's niece. After seeing him in a fight with Hansbro, rancher Kate Canaday hires Lockhart. A grudging respect develops between Lockhart and Hansbro, but the latter's hopes of taking over the Waggoman spread are dashed when the old man announces that unpredictable Dave will be his heir. While riding along the trail, Alec discovers that Hansbro and Dave sold guns to the Indians. In a struggle with his foreman, Alec falls off a cliff, but survives to implicate the gun runners. Hansbro kills Dave in a quarrel over the guns. The shots arouse the Indians, and they kill Hansbro.

Although Alec Waggoman appears to be the strongest man in the territory, he doesn't possess the knowledge which is the true power in *The Man from Laramie*. Scenarists Philip Yordan and Frank Burt and director Anthony Mann depict the fears which haunt the aging cattle baron: going blind, he is worried about the future of his land in the hands of immature Dave. He also has nightmares about a man coming to kill his son. The source of the tension between Waggoman and Will Lockhart is the same, although neither of them knows it. Each man struggles with his own personal demons. Lockhart's are exorcised by the deaths of Vic and Dave, but Waggoman's can only be released by his own demise.

As he did in *Johnny Guitar*, writer Yordan brutally illustrates the lifestyle of the rich and influential. On the salt flats, Lockhart asks the identity of the men who have just appeared. "That's the only introduction you need, mister," says Dave Waggoman, pointing to the brand on a horse. But later Lockhart proves, fist for fist, that he is at least the equal of Vic Hansbro.

When all else fails for those obsessed with gobbling up the opposition, they become irrational. One of the most riveting scenes in the Western takes place on the prairie, where Will and Dave engage in a gun duel. Lockhart has bested the young tough. Using a series of darkened images, director Mann shows how Dave orders a couple of cowboys to grab Lockhart and hold out his hand. As Hansbro looks on in disgust, Dave sadistically pumps a bullet into the outstretched palm. "You scum," Lockhart screams in agony.

Despite the incredible psychological tension which runs through *The Man from Laramie*, the film is also imbued with an ethereal quality, as when Waggoman tells Will about his nightmare, and especially in Anthony Mann's landscapes. Many of the objects in the images are brown—the land, the distant mountains, the cattle, the wooden structures, even Lockhart's outfit, which is touched off by a red scarf. The sky often provides a brilliant blue backdrop. So when any character rides through the territory, it is as if he moves through an unchanging universe, a vacuum which defies time and space. Yet such cinematography does not weaken the hard-driving motion of the script, for it never draws undue attention to itself.

James Stewart's Will Lockhart is the last of five lean, laconic Westerners he portrayed in films directed by Anthony Mann. By 1955, the star had long since proven he could ride in the saddle with the best of the cowboy stars. And he offered something more. That warm innocence which he exploded into leather when the time was right gave him a range far wider than most movie cowboys. On the prairie, when surprised by the shady Chris Boldt, he confronts the man, then says with a cat's purr which is wise, definite, and angry, "Don't you ever sneak up behind me again."

The Man from Laramie is a wood-hard Western carved into a story of passion, prophecy, and pragmatism.

The Making of *The Man from Laramie*

Anthony Mann's contract with Universal had just expired. Seven of his last eight films starred James Stewart. Four of these were tough, picturesque Westerns which established Mann as one of the finest filmmakers in the genre in the 50s, and which amplified the tense, sometimes passionate screen persona Stewart had developed in *Broken Arrow* (Fox, 1950).

The director was aware of the significance of Stewart's contribution to his work, and when he signed a two-picture deal with Columbia, Mann wanted very much to continue his association with the star. He also wanted *The Man from Laramie* to be something of a resume of his work with James Stewart. Here he decided to repeat old themes about the land and man's obsessions, but with

James Stewart and Cathy O'Donnell

Cathy O'Donnell, Arthur Kennedy, and James Stewart

a new intensification, an added jolt missing in their previous Westerns together.

The making of *The Man from Laramie* was a tough enterprise which rivalled some of the daily living done by the people in his story. Although he surrounded Stewart with a host of fine supporting players, the director didn't expect them to bear the weight of the production by themselves.

The land would always be there to help. One of Mann's greatest assets as a filmmaker was his ability to photograph nature: the mountains, plains, rivers, crags in rocks, ripples of water, the bending sky all took on a significance, a magnificence which did not have to be referred to in dialogue. In addition, he could use his actors' faces better than most. Mann brought out meanings hidden between the lines of a script by framing a performer's expression just right.

Yet it was the land that attracted Mann and, in a way, symbolized his approach to the cinema. He believed violence was an omnipresent force in Hollywood films, but when action occurred outdoors, the director thought it to be an aid to an actor's believability. Crew members also seemed to be invigorated by the challenge of working with and against the elements. The medium of film told a story best in images, not words, and shooting on location only pointed that out more to one of the foremost makers of Westerns in American movie history.

Cast and crew travelled to New Mexico to lens events which occurred in the state in the 1870s. Totally giving himself to a love of locations, Mann planned to utilize six sites, but by the end of the twenty-eight-day schedule, the company moved back and forth between an additional dozen settings. They journeyed a reported total of 2,954 miles making *The Man from Laramie*, with two prime spots 104 miles apart. It seemed that Mann would go anywhere for the right background.

However, all locations were within a hundred-mile radius of Santa Fe. The crew erected a replica of the Big Barb Ranch, thirty-two miles from Santa Fe, and also the Half Moon spread, built on the site of the old mining town Bonanza, then occupied by the 90,000-acre Jarrett Ranch. Mann also filmed some scenes at the Pueblo Indian village of Tesuque.

One of the problems faced concerned the distinctly 20th-century appearance of some of the areas. Fourteen poles of electric wires were taken down. All locals were requested to remove television aerials from the roofs of houses which might be seen by the camera. One man refused to accommodate the people from Hollywood, so the director pulled a trick to bring the land back into the 19th-century. One of the crewmen stretched out a branch from a

Aline MacMahon and James Stewart

James Stewart (center) and Alex Nicol (center right)

James Stewart and Cathy O'Donnell

cottonwood tree over the irksome aerial, which clung to the metal device by wires invisible to the camera.

In order to help James Stewart feel the role of the westerner, Columbia obtained a rare Henry repeating rifle for use in *The Man from Laramie*. The antique was one of only three of its kind in California. The researchers made sure the weapon could have been used by a man in the 1869 West. The rifle was first marketed in 1866. This type of scrutiny was not at all unusual while the studios were still large enough to retain a research staff. Stewart also wore what might be called his "lucky sombrero" during production. He also donned the hat in other films, and considered it valuable enough to be locked in a fireproof vault between assignments.

Aside from their general chemistry as a star/director team, Stewart and Mann worked well together in a tough genre because the actor himself insisted on doing many of his own stunts. One scene required Stewart to ride down a treacherous ninety-degree slope on a disheveled mesa. He did so with the scorching New Mexico sun beating down on his back. In a rough fight which recalls the battles of the various *Spoilers* Westerns, the star received a brutal blow to the mouth by co-star Arthur Kennedy, and fell back into a corral of cattle. A third task which taxed his endurance involved riding directly at the camera on horseback. Stewart needed to control the horse, gallop in a straight line, and make sure he didn't send cameraman Charles Lang flying through the air while the equipment smashed in the dirt. Usually studios are extremely hesitant about letting non-stunt personnel, especially expensive stars, perform such deeds. But Stewart was insistent, and director Mann had an easier time shooting the scenes because the actor's presence freed him to do close-ups as well as longer shots which might ordinarily disguise a stunt man's identity.

Stewart wasn't the only one who performed with extreme dedication. Donald Crisp, who emoted in front of cameras hundreds of times during a fifty-year career, was smart enough to perceive the challenges of his role as Alec Waggoman, the tough empire builder who is going blind. As part of the publicity campaign for *The Man from Laramie*, Crisp spoke about acting:

> The best way for an actor to stunt his professional growth is to accept every part that's thrown at him. If an actor is not a good judge of parts or scripts, he's in for trouble. An actor's job is to create an illusion, giving him his hold on the public. If he destroys it, he betrays his audience and they don't forgive him. In *The Man from Laramie*, for example, I play a hard, selfish man who is blinded by an inordinate love for his spoiled, wayward son. He is not an admirable character, but he is human

and understandable and, in the end, sympathetic.

The roles I've played throughout the years have had a saving grace, and it is by this that audiences have come to know me. Believe it or not, I still get fan letters, even at my age [75], and it is that spark of goodness in my screen roles that keeps people writing.

When an actor's been playing heavies and suddenly appears as a hero, audiences love him. But when the hero becomes a villain, he's a dead duck.

At the end of a month's shooting, *The Man from Laramie* company returned to Hollywood, where Mann did some post-production work. In general the director was satisfied with his latest Western. He particularly liked the scene in the marketplace, where Vic Hansbro brings Dave Waggoman's body to town. And the Cinemascope effect gave added emphasis to the outdoor sequences.

A modest advertising campaign emphasized Stewart in the title role, rather than the extremely violent ambience of the Western:

This is THE MAN . . .
who came a thousand miles to
kill someone he'd never seen!

THE MAN You'll Never Forget!

The Man from Laramie received a mixture of good and bad reviews:

Christian Science Monitor, John Beaufort:

The Man from Laramie possesses more than its share of resultant violence, under Anthony Mann's direction; some of this is inexcusably gruesome. . . . The violence itself, although shocking, does not succeed in concealing the clumsiness with which Lockhart's story is told. Too many elements are introduced; some of them are never explained. . . . To the extent that the writing makes it possible, the performers are convincing.

New York Herald Tribune, Paul V. Beckley:

It is not a great picture, but it is a good one, made with a cunning eye for the architecture of suspense.

New York Times, Bosley Crowther:

. . . the main body of the picture is wholly and tempestuously filled with Mr. Stewart's uncomfortable relations with the highly unsociable elements in town. . . . William Goetz has produced the picture in excellent color and Cinemascope, which enlarges the Western vista. This makes up for the things that are obvious and banal, of which there are a number in this stoical Western film.

Variety:

The Man from Laramie, initialer for William Goetz' Columbia releasing deal, is rugged Western filmfare, using good characterizations to make the dramatic points as a story of vengeance is unfolded with explosive violence.

In 1957, James Stewart returned to Universal to star in a Western titled *Night Passage*, to be directed by Anthony Mann. The script looked promising, with Stewart as a railroad employee trying to prevent his brother's gang from robbing the train. Conflicts arose and Mann left the production. James Neilson took over and turned out a solid oater. But Stewart was upset with Mann for quite some time afterward. Eventually the two made up, although they unfortunately never worked together again.

Anthony Mann said character conflicts provided the roots for all his Westerns. The director liked to illustrate how much in common some opponents shared, as with the similar traits of Will Lockhart and Vic Hansbro: the sense of fair play, the ruggedness, the obsession. Such men enhance the audience interest in a story, especially when they inevitably turn against one another.

Mann's unique approach to characterization is in part why James Stewart shot into the Top Ten Hollywood stars of the 1950s. And the director's talent for bringing out incisive points about his fictional men and women is one of the reasons he's respected as one of the greatest makers of Westerns, never so evident as in *The Man from Laramie*. The people and the land are all there in that special Mann way.

Randolph Scott and Maureen O'Sullivan

CHAPTER EIGHTEEN

The Tall T

Year Released: 1957
Studio: A Columbia release of a Scott/Brown Production
Producer: Harry Joe Brown
Director: Budd Boetticher
Screenplay: Burt Kennedy, based on the story *The Captive* by Elmore Leonard
Cinematography: Charles Lawton, Jr.
Music: Mischa Bakaleinikoff
Art Director: George Brooks
Editor: Al Clark
Sound: Ferol Redd
Color, 77 minutes

Cast:

Pat Brennan	RANDOLPH SCOTT
Usher	RICHARD BOONE
Doretta Mims	MAUREEN O'SULLIVAN
Ed Rintoon	ARTHUR HUNNICUTT
Billy Jack	SKIP HOMEIER
Chink	HENRY SILVA
Willard Mims	JOHN HUBBARD
Tenvoorde	ROBERT BURTON

The Tall T helps prove that the "B" Western could be as vital a force as any in the Hollywood cinema. The story of a man acting alone in a maze of circumstances out of his control is fleshed out by complex characters who can be forgiven their indiscretions, even if they must die for them.

Saddle-tramp Pat Brennan loses his horse in a bet and hitches a ride on a stagecoach driven by a friend who is taking the newlyweds Doretta and Willard Mims on their honeymoon. The stage is held up by three outlaws who mistakenly believe there is a large gold shipment aboard. When they learn that Mrs. Mims is an heiress, the entire group is kidnapped and taken to a nearby cave, where Mr. Mims is later shot down trying to escape. Brennan and outlaw leader Usher develop a strange mutual respect. After instigating distrust among the bandits, Brennan is able to kill them.

In *The Tall T* Budd Boetticher continued his series of fast-paced "B" Westerns with Randolph Scott which embrace an action-filled framework with twists of character and plot. As Brennan, Scott exudes a confidence typical of stalwart sagebrush heroes, but he is not without a philosophical sense of humor about the West and himself. The early scene where Brennan is rudely dumped from the bull establishes the fallibility of the ego as a guarantor of success. Brennan is left to endure a prolonged walk through the desert, dragging his saddle until the stagecoach happens by. When the Ringo Kid was introduced twenty years earlier in *Stagecoach*, he stood on the road awaiting the oncoming vehicle. But then John Wayne posed proud and strong, flipping a rifle as George Raft tossed a coin in *Scarface*.

Unlike most Westerns, *The Tall T* features a hero and villain (Usher) as equals. Scott, with the hard, serious, bronzed features reminiscent of William S. Hart, a man on even keel in the most hazardous situation, and Boone, the curly-haired, deep-voiced mustachioed ringleader with an unbalanced sense of morality, make a good match. Both men are clearly superior to the psychotic Chink, the snivelling Billy Jack, or Willard Mims, a man who deserts his wife to secure his own freedom.

Despite the aberrant nature of some of the characters, the feeling persists that Burt Kennedy's script is all part of a universal shell game. The winners win, the losers lose, and that's the end of it. There is no moralizing against psychosis. As in all the best American genre productions, the actions speak for the characters and the makers. Yet here this is seemingly done even more than in, say, the average Howard Hawks picture, because the illness of Usher, Chink, and, to some extent, Willard Mims exceeds that of the "normal" Hollywood criminal.

As the balance of power shifts between Brennan and the Usher

Randolph Scott and Maureen O'Sullivan

Maureen O'Sullivan, Randolph Scott, John Hubbard, and Arthur Hunnicutt

gang, morality is clear but almost unspoken. "Some things a man can't ride around," says Brennan to Mrs. Mims, coining the only righteous dialogue in the film when he advises her to escape. The import is man's ability to survive. Chink and Billy are okay to Usher until they become useless. Mrs. Mims loves her husband, but it is clear that he married for money and he leaves her the first chance he gets to save his own life. Usher is sickened by the act, but once Mims is killed, all is forgotten.

Budd Boetticher's simple camera style moves everything along at a tight pace. He doesn't waste motion with flashy pans to establish atmosphere. Instead there is a sense of extreme control, something the characters don't have. People and objects always fill the frame, sometimes with striking angularity. When Mims pleads for his life, he and Billy are in the background, framed in front of a disgusted Brennan and Usher. The shot is quite economical and expressive.

The Tall T is part of a low-budget Western series which was an important force in the progression of the genre in the 1950s. The contributions of Budd Boetticher, Randolph Scott, and Burt Kennedy have made *The Tall T* one of the most vibrant oaters made in the decade before the West was revolutionized on screen by Sam Peckinpah.

The Making of *The Tall T*

Seven Men from Now (Warner Bros., 1956), a "B" Western, had done well with the critics and public. The film offered a chance for old and new talent to grow, to freshen itself, or, in Budd Boetticher's case, to blossom.

Boetticher lensed his first feature, *One Mysterious Night*, for Columbia in 1944 under his real name Oscar Boetticher. This little "B" started him on a successful career through the 1940s with economic productions sometimes colored by the director's wit and sense of irony. In the 1950s, when he changed his screen name from Oscar to Budd, Boetticher's talent grew, even if the budgets for his movies remained the same. After ten productions at Universal over the years 1951-55, he made the second of his trio of works on bullfighters. Called *The Magnificent Matador* (Fox, 1955), the zesty story showed, as did *The Bullfighter and the Lady* (Republic, 1951), that Boetticher could direct extremely personal films as well as genre assignments.

The Killer Is Loose (UA, 1956), a modern thriller, has the hints of downbeat irony, complex characters, and psychological tension which erupted in *Seven Men from Now*, and the team that made that fine Western was reunited in *The Tall T* under producer Harry Joe Brown—director Boetticher, writer Burt Kennedy, and star Randolph Scott, who was a long-time partner of Brown.

Although another studio had rights to an Elmore Leonard Western story called *The Captive*, Harry Brown managed to acquire them, and Burt Kennedy fashioned a script Columbia decided to call *The Tall T*. Director Boetticher had no idea where the title related to the story. Advertisements for the oater claimed the "T" stood for "terror."

Seven Men from Now was adapted by Kennedy from his own novel. The assignment provided a meaningful start in Hollywood for the writer, which eventually led to his directing many action films on his own, with an emphasis on Westerns. Working with Boetticher on *Seven Men from Now, The Tall T,* and the subsequent *Ride Lonesome* (Columbia, 1959) and *Commanche Station* (Columbia, 1960) was a rewarding experience for Burt Kennedy. Both men fused into a cohesive unit which allowed freedom of expression and produced material as a group offering, so much so that it is difficult for Kennedy to discuss who contributed exactly what to each picture. "Budd Boetticher is a dear friend and a great director," Burt Kennedy told me recently. "As for what part of *The Tall T* was his and what was mine it is hard to say. All I know is that we worked well together."

Although Randolph Scott had shuffled between major roles in "B" films and second leads in prestige productions, he never achieved any sort of solid screen personality until his 1950s Westerns in general and the work for Boetticher in particular. He was the good-natured stalwart onscreen, always hanging around, ready to do a good deed, even on those rare occasions when he played a villain.

The Westerns made by Scott, Boetticher, and Harry Joe Brown capped Brown's long Hollywood career. He had been a jack-of-all-genres, making production decisions on all kinds of films for many studios. By 1950 Scott/Brown Productions was formed, and together they made a handful of oaters before Boetticher came along. While the earlier pictures are certainly solid, the presence of Boetticher and Kennedy brought the Scott/Brown movies from a workmanlike appearance to the top of the Western heap by the end of the 1950s.

The Tall T was also important to the career of Maureen O'Sullivan, whose first color picture this was after scores in black and white. After the early 1940s, the MGM player known for her portrayal of Jane in the studio's "Tarzan" series retired to raise a family. For her husband, director John Farrow, she had made periodic appearances onscreen between then and *The Tall T*, but the West-

A stuntman for Richard Boone (left) and Randolph Scott

Maureen O'Sullivan, Randolph Scott, and Richard Boone

ern remains one of her personal favorites. Boetticher permitted her to act without makeup, a decision she greatly appreciated.

Like Maureen O'Sullivan, Randolph Scott was physically prepared to film without heavy preparation. Invariably immaculately groomed, the cowboy star possessed the granite good looks and staunch figure that always imparted an air of dignity which above all else was clean. By the time *The Tall T* began production, Scott needed little makeup. The actor's bronzed skin which covered those stony features Andre Bazin likened to William S. Hart was more than ready to be photographed by Boetticher's Technicolor cameras.

The production company of *The Tall T* remained a flexible crew of actors and technicians who let each other grow. They obviously listened to suggestions. Maureen O'Sullivan enjoyed the opportunity to mold her role a little more than had been the norm at MGM. Boetticher and Burt Kennedy were of essentially one mind during the conception and making of the Western. In later years, Kennedy remembered the sense of ease on the sets in comparison with the "A" productions. "I work pretty much the same as Budd," Kennedy said. "But I've been thrown in with some tough fellas that Budd never had to face—like Wayne, Kirk Douglas, Frank Sinatra. Budd had the luxury of telling his actors what to do without saying 'please.' "

The film was lensed at the foot of the Sierra Nevadas. As usual with the location of a Hollywood Western, many artifacts of frontier existence were employed. Boetticher used a Concord stage of the 1860s, but had to fit the coach with shock absorbers and foam-rubber cushions. Even so, Scott and O'Sullivan could often be found standing between scenes!

Tough production conditions are an occupational hazard with Westerns. The weather was quite warm during the shooting, and at least once when the cameras rolled the make-believe world of the movies collided with reality. An early scene has Randolph Scott toting his saddle across the desert. The sweat on the actor's brow and the fatigue on his face were real enough to motivate an eleven-year-old girl to rush into the shot and wipe the perspiration from the star's forehead.

Despite working on this economic budget, there was no question that Scott enjoyed star status in the eyes of area residents. They continually flooded him with well-wishes and requests for autographs throughout the course of the filming.

Along with the more charming mishaps, director Boetticher contended with one big miscalculation which put him in jeopardy with the city of Los Angeles. The filmmaker ordered a well dug in a certain spot. No sooner was this done than it was discovered that the crew had tunneled into part of the large underground reserve of Owens Valley, property of Los Angeles. Boetticher quickly made amends to city fathers, had another well set up above ground, and trucked in water.

Since several of the characters were extremely complex individuals, the actors had to have a clear understanding of their roles. Richard Boone, who plays the deadly Usher, spoke about the screen heavy for Columbia publicity people:

> A villain is difficult to play because most members of the audience find the pathological premise for such characters foreign to their own experience. They are familiar with the psychology of what is considered a "regular Joe," a nice guy with reasonable desires and objectives. Most people are like that, and so they find it hard to identify or affiliate themselves with psychiatric cases. My impersonation, if overdrawn, could draw hisses from spectators as though they were watching an old-time melodrama. However, the part is so well-written that it became a matter of underplaying, to suggest the strength of the character.

That kind of thinking is representative of the mood of *The Tall T*. Publicists had an obvious course for advertisements. Psychopathology, obsessions, and passions were emphasized, in keeping with the 1950s trend in Hollywood of focusing on the deviant nature of crime and criminals.

"T Is For Terror," exclaimed an ad for *The Tall T*, which gave one explanation for the meaning of the lone letter in the title. "He was gunning for three outlaws: the dark one, who killed for the love of it; the big one, who loved only the smell of gold; and the young one, who only wanted the woman."

Some reviewers appreciated *The Tall T*:

Variety:

> An unconventional Western, *The Tall T* passes up most oater cliches to shape up as a brisk entry for the general market. Co-producer Randolph Scott, who tops the cast, is a familiar name to outdoor fans and the lush Technicolor mantling will be another asset, particularly at drive-ins. . . . There's a wealth of suspense in the Burt Kennedy screenplay based on a story by Elmore Leonard. . . . Under Budd Boetticher's direction the story develops slowly, but relentlessly toward the action-packed finale.

The Tall T shows Boetticher, Kennedy, Scott, O'Sullivan, Boone, and Harry Joe Brown at their best. The director was extremely impressed with the work of both Boone and O'Sullivan, in their sole efforts with Boetticher. Burt Kennedy is preparing a volume of the scripts of the films he and Boetticher made together. "I think they would be material for young writers to study," Kennedy recently wrote in a letter to me, "not for their value as stories but how to put their ideas into screenplay form."

The Tall T and his other 50s Westerns solidified Budd Boetticher's reputation as a top action director, perhaps the man who bridged the gap between the romanticism of John Ford and the cynicism of Sam Peckinpah. Boetticher knew the value of the oater to himself and to Hollywood. For the publicity of *The Tall T*, the director related his feelings:

> Throughout the history of the motion picture industry, Western films have served as the staple entertainment commodity despite the multitude of vogues and changes. And Westerns will become more and more popular as time goes on. Time itself enhances the color and adventure of a form of life in the United States that will never be lived again. Already the Western has become a form of folklore, based primarily on the American pioneer spirit. As technological achievements bring us closer and closer to push-button automation, the need for the Western film for complete escape will become more apparent.

It gets more apparent every day. Maybe that's one reason why *The Tall T* remains one of the finest Westerns of the 1950s. Its complexity, wit, and irony keep getting better all the time.

John Wayne

CHAPTER NINETEEN

Rio Bravo

Year Released: 1959
Studio: Warner Bros.
Producer: Howard Hawks for Amanda Productions
Director: Howard Hawks
Screenplay: Jules Furthman, Leigh Brackett from a story by B. H. McCampbell
Cinematography: Russell Harlan
Music: Dmitri Tiomkin
Art Director: Leo K. Kuter
Editor: Folmar Blangsted
Color, 141 minutes

Cast:

John T. Chance	JOHN WAYNE
Dude	DEAN MARTIN
Colorado Ryan	RICKY NELSON
Feathers	ANGIE DICKINSON
Stumpy	WALTER BRENNAN
Pat Wheeler	WARD BOND
Nathan Burdette	JOHN RUSSELL
Carlos	PEDRO GONZALEZ-GONZALEZ
Consuela	ESTELITA RODRIGUEZ
Joe Burdette	CLAUDE AKINS
Harold	HARRY CAREY, JR.
Jake	MALCOLM ATTERBURY

Matt Harris	BOB STEELE
Cowboy Murdered in Saloon	BING RUSSELL
Burdette Henchman	MYRON HEALEY
First Burdette Man	EUGENE IGLESIAS
Second Burdette Man	FRED GRAHAM
Henchman	TOM MONROE
Messenger	RILEY HILL

Rio Bravo's 1959 release marked the temporary shift of the Western from a genre imbued with complex psychological and thematic narratives to one stressing the entertainment value in a story. Although Howard Hawks' third Western reveals the natures of its leading characters, inner motivations are not deeply investigated. *Rio Bravo* takes F. Scott Fitzgerald's dictum that action is character to its logical extension by emphasizing plot, fighting, loving, and comedy.

Marshal John T. Chance of Tucson, Arizona, jails a hoodlum despite threats from the man's cohorts. Chance prepares to fight the battle alone but many townspeople rally to his aid, and former deputy Dude, who became an alcoholic over the loss of his lady love, sobers up to stand by his old boss. They are joined by an ornery old cripple named Stumpy and, after holding out, young gunfighter Colorado throws in his lot with Chance. A saloon girl tries to romance Chance, but the marshal's mind is on his prospective opponents. When the gang kidnaps Dude and offers to exchange him for the jailed man, Chance, Colorado, and Stumpy use rifles and dynamite to blast the bad guys into submission.

In 141 sprawling minutes, *Rio Bravo* stays arresting because it is a film about hard, courageous men who are not above being victims of the merciless Hawksian sense of humor. The length of the Western allows for detailed exploration of character relationships, although such scenes are always predicated on their value to the story, and subject to inversion from drama to comedy, or vice versa.

Dean Martin's Dude is a constant source of humor. The opening scene features Chance astride a horse, looking down disdainfully at his former deputy, now wallowing in the Tucson dust. Director Hawks' use of the simple shot-counter-shot technique of filming, where the camera moves back and forth between the subjects, beautifully summarizes their association. Even when Dude musters the nerve to give up booze, his actions are comic. Sitting in a shabby room, Dude looks at the drink he has just poured. Instead of simply walking away to join Chance, or knocking the liquor to the floor, Dude daintily pours the whiskey into the bottle.

It is that strength of character which gives impact to the leisurely paced drama, as well as providing incentive for more comedy. As John T. Chance, John Wayne is self-assured on the field of fire but, when he steps inside, discards the badge, and becomes a mere man relating to a woman, Chance is reluctant to take action of any kind. The actor's deft footwork between the lawman as tough guy and Chance the potential lover makes the marshal one of Wayne's more memorable screen roles. Angie Dickinson's Feathers is a young, vital woman, as determined to have Chance as he is to round up the gang. Their dickering back and forth reveals his vulnerability. It makes him a funny man as well as a hero.

Even the violence in *Rio Bravo* dangles comic strings. In one bit, Chance pummels a cowboy across the face. Dude tells him to take it easy. Chance replies that he's not going to hurt him. In addition to having that comic touch, the film offers the type of action that shatters the myth about celluloid cowboy heroes being saintly in their efforts to give opponents a fair shake. While battling the gang, Chance and the others make no pretense about walking down the middle of the street, guns holstered, trying to stare down the baddies. The gentlemanly rules of boxing or dueling don't apply on Hawks' frontier. So the upholders of law and order instinctively utilize every means at their disposal to decimate the gang. Dynamiting the family is something the jailed man's kin would have done had they the equipment. Scenarists Jules Furthman and Leigh Brackett make that clear.

Rio Bravo helped shape the Western hero into a stronger, more determined man than those who rode the frontier the previous decade. Yet the Hawksian good guy is more than a mere righter of wrongs. He is a real person who reveals weakness as well as macho muscles, and he will readily employ man's instinct for survival without fear of sullying his protagonist purity.

The Making of *Rio Bravo*

Howard Hawks didn't like *High Noon*. He also didn't like Delmer Daves' *3:10 to Yuma* (Columbia, 1957). Both Westerns feature a lawman who seems to be something less than Hawks thought frontier marshals should be. Will Kane running around asking the people of Hadleyville to help him rout a trio of bad guys wasn't realistic to Hawks. Instead, Kane should have turned down any help offered, saying that the average man cannot deal with a gunfighter. In *3:10 to Yuma*, a sheriff is intimidated by an outlaw he is bringing in for trial. Hawks believed the average lawman would have shut up the criminal one way or another. Somebody asked Hawks to

Walter Brennan and John Wayne

John Wayne

John Wayne

make a Western the way he felt it should be done. So he decided to film *Rio Bravo*.

The thinking was typical of Hawks. His work reflects that very practical logic, encased in an aggressive, positive action format. A frontier sheriff who had any integrity simply wouldn't go around asking the people of his town for help in doing the job he was paid for. Of course, Hawks didn't take into account, or wasn't convinced of the very valid argument, that *High Noon* exists on a symbolic level as well as a real one: that its story could have occurred in another place, at another time, as producer Stanley Kramer has pointed out.

The casting of *Rio Bravo* made a multi-faceted rumble in Hollywood. Hawks wanted John Wayne to portray the tough, clear-thinking marshal. They had last worked together a decade earlier on *Red River*, Hawks' first Western. But time had naturally changed Wayne's appearance. The director didn't want his star spending a lot of screen time romancing young girls. It wasn't appropriate for a lawman, or the aging Wayne. Since Hawks often made the female leads in his productions the aggressors (as in the great *Bringing Up Baby*), he decided to strengthen the role of the saloon girl who loves the lawman. Howard cast twenty-six-year-old Angie Dickinson as Wayne's romantic interest. The two would act scenes in which they do battle by innuendo and implication, as thunder foretells the rain, but, in this case, a rain delayed over and over again. The waiting builds the tension.

Dean Martin wanted very much to play Dude. The singer had broken up a musical comedy act with comedian Jerry Lewis several years before and was trying hard to shed the image of the plastic romantic lead he'd played in so many Martin and Lewis films. And Martin loved Westerns. So Hawks told him to dress in an appropriate costume. The eager crooner appeared on the set in the spic and span garb of a "B" movie gunfighter. The director informed him that drunks never looked that good. Martin returned looking like a derelict who'd just stepped out of a Western Bowery. He wore a stained and torn jacket and shirt. His hat flopped over his face like the ears of a beagle. Martin looked so awful that Jack Warner didn't recognize him. When Hawks apprised the mogul of Martin's identity, Warner couldn't believe it, but he was convinced the image was right.

Hawks saw Ricky Nelson, then only eighteen, in the long-running television series "Ozzie and Harriet," and decided that Nelson's youth, popularity with teenagers, and genuine acting talent made him a good choice to portray the young gunfighter. So Howard Hawks had two famous singers with limited screen experience cutting their Western spurs in an oater which began as a

Dean Martin in an action pose

reaction to other productions and that starred John Wayne, perhaps the cinema's greatest cowboy.

Walter Brennan, who had worked with Hawks in *Red River,* signed to portray the cantankerous Stumpy. While doing *Rio*

Bravo, Brennan also was playing the irascible but kindly Amos McCoy on the teleseries "The Real McCoys." When *Rio Bravo* began production, Hawks found Brennan doing the TV character rather than the more spiteful Stumpy. So filming stopped, and the director advised Brennan to play the man like a hard, grumpy Westerner who could back up Marshal Chance, throw fear into bad guys, and come out with some downright cruel remarks. Hawks got what he wanted.

The filmmaker felt that all the actors around John Wayne would have to work at maintaining their footing in the face of the star's powerful presence. A decade earlier, Hawks had believed that the underplayed performance of Montgomery Clift in *Red River* was an essential component to the balance of Clift and Wayne. Since the acting would have to be formed with special care, it required an occasional script change. Any writer who ever worked with Howard Hawks knew the director often rewrote the day's material on the morning it was to be filmed, so by 1959 flexibility was a natural part of the filmmaking process on a Hawks production.

Action, in Hawks' mind, came before dialogue. He had to know what the characters were going to do before deciding what they would say. The easy-going look of *Rio Bravo* is very different from the usual tightly constructed Hawks picture. The director and others often found themselves making up bits of business, dialogue, or whole scenes as the shooting progressed. If Howard thought of several good things he'd like to include in a Western, one might be used and the others stored away for future reference. At one point, a shootout produced too many dead bodies; it was beginning to look like slapstick comedy. So Hawks cut some shots and successfully redid them eight years later in *El Dorado*.

For a Western which has come to be regarded as a classic, *Rio Bravo* received surprisingly lackluster reviews:

> *London Observer:*
>
> It is, however, based on a short story and feels as if it were. . . . The film starts with a fine burst of action, dwindles off, and long before the end becomes confused and repetitious.
>
> *Cue:*
>
> To his [Howard Hawks'] long list of celluloid screen-wallopers, now add *Rio Bravo*, a rollicking Western built along familiar suspense plot-lines but drawn taut as a fiddle string screeching into high-E for Excitement.
>
> *Punch:*
>
> . . . it is absolutely shameless hokum, and an amusing

curiosity for that reason. It is a very long, spectacular, highly coloured Western, built round John Wayne as a box-office star.

Saturday Review:

Rio Bravo is just about as standard Western fare as has ever turned up on a Hollywood menu. . . . There is excitement, tension, the pleasure of looking at Western landscapes, and the age-old gratification when the good guys beat the bad. . . . The good guys, in this instance, are John Wayne and Dean Martin; and while Wayne swaggers through his role with a contentment bred of familiarity, Martin succeeds in making something quite fresh and fascinating out of his portrait of a gunslinger determined to redeem himself after a two-year bender.

Variety:

While somewhat long, interest is sustained and net effect is one of the better class oaters of the year.

Rio Bravo is a classic Western which also happens to be a unique film. It started Howard Hawks off on his trilogy of Wayne Westerns. It altered John Wayne's screen image slightly without diminishing the movie star's great popularity and, in fact, gave him a new dimension which enabled him to play extremely funny characters. It gave Dean Martin a chance to prove he could act. And it is one of the few great films to be made as a direct reaction to (as opposed to simply cashing in on a trend) another fine work, *High Noon*. *High Noon* and *Rio Bravo* may take different paths, but both lead to excellence.

Brad Dexter and Yul Brynner

Eli Wallach

CHAPTER TWENTY

The Magnificent Seven

Year Released: 1960
Studio: United Artists release of a Mirisch Production
Executive Producer: Walter Mirisch
Producer: John Sturges
Associate Producer: Lou Morheim
Director: John Sturges
Screenplay: William Roberts, based on the film *Seven Samurai*, by Akira Kurosawa
Cinematography: Charles Lang, Jr.
Music: Elmer Bernstein
Art Director: Edward Fitzgerald
Set Decorator: Rafael Suarez
Editor: Ferris Webster
Production Manager: Chico Day
Assistant Directors: Robert Relyea, Heimie Contrarez
Makeup: Emile LaVigne, Daniel Striepke
Special Effects: Milt Rice
Production Supervisor: Allen K. Wood
Color, 126 minutes

Cast:

Chris	YUL BRYNNER
Calvera	ELI WALLACH
Vina	STEVE McQUEEN
Chico	HORST BUCHHOLZ

O'Reilly	CHARLES BRONSON
Lee	ROBERT VAUGHN
Harry Luck	BRAD DEXTER
Britt	JAMES COBURN
Old Man	VLADIMIR SOKOLOFF
Petra	ROSENDA MONTEROS
Hilario	JORGE MARTINEZ de HOYOS
Charmlee	WHIT BISSELL
Henry	VAL AVERY
Robert	BING RUSSELL
Sotero	RICO ALANIZ
Wallace	ROBERT WILKE

The Magnificent Seven comes across like a riveting cold stare. Featuring seven tough poker faces who right wrongs for a fee, the Western is one of the most solemn oaters ever produced in Hollywood. For all its iconoclasm, *The Magnificent Seven* initiated the cinema trend to depict the actions of networks of men expert at the methodology of death and mayhem.

A peaceful Mexican village is terrorized by bandits led by Calvera. The farmers hire a gunfighter named Chris to defend them, and he in turn chooses six mercenaries to aid in the fight to thwart the gang. Each of the defenders has his own specialty, and they are molded into a formidable unit. Calvera captures the seven but permits them to ride away. At first Chris, Vina, Chico, O'Reilly, Lee, Britt, and Harry Luck willingly exit a dangerous situation, yet they return to help the villagers repel the aggressors.

Perhaps the first thing that comes to mind when thinking about *The Magnificent Seven* is its sweeping musical score. The grandiose theme was heard in several of the film's sequels and then was borrowed for the Marlboro cigarette commercials. The melody seems to follow the rhythm of the seven galloping over Mexico to help the downtrodden farmers. The Elmer Bernstein score defines the glorious tone of the Western, and propels it through the bittersweet ending. Something great is happening onscreen and there isn't much time for sidetracking except for character delineations.

That something is the casting of the noble gunfighter who first appeared in the form of William S. Hart in bronze as a monument to the West. Like the seven, Hart might have ridden across the river to escape a life and death conflict but he would have returned quickly. The half-dozen plus one good/bad men begin strictly as mercenaries—practicing their deadly crafts for pay—but ultimately throw their lot onto the side of the victims. The bandits don't need any help exploiting the poor farmers. Calvera defines the heartless blitzkreig tactics of the gang. "Why are you poorer and poorer every time I come here? This time there is practically nothing in the poor box in your church—but I took it anyway," he snarls.

In the manner of Sergio Leone's later *Man With No Name*, the seven mercenaries look pretty good because the opposition is so evil. Calvera strikes and strikes again in a ruthless manner. Since Calvera is a gregarious, though blood-thirsty murderer, it might be expected that the seven would be less than charming rogues. While Britt, the knife-throwing expert, is the most taciturn, the other six don't exactly warm the hearts' cockles with their giving lifestyles. O'Reilly might be more able to touch basic human emotions than the others, but such sentimentalizing goes no further. There is wit in *The Magnificent Seven* but nothing resembling the comic relief which helped shape so many other Westerns centered around larger-than-life heroes prominent before the complex protagonist replaced them in the 1950s.

So there are relatively few digressions in William Roberts' script. The lean quality aids the film's sturdily somber tone. The philosophizing of the men brings the Western to a level untouched by the simple good guys of past oaters. The sagebrush tale used to feature cowboys who revealed their attitudes about life by acting out their thoughts. Roberts allows the seven to discuss morality, putting *The Magnificent Seven* on a more intellectual plateau from which the characters can look (physically) down on the role models their very words codify as genuine myths. The feeling is always around the corner that Chris, Vina, and the others have a bit of the Greek tragic hero in them. They know their fate. Can they change it? The answer is elusive. But an old Mexican puts things in perspective after the village has been freed from Calvera. "Only the farmers have won," he says. "They remain forever. They are like the land. You are like the wind . . . a strong wind [chasing] the locusts . . . blowing over the land and passing on. Vayan con dios."

The brilliant casting of *The Magnificent Seven* reflects John Sturges' talent for picking performers—a talent as intuitively accurate as John Huston's eye. The most outstanding performance comes from Eli Wallach. The New York-based actor had never appeared in a Western, yet his characterization of Calvero is *the* archetypal Mexican bandido of the last two decades, enlarging the scope of the south-of-the-border villains in Huston's *The Treasure of the Sierra Madre* (Warner Bros., 1948). The unctuous surface charm combined with the poor-boy appeal masks a cutthroat

Yul Brynner

nature and a streak of sadism. If there is comic relief in the Western, it comes from Wallach, the killer, the oppressor, and his earthy witticisms only add to his dark nature, which hardly provides relaxation. Yul Brynner's Chris is cool and detached at first, but once you get past that bald head and look into those quick, piercing eyes, Chris becomes something of a lost hero, an Odysseus leading his followers in a search for home. As Vina, Steve McQueen is something of a Western hipster, a man whose face and hands are always in motion, large or small. It is easier to see through him. Chico is a youngster trying to hang out with the big boys, so Horst Buchholz makes the character extremely accessible—it is easy to feel for him. The *raisons d'etre* of Lee (Robert Vaughn), Harry Luck (Brad Dexter), and especially Britt (James Coburn) rest in their faces. The sophisticated look of Vaughn's angular countenance and perfectly shaped haircut, Dexter's simple man-of-the-earth power, and Coburn's memorable yet enigmatic features that stay in the back of the mind without purpose are like untitled pen-and-ink drawings minus an explanation: they simply exist.

The Magnificent Seven sets down Western legends in concrete with a taut, action-filled story which reveals the mechanics of its mythology as well as the reality of those being turned into folk heroes.

The Making of *The Magnificent Seven*

The Magnificent Seven is a hard Western, and it was a tough one to film. An actors strike and government censorship tried to shape the production. Both failed.

The problems of shooting this cowboy morality tale began long before anyone in Hollywood thought to make the picture. John Sturges' Western *The Magnificent Seven* is a remake of Akira Kurosawa's *Seven Samurai*, also known as *The Magnificent Seven*.

In 1954, Japanese director Kurosawa and scenarist Shinobu Hashimoto penned a script they considered to be quite a departure from most other films made in their nation. Japanese cinema was too quiet for them. With *Seven Samurai*, they wished to bring a bold, colorful, rich tapestry of Japan's history to the screen. It is said that all directors, regardless of nationality or focus, want to make *the* big film, a movie with a cast of thousands and a budget of millions. In a way, this is what Kurosawa did with *Seven Samurai*.

There were many objections from the front office. *Seven Samurai* was a much bigger production than Toho Films was used to making. Executives didn't like the idea of Kurosawa doing so much work in a far-off location, out of reach. The director wanted to make an epic, and it made the men in power at Toho nervous. Nothing like it had ever been done in the Japanese cinema.

It took Kurosawa over a year to finish *Seven Samurai*. Much of this time was spent on location. Bad weather, friction from top executives, and a myriad of production setbacks didn't dampen the enthusiasm of the cast and crew. Kurosawa felt that everyone on the picture contributed far more than had been expected. And they had to surmount some enormous troubles. While on location, the rain never seemed to stop, and its constant flow ruined the shooting schedule. Kurosawa wasn't always able to obtain enough horses for his epic. Adjustments had to be made. Back in Tokyo, Toho Films sent him many telegrams ordering the director to stop production. But then, with its budget already way beyond the original figures, executives undoubtedly felt it better to let *Seven Samurai* alone, rather than shut down filming and lose all that money or hire another director and waste additional time. And Kurosawa's artistry was respected enough to prevent mixing his style with that of another filmmaker, thus turning what could be a masterpiece into a pieced-together mishmash. That would be important if the production was to be profitable.

Hollywood mythmakers say that you can't remake a great film. Cinema history has proved the notion more right than wrong. But producer Walter Mirisch and director John Sturges decided to break the rule and make a version of *The Magnificent Seven* set in the American West. The Japanese picture was later retitled *Seven Samurai* in the U.S. to prevent confusion.

Originally Yul Brynner reportedly planned to lens a Hollywood version of Kurosawa's epic. Arrangements were made to have Anthony Quinn co-star in the picture to be produced by Brynner's Alciona Productions. When Brynner sold the property to Mirisch Productions, Quinn sued for breach of contract. The suit was settled, and Quinn was off the project.

Seven Samurai went on to world-wide critical acclaim and won an Oscar as Best Foreign Film of 1955. It is truly one of the classic films of the Japanese cinema. How could anybody top it?

John Sturges loved Kurosawa's production and desired to make it into a Western. The director was fascinated by the idea of setting a 17th-century narrative of Samurai warriors in Japan in a 19th-century tale of American gunfighters in Mexico. Recently, Sturges informed me, "My thought was that the original film held the basis for a story and characters that would make a very good Western. We developed that story to the best of our ability without regard as to whether or how it differed."

Fortunately for the makers of *The Magnificent Seven*, nobody wanted to make an entirely new creation out of already successful screen material. They evidently didn't feel change was necessary for its own sake. As fellow director Mervyn LeRoy might have commented, Sturges didn't "improve the story into a flop," or alter the qualities of a property so much that it no longer possessed the touch which made it so cinematically attractive in the first place. Nevertheless, a number of alterations were made, such as the reshaping of the opening of the Western.

Sturges was under pressure to cast the production by a certain date, due to an impending strike of the Screen Actors Guild. Since most of the roles were set and Sturges planned to film in Mexico, he didn't have a great deal to worry about but, concerned that some might say he fled the country to avoid dealing with the strike, he went to the Guild and explained that while they had no jurisdiction out of the United States, he did not want them thinking *The Magnificent Seven* was originally going to be made in Hollywood. The Guild conceded that as long as he had his cast by the time of the strike, nothing would be implied or stated.

Yul Brynner, Steve McQueen, Horst Buchholz, Eli Wallach, Charles Bronson, Robert Vaughn, and Brad Dexter had already agreed to appear in the picture. They made an impressive line-up of talent even in 1960, although only Brynner was a "star." Unquestionably John Sturges is a master at choosing the right actors for his characters. He'd been doing it for years. Bob Relyea, the director's assistant and friend, talked about Sturges and actors. "John casts brilliantly, particularly in what we call the 'gut' of the picture. If it's a Burt Lancaster picture, or a Marlon Brando picture, or a Bob Redford picture, you know what the structure of the head of the animal is. John has the ability to cast in the center of the picture. If you look

Brad Dexter, Steve McQueen, James Coburn, Horst Buchholz, and Yul Brynner

through his films, you see people that are old hat to you and me now, but nobody ever heard of 'em. I'm talking about the heavies in *Bad Day at Black Rock* (MGM, 1954). Borgnine and a guy called Lee Marvin, whom nobody ever heard of."

Brynner brought the property to Mirisch, and was Chris from the beginning. Steve McQueen had co-starred in Sturges' *Never So Few* (MGM) the year before, and the director felt that the actor's future was most promising. Charles Bronson and Brad Dexter quickly accepted supporting parts based on previous associations with Sturges. Eli Wallach's appearance as Calvera became a real coup. "John made every casting decision on the picture," Relyea told me. "John will get a fix on a character, in the gut, not above the title, and he will come up with ideas that are not the standard Mexican bandito. I don't think Eli'd ever been on a horse before. . . . John said he's such a magnificent actor, and the look is right. It was just one of those things."

But the role of Britt hadn't been set yet. Britt, the quiet man who threw a knife rather than fire a gun, needed to be played by an actor whose countenance was expressive enough, even when there was no expression, to hold a viewer's attention.

James Coburn wanted very much to play Britt. Coburn had a background in television prior to *The Magnificent Seven*, co-starring in the short-lived teleseries "Klondike" and "Acapulco." His bad guys could ooze evil, or be slickly sinister. After making *The Magnificent Seven*, Coburn slowly built himself into a star.

But getting that part of Britt wasn't easy. The actor phoned his agent, who contacted John Sturges and made an appointment for Friday, the last possible day the picture could be cast. The trade papers had announced the names of most of the actors who had already signed to appear. After a brief interview, Coburn went home. Three hours later, Sturges' secretary phoned with the news that he was to portray Britt. Later Coburn found out that two bigger names had lost the role because of salary disputes.

Britt speaks only fourteen words in the movie. Yet they were important enough to help the actor get more and better roles. Coburn was wise enough to know that a good screen character can't be measured by billing, salary, or how much screen time is involved. And his director understood that a person in the movies doesn't have to talk frequently to be noticed.

With the cast set, Sturges and company journeyed to Mexico. Their troubles were far from over. Six weeks before the production began, Sturges followed Mexican government procedure by submitting his script for their approval. Jorge Ferretis, the official censor, thought the material was anti-Mexican. Reportedly Ferretis, without even reading the scenario, demanded that Sturges make numerous changes in the plot and characters. A large battle between the director and the censor ensued.

John Sturges elaborated on the censorship problems. "The idea of Americans coming into Mexico to do a job involving physical prowess and courage for Mexicans presented an instant censorship problem. We had difficulty selling the idea that the villagers were farmers, men of peace—not an aspect limited to Mexicans! Even a line explaining to the village wise man, 'We know how to plant and grow, not how to kill,' met with objections. Mexicans can kill as well as anyone, certainly a non-sequitur. Another exchange, 'Hire gunfighters,' 'Gunfighters are very expensive,' 'Find hungry gunfighters,' hit the rocks."

And this particular incident occurred after the filming had begun. As expected, a representative of Mexico's censorship board was on the set daily. Only when Sturges was about to lens the scene in question were there any objections. "This censor did not want this. He said he would not have us saying that Mexicans could not afford high-priced gunmen. Mexicans don't have to be second best. And so on and so on. We persevered through endless discussions and showdowns without being mortally hurt. This attitude characterized the censor, but not the rest of the government or the Mexicans who worked on the film."

Although Sturges and company had problems with Ferretis, his representative on the set was remembered by assistant director Bob Relyea as a very pleasant woman. She would simply observe the day's shooting, then each night sign the film cans which would be sent to the United States for developing. That symbolized the government's stamp of approval.

The Hollywood crew had a happy experience with their Mexican counterparts. As soon as a foreign production company decides to shoot in Mexico, the technicians are matched man for man. For instance, Sturges' opposite number was Emilio Fernandez, the great actor, and director of such fine films as *The Pearl* (1948). Fernandez choreographed the dances and scouted extras. Heimie Contrarez was Bob Relyea's counterpart, a man the assistant recalled as a colorful person who was married about nine times. "My relationship with Heimie was at first a little bit strange because you don't know how that kind of thing is going to happen," Relyea reminisced. "But then, water finds its level, and you sort it out. As any American first assistant, I was at that time aggressive, and ran the set. Heimie helped me a great deal because my Spanish is very limited. He worked more like a second assistant and interpreter . . . and it worked out just fine and we became good friends. As a matter of fact, every time I went back, regardless of what my position became eventually, I always asked for Heimie. And he would always say to me, which I shall remember forever, 'Boy, you forgot that Abraham Lincoln freed the slaves!' What he meant was, all work and no play makes anybody dull. Heimie was quite good at living it up."

The Magnificent Seven company had the luxury of a valuable Mexican crew to help balance the censorship problems. Although he appreciated the assistance obtained south of the border, Sturges adamantly opposed the censor. He spoke of it in 1960:

> The censor is an autocrat who lives in a dream world. The regulations laid down by the Mexican government are practical and workable. But he operates on the basis of whimsy. He is confused, petulant, and goes on the theory that anything debatable should be stricken out.
>
> The censor was just picking on anything that might be objected to by some member of the lunatic fringe. I think his only concern was that there must be nothing that someone in Mexico might conceivably consider anti-Mexican.

Sturges wryly summarized the state of cinema affairs for a foreign production company in Mexico. "If it weren't for the censor, Mexico would be a wonderful country for making movies. But as it is now, it is okay so long as you are making movies about an American or about a boy and his dog."

While taking on the censor, Sturges reportedly served as a mediator for the conflicts between Yul Brynner and Steve McQueen. Reports filed stated there was a personality difference which almost led to real friction between the pair. Brynner, of course, was still riding on the crest of popularity from his Oscar-winning performance as the egotistical monarch in *The King and I* (Fox, 1956). The actor brought a new breath of European sophistication to the American cinema, and his bald pate made him a unique leading man in itself. The role of Vina in *The Magnificent Seven* was Steve McQueen's second important part. It followed a co-starring role in Sturges' *Never So Few* with Frank Sinatra. So the new Western could maintain Brynner's bright image and confirm McQueen as one of the screen's somber anti-heroes, a man of few words whose presence can extend far beyond the last row of a movie theatre.

In his book, *Steve McQueen: The Unauthorized Biography* (New American Library), Malachi McCoy reported that the star was less than thrilled with Brynner and felt resented by the European. Supposedly Brynner's concern about news of their alleged troubles caused him to ask McQueen to send a letter to the press denying reports of strife between them. Undoubtedly the fact that Yul

John Sturges

Brynner was slated to marry on the set of *The Magnificent Seven* made him more vigilant to avoid any unpleasantry with cast and crew.

Bob Relyea didn't recall any major discord between Brynner and McQueen:

> That's been blown up. . . . I think that happens on any picture where you have volatile stars. . . . Now, once we got the band together, we headed for Mexico. From the first take, which was a shot of them during the trek, crossing a little river bank, John got it all lined up. There were a couple of rehearsals for the camera, and everything was fine. John said 'roll 'em,' and they came single file and each got in front of the camera. They did a couple of acts from *Hamlet*! Some people scooped water out of the stream with their hat, others adjusted their gunbelt. There was so much going on that the look on Sturges' face was incredible. I think those rumors come from the fact that everybody in the seven was in a different way, and there were seven different personalities all working very hard to make it their big picture. And I don't think there's anything wrong with that. If they weren't trying hard, they should be in another business. I don't think that Steve and Yul were ever close, but I don't feel that there was ever any animosity. Number one is, Yul is in an entirely different lifestyle. He was preparing to marry. Steve was in his second picture, and young . . . and used to play around with Bronson and Coburn. Brad liked to play gin rummy, so he and Yul became close friends. They were about an even match in gin, although neither one would admit that. Horst was somewhat of a loner, still working on his English. I think the stories which I've heard about rivalry between Yul and Steve, having been there, I would have to say rivalry is the best word you can use. But no more so than between, say, Steve and Charlie, who were probably closer personally because their lifestyles were more the same.

Fortunately for John Sturges, there were no major weather problems or delays due to equipment breakdown or injury. He didn't feel there was a feud between McQueen and Brynner. In any case, keeping all those aggressive performers in proper perspective for an entire production must have required a confident and sure hand.

The Magnificent Seven received some praise and some criticism from reviewers. Few called it an unqualified success or a dismal failure:

Cue:

As a straight, hard-shooting, hard-riding Western, this film has many thrill-packed moments. There's enough heroism and action to satisfy any horse opera addict. But the re-written story now is far too theatrical and weakly motivated to be creditable.

The Illustrated London Daily News:

The director, John Sturges, has done a thrilling job, and the color . . . is of quite exceptional charm and enhancement. . . . Much of the film is unusually witty for a Western—or rather, an Eastern-Western.

London Observer, Penelope Gilliatt:

As expositors of the code that makes the Western hero tick, John Sturges and William Roberts are well equipped to write a thesis, but by attributing the same perception to their characters they vitiate the film, for it is part of the essence of the epic hero that he should not be able to hear himself ticking.

Time:

Color, camera work, acting and directing are competent. But the script is what gives the Western its special dimensions, inwardness and dignity. Expert but sensitive, the writer searches even more intimately than Kurosawa did, into the nature of that fateful tie that sometimes is pity, sometimes is cruelty, sometimes is love, but always inevitably binds the strong to the weak.

Variety:

Until the women and children arrive on the scene about two-thirds of the way through, *The Magnificent Seven* is a rip-roaring, rootin'-tootin' Western with lots of bite and tang and old-fashioned abandon. The last third is downhill, a long and cluttered climax in which *The Magnificent Seven* grows slightly too magnificent for comfort.

Some of the criticism of *The Magnificent Seven* inevitably centered around how the Western compared with Kurosawa's *Seven Samurai*. Some implied it was wrong of the Mirisch Company to even attempt to improve upon the Japanese epic. Director Sturges maintained he simply attempted to make a Western out of Kurosawa's film. *The Magnificent Seven* was extremely popular throughout Europe. When John Sturges received a ceremonial sword in the mail from Akira Kurosawa, attached to a note stating the Japanese filmmaker had just seen the Western and loved it, Sturges felt extremely satisfied. Kurosawa's opinion was the one he cared most about. Regarding Kurosawa's classic film, Bob Relyea said, "I think if you ask John which picture he likes better, he'd probably answer *Seven Samurai.*"

All but one of the original "gunfighters" was a star of one magnitude or another by the end of the 1960s. Yul Brynner continued to be a major star, despite many of his subsequent movie roles. Steve McQueen consolidated his growing appeal in Sturges' *The Great Escape* (UA, 1963), also with Coburn and Bronson, *Soldier in the Rain* (Allied Artists, 1963), and *Love with the Proper Stranger* (Paramount, 1964), while Horst Buchholz reached his peak in the early 1960s with *Fanny* (Warner Bros., 1961) and Billy Wilder's *One, Two, Three* (UA, 1961). Rugged Charles Bronson built up his image in a series of supporting roles throughout the decade, then went to Europe and became a star in *Adieu Ami* (1968) and *Rider on the Rain* (1970). James Coburn was allowed to speak more in a number of pictures which portrayed him as the super-hip, sexy, usually scrupulously fair anti-hero. *Our Man Flint* (20th, 1965) and *Dead Heat on a Merry Go Round* (Columbia, 1966) are two of his best. Robert Vaughn went on to TV fame as Napoleon Solo, the debonair spy on "The Man from Uncle." The only member of the outlaw band who failed to become something of a household name was Brad Dexter, who continued a career in acting and, after saving him from drowning during the filming of *None But the Brave* in 1965, became one of Frank Sinatra's cronies and business associates.

The Magnificent Seven is still enormously popular throughout the world and it spawned several increasingly less successful sequels: *Return of the Seven* (1966), *Guns of the Magnificent Seven* (1969), and *The Magnificent Seven Ride* (1972).

In a recent survey quoted in *TV Guide, The Magnificent Seven* ranked as the most popular old movie to appear on television. It remains a classic example of a film that is loved by the public after being received coolly by many critics. It has become a cult favorite and has been so successful that it has signaled a series of carbon copy ripoffs cashing in on its title. Primarily, though, it represents the triumph of art over adversities.

Clark Gable and Marilyn Monroe

CHAPTER TWENTY-ONE

The Misfits

Year Released: 1961
Studio: United Artists-Seven Arts
Producer: Frank Taylor
Director: John Huston
Screenplay: Arthur Miller, based on his story
Cinematography: Russell Metty
Music: Alex North
Art Directors: Stephen Grimes, William Newberry
Editor: George Tamasini
Production Manager: C. O. Erickson
Assistant Director: Carol Beringer
Second Unit Director: Tom Shaw
Set Decorator: Frank McKelvy
Sound: Philip Mitchell
Assistant to Producer: Edward Parone
Hair Styling: Sydney Guilaroff, Agnes Flanagan
Makeup: Allan Snyder, Frank Prehoda, Frank LaRue
Script Supervisor: Angela Allen
124 minutes

Cast:

Gay Langland	CLARK GABLE
Roslyn Taber	MARILYN MONROE
Perce Howland	MONTGOMERY CLIFT
Guido	ELI WALLACH

Isabelle Steers	THELMA RITTER
Old Man	JAMES BARTON
Church Lady	ESTELLE WINWOOD
Raymond Taber	KEVIN McCARTHY
Old Groom	WALTER RAMAGE
Young Bride	PEGGY BARTON
Fresh Cowboy	J. LEWIS SMITH
Susan	MARIETTA TREE
Bartender	BOBBY LaSALLE
Man in Bar	RYALL BOWKER
Ambulance Attendant	RALPH ROBERTS

The Misfits is about people who are alienated from modern society. They wander aimlessly about the mid-20th-century Western prairie. Scenarist Arthur Miller and director John Huston bring out their humanity beautifully.

The setting is Reno. Roslyn Taber has just been granted a divorce from her husband Raymond. Gay Langland is an out-of-work wrangler. Perce Howland is a cowboy who is nervous and unsure of himself. Guido is a former bomber pilot who works as a garage mechanic. Roslyn meets Guido through her landlady, and Guido introduces her to Gay. Later they meet Perce, and the four agree to go after wild stallions. Gay and Roslyn develop a romantic relationship. Roslyn treats Perce like a son. Roslyn becomes disgusted by the job they set out to do and persuades Gay to free the horses.

Gay, Roslyn, Perce, and Guido are all desperately trying to maintain a footing in the world. *The Misfits* is one long, brilliant mood piece about that struggle. Gay is the strongest, but he is trying to amble over changing turf. The aging cowboy comforts Roslyn, who in turn cares for Perce. They all give Guido some security. "I can't make a landing and I can't get up to God," former flyer Guido says at one point, thus defining the group position. They are all floating in a holding pattern. The job of lassoing the stallions is something tangible, but even that creates a rift when Roslyn finds out the horses are to be butchered. "Freedom. You and your God's country," Roslyn says. Huston's camera then moves to a colt grabbing at a mare's throat. If nothing can be the same forever, the quartet does achieve a temporary cessation of aimless wandering in each other's company. Gay and Roslyn spend the night together. Roslyn holds Perce the way she might comfort a little boy.

As Arthur Miller's script caresses the characters, John Huston's camera portrays the harsh prairie winds, the ramshackle dwellings, the scattering dust as a unit of historical integrity. While Martin Ritt depicts the transforming earth as something warped with his brilliant imagery in *Hud*, Huston uses the modern frontier as an extension of his characters' loneliness. There is no sharp edge to Huston's frames, no disfigured tree branches, distinctly barren skies, or cracked earth. The land isn't particularly exciting and it does not at all compete with the people in the film for attention. It just exists, as always. If *Hud* surges forward in its illustration of the present-day West, then *The Misfits* simply winds over the plains likes a drifting mesquite bush.

The most telling shots in *The Misfits* are those which show the group chasing horses in a truck. They lasso the stallions from the back of the pick-up, zooming over the prairie, kicking up dust, like something created in a time gap. Twentieth-century men on a 20th-century machine doing 19th-century wrangling symbolizes the status of the misplaced four.

The cast is brilliant, from the stars to the supporting players. Picking the right actors has always been one of John Huston's talents, and he used it to full potential here. Clark Gable's Gay Langland is a man caught out of his time, but a courageous man nonetheless, facing his obsolescence with dignity. Gable's clipped intonation and craggy, handsome features are perfect for Gay, whose few words of wisdom are backed by years of experience finding out what's right. As Roslyn, Marilyn Monroe can be airy and complex, almost interchangeably. Roslyn is throbbing from her divorce, and yet reaches out to love Gay and comfort Perce. Her character really comes into focus, gets a grip on itself, when she is revolted by the future slaughter of the stallions. Perce's early telephone conversation with his mother defines a sad, troubled man. Montgomery Clift's searching eyes, and vocal style which seems to pour over every word carefully, give an extra dimension to Perce's indecisiveness. It is as if he can't decide even what to say. Eli Wallach's Guido is full of zest, perhaps motivated by Gay's belief about just plain living each day, even though Guido too acknowledges the horrible empty feeling.

The Misfits is a rich and powerful cinema tone poem, a Western which so reflects its characters that the plot is almost incidental. The fact that things happen is memorably overwhelmed by the people to whom they're happening.

Thelma Ritter, Clark Gable, and Marilyn Monroe

Estelle Winwood (second from left), Eli Wallach, Montgomery Clift, Marilyn Monroe, and Clark Gable

The Making of *The Misfits*

Arthur Miller published a short story in 1957 set in the present-day West. It concerned four people—two cowboys, a divorcée, and a garage mechanic—who band together out of loneliness and are hired to capture wild stallions by a dog-food manufacturer.

Although Miller was one of the most important playwrights to emerge in post-war America, with classics such as *All My Sons* and *Death of a Salesman* to his credit, he never had written a screenplay. He now wanted to create a vehicle for his wife, Marilyn Monroe. Miller desired to take a more active part in his wife's career, to give her dialogue which would reveal the depth of her talent, and to perhaps lessen the influence of the Actors' Studio on Marilyn's work. Miller just didn't agree with the school's theory of acting. Monroe needed the discipline of a tight script and direction, not a method of performing which relies primarily on an actor's feelings to do a scene.

Up to then she'd proceeded to hone her comedic ability to frothy sex comedies which promoted the star as a blonde bombshell who sometimes made the average male moviegoer forget about "little" things like plot and character. Despite movie executives' inability to look past the star's beautiful form and into the real acting potential she occasionally displayed, Marilyn Monroe did make a number of fine and funny films throughout the 1950s, including Howard Hawks' *Gentlemen Prefer Blondes* (Fox, 1953) and Billy Wilder's *The Seven Year Itch* (Fox, 1955) and *Some Like It Hot* (UA, 1959). *Bus Stop* (Fox, 1956) showed Monroe capable of giving a sensitive dramatic portrayal. Miller wanted to bring that bright promise to fruition in the screenplay called *The Misfits*.

By July 1958, the script was completed. Miller gave the material to a friend, film producer Frank Taylor, who then took it to director John Huston. Having seen and admired several of Huston's pictures, Miller approved the selection, as did Marilyn Monroe, who had liked Huston ever since he gave the actress her first important screen role in *The Asphalt Jungle* (MGM, 1950). Huston hadn't made a movie in the United States since the controversial *Red Badge of Courage* (MGM) in 1950 but thought *The Misfits* was magnificent and happily agreed to direct.

In the meantime, Marilyn Monroe needed money and signed to play a member of an all-female jazz band of the 1930s in Wilder's *Some Like It Hot*. The shooting took her away from *The Misfits* project but didn't prohibit her from voicing objections about her character of Roslyn Taber. The star felt the woman to be too weak, that the lonely divorcée who reaches out to an aging cowboy needed more development. Conflicts over the nature of the role weren't the first personal/professional differences which threatened the Millers' marriage, but rather capsulized a relationship which ultimately sputtered along for the sake of *The Misfits* and ended once the film went into the editing room.

Although in retrospect Miller seems to have written the rest of the characters in *The Misfits* with certain actors in mind, those performers didn't see it that way. Clark Gable was sought to play Gay Langland, a middle-aged cowboy who finds himself an anachronism in the modern world. Langland is a tough, experienced man looking for a foothold in life. Gable, of course, had been a star for more than a quarter of a century. He left MGM in the mid-1950s to freelance but, while the pictures in which he subsequently starred were sometimes quite good, they just weren't the same. Gable had to move over to make room for the Brandos, Newmans, and Deans.

He wasn't quite sure he liked Gay Langland and didn't understand Miller's script, feeling that the cowboy seemed to be left behind. Perhaps Gable came to understand the fictional man as well as anybody. He accepted the role.

At first, Miller couldn't see Gable as Langland, and in fact confessed he was never able to visualize a specific actor portraying one of his characters. When the writer and star met, Miller changed his mind. It was Gable's tough exterior masking a truly sensitive personality that Miller realized was so right for the cowboy.

For starring in *The Misfits*, Clark Gable was to receive ten percent of the film's gross, with a guarantee of $750,000. His work day would run from nine to five, and overtime pay was set at $48,000 per week. There was to be much overtime during the making of *The Misfits*.

Montgomery Clift was approached to play Perce Howland, another lonely cowboy. At the time the actor was suffering from a myriad of personal problems, many brought on by his alcoholism and pill popping. After a distinguished start in Hollywood as a thoughtful G.I. in Zinnemann's *The Search* (MGM, 1948) (released prior to *Red River*, which was actually Clift's screen debut), the performer followed up with Stevens' *A Place in the Sun* (Paramount, 1951) and Zinnemann's *From Here to Eternity* (Columbia, 1953), among others. In the late 1950s Clift's erratic behavior had made it more difficult for him to obtain quality roles.

In his biography, *Monty* (Arbor House), author Robert LaGuardia states that Clift had reservations about the script but was convinced by friend Nancy Walker that he was perfect for the part. The actor would pick up a screenplay and dissect character, plot, and dialogue line by line, the way a prospector would pan for gold in a river. So anything he accepted was more often than not the right choice. Clift was a perfectionist, which is one of the reasons his unique talents were only utilized in a relatively small number of films in his almost twenty years as a screen star. But the roles he did compose one of the most distinguished acting careers in post-war American cinema. Clift's performance as Perce would be one of his finest.

Clift decided to do *The Misfits*, he told reporters, because his first scene began on page fifty-seven. In his previous productions, he had been onscreen what he considered an excessive amount of time. After reading ten pages of *The Misfits*, Clift agreed to co-star in the project. He was particularly impressed by Perce's telephone conversation with his mother.

That scene in the phone booth struck ironic tones. Perce is telling his mother that he's never been the same since a serious accident. In this moment, it could be Montgomery Clift talking about the automobile crash which nearly killed him in 1956. A number of years later a writer in *Esquire* chastised Arthur Miller for the author's supposed bad taste in penning a sad scene which so closely resembled a horrific episode in the real life of its speaker. The playwright strongly denied having Clift in mind when he conceived the phone conversation. Miller's statement that he could never mentally cast his characters bears out the denial somewhat, and his assertions make sense if considered from a theoretical standpoint. Miller didn't approve of the kind of acting which comes from a performer's being or personal life, at the expense of the script. He not surprisingly wanted the writing to motivate a performance. This is one of the reasons he created a screenplay for his wife, to wrestle her away from the Actors' Studio's method of inspiring a performer. Thus, an accusation that the author was inspired to write the scene by Clift's tragedy has little validity. Nevertheless, the moment in question takes on a chilling quality when one realizes what is said on film is so real to the actor saying it. Yet on the basis of that segment, Clift agreed to do *The Misfits*.

With Monty Clift signed at a salary of $200,000, the rest of the cast was assembled. Eli Wallach, another New York stage actor, readily agreed to portray garage mechanic Guido, who makes up the last part of the foursome that ride across the plains in a beat-up truck roping wild horses for the dog food manufacturer. Thelma Ritter, Estelle Winwood, James Barton, Marietta Tree, and Clift's friend Kevin McCarthy rounded out the brilliant group of players.

Perhaps *The Misfits* would provide new life for its participants. A fresh direction for Arthur Miller, a return to filmmaking in America for John Huston, and the rebirth of the careers of Clark Gable, Marilyn Monroe, and Montgomery Clift were the potential rewards for making the modern Western.

Clift took his opportunity quite seriously, as did the others. The actor flew to the production site at Reno, Nevada, before the July 1960 starting date to learn about the lives of rodeo cowboys. And he wasn't totally unprepared. A decade earlier the actor was taught to ride a horse for his co-starring role in *Red River*. In researching Perce Howland's environment and the associations a real-life cowboy makes on and off the range, Clift couldn't avoid taking on the characteristics of his role. Coincidentally, as he helped a cowboy mount a Brahma bull, Clift received a painful nose injury. The same thing happens to Perce in *The Misfits*.

Although the production was filled with bright promise, everyone realized numerous obstacles would have to be overcome before anything of quality could emerge. One trouble spot was the Millers' failing marriage, another Clift's erratic behavior. A third, and most enveloping possible area of friction, was the personal and professional differences between Gable and Clift, and Gable and Monroe, and the distance New York-based actors sometimes feel from their Hollywood counterparts. Since even Monroe had worked at Lee Strasberg's Actors' Studio, the odds were geographically stacked against Gable. Compared with the years of study and/or theatrical backgrounds of Clift, Monroe, and Wallach, one might have thought that Gable was a comparatively untrained movie star who had spent his career playing variations on the same character.

John Huston noticed that his co-stars were less than awed by Gable at first but, despite the misgivings of the others, the director knew that the man who once sat on the throne at Metro was right for the role of Gay Langland. And his faith was justified.

In a way, Gable, Clift, and Monroe had to prove themselves to one another in *The Misfits*. Gable had to convince the New York actors of his talent, Clift needed to show himself to be a reliable performer who showed up to work sober and on time, while Monroe's task was to fulfill her potential as a dramatic actress.

If Clift had suspicions about Gable's capabilities, so was Gable not quite sure about Clift's. The situation resolved itself once shooting commenced. As irony piled on irony, the first scene Huston took was the telephone conversation between Perce and his mother, perhaps the most harrowing part of the script for Clift. It is said Clift felt he was auditioning in front of the cast and crew, to show them that a near-tragic accident and enormous personal problems hadn't worn out his talent. Perce's speech is long, full of awkward stops and starts. Clift surprised everyone by getting it perfect on the first take. Clark Gable was impressed. *The Misfits* production company, it began to appear, might actually get along and do exactly what they had assembled to do—make a movie.

John Huston in 1975

Some say John Huston also had to illustrate his worth. None of his films had done well at the box office in recent years. Huston's last work, *The Unforgiven* (UA, 1960), was a moody period Western starring Burt Lancaster and Audrey Hepburn which was less than enthusiastically received. And the director was rumored to be a difficult man on the set. Perhaps he considered working with Monroe and Clift, two top performers who were reported to be "problem" actors, to be part of the price for his "comeback," as well as proof that he could be more patient with stars than some indicated. Recently Arthur Miller gave me an opinion of the director's value to the production. "Huston, despite understandable frustration with delays due to Marilyn's illness, kept his cool and did get the film finished. Like everyone else, he probably contributed to the problems, but more, I think, to the solutions."

John Huston began filming *The Misfits* on July 18, 1960, and didn't finish until November 24. It seemed as if there was no end to the clashes on and off the set. The working day, as stipulated in Gable's contract, began at nine sharp. Most mornings filming didn't begin until eleven. The cast and crew would often waste mornings, afternoons, and sometimes entire days waiting for differences of opinion to be resolved. Yet at least these situations reflected a company of moviemakers who were willing to give and take: one would make a suggestion, the others then mulled it over. After the picture was completed, Clift said that one of the things he enjoyed about *The Misfits* company was the freedom to comment on the work and not be ignored. This may be the key to understanding why *The Misfits* is such an excellent film, despite the inner turmoil which might have shut down another production.

Sometimes the flexibility went too far and just created more tension. After a while, Marilyn Monroe reportedly came to the conclusion that her husband and Eli Wallach secretly planned to build up Wallach's role at the expense of her part. She therefore insisted that Miller rewrite some scenes. He refused. And she still didn't feel completely comfortable with Roslyn. Monroe insisted that an audience would never sympathize with a woman who makes love to two men in a film. Of course, this objection probably wouldn't be made today, but in 1960 it had validity.

When artistic differences didn't hold up production, Marilyn Monroe did. She was by then addicted to sleeping pills and given to dropping off for hours. Costs mounted because of her inability to take care of herself, but director Huston was patient. Arthur Miller and Monroe became increasingly distant as the shooting progressed. At one point, he even took a separate hotel room. She rarely saw anyone, except friend Montgomery Clift. Miller has asserted the two got along well together because both were lost souls who were a comfort to each other. Apparently, no one else could help the actress—not her husband or her acting coach Paula Strasberg. But Clark Gable treated her sympathetically, and Huston was extremely sensitive to the actress' needs. When finally

Marilyn's drug intake became more than her body could handle, the director terminated production for two weeks and placed Monroe in a Los Angeles hospital. Marilyn Monroe's mother kept a picture of Gable on her bureau, and it is said the actress saw the aging idol as a surrogate father. She did respond well to the actor.

At one point in the script, Gable gives a poignant speech to the divorcée which may very well represent the attitudes of those who made *The Misfits*. "Honey, we all got to go sometime, reason or no reason. Dyin's as natural as livin'. Man who's afraid to die is too afraid to live, far as I've seen. So there's nothin' to do but forget it, that's all—seems to me." That's what Gable, Monroe, Clift, Miller, and Huston tried to do—forget their problems, anxieties, conflicts, and get the job done.

There was one more scene where the stars' strife-torn reality momentarily disappeared and the business of being a dedicated artist in a make-believe world reigned supreme. And irony was once again the definitive retrospective tone. While Monroe continually tried Huston's patience with her inability to remember the dialogue of even the shortest scenes, both she and Clift amazed everyone by doing a five-minute one-shot segment in only six takes. It occurs in the saloon, where Gay, Perce, and Roslyn are dancing. Perce becomes dizzy and Roslyn takes him outside for a breath of air. Those minutes are among the most moving in *The Misfits*.

This may be the scene which prompted Huston to hug Marilyn. Since reports of the troubled production had been making news regularly, the actress asked someone to take a picture of herself and the director, to show their relationship wasn't all bad.

On other occasions, the shooting became harder. Huston knew that censors wouldn't pass a particular Monroe action. In the scene showing Gay and Roslyn after they have made love, Monroe was naked under the sheet, being filmed by two cameras. It was the seventh take. Gable kissed her and she exposed her breasts.

During the making of *The Misfits*, the location was like a flaming meteorite, fueled by the finest creative flourishes which should come from artists, or out-and-out warfare between the participants. The constant tension had its consequences. Arthur Miller reportedly lost $50,000 at Reno crap tables. Monroe relied on sleeping pills to get her through the day and night. Clift drank vodka and grapefruit juice. And the strain showed on Gable. In addition to the irritation suffered by numerous delays, Gable was physically tired from doing a series of stunts at his own insistence.

A happy moment occurred when the fifty-nine-year-old star announced he would become a father for the first time. With that prospect to steel him, Gable was always more than courteous to

Marilyn Monroe

Monroe and achieved a friendly rivalry with Huston, another hard-living movie man. Gable and Clift shared a mutual respect. But the strain proved to be too much. The final scene of *The Misfits* was lensed on November 24. Clark Gable suffered a heart attack three days later.

Marilyn Monroe and Arthur Miller officially separated at the end of the production. The playwright became involved with Inge Morath, a photographer who shot stills of the production. Soon after they married.

In October, cinematographer Russell Metty voiced his displeasure over the strife on the set. He told the press in sarcastic terms about his disdain for the confusion caused by so much fighting. Inevitably, others saw the situation differently. Producer Frank Taylor said he was most satisfied with the results. John Huston spoke well of all the actors and praised Arthur Miller's script. Although the normal alterations were made by the director during the course of filming, the writer's material appears on screen pretty much intact. Of course Huston was not shy about discussing his aggravation at all the unpleasantries, but considered the finished product to be the main concern.

The critics had varied comments about *The Misfits*:

Cue:

Miss Monroe, on screen, is again the dumb blonde trying to act interpretively and introspectively. But the wonderful intuition of her earlier career is gone; and the cerebral method has now taken over. You can see the wheels working behind those wide eyes and furrowed brow: Mr. Gable in his last picture, was, as always, an old pro—wonderfully expert—as the ex-pilot, Wallach is splendid, and so is Clift as the rodeo rider. John Huston directed with great power, sensitivity, pictorial excitement—and, I have been told, much patience.

New York Herald-Tribune, Paul V. Beckley:

It has a vitality so rich that I dare say it can scarcely be taken in at one viewing. It gives that sense of warm, almost fleshly contact with reality that one never experiences except where a film has grown out of somebody's response to life.

New York Morning Telegraph, Leo Mishkin:

John Huston, the director of the film, has drawn brilliant characterizations from each of the actors taking part in the film. Certainly Marilyn Monroe now stands forth not only as one of the great beauties, one of the great sex symbols of the age, but also as an actress of rare and hitherto unsuspected gifts. Clark Gable, in the last appearance he made on screen, exhibits a volatile, dynamic and explosive performance such as he never gave in his whole long career. Eli Wallach as that Air Force pilot, Montgomery Clift as the rodeo rider, and in lesser assignments, Thelma Ritter as a friendly landlady, James Barton as a boozy saloon-drinker and Estelle Winwood as a strolling charity fund raiser, all contribute effectively to the general idea.

New Yorker, John McCarten:

The casting of the film is almost impeccable. . . . It must be clear by now that all severe doubts about *The Misfits* center on Arthur Miller's screenplay, which seems to be obtrusively symbolic and so sentimental. . . .

Village Voice, Jonas Mekas

Marilyn Monroe, the saint of Nevada Desert. When everything has been said about how bad the film is and all that, she still remains there, a new screen character. Marilyn Monroe, the saint. And she haunts you; you'll not forget her.

Clark Gable never lived to see the completed version of *The Misfits*. He died of a heart attack on November 30, 1960. He was buried at Forest Lawn Cemetery beside Carole Lombard, his former wife, who had been killed in an airplane crash in 1942. His widow, Kay Spreckels Gable, subsequently gave him the son he had always wanted. John Clark Gable came into life several months after his father's death.

All the world mourned the loss of Clark Gable, the King. With his last film, *The Misfits*, Gable achieved his greatest heights. United Artists wanted to do something for his memory. So they rushed the picture into release near Christmas, to qualify for Academy Award consideration. Gable had seen a partially edited version of the Western, and thought it to be the best work he'd ever done. John Huston wanted the star to receive a posthumous Oscar for playing the role of Gay Langland.

The Misfits also was Marilyn Monroe's last completed film. Under George Cukor's direction, she had begun doing a comedy called *Something's Got to Give*, co-starring Dean Martin. She didn't live to complete it. Some say she committed suicide; others insist Marilyn's death resulted from an accidental overdose of sleeping pills.

After *The Misfits*, Montgomery Clift's health grew steadily worse. Only three more films could claim Clift's name on the credits before he died of a heart attack in 1965. His death at age forty-five was certainly hastened by his abuse of alcohol and pills. Another member of *The Misfits* cast, James Barton, also died not long after completing his role.

An Arthur Miller screenplay hasn't been filmed since *The Misfits*, although Sidney Lumet lensed a screen version of *A View from the Bridge* (Continental, 1961).

The next decade was a professionally tumultuous one for John Huston. Some of his films made money, but many were received coolly by both critics and the public and his work continued creating controversy. In the 1970s, after spending some time in front of the camera as an actor, Huston has been more successful at the box office and in reviews with two fine pictures, *Fat City* (Columbia, 1972) and *The Man Who Would Be King* (Allied Artists, 1976).

Almost lost in the maze of adverse publicity, Eli Wallach continued performing in the cinema and theatre and on TV. He became the archetypal Mexican bandit of the 1960s with his portrayals in *The Magnificent Seven* (UA, 1960), *How the West Was Won* (MGM, 1962), and *The Good, the Bad, and the Ugly* (UA, 1967).

Shooting *The Misfits* was such a dramatic enterprise in itself that James Goode wrote a book about it. This was the second time that the filming of a John Huston production resulted in a volume being published on its making.

As Russell Metty pointed out, *The Misfits* was an appropriately named production, from start to finish, from theme to characters to makers. Yet even though the set flamed with clashes, they were battles waged by fine artists, attempting to overcome flaws which afflict us all in one way or another. Monroe, Miller, Huston, Gable, Clift, Wallach, and Metty fought each other, but nevertheless harnessed their emotions, pooled their resources once the cameras rolled, and made a movie. It was what they were there to do—to engage in their arts. It was an heroic struggle. In a very real way, *The Misfits* created portraits of artists as heroes, mortgaging their very existences in some cases to bring Miller's brilliant script to life. They fought over it, and for it. And, despite the terrible price of producing *The Misfits*, the moviemakers won. The victory is on film.

Joel McCrea and Randolph Scott

Randolph Scott, Ronald Starr, and Joel McCrea

CHAPTER TWENTY-TWO

Ride the High Country

Year Released: 1962
Studio: MGM
Producer: Richard Lyons
Director: Sam Peckinpah
Screenplay: N. B. Stone, Jr., Sam Peckinpah
Cinematography: Lucien Ballard
Music: George Bassman
Art Directors: George W. Davis, Leroy Coleman
Editor: Frank Santillo
Set Decoration: Henry Grace, Otto Siegel
Assistant Director: Hal Polaire
Sound: Franklin Milton
Color, 93 minutes

Cast:

Gil Westrum	RANDOLPH SCOTT
Steve Judd	JOEL McCREA
Heck Longtree	RONALD STARR
Elsa Knudsen	MARIETTE HARTLEY
Billy Hammond	JAMES DRURY
Joshua Knudsen	R. G. ARMSTRONG
Judge Tolliver	EDGAR BUCHANAN
Kate	JENIE JACKSON
Elder Hammond	JOHN ANDERSON
Sylvus Hammond	L. Q. JONES

Henry Hammond	WARREN OATES
Jimmy Hammond	JOHN DAVIS CHANDLER
Saloon Girl	CARMEN PHILIPS

What happens when two veteran Westerners find themselves being eased out of a frontier they helped civilize? Questions arise about the way a man has lived his life. In *Ride the High Country,* the crisis of two cowboys who are losing their place in society spirals to an apocalypse of the movie Western. It is the final chapter in a segment of cinema history.

Steve Judd is hired to carry a gold shipment from a mining camp to town. Realizing he's gotten too old to do it alone, he hires old friend Gil Westrum and Westrum's youthful sidekick, Heck Longtree, to assist him. Along the trail Westrum and Longtree plot to steal the $20,000. Westrum tries in vain to persuade Judd to split the gold three ways. The trio stops at the home of religious zealot, Joshua Knudsen, whose daughter Elsa yearns for a life free from her father's oppressive restrictions. The men take her to marry Billy Hammond in the mining camp, but the bridegroom turns out to be a callous man with a brutish family. After a bawdy wedding ceremony, Elsa flees the camp with Judd, Westrum, and Longtree, with the Hammonds in hot pursuit. Westrum and Longtree, meanwhile, attempt to steal the gold, but Judd thwarts their efforts and vows to bring them in for trial. Elsa and Longtree become romantically involved. But the Hammonds are getting closer. A final showdown is necessary. Westrum rides off, then returns with Judd to face the Hammonds. Judd is mortally wounded in the gun battle, but gets Westrum to promise to bring the gold to town.

The casting of Randolph Scott and Joel McCrea gives a double edge to the death of the West theme which lurks in the background of *Ride the High Country*. Both actors were winding up three decades of Hollywood stardom, each devoting the latter part of his career to Westerns. The actors had slowed down as their characters ceased to be the men they once were. In the opening scene of the film, Sam Peckinpah illustrates the changing frontier with a moment which is ironic, beautiful, funny, and a bit cruel. Judd rides into town to see a cheering crowd, and he thinks the celebration is for him. In reality the people are there to watch an auto race. "Watch out, old timer," someone yells as he lopes by. Time in the form of automobiles is quickly and harshly passing him by.

Such detachment from a life once relished brings on a *crise de conscience* for Judd and Westrum. Each knows this assignment may be his last. Twenty thousand dollars split three ways would make an easy retirement for the veterans and a nice nest egg for

Heck Longtree. But Judd is adamant about doing the honorable thing. Westrum is more practical. Yet director Peckinpah keeps the men equal. The battle of morality versus money is waged by two frontier giants, jousting with the same strong weapons. There is no obsession in either character, which is a departure from the 1950s Western protagonist.

With the personalities of Westrum and Judd etched in solid steel, the graphic nature of the frontier and neurosis prevalent in post-war Westerns emerges for a spell in the mining camp and in the characters of Joshua Knudsen and the Hammonds. Knudsen confines his daughter to a solitary life on their modest farm. The mutual attraction of Elsa and Longtree oddly enough leads to her decision to leave home for Billy Hammond. Upon arriving in the mining camp, Peckinpah reverses the conservative tone of the scenes in Knudsen's dwelling by depicting the wedding of Billy and Elsa as something out of a Fellini film. The loving, the boozing, and the eating at the wedding party held at a brothel anticipate similarly unabashed excitement in *McCabe and Mrs. Miller*. The bawdiness and sexual violence themselves distinguish *Ride the High Country* from earlier Westerns, and their intensity hints at the graphic depiction of murder and mayhem in Peckinpah's *The Wild Bunch*. After the camera pans the room, sweeping by the whores dressed in their finest lace and the assorted crater-faced rowdies, a disgusted Westrum grabs the marriage certificate and whisks Elsa away.

The final gun fight is not only the climax to an action-packed Western but serves as a denouement for the entire genre. Westrum has ridden away, leaving Judd, Longtree, and Elsa to defend themselves against the enraged Hammonds. Hearing the shooting, he returns, just as the free-lance army comes back to help the farmers in *The Magnificent Seven*. "Where's the rifle?" Westrum asks Judd. "On the horse." He retrieves it. The Hammonds are holed up in a cabin. Judd wants to battle them face to face to end the violence quickly. The Hammonds emerge, scared, with anxiety and passion pushing them toward the showdown. As Judd and Westrum walk together the camera hovers over them, leaving enough room in the image for large shadows of the men to form in front of them. The firing begins. Peckinpah zooms in on each Hammond. Judd is shot but the Hammonds are killed. Judd knows he is dying. "I don't want them to see it. I'll go it alone," he tells Westrum. "I'll see you later," says Westrum and leaves Judd to die in peace. This is the end of the old movie cowboy, the man of virtue. Historically, the sagebrush heroes lived and rode alone and, as Westrum rides into the sunset, he leaves a solitary set of hoofprints as a mark in the earth.

Earlier in the tale, Judd begins to feel like the man he used to be.

Randolph Scott

"Now I'm gettin' back a little respect for myself," he proclaims. Then he reiterates the creed of all honorable men of the West. "All I want is to enter my house justified."

He does that. McCrea and Scott keep their integrity as actors and as cinema Westerners. Their performances are genuine, based on years of experience in the saddle. This is the main element which distinguishes Peckinpah's glorification of the movie cowboy from Sturges' in *The Magnificent Seven*. Peckinpah's characters radiate simple humanity while Sturges' go off in an equally valid direction as philosophers who talk about their roles on the frontier. Judd and Westrum just live their lives.

Scott's sculptured face looks gentlemanly and moral from any direction. The flourish of charming villainy in the film is something he had perfected over the years. McCrea is the direct one, with the friendly countenance, a man incapable of doing the wrong thing. Screen newcomer Mariette Hartley reflects a similar innocence. Elsa is a confused victim of both Josh Knudsen's repression and the Hammonds' vulgarity. She is in a constant daze until the trio arrives to free her.

The Western did not die after the release of *Ride the High Country*. Scott retired. McCrea has worked infrequently in films since. Yet this zesty oater with streaks of sentiment pointed the way for the genre. *Ride the High Country*, capturing the spirit of the American West, is a monument to what has been and a prophecy of what will be.

The Making of *Ride the High Country*

Ride the High Country was produced by people who loved the West and Westerns. Director Sam Peckinpah and stars Randolph Scott and Joel McCrea had a particular affection for the frontier which helped turn a low-budget property into a classic.

Producer Richard Lyons found a story called *Guns in the Afternoon*, and aroused Randolph Scott's interest in the tale of two old friends hired to deliver a gold shipment. Scott sent the material to his long-time pal, Joel McCrea, who was equally enthusiastic about the project. Scott told his fellow veteran actor to choose a part for himself, and McCrea decided to play Gil Westrum. In the meantime N. B. Stone, Jr. penned a script which did not satisfy either Lyons or MGM studio head Sol Siegel. With the blessing of Scott and McCrea, Sam Peckinpah, whose background had been in television as a writer and director, was hired to redo the screenplay and direct the new approved narrative called *Ride the High Country*.

Peckinpah's credentials were impressive and well-suited to making a "B" film in the manner expected—fast and cheap. He knew the business from just about every angle. Starting in Hollywood sweeping sound stages led to a stint as Don Siegel's dialogue director. From there he began writing scripts, using facts and stories about the West accrued since he was a boy living with his family on the side of a mountain in Madeira County, California.

Television producers became interested in the unknown writer who penned tales, steeped in the day-to-day rugged reality of the 19th-century West, which possessed colorful plots and characters. Before long he was writing for a new CBS series called "Gunsmoke" (he created thirteen scripts for the series). He later sold several pilot screenplays, including the highly successful "The Rifleman," with Chuck Connors, and the short-lived but critically applauded "The Westerner," featuring Brian Keith. Peckinpah also directed many of his own scenarios, turning out a program in an average of two or three days. He learned the value of shooting quickly and economically, as television shows which went over-budget and came in late could easily lead to the unemployment line for a director.

He showed TV producers he could bring in a quality thirty- or sixty-minute program on time. The little seen *The Deady Companions*, co-starring Maureen O'Hara and Brian Keith, marked his debut with a theatrical feature and proved that his talents extended to doing a creditable job with a script he hated.

While Peckinpah reworked Stone's material, Scott and McCrea prepared for their roles. Both actors had spent the previous decade almost exclusively in oaters: Scott had starred in a handful of tough little productions made by his own company and helmed by Budd Boetticher, which are now recognized as among the finest in their genre of the 1950s; McCrea's work during the period had received less acclaim, but maintained a fine professionalism. By the time *Ride the High Country* was ready for release, Metro publicity men calculated that McCrea and Scott had starred in a total of 230 motion pictures over the past thirty years, fired 150,000 bullets, ridden 200 horses, shot 130 bad guys, and worn out 250 pairs of boots, chaps, and pants.

Mariette Hartley was captivated by Western lore. Although she made her screen debut from the ranks of many who tested for the part of Elsa Knudsen, the actress was no amateur. Mariette had been acting since she was twelve years old. At twenty-two, the performer received her first big chance in the movies.

In addition to McCrea, Scott, and Hartley, the cast was rounded out by veterans Warren Oates, Edgar Buchanan, and R. G. Armstrong, together with James Drury (soon to win fleeting fame in the title role of TV's "The Virginian") and newcomer Ron Starr as the third member of the trio who transport the gold shipment.

With the casting settled, there remained the question of billing. Who would be on top—McCrea or Scott? Although McCrea had won fame as a leading man in the early 1930s, Scott had had to wait until the 1950s to really come into his own. Yet Scott more recently had done his best work for Budd Boetticher. Somebody came up with a simple solution to a touchy problem. Scott, McCrea, Peckinpah, and Richard Lyons were lunching in the Brown Derby. A coin was flipped, and Scott won the toss. His name would appear at the head of the credits. Everyone seemed happy at the result.

MGM constructed a Western set on a back lot, but most of the shooting was done on location at Mammoth Lake in the High Sierras, Conejo Valley, and Frenchman's Flat.

The cinematographer was Lucien Ballard. Both Ballard and Peckinpah respected each other's professionalism. They would work together again on the controversial *The Wild Bunch* (Warner Bros., 1969) doing the same kind of preparation as for *Ride the High Country*. The director and his cameraman pored over books and old photographs, studying Western culture of the 1880s. The scenes in the mining camp have added impact because they look so real. Peckinpah credited Ballard with giving these segments a graphic atmosphere. Art Director Leroy Coleman employed old sails from *Mutiny on the Bounty* to make the tents, and everybody assisted in the creation of the dowdy camp.

Things went well until the first day of shooting. Scott played the

Ronald Starr, Randolph Scott, Mariette Hartley, Joel McCrea, and R. G. Armstrong

middle-aged ex-marshal hired to bring the gold shipment from a mining town to a bank. McCrea was cast as his friend, a man who decides to steal the wealth. Joel McCrea had never played a villain before. Even though the role was much more than a cardboard black-hat type, it didn't feel right. Conversely, Scott had portrayed baddies occasionally throughout his long career. He had been an outlaw in *Belle Starr* (Fox, 1941) and Errol Flynn's adversary in *Virginia City* (Warner Bros., 1939) but he never failed to charm, even while trying to do the hero in. So Joel McCrea and Randolph Scott switched roles.

During the making of *Ride the High Country*, Sam Peckinpah was everywhere, into everything. Of course he needed the help of the other men behind the camera, but he felt totally responsible for what appeared onscreen. He was as demanding of himself as he was of others. Joel McCrea remembered Peckinpah as "a very gifted writer . . . he was fine to work with. I hear he got tough later on, especially with the crew, but with us he was fine—a real talent." The star put Peckinpah in a category with such top filmmakers as Alfred Hitchcock, Howard Hawks, King Vidor, William Wyler, Preston Sturges, William Wellman, George Stevens, and Henry King, some of the directors who have guided him. Assistant director Hal Polaire also recalled Peckinpah's strong sense of dedication:

> I found him very demanding, but justifiably so. He expected everybody to perform at his maximum capacity, which I agreed with. People in the motion picture industry, I think, are well paid, better paid than in most industries and, as a result, you try to get the best people you can and expect them to give a maximum performance for you. I think he's entitled to that. That's the way I feel and, as a result, he and I had a good relationship. His demanding was a lot heavier . . . than a lot of directors, and his patience . . . didn't have a great longevity . . . and if a person did not really perform for him, he didn't want him around. He was a little rough on people but, at that particular time, which was his first major film, he was, in my estimation, dealing rather fairly with people even though he was demanding.

Polaire gave me an excellent summary of the function of an assistant director and of his own work on *Ride the High Country*:

> At that time in the movie industry, people like myself were actually doing two jobs . . . production manager and assistant director . . . which meant you ran the company from its operational standpoint and its logistic standpoint. You were respon-

sible for all the money that was spent. You ran the set. . . . The assistant assists the director in everything he does, like a first sergeant in the military. He motivates the company. He keeps it moving. He plans the schedules day by day. . . . In addition to that, he sets up all the background movements for the director, so the director can concentrate on his principal actors—staging them. Now, in a Western this can include a lot of things—horses, wagons. If there is a fight sequence going on, he makes sure everybody is prepared. . . . If there are stunts involved, if there are gunshots involved, the special effects people must be prepared and ready to rig up all the special effects that need to be done . . . for a second, a third, and a fourth time, depending on how many times it's necessary. In addition he makes sure that the makeup people are there, particularly if there are wounds involved, and that the sound men have all their equipment in place.

We were up in Mammoth shooting some of the big scenes for the film where there was great scope, and I had to follow the weather reports very carefully. It was a very dry season, and I had a weather report come in indicating we could be hit with a snowstorm. So I had to make a decision as the production manager to keep the company up there or pull them out, because if I made the wrong decision and we got hit with a snowstorm we could have been snowbound. I made the decision to pull out and to me it was the right decision because three hours later there was a snowstorm, one of the worst they'd had in many years up in Mammoth. . . . Those are the kind of decisions a person doing that kind of a job has to make.

Obviously any film cannot afford lengthy delays due to inclement weather, but a production such as *Ride the High Country*, with a twenty-four-day shooting schedule and an $800,000 budget,* might just have been shut down if the cast and crew had been locked into the mountains.

Since all involved were so well prepared to do their jobs, director Peckinpah felt free to improvise if he felt it necessary. Shooting the boisterous wedding scene involved much give and take among the actors and crew. Warren Oates, L. Q. Jones, and several other performers had worked with Peckinpah in television, so he knew their capabilities. After the cameras rolled, the players were allowed to really enjoy themselves, go with their feelings, move around, and try to make the make-believe party as real as possible.

Hal Polaire remarked to me about the value of *Ride the High Country* in general and that wedding fracas in particular. "I think

*Sam Peckinpah's salary was $15,000.

Sam Peckinpah in 1973

there was something that Sam Peckinpah kind of started at that time which became full blown in the years to come. And that was the kind of violence he portrayed. . . . You didn't see a great deal of that in films in those years. . . . In the wedding scene itself, there was going to be a gang rape and, at that time, I don't recall any other films [having one], and the fight sequence of the wedding scene also. . . . It was very violent for those times."

Although most of those involved with the Western's production didn't realize they were making a classic film, there was a general feeling that *Ride the High Country* was the swansong of McCrea and Scott. Both men evidently felt it would be their last picture. McCrea told me that the Western was one of his all-time favorites.

After Peckinpah and editor Frank Santillo finished readying the production for release, they discovered that *Ride the High Country* no longer fit into MGM's distribution plans. During the filming, Sol Siegel had left the studio and his replacement evidently had little faith in the "B" Western. The new feeling at MGM was that the story suffered from bad construction, the brothel scene from bad taste, and the Hammond brothers from poor development.

Peckinpah, of course, defended his film. The director believed that while the wedding scene certainly jolted what had been a relatively quiet story, the contrast to what preceded it worked very well. The purpose of the great difference was to compare the life on Knudsen farm with the coarse existence in the mining camp. And Peckinpah knew people like the Hammonds. They were not exaggerations.

Despite everything, *Ride the High Country* was released as a second feature in the summer of 1962. Soon it found its way to the bottom half of double bills at drive-ins. The cast and crew of the Western were bitterly disappointed.

Of course *Ride the High Country* did receive some publicity courtesy of MGM, but its heart was half-missing.

"TWO WESTERN STARS IN ONE GREAT MOVIE!" screamed MGM ads for the film, as if they actually believed it. Others read:

> They'll set Fire to your box office with this brand . . .
>
> They each had a gun and a last chance to make good—on one side of the law or the other.

Reviews were generally very favorable:

Newsweek:

> In fact, everything about the picture has the ring of truth, from the unglamorized setting to the flavorful dialogue and the natural acting. Within the standard cowboy framework, director Sam Peckinpah and writer N. B. Stone, Jr. have created a Western that can be believed.

Time:

Ride the High Country has a rare honesty of script, performance and theme—that goodness is not a gift but a quest. In the unhurried tempo of their speech, their ease of bearing, the firm-lipped gravity of their faces, actors McCrea and Scott give the action strength and substance.

Variety:

It remains a standard story, albeit with some interesting gimmicks and some excellent production values, but is in the hard-to-sell area in between an expensive "B" and the big ones. It is doubtful if Randolph Scott or Joel McCrea, teamed for the first time, can draw the mainstream crowds. If so, this limits the film.

But that wasn't the end of *Ride the High Country*. The Western (called *Guns in the Afternoon* in Great Britain) went on to win first prize at the Venice Film Festival and capture the Grand Prize at the Brussels Film Festival, beating out the dazzling *8½*. In comparing the two films, one commentator referred to Peckinpah's action tale as "life," and Fellini's portrait of the artist as "intellect." Film journals ran articles which praised *Ride the High Country*. Writers in the British periodicals *Sight and Sound* and *Films and Filming* were among the early supporters of the Western. Peckinpah's little "B" production remained a favorite in Europe for years, where it ranked as one of MGM's most profitable pictures in the early 1960s.

Ride the High Country started Sam Peckinpah on a successful career as a film director. It is chock full of the things Peckinpah cares about—the West, the progression of time, violence, men, and women on the periphery of society.

While *Ride the High Country* provided a classic end to Randolph Scott's cinema work, it was to be Joel McCrea's last picture too, until he surprised everyone by coming out of retirement to star in 1975's *Mustang County* (Universal). Prior to that, the veteran appeared briefly in *Cry Blood, Apache* in 1970 as a favor to son Jody, who produced and played the lead, and narrated a 1974 documentary, *The Great American Cowboy*.

Most of all, *Ride the High Country* is a brilliant comment on man and civilization, a compendium of all the best ingredients of the Hollywood Western and a tribute to the tenacity of dedicated filmmakers.

Patricia Neal and Paul Newman

Brandon de Wilde, Paul Newman, and Melvyn Douglas

CHAPTER TWENTY-THREE

Hud

Year Released: 1963
Studio: Paramount
Producers: Martin Ritt, Irving Ravetch
Director: Martin Ritt
Screenplay: Irving Ravetch, Harriet Frank, Jr., based on the novel *Horseman's Pass* by Larry McMurtry
Cinematography: James Wong Howe
Music: Elmer Bernstein
Art Directors: Hal Pereira, Tambi Larsen
Editor: Frank Bracht
Set Decorators: Sam Comer, Robert Benton
Assistant Director: C. C. Coleman, Jr.
Costumes: Edith Head
Makeup: Wally Westmore
Second Unit Camera: Rex Wimpy
Sound: John Carter, John Wilkinson
112 minutes

Cast:

Hud Bannon	PAUL NEWMAN
Homer Bannon	MELVYN DOUGLAS
Alma Brown	PATRICIA NEAL
Lon Bannon	BRANDON DE WILDE
Burris	WHIT BISSELL
Hermy	JOHN ASHLEY

Jesse	CRAHAN DENTON
Jose	VAL AVERY
Thompson	SHELDON ALLMAN
Larker	PITT HERBERT
George	PETER BROOKS
Truman Peters	CURT CONWAY
Lily Peters	YVETTE VICKERS
Joe Scanton	GEORGE PETRIE
Donald	DAVID KENT
Dumb Billy	FRANK KILLMOND
Patron	N. CANDIDO
Cowboys	MONTY MONTANA
	JOHN M. QUIJADA
	JOHN INDRISANO
Greased Man	SY PRESCOTT
Proprietor	CARL SAXE
Announcer	ROBERT HINKLE
Myra	SHARYN HILLYER

Hud is a modern Western about a man with no morality. This powerful film features men and women who have their own peculiar ways of coping with a world they don't understand. While *Ride the High Country* blows a memorial trumpet for the old time cowboy hero, *Hud* contains a devastatingly cynical portrait of the Westerner who replaces him.

One morning young Lon Bannon is sent by his grandfather, Homer, to find his uncle, Hud, a cowboy who lives by his desires. Lon discovers Hud in the home of a woman whose husband is out of town. There is an uneasy atmosphere at the Bannon ranch. Homer is an aging man who believes the world has lost its honor, and sees the apathy and immorality of the new Western man in the form of his nephew Hud. Lon worships Hud, but remains loyal to his grandfather. Hud is attracted to Alma, their housekeeper. She in turn is simultaneously fascinated and repelled by the modern day cowboy's incredible ego. The Bannon herd has become diseased and must be destroyed. Ultimately, Hud alienates both Lon and Alma with his selfishness. Alma leaves the Bannon house. When Homer dies, Lon packs up and moves out too, leaving a confused Hud alone.

Although there is very little action in *Hud*, the story is propelled by the dynamic interplay between the characters. The theme of the killing off of the virtuous Westerner, the cattle, and the land is personified in the form of Hud, a cowboy who feels no communal attachment to the ranch or the ancestral tradition of familial ownership. While Homer has lost his way in a changing age, Hud could never feel the naked pain of that deprivation because his spiritual values are nil. He has little of substance to lose. The earth and the sky in *Hud* are different from the usual beautiful John Ford landscapes. The terrain symbolizes the real Hud, a Western Dorian Gray whose surface beauty masks a diseased soul brought out in the land.

Yet Paul Newman's Hud can be devastatingly charming, exuding that animal magnetism at will. *Hud*'s power source is Newman's portrayal of a texturally rich character possessing contradictory personality traits which run through him like a maze. The handsome stud on the outside hides the poor soul who has no friends and can't understand why Homer hates him. "You're an immoral man, Hud," states Homer. "You don't give a damn." Newman looks at Melvyn Douglas with those hurt eyes, surrounded by an insolent face. It's the countenance of a little boy whose meanness comes from spite but really agonizes in a loveless existence.

Several scenes involving Newman and Patricia Neal work particularly well on a sensual level, recalling Bogart and Bacall in their best Warner pictures of the 1940s. Hud is commencing his pursuit of Alma. "Still get the itch?" he asks impishly. "Now and then," she replies. "Let me know when it starts itchin' again." Alma smiles. The itch will be there. But Hud is impatient. He makes a strong pass. "Don't you ever ask?" "The only question I ever asked a woman is 'What time's your husband comin' home?' " Hud replies with conviction. Their relationship comes to its inevitable conclusion in *Hud*'s most explosive scene. In a drunken rage, Hud bursts into Alma's room. They fight. The heat of the night mixes with Hud's sweat-soaked T-shirt and his alcoholic breath to create a frenzied reaction in Alma. Director Martin Ritt has cameraman James Wong Howe shoot the scene in staccato-like, unevenly lit pieces. The extremely close shots are often out of focus. The actionless narrative has lost control, detonated into a rage of climactic emotions.

The killing of the diseased cattle is photographed and edited with the same jumpy technique as the rape scene. The procedure follows a rigid format. The riflemen wear slickers to catch the splattering blood. They stand over the animals moving in a pit which will be their grave. The carcasses are then strewn with lime and dirt. "It don't take long to kill things," laments Homer. "Not like it does to grow." While Hud's brutal behavior destroys any possibility of an

Patricia Neal and Brandon de Wilde

Patricia Neal and Paul Newman

intimate friendship with Alma, the extermination of the cattle may very well have taken the life out of Homer Bannon.

The land is unquestionably in the throes of decay. The skies are flat and cloudless. The earth is parched. The trees are gnarled as in a nightmare. The Bannon ranch has symbolically become Hud, as Hud has been shaped by his environment. Somewhere in the middle of the film, Homer Bannon philosophizes: "Little by little, the look of the country changes by the men we admire." *Hud* gives a striking chronicle of that change and laments the times past.

The Making of *Hud*

Martin Ritt had never directed a Western before. After years of work in theatre and television as an actor, writer, and director, Ritt made an impressive film debut with the realistic *Edge of the City* (MGM, 1957). Seven productions followed, none truly fulfilling the promise shown in his first.

Two friends of Ritt's, Irving Ravetch and his wife Harriet (Frank, Jr.), both writers, suggested the director read a novel called *Horseman's Pass* by Larry McMurtry, with the idea of making it into a movie. The book is about conflicts wrought between the generations against a backdrop of changing times. The main characters are an old man and his grandson, with a black housekeeper and other minor people fleshing out the story.

Ritt became interested in one of the ranch hands, a rather cynical cowboy. There was something about the man which fascinated the director as much as the more prominent characters. The Ravetchs were interested as well.

"We had always wanted to make a picture," Martin Ritt told me recently. They discussed taking the wisecracking anti-hero that Clark Gable always portrayed for half a film before becoming a bastion of virtue. "We said, 'Let's carry him to his logical end.' And so that character was inserted." The man called Hud would be featured in the Ravetchs' screenplay, instead of the lyrical, bittersweet relationship shared by the boy, Lon Bannon, and his grandfather, Homer. Hud was to emerge as an overaggressive, supermacho stud, a personification of the deepest implications of Gable's first-half-of-the-picture dynamics.

Little doubt existed as to who should play Hud. Everyone wanted Paul Newman. Newman liked the script and the character, but his agent felt it would be too dangerous to let his client appear on screen in a totally amoral role. "But Paul had more sense than that," Ritt recalled.

Certainly Newman took a small risk signing to play the title role in *Hud*. Although the anti-hero had been a staple of the American cinema since the advent of William S. Hart in 1914, the man Hud took such traits a step farther, off the white horse, and onto something villainous which most leading men of the early 1960s and before might not have touched.

But Newman believed in taking chances when the project warranted it. He had used a flat, growling vocal pattern in *Somebody Up There Likes Me* (MGM, 1957) to bring out the animal-like intensity of prizefighter Rocky Graziano, starred as an impotent former athlete in *Cat on a Hot Tin Roof* (MGM, 1958), and tackled comedy respectably in *Rally 'Round the Flag, Boys* (Fox, 1958), a task few performers trained at the Actors' Studio had enacted gracefully until then.

Newman and Ritt shared a mutual respect achieved on the set of *The Long Hot Summer* (Fox, 1958) and continued through *Paris Blues* (UA, 1961) and *Hemingway's Adventures of a Young Man* (Fox, 1962). So the agent's quite logical objections were overridden and Paul Newman went to work on his next assignment.

The star sent a copy of the script to Patricia Neal. Director Ritt insisted she was right for the role of the housekeeper, Alma, changed from a black woman to white. Ritt and the Ravetchs believed the switch necessary to maintain a proper focus on Hud. The cowboy's dark nature worried Paramount and Newman's agent. The writers were taking a chance in making him so unsympathetic. The thrust of the film would have to concentrate on understanding Hud's motivations and evoking the tragic price his immorality has taken on his family and himself. There seemed to be no place to develop a full romance between a white man and a black woman in 1962 Texas.

Ritt also wanted Patricia Neal to play Alma. He explained his reasons for me. "She'd been in Hollywood for some time, in quite a few films—nothing nearly as good as this. But I had seen her on Broadway, and knew she was really a first class actress. And when this part came along and I needed that kind of wry, American humor, I didn't know where else to go. As a matter of fact a similar part came up in a film I did called *Hombre* (Fox, 1967). I went to England to get Diane Cilento. It's a tough kind of character. We have more of those ladies now. We have [Louise] Fletcher, Ellen Burstyn. But we didn't have them then. Maybe it wasn't the time. Pat was the only one I knew. That's how she got the part. I had seen her in *Another Part of the Forest* in New York. I did anything to get her in the part. I agreed to let her go to England to see her family. I did everything. I knew she would be marvelous."

The actress decided to portray Alma. She'd done only a few films in the last half-dozen years. Feeling her duty was to husband

Ronald Dahl and her children, the performer only accepted a role when it really suited her. Alma fit her perfectly. The housekeeper was a warm, witty woman, who could turn tough or soft like a chameleon when the occasion demanded. Parts in *A Face in the Crowd* (Warner Bros., 1957) and *Breakfast at Tiffany's* (Paramount, 1961) were basically solid, but she had yet to realize the potential indicated in *The Fountainhead* (Warner Bros., 1949) and *The Breaking Point* (Warner Bros., 1950). *Hud* gave her the chance.

As the director indicated, Patricia Neal would only do *Hud* if allowed to travel back and forth to her family. She spent four weeks shooting, then went home for three, and returned for another four in Hollywood. Although she was pleased with the production, her favorite bit ended on the cutting room floor. Lon comes to her cabin and asks what life is all about. "Honey," she says, "you'll just have to ask someone else." That scene would have defined Alma as a very positive woman who realized there was much she would never know: this is the source of her wisdom. The feeling persists throughout that Alma is by far the smartest person living on the Bannon ranch, and therefore a moment with such an obvious message, however well played, seems unnecessary.

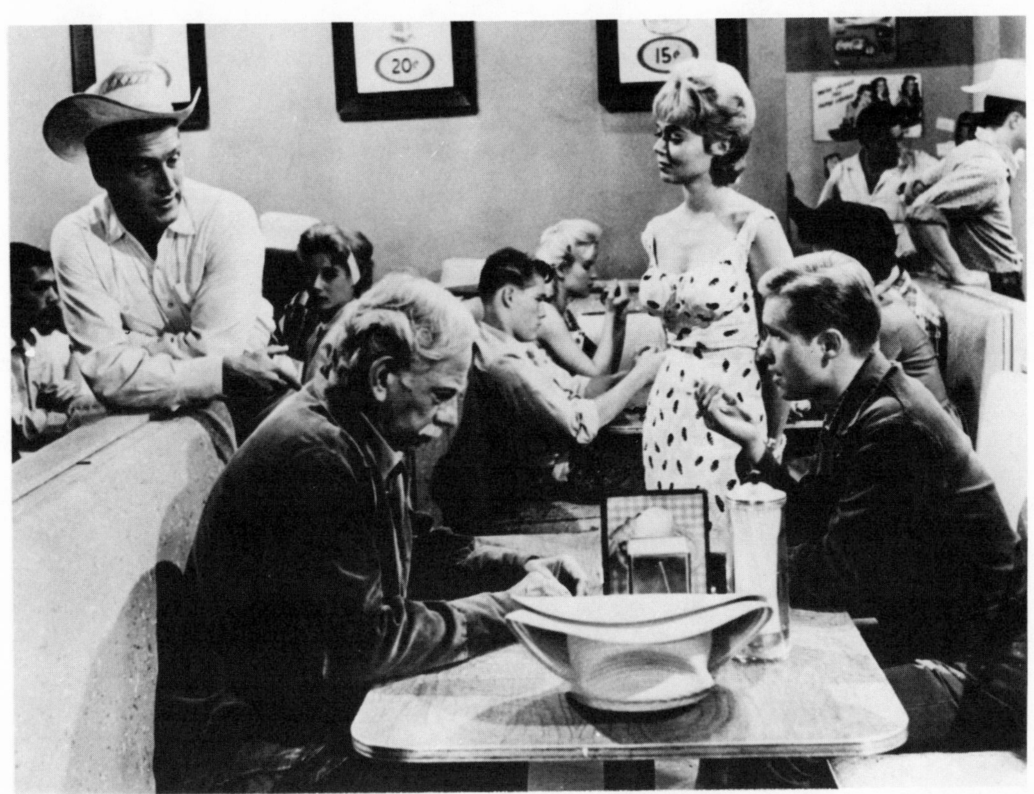

Paul Newman, Melvyn Douglas, and Brandon de Wilde

Not that *Hud* was made in the cutting room, or on the set either. "Once a script was written, we didn't take too much liberty with it," Ritt said. "I don't do that generally. If I have good writers, they write much better than I could." As a co-producer, he certainly possessed the power to make changes, so it was the director's good sense which told him to shoot the material as written. Martin Ritt is a filmmaker who realizes the significance of good co-workers—cameramen, writers, actors. The man who has performed many jobs in theatre and film doesn't believe all a director's films should be respected simply because they were made by the same man. This may seem an obvious point, but the auteur theory of cinema which reached its zenith in the 1960s and early 70s had and still has proponents who sometimes go overboard in praising one man's work.

Yet Ritt insisted on executing *Hud* the way it was conceived, from script, to cinematography, to casting. He fought to have Melvyn Douglas essay the part of Homer Bannon. Douglas had returned to the screen after a decade's absence to perform a supporting role of an old sailmaker in *Billy Budd* (Allied Artists, 1962). The combination of a heart condition which made it difficult for studios to insure him and the personal desire to slow down made Douglas an infrequently seen figure on screen. Despite the veteran's fine performance in *Billy Budd* and demonstrated ability to stay healthy during production, Paramount nevertheless balked at signing him.

"I don't know how tough that really was," the director commented as to whether or not Douglas' physical condition made the studio wary of using him. "But I did want him very much. I feel very strong about the actors I want. I know how important they are to a film. And I wanted him. There was some resistance. Whether it was his heart, or whether they'd felt he'd had it, who the hell knows. You never know what the studios really mean anyway. And you never get a straight answer. You just have to stick to your guns and get what you want."

Ritt chose veteran James Wong Howe to be the director of photography for *Hud*, another selection which worked out brilliantly. Ritt's camera style has never been obtrustive. He doesn't like such attention-getting devices as the zoom lens. The films of Martin Ritt are at their best in the realist tradition which developed in Hollywood after World War II. *Edge of the City, Hud,* and *The Spy Who Came in from the Cold* (Paramount, 1965) are three graphic, honest depictions of institutions and people. James Wong Howe understood what the director sought. The cameraman had lensed *Body and Soul* (UA, 1947), *The Rose Tattoo* (Paramount, 1955), *Sweet Smell of Success* (UA, 1957), and *The Last Angry Man* (Columbia, 1959) in that fashion.

There were few differences of opinion between Ritt and Howe.

The first came quickly. When Howe came onto the project, Ritt had already taken some footage of flat, cloudless skies and asked the cameraman if he could double print in some clouds. Howe and Ritt discussed the situation, and decided to give *Hud* a stark look. Whenever Howe saw clouds on location, he put a filter on the lens to remove them from the image. The sky photographed very light that way.

Ritt recalled his relationship with Howe. "There was no real conflict. What happened was that Howe wasn't a man who could read scripts and understand a picture immediately. He had to get a feel of the picture. So when he read the script I don't think he totally understood the film. But after we were shooting about a week he understood.

"Because we felt we had to have a sense of space, most of the film had to be back-lit, in terms of the exteriors too. So we kept chasing the light in those terms and once he caught on to that there was nobody better than he. We never had any conflict about it. It's just that I don't think Jimmy totally understood that at the beginning of the film, and maybe I didn't either. But it became clear to us that we needed that soon after we started the film and then we began to search for it."

And search they did. With a firm concept the crew strove more readily to obtain the effect needed, no matter how long it took. Howe spent more than eight mornings, for instance, trying to get the first shot of the truck on the horizon.

"The country that we shot was a kind of high plateau," Ritt informed me, "and the natives very often say that there's nothing between here and the North Pole but barbed-wire fence." It was exactly what he wanted. "In terms of the execution of the cattle sequence, in terms of all the big exteriors, I had a sense that I needed that real sense of space from the beginning."

Under Ritt's guidance, Howe made many creative suggestions. "In all the personal scenes, as I always do, I staged them first. And that dictates how you're going to shoot. In other words, I don't arbitrarily decide where I'm going to put the camera, and then put actors in, because I don't want to inhibit any creative impulse that an actor might have. And if I think he's right, I'll let him go. Then I would adjust to that."

The flexibility applied to cameramen as well. There was one shot Howe particularly liked because he was free to solve a tricky problem. Paul Newman and Brandon de Wilde were standing near a water trough. Both were drunk. Howe employed incandescent lights and took condensers out of the interior arcs to obtain sharper shadows.

This is exactly the kind of thinking Ritt wanted. "He was helpful to me on certain things in other films. For instance, in *The Molly Maguires* (Paramount, 1970), when I didn't have clouds in the sky he painted them in in a way that I had never seen a cameraman do. He used vasoline in a certain way on his lenses. He was a very creative guy. And a lovely man, although he always had trouble with crews. But we complemented each other perfectly because he understood that I knew what I wanted, and that I knew my script, and that I knew the actors, and that I would depend on him for a lot of the physical life of the picture."

Hud took about eight weeks to shoot, plus time in the editing room. Once the casting was done, and a unified look for the production defined, things proceeded relatively smoothly. Everyone involved thought *Hud* to be a fine film. Yet other Hollywoodians were skeptical about its box-office potential.

Martin Ritt knew he had a good picture. But he didn't expect audiences to sympathize with the plight of a macho cowboy and certainly could not foresee young people responding positively to Hud. "I must admit I was surprised by the way the young audience responded to him. They ended up supporting him. They saw something in him they identified with."

Perhaps the director expected male viewers to empathize with a person who was roughly their age. For the young, there was Brandon de Wilde as the confused Lon, caught between a moral, stern, but sensitive, grandfather and the more readily appealing, but callous, Uncle Hud. Those gradually slipping into middle age might better understand the problems of Homer Bannon, a rancher whose world is transforming into a space whose rules he doesn't understand. Women could see some of their questions about relating to men and society answered in the character of Alma. At one point, Patricia Neal tells de Wilde that she had no idea of what motivates people. Yet Alma has that special knowledge of self, of right and wrong in her own life, which gives her the strength to resist Hud's advances and to leave the ranch to get away from him. She has maintained her integrity as a woman and provided a sound role model.

But Paul Newman's Hud elicited the most sympathy.

"They [young people] liked him," Martin Ritt said. "If I had really properly understood that, perhaps I would have known that Haight-Ashbury was coming, and the terrible sixties were going to erupt. Because they were really very cynical, and they had many reasons to be that way of course. Yes, I was surprised. I didn't have any high regard for Hud, as a human being.

"I went through the McCarthy period . . . and if it finally came down to dramatizing why people acted well and why people acted badly, I feel always that people acted badly because they followed

Paul Newman

their appetites, and their appetites controlled them. And that's what Hud did. Hud followed his appetite all the time. He had no morality, and therefore there was no censoring his appetite. All people who follow only their appetite finally are inhuman and indecent. And if your appetite leads you into areas of immorality—and I'm not even talking about it sexually at all, I'm talking about inhumanly—forget the rest of the world, whatever it is. That's the basis of Hud. Hud was a man who believed that what was good for him was the only thing that was important. Nobody else in the world mattered. And he could not understand that anybody had any other kind of morality. And at the end where he proffered friendship to the young boy, and the boy said no, he more or less said to the boy, 'What do you know? You'll be back on your knees for a handout.' That's really what he felt."

Nothing bears out the strength of *Hud* more than the fact that an audience could feel for such a brutishly self-involved person.

Hud's release prompted an avalanche of generally enthusiastic reviews:

New York Mirror, Justin Gilbert:

Hud is so many things—morality screenplay, graphic Americana, a study of today's sex mores and powerful drama—that it can only be labelled the best American-made movie seen this year. . . . The major credit for the incredibly arresting, earnest and commanding drama, full of reckless passions and moral persuasion, belongs to Martin Ritt, who directed and co-produced it. . . . From the stunning screenplay fashioned by Ritt and Harriet Frank, Jr., he has at last wrought a film that marks the measure of his worth.

Esquire, Dwight MacDonald:

. . . on the international scale *Hud* doesn't weigh much. The uncompromising realism is mostly in veteran James Wong Howe's photography, which does give an unretouched picture of the arid, scrubby landscapes of West Texas, its neon squalid towns and its cheap clapboard houses, belligerently charmless inside and out.

New York Morning Telegraph, Leo Mishkin:

Paul Newman and Melvyn Douglas are matched toe-to-toe in their slugging match between youth and age; Brandon de Wilde appears once again in his now familiar role of a hero-worshipping teenager with doubts beginning to form, and Patricia Neal is a raspy-voiced, slatternly, and utterly convincing hired girl in one of the most vivid roles in her career. . . . You may find some faults in the way *Hud* tells its story, but you'll be so tightly held by the people herein, and the way the speakers behave, you'll hardly notice it.

Washington Post, Richard L. Loe:

Hud is an extraordinarily powerful, provocative movie. Fine performances, a probing script, and exceptional atmosphere distinguish the tale of modern Texas.

Village Voice, Andrew Sarris:

The whole film, in fact, displays that hungover look which is almost invariably confused with honest realism. Hence the visual correlative of decadence is dust, even though Texas was dusty long before the Alamo. . . . Frankly, I thought the real villain of *Hud* was the self-righteous father, possibly because Melvyn Douglas gave the worst performance.

Hud was tremendously successful in its initial run and was re-released by Paramount several years later. Advertisements referred to the title character as "The Man with the Barbed Wire Soul," and offered a picture of an insolent-looking Paul Newman to prove its point.

Hud won three major Oscars. Patricia Neal capped her career by winning the award for Best Actress, Melvyn Douglas began a new screen life by being named Best Supporting Actor, and James Wong Howe copped the prize for Best Cinematography of a black-and-white film. Many people were annoyed that Douglas didn't get nominated as Best Actor—he was second-billed to Newman—not to mention that Newman, Ritt, nor the film *Hud* failed to win anything. But it was the year of *Tom Jones.* The bawdy adaptation of Henry Fielding's novel was named Best Film.

However, *Hud* placed as one of the ten best films of 1963 by *Film Daily* and the National Board of Review. Neal and Douglas were honored by the Board for their performances. Neal also received an award as Best Actress from the New York Film Critics.

Hud stands out as one of the best Westerns of the 1960s. As a cinema depiction of the modern West, it has yet to be topped and ranks with *The Lusty Men* (RKO, 1952), *The Misfits, Lonely Are the Brave* (Universal, 1962), and *Junior Bonner* (Cinerama, 1973) as a fascinating study of the 20th-century cowboy, a figure often alienated from society, off in his own world, whether he knows it or not. Hud Bannon doesn't know it. The shadow of Hud's affliction is reflected brilliantly in Martin Ritt's film, from the stark, cold countryside to the anxiety the Westerner causes all around him.

Lee Van Cleef
and
Klaus Kinski

Lee Van Cleef
and
Clint Eastwood

CHAPTER TWENTY-FOUR

For a Few Dollars More

Year Released: 1965 (1967 in United States)
Studio: United Artists
Producer: Alberto Grimaldi, for PEA, Arturo Gonzales, and Constantin Film
Director: Sergio Leone
Screenplay: Sergio Leone, Luciano Vincenzoni
Cinematography: Massimo Dallamano
Music: Ennio Morricone
Art Director: Carlo Simi
Editor: Alabiso Serralonga, Giorgio Serralonga
Assistant Director: Tonino Valerii
Costumes: Carlo Simi
Color, 130 minutes

Cast:

Man With No Name	CLINT EASTWOOD
Colonel Mortimer	LEE VAN CLEEF
Indio	GIAN MARIA VOLONTE
Old Man	JOSE EGGER
Colonel's Sister	ROSEMARY DEXTER
Hotel Manager's Wife	MARA KRUP
The Hunchback	KLAUS KINSKI
First Man	MARIO BREGA
Second Man	ALDO SAMBREL
Third Man	LUIGI PISTILLI
Fourth Man	BENITO STEFANELLI

For a Few Dollars More, like its predecessor *A Fistful of Dollars,* examines Western myths in a framework which runs the gamut between outright parody to the squint-eyed seriousness of two men squaring off for a gunfight. Yet there is more life, more tension, and a bigger plot in *For a Few Dollars More.*

A cowboy, riding across the plains, is shot off his horse. Smoke from the murder weapon forms into letters. A title reads, "When life had no value, death sometimes had a price. That is when the bounty hunter appeared." Colonel Mortimer is a passenger on a train. The conductor informs him they are not scheduled to stop at Mortimer's destination. "This train'll stop at Tucomcari," the Colonel states, then proceeds to pull the emergency cord. The next image shows the Colonel leading his horse down a plank and into the station. Soon he discovers the whereabouts of his next bounty. Mortimer calmly slides a wanted poster under the door to the hotel room where the bandit is making love. The hunter then kicks the door open, to find that the outlaw has fled out a window. "Pardon me ma'am," he says politely to the startled woman. The Colonel nonchalantly walks down the stairs, pulls out a sawed off rifle, and shoots the quarry as he attempts to escape.

The Man With No Name rides into town. He corners his wanted man in a saloon, a gunfight ensues, and the outlaw is killed. While watching the mechanics of a bank robbery, the bounty hunters discover each other. The Man With No Name and Mortimer decide to work together. The nameless gunman will infiltrate the gang of the notorious bandit Indio. It is later revealed that Indio had murdered the Colonel's sister and brother-in-law years earlier. Mortimer possesses one of two watches with a chime and photo of his sister. Indio has the other one. After a while, the Man With No Name's cover is blown. Mortimer comes to his rescue. The unnamed hunter returns the favor by getting the drop on Indio, who was about to kill the Colonel. Following a fierce battle, Indio is the only surviving criminal. As the bounty man "umpires" the showdown, the Colonel beats Indio to the draw. With justice served, Mortimer leaves the rewards for the entire gang to his partner.

For a Few Dollars More isn't quite complex enough to be a satire on the Western. The film certainly doesn't point up the failings of the genre, characters, or stories. It revels in them, but with a sense of humor. Director Sergio Leone, long an admirer of Hollywood's cowboy movies, has corraled all the melodrama inherent in the oater since its earliest cinema days. The larger-than-life Westerners are exemplified by the Man With No Name, the tall, gaunt, ruffled, laconic figure who lets his guns do the talking. He can shoot down as many as half a dozen men at one time (as in *A Fistful of Dollars*), without batting an eye or losing the ash at the end of his cheroot. Compared with the anonymous gunfighter, Colonel Mortimer is a Socrates of the prairie. The retired officer is relatively easygoing and wise, wasting few words or body movements, and counsels his partner in the ways of the criminal mind. When it counts, both men are equal on the field of hunting. And they do need each other. That is a dose of humanity which provides a source of conflict missing in *A Fistful of Dollars*.

The scene which capsulizes their friction and sums up Leone's serio-comic attitude toward his tale of two legends occurs in a duel of marksmanship. One evening, they stand on the street, about to face each other in a gunfight, whose outcome will decide which man hunts the outlaws. To demonstrate the superior fire power of his sawed-off rifle, Mortimer shoots the opposition's hat all over the dusty street. As though in a contest, the Man With No Name matches his feat. They drive to distraction an old Chinese who has been hired by the Colonel to transport the other gunfighter's belongings to the station. "Take it to the station," Mortimer commands. "Take it back," the other counters. The aging Oriental finally runs away screaming.

Indio is a legend of another sort. His character is much more remote than the men who pursue him. The bandit spends an enormous amount of time in contemplation, a soft period mellowed by marijuana. In a flashback, he recalls seeing a pair of lovers. Against the music of the watch, Leone frames Indio's longing face peering through a delicate window coated with rain. The husband runs for a gun but is shot down. The moment has the far-away feel of a dream. This is Indio, with his mask of a reflective man, almost a philosopher, his yearnings those of a little boy, and his mind that of a psychotic. Indio is perhaps the most fascinating villain in the Westerns of Sergio Leone. The bandit's presence gives *For a Few Dollars More* a strong three-way clash absent in Leone's previous Western. The same triangle is slightly de-emphasized later by the magnificent spectacle in *The Good, the Bad, and the Ugly* (UA, 1968) and *Once Upon a Time in the West* (Paramount, 1969).

The climactic gunfight between Mortimer and Indio, as refereed by the Man With No Name, contains all the excitement of duels of Westerns past. This is where Leone leaves the parody and aims for the heart of the genre. Along with the battle in *The Good, the Bad, and the Ugly*, the final contest here epitomizes Leone's hard, no-nonsense approach to the most trite of structural components of the oater. With the gentle chimes of the watch playing, Leone cuts between close-ups of the men, to their guns, nervous hands, faces, and extremely close shots of anxious eyes, another Leone trademark. When the chime runs out, the guns blaze.

For a Few Dollars More, as the second of the three Westerns fea-

Lee Van Cleef

Lee Van Cleef, Clint Eastwood, and Gian Maria Volonte

turing the Man With No Name, is not surprisingly in the middle ground between *A Fistful of Dollars* and *The Good, the Bad, and the Ugly*. It has the atmospheric reality, ostentatious violence, and grim humor of the first woven into a richer plot. *For a Few Dollars More* lacks the epic background of the Civil War in Leone's third Western, and, as such, features a more perfect balance of the filmmaker's view of frontier history and legends, along with the bloodletting and comedy which are parts of the formula.

The Making of *For a Few Dollars More*

Sergio Leone was ready to direct another Western. He had just led Clint Eastwood to stardom the summer before in *A Fistful of Dollars*, a film whose title grossly underestimated its box-office value. Leone, whose first Western recorded huge profits all over Europe and America, deserves much credit not only for extending the parameters of the cowboy movie in the 1960s but also for creating a new screen sub-genre, the "Spaghetti Western." The success of his films starring Clint Eastwood proved that realistic oaters could be made on foreign soil and be popular with American audiences. He showed the genre might beautifully embrace the ironies, abstract quality, and humor of the work of modern masters such as Federico Fellini and Michelangelo Antonioni.

Leone's cinema background had prepared him for making Westerns. He had already worked on almost sixty films, assisting notable American filmmakers Fred Zinnemann, William Wyler, Raoul Walsh, and Robert Wise when they shot in Italy. In 1960, he directed *The Colossus of Rhodes*, one of the most intelligent of the hordes of Italian muscleman epics churned out in the last two decades.

Then Leone decided to do a Western trilogy. In the manner that Martin Ritt's *The Outrage* came from Kurosawa's *Rashomon* (1951) and John Sturges' *The Magnificent Seven* was reworked from Kurosawa's *The Seven Samurai* (1956), *A Fistful of Dollars* was taken from another Kurosawa Japanese film, *Yojimbo* (1962), itself based on a detective story. These roots were often used as the basis for criticism of the Westerns when they were released in this country. It was somehow deemed dishonorable to unofficially utilize material from another film, especially a classic, for what some of the director's detractors must have labelled "just another Western." Of course, the criticism doesn't take into account the numerous times Hollywood studios borrowed stories in part or whole from previous productions, or remade a basic property and released it with a new title and a few alterations. Sometimes a better movie resulted, sometimes not. In this case, it is not a matter of quality, as *Yojimbo* and the "Dollars" Westerns are all unique, exciting works of art. Leone took similar plot lines and, to paraphrase Ezra Pound when the poet spoke of the duty of his generation of literary writers, made them new again. And the filmmaker accomplished this difficult task by recycling the very characters which had become worn-out fixtures in the Western.

Sergio Leone wanted to film the birth of America. He sent scenarist Luciano Vincenzoni to research the American West. Vincenzoni studied reams of frontier newspapers of the 1880s, the time when the bounty hunter was a potent force in the wilderness, and discovered that many Westerners did not bear the slightest resemblance to cowboys depicted on the movie screen. The real gunslingers, sheriffs, bounty hunters, goldminers, and assorted wanderers usually looked as if they were carved out of rawhide. Their wardrobe was often bland and ill-fitting.

Leone believed the 19th-century Americans had more character in their faces than his actors. But what faces on those actors! The cast of *For a Few Dollars More* looks like it was recruited from a Fellini movie, or picked out of a police line-up. The figures of Clint Eastwood, Lee Van Cleef, Gian Maria Volonte, Klaus Kinski, Mario Brega, and the others could very well be the stuff of nightmares or the work of a sculptor creating a museum of frontier faces.

Eastwood, the handsomest of the leading actors in the Western, looks like a hermit. With the week-old beard, the squinted eyes, the cigar stuck in his mouth like a tree stump to earth, the wrinkles formed not so much by age but by the sun and a strenuous, violence-hewn lifestyle, the Man With No Name tells his story with his face. Lee Van Cleef, with the nose of an eagle and the eyes of a vulture, instills fear when his bony countenance freezes into a penetrating stare. His character is a man determined to capture the outlaw Indio, who murdered Colonel Mortimer's sister and brother-in-law so many years before. As Indio, Gian Maria Volonte lives in a drug-smeared world of murder and theft and drinking and laughing and sex. When Volonte goes off on a cannabis-induced dream he might as well be catatonic. The grubby face staring into space is haunted by so many memories. Two of Indio's men, played by Klaus Kinski and Mario Brega, seem straight out of a Tod Browning scenario. Kinski with the skull-face and marble-eyes, sneering at the world with every move, and Brega with his girth, looking like he is about to burst his guts every time he swaggers or beats someone senseless, lurk in the background of Leone's gallery of moving Western portraits.

It was natural for the director to want Clint Eastwood to repeat his role as the nameless bounty hunter of *A Fistful of Dollars*. The actor happily agreed to do a sequel to the production which would make him an international star. Prior to working with Leone, Eastwood's main credit was eight years as co-star of the Western teleseries "Rawhide," which aired for a total of 250 viewing hours. He had appeared in small roles in ten films between 1955 and 1958 as a Universal contract player before "Rawhide" came along. Then Leone followed with an offer of $15,000 to star as an unkempt man of the West. By the time of *For a Few Dollars More*, Eastwood's fee reflected the title. He earned $50,000 for the second appearance in the saddle of an Italian oater.

Leone originally sought Henry Fonda to play Colonel Mortimer, who teams up with Eastwood to track down Indio and his gang. Fonda's agent in Italy apparently didn't think the project worth mentioning to his client, or forgot about it, and therefore Leone looked elsewhere.

When Fonda discovered Leone had asked for his services, it was too late. Lee Van Cleef had signed for the role. Fonda finally obtained what turned out to be one of the most memorable parts of his later career as the ruthless gunfighter in Leone's *Once Upon a Time in the West*. Even after the production on that film began, the veteran actor was highly appreciative of Leone's very strong directorial personality. Because his intuition was usually correct, Sergio Leone invariably got what he wanted. He had seen Van Cleef in a number of supporting roles in Westerns over the years, including *High Noon*, in which he was one of the outlaws out to gun down Gary Cooper, and *The Bravados* (Fox, 1958). So in 1965 Leone came to America to interview Van Cleef. The director could hardly speak English, but managed to communicate his desire that Van Cleef portray Mortimer. Perhaps part of the reason rested on the actor's professional stamina. Between his motion picture debut in *High Noon* in 1952 and *For a Few Dollars More* thirteen years

Lee Van Cleef, Clint Eastwood, and Gian Maria Volonte

later, Van Cleef had performed (usually as the villain) in fifty-seven films, thirty-eight of which were Westerns. In 1959, Van Cleef had lost his left kneecap in an automobile accident and doctors told him he'd never ride a horse again. The blow which could have seriously damaged his career turned out to be nothing more than a glancing shot. The actor was back in the saddle within six months. Yet as the 1960s progressed, he found himself cast in fewer and fewer productions, perhaps because of overexposure. Van Cleef's face was striking enough for Leone to put him in a cast of unusually endowed men and women in a film which would contain every possible Western stereotype. By 1965, Van Cleef qualified as the cliche of the genre, although at the time Leone spoke with him the actor was living on unemployment, television residuals, and his wife's salary as an employee of IBM.

With a cast and crew set, Leone went to work filming *For a Few Dollars More* in 1965, with a budget of $550,000 as opposed to the mere $80,000 he'd had to make *A Fistful of Dollars* the year before. One of the most important carryovers would be the number of people shot down by the Man With No Name. The Western's distributors felt many gun battles were an essential ingredient in the picture's success.

While the interiors were lensed at Cinecitta in Rome, the rest of the production took place in a series of villages, constructed near Rome, in Madrid and Almeria, Spain. The company was an international mix. Eastwood and Van Cleef came from America, Klaus Kinski was from Germany, and Leone, Volonte, Brega, and many others represented Italy. And of course there were many Spaniards working behind the scenes. Naturally a visitor to the set on any day would likely be bombarded with people speaking many different languages and dialects, all of which presented a problem during the filming. How was Leone going to relay his instructions to the actors and crew? Somehow the director understood enough of each language to convey instructions. But the actors spoke their lines in their native tongues. There was comparatively little dialogue to be learned, although it contained more than *A Fistful of Dollars*. A scene in *For a Few Dollars More* sometimes featured as many as five different languages as the cameras rolled. Leone had to make sure those speaking English, Italian, Spanish, German, and even Greek read their lines correctly, and that the actors who listened appeared to understand the conversation! After the Western was completed, the soundtrack was dubbed in the language of the country in which the film was to be shown.

Perhaps the inherent difficulty of trying to direct a picture in a half-dozen languages became easier due to the strength of Leone's vision. No doubt existed about the theme of the movie, its plot, and its characters. The filmmaker felt the bounty hunter of the 1880s was one of the most dangerous of men. Leone saw his character as a modern myth, a man who dresses and acts strangely. He has no friends and only a few living enemies. Although the director exaggerated the significance of his main character in that he was rooted in the basic anti-hero which had been a force in cinema Western lore since William S. Hart, there was little question that the Man With No Name brought that kind of protagonist farther into the realm of mythology than most. Leone's ironic treatment of the subject gave the character a fresh air.

Even though he loved Westerns, Sergio Leone made the "Dollars" productions something of a comment on the political pessimism in his native Italy. To Leone, the political situation in his country is an absurdity. He conceded that the world shared the same problems, but that in Italy they are far worse. An excessive amount of compromise caused Italy's troubles. After living with Fascism for years, Leone felt his country might very well have to face that same situation once again. As an artist, he chose to create fables, tales of legendary giants to combat the evil. He picked the American West because he considered Italian political films to be too nationalistic, with little impact elsewhere. A film such as Elio Petri's *Investigation of a Citizen Above Suspicion* (1970) had small significance elsewhere in the world.

Clint Eastwood believed the Man With No Name shared some of the characteristics of James Bond, in that both creations were real super heroes. Eastwood considered the gunfighter only a breath away from the traditional villain. Lee Van Cleef concurred.

With *For a Few Dollars More*, Sergio Leone felt that he had taken on an important theme for the first time. Like director Howard Hawks, Leone was fascinated with the ways in which a friendship between two men develops and how it can affect their lives, and he particularly cared about the generational aspect of the relationship. The Man With No Name was somewhere in his thirties, Colonel Mortimer fifteen or twenty years older.

The director believed he returned the traditional flashback to its former eminence with the lyrical scenes set in the past in the second part of the Western trilogy. While it is certainly true that Leone used the flashback technique well, he can hardly be credited with rediscovering the cinema's ability to have characters relive moments from times past. If anything, Leone's contribution was to make good use of this method of playing with time, even though French director Alain Resnais has explored time and memory in more original ways.

For a Few Dollars More made its European debut in 1965. It was not seen in the United States until 1967, soon after the highly successful run of *A Fistful of Dollars*. By then Leone and Eastwood were at work on *The Good, the Bad, and the Ugly*.

THE MAN WITH NO NAME IS BACK . . .
. . . THE MAN IN BLACK IS WAITING! warned a poster.

As if one wasn't enough . . . as if death needed a double!
It's the second motion picture of its kind!
It won't be the last!

Reviewers were not particularly impressed:

Films and Filming, Richard Davis:
The return of the anti-hero to end all anti-heroes. Come to that he deserves too: he is so completely negative and undeveloped in character, a mere sop for the gratuitous violence beloved by the makers of these bastardized Westerns, that the fashion for anti-heroism might well play itself out, exhausted by misuse.

London Observer, Penelope Mortimer:
From the first whining bullet to the last this film is a prodigious, straight-faced hoax. As such, with its howling, manic music, its startling photography, its operatic direction by Sergio Leone, it should be extremely funny, in the same way that the Bond films, seen through half of a sane eye, are extremely funny. . . . But no such luck.

New York Daily News, Ann Guarino, 2½ stars:
More than two dozen people get killed in one way or another, so the cast is large. Sets have an empty look and seemed to be as lightly constructed as the plot.

New York Times, Bosley Crowther:
But the fact that this film is constructed to endorse this exercise of murderers, to emphasize killer bravado and generate glee in frantic manifestations of death is, to my mind, a sharp indictment of it as so-called entertainment in this day.

Washington Post, Richard L. Loe:
Somehow, though there are some snickers at Western absurdities, the "Dollar" films don't come out as satires. They come out as Europeans' ideas of what our West was like and, concomitantly, what we are like. I don't know which is sorrier, their notion of us or their pitiable ignorance.

Sergio Leone tried to answer criticisms that his characters were undeveloped by countering that the West was full of simple men whose psychology was not as complex as some present-day filmmakers try to illustrate. The director didn't feel Westerners should be understood by modern standards, but by their own. This notion is akin to the statements made by Fellini about his *Satyricon*, a sensual film set in Roman times.

Lee Van Cleef believed it absolutely essential that violence on screen be true to life. Perhaps this is a variation on Sam Peckinpah's thesis that illustrating graphic bloodletting is in its way an anti-violence statement, because the viewer becomes sickened at what appears on film. Van Cleef also felt *For a Few Dollars More* added a welcome tongue-in-cheek air to the standard horse opera.

Clint Eastwood knew the audience somehow identified with the Man With No Name. Since his personality featured few outstanding characteristics, a moviegoer could pretty much establish the motivations for the gunfighter. The bounty hunter could be practically anyone.

A Fistful of Dollars grossed $8,500,000 as did *For a Few Dollars More. The Good, the Bad, and the Ugly* made $10,000,000 in domestic distributors' rentals.

The people who made *For a Few Dollars More* profited immensely from their association with the Western. Sergio Leone went on to direct a stunning epic about the growth of the West in *Once Upon a Time in the West*, which received many negative reviews, but has since become respected as a brilliant exploration of frontier myths and realities.

Clint Eastwood's fee for *The Good, the Bad, and the Ugly* was $250,000 plus a percentage of the profits, a far figure from the relatively paltry $15,000 he received for *A Fistful of Dollars*. Eastwood went on to make $20,000,000 for United Artists. He received $400,000 along with a twenty-five percent of the gross for his first starring American Western, *Hang 'Em High* (1968), under the direction of Ted Post, a friend from their TV "Rawhide" days. The star has since directed many of his own pictures for his own Malpaso Productions.

Lee Van Cleef co-starred again with Eastwood in *The Good, the Bad, and the Ugly*. The veteran supporting actor-turned-leading man then was top-billed in a solo effort, *The Big Gundown* (1967), another popular Spaghetti Western which grossed over $2,000,000 in America. After that, Van Cleef was named one of the five most popular actors in Europe. Currently the actor can command about $300,000 per film and a percentage of the profits.

For a Few Dollars More was the second part of Sergio Leone's three-sectioned endeavor to change the face of the movie Western. He succeeded in electrifying the genre with new life and making stars out of two of the most unlikely candidates to ride the celluloid range of Hart and Wayne.

Lee Marvin and
Burt Lancaster

Lee Marvin,
Claudia Cardinale,
Robert Ryan, and
Woody Strode

CHAPTER TWENTY-FIVE

The Professionals

Year Released: 1966
Studio: Columbia
Producer: Richard Brooks
Director: Richard Brooks
Screenplay: Richard Brooks, based on the novel *A Mule for the Marquesa* by Frank O'Rourke
Cinematography: Conrad Hall
Music: Maurice Jarre
Art Director: Edward S. Haworth
Editor: Peter Zinner
Assistant Director: Tom Shaw
Set Decorator: Frank Tuttle
Makup: Robert Schiffer
Wardrobe: Jack Martell
Sound: Charles J. Rice, William Randall, Jr., Jack Haynes
Special Effects: Willis Cook
Color, 117 minutes

Cast:

Bill Dolworth	BURT LANCASTER
Henry Rico Farden	LEE MARVIN
Hans Ehrengard	ROBERT RYAN
Captain Jesus Raza	JACK PALANCE
Maria Grant	CLAUDIA CARDINALE
J. W. Grant	RALPH BELLAMY
Jacob Sharp	WOODY STRODE

Ortega	JOE DE SANTIS
Fierro	RAFAEL BERTRAND
Padilla	JORGE MARTINEZ DE HOYOS
Chiquita	MARIA GOMEZ
Revolutionaries	JOSE CHAVEZ
	CARLOS ROMERO
Banker	VAUGHN TAYLOR
Bandits	ROBERT CONTRERAS
	DON CARLOS
Mexican Girl	ELIZABETH CAMPBELL
Mexican Servant	JOHN LOPEZ
Hooper	DARWIN LAMB
Man at Door	DIRK EVANS
Sheriff	JOHN McKEE
The Prisoner	EDDIE LITTLE SKY
Lady	LEIGH CHAPMAN
Deputy Sheriff	PHIL PARSLOW
Bits	FOSTER HOOD
	HENRY O'BRIEN
	DAVE CADIENTE
	VINCE CADIENTE

Disillusionment with the American dream has been a popular theme in Hollywood for the past twenty years. From *A Face in the Crowd* (Warner Bros., 1957) through *Easy Rider* (Columbia, 1969), *The Godfather* (Paramount, 1972), and beyond, the rich and powerful are often depicted as irreversibly corrupted. The Western long has been a fertile genre for developing such notions, as the frontier agonized in the throes of the transformation from the wilderness to a strong, complex industrial society where business motives were more enigmatic than the plowing of the land. It is in this state of change that the conflicting lifestyles can be explored.

The Professionals reflects a distaste for the omnipotence of the wealthy. In a violence-hewn but entertaining narrative, the film promotes the jousting of men who face each other in a straightforward manner, even though they may utilize trickery and deceit. It is all part of their shared game plan.

Powerful rancher J. W. Grant hires trouble-shooting mercenary Henry Rico Farden to rescue his wife, Maria, who has been kidnapped by Captain Jesus Raza, a Mexican revolutionary who happens to have been a former saddle partner of Farden and Bill Dolworth. Along with Farden and Dolworth, Grant employs Hans Ehrengard and Jacob Sharp to form a team of professionals for the mission. When hired men ultimately reach Raza's camp and take him prisoner, they realize the bandit leader and Maria Grant are lovers. Maria actually has prostituted herself by marrying the rancher in order to raise money for Raza's revolution. On the way back, some of the professionals express doubts about handing over Maria and Raza to Grant and, at the exchange site, Grant's callous attitude toward Maria and the wounded bandit prompts the men to release what they have come to understand are two captives.

The major characters in *The Professionals* are built on ideals. As a revolutionary in Mexico, Bill Dolworth was in love with the *idea* of revolution, not the day-by-day struggle for change. Raza is a practical fighter for freedom. He masterminds the scheme to get money for arms by having Maria marry Grant. Although she has corrupted herself, it is to bring her ideals to fruition. Farden is an honorable man looking to break with his past. J. W. Grant believes money is power.

Producer/director/writer Richard Brooks illustrates the divergent thoughts of his characters by surrounding their beliefs in a mirrored maze, where those who compromise appear to take on a chameleon quality. They are transfigured as the story progresses, shattering a series of varying images in the mirrors until the true nature of the men and women are revealed at the end.

The scene which implies Grant and the professionals will ultimately be at odds is the one in which the rancher describes their duties. He asks if the others have any qualms about working with a black man (Sharp). Slight disdain for Grant is the answer. When Brooks repeatedly cuts between Grant and the others, all are neatly framed except Grant. His image spills out of the frame, rocking back and forth, like some mighty power trying to break out of the screen.

The twists of plot and character make for a compelling narrative with the irony of the Trojan War. Menelaus and a host of Greek heroes battle for a decade to rescue his wife Helen from the city of Troy. When the war is over, she no longer wishes to return to her husband. In *The Professionals,* the switch is double-jointed, as Maria's marriage was only part of Raza's strategy.

Along with the attempts to free Maria, it is the breaking of impressions which gives the Western the thumping drive of the brass and percussion sections of an orchestra. Raza is introduced while he and his gang rob a train. The leader then instructs his men to shoot down the passengers. Hans Ehrengard is disgusted at the merciless behavior. Later it is discovered the train contained a group of Mexican torture experts. Therefore, Raza is elevated from the status of butcher to that of angel of mercy in a devil's guise. Dolworth, a disenchanted romantic idealist, is first seen by his friend Farden stripped down to his underwear and in chains. Dolworth had been arrested for being intimate with a townsman's wife. Farden details the job to Dolworth. "You won't lose your pants. Your life maybe. But what's that?" "Nothing at all," smiles Dolworth.

For all his masculinity, Bill Dolworth is constantly defeated by those who act with cold professionalism, as when Maria attempts to seduce him to steal his gun. Even oil man Grant, who claims to be a personification of the frontier ethic, is really offering a false front. Once he became an owner, Grant obviously lost the sense of justice that comes with men and women who possess only themselves. This is never so evident as when the baron slaps Maria around, plies her with promises, and attempts to kill Raza. At the finish, J. W. Grant is left without his wife and the respect of the professionals. "You, sir, are a self-made man," deadpans Farden, speaking what has got to be one of the sharpest plays on words in the history of the Western.

In *The Professionals,* Richard Brooks proves that people must sometimes take bizarre courses to achieve their goals. It is only when these strategies are completed that things become clear. The journey between confusion and enlightenment sparks the brilliance of *The Professionals.*

The Making of *The Professionals*

The Professionals is an aptly named production. It is a movie about men who knew what they were doing, made by people who had a clear view of the job to be done and did it.

For the last decade, producer/director/writer Richard Brooks had often adapted literary material for his films. Through Brooks' efforts, the work of Dostoyevsky *(The Brothers Karamazov),* F. Scott Fitzgerald *(The Last Time I Saw Paris),* Sinclair Lewis *(Elmer Gantry),* Tennessee Williams *(Cat on a Hot Tin Roof, Sweet Bird of Youth),* and Joseph Conrad *(Lord Jim)* appeared on the screen in expensively mounted, impressively cast productions. The literature of Lewis and Williams fared well under Brooks' guidance, but not that of Dostoyevsky, Fitzgerald, or Conrad. *Lord Jim* (Columbia, 1965), the director's last work prior to *The Professionals,* is a heavy-handed spectacle with little of the subtlety or power of Conrad's first-person prose.

So Brooks reversed his personal trend and, for his second Western, fashioned a screenplay from Frank O'Rourke's Western novel,

A Mule for the Marquesa. Brooks also wrote the script for the fine, thoughtful action film *The Last Hunt* (MGM, 1956). For a filmmaker who had worked so often in action genres early in his career, it is odd indeed that he had made only one previous cowboy saga.

The script of *The Professionals* gives more emphasis to the philosophical battles between the characters than exists in O'Rourke's novel, but both versions contain solid story values and taut action. Since the fictional people are hearty, earthy, magnetic men and women of the soil all the way down the line, the actors chosen to portray them would have to be capable of rendering a rawhide gusto to their line readings. They would have to possess a presence which could fill a movie screen, a face that stands out like those on Mount Rushmore. What Brooks didn't need was a series of Hollywood pretty boys, vacuous magazine cover girls, or introspective method actors.

He required very strong men and women, and he got them. Not, save Lancaster, from the ranks of the leading men, but from an endless list of those who stand behind the stars, sometimes supporting an idol-of-the-moment's awkward characterizations, occasionally making a sour script palatable, always adding color and verve to a picture.

Burt Lancaster was chosen to play Bill Dolworth, explosives expert and tarnished romantic. *The Professionals* teamed Brooks and Lancaster for the second time. Their first encounter resulted in a revival of the actor's career and an Oscar for his portrayal of the charlatan minister in the title role of *Elmer Gantry* (UA, 1960). That handsome but weathered face and sparkling smile could add emphasis to the already witty dialogue written by Richard Brooks for Dolworth, the husky-voiced Westerner with the twinkle in his eye.

Lee Marvin, fresh from his Oscar-winning dual role in Elliot Silverstein's comic Western, *Cat Ballou* (Columbia, 1965), agreed to play Henry Rico Farden, a veteran of the Mexican and Spanish-American Wars. With his granite face and commanding tones, Marvin would lend authority to the very moral Farden, and the performer's ability to essay unsympathetic and snivelling characters might also provide the range to express the warrior's doubts without losing his power.

Hans Ehrengard, a master with horses, came to life in his Robert Ryan portrayal. After many performances as hard men and a number of forays into psychopathic parts, Ryan's stately, wrinkled presence as a professional skilled with animals and given to kindness presented Ehrengard with a welcome double-edge.

Hawk-faced Jack Palance enacted Raza, the philosophical outlaw. Palance's earthy appearance and sensitive intellect would be used to bring Raza from the boisterous-type Mexicans often played by Eli Wallach to a person more refined, but just as deadly.

Striking Claudia Cardinale would co-star as Maria Grant, with J. W. Grant given staunch patriarchal airs by Ralph Bellamy. Woody Strode rounded out the professionals as Jacob Sharp, tracker and scout with a hard face and penetrating stare.

Although all the performers were enthusiastic about *The Professionals,* Claudia Cardinale in particular appreciated the opportunity to act a role with more depth than earlier assignments. Cinematographer Conrad Hall was most impressed with the actress, feeling he had an easy assignment photographing her because of her beauty. As he did with all the actors, Hall backlit Claudia Cardinale in close-ups and employed a sharp cross-light to highlight her face. Perhaps lensing Cardinale's performance was the only easy thing about making *The Professionals.* Hall, who has since shot such finely photographed films as *In Cold Blood* (Columbia, 1967), *Butch Cassidy and the Sundance Kid* (Fox, 1969), and *The Day of the Locusts* (Paramount, 1975), found himself up against some difficult production circumstances in making Brooks' second Western. But he had the blessing of a director who knew exactly what he wanted and believed in planning ahead. Hall was assigned to *The Professionals* two months before actual production began. He and Brooks travelled to the prospective locations to map out the shooting schedule. Other technicians were also permitted to prepare in advance, something which does not always occur in the motion picture industry. By being involved in the project almost from the start, Hall was able to achieve a more complex view of exactly how *The Professionals* should be photographed. Often a cameraman comes onto a picture shortly before the cameras are to roll and therefore his main assignment is to carry out plans already made. On this property, Hall was able to take more responsibility for the physical look of the Western. He could tell Brooks how a particular effect could be executed and if it could be done at all.

Director Brooks decided his Western should run no more than two hours. A number of cameras were to be used to photograph the scenes. That way the filmmaker and his editor Peter Zinner could eliminate certain shots from a particular sequence without seriously damaging its photographic quality.

Except for some interiors and one night exterior, *The Professionals* was lensed on location at Death Valley, the Valley of Fire State Park (near Lake Mead, Nevada), and at a rail spur line fifty miles east of Indio, California. Principal photography began in Death Valley, showing the retreat toward the border after Raza has kidnapped Maria Grant.

During the shooting, dust storms occasionally swirled about,

Woody Strode,
Lee Marvin,
Robert Ryan, and
Burt Lancaster

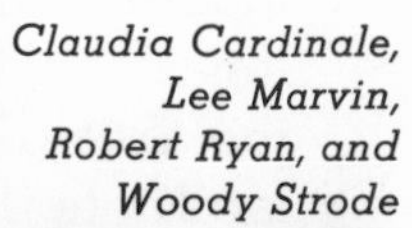

Claudia Cardinale,
Lee Marvin,
Robert Ryan, and
Woody Strode

reaching such a ferocity that the camera operator had to frequently brush off and clean all the working mechanisms of his machine. At other times sandstorms were created by throwing sand and a substance called "Fuller's Earth" in front of huge wind machines.

Many of the night scenes had to be filmed during the day due to the vastness of the landscape. Ordinarily, a modern production company is able to do a scene at the point in day or night in which it occurs. In his case, however, Brooks was forced to employ the formerly traditional day-for-night technique. He had to shoot while the sun was out and use filters to simulate evening hours. The sprawling nature of the landscape made it impossible for cameraman Hall to get any kind of depth in the images. Faces, bodies, and objects up close would appear, but nothing else. Thus the land would be wasted in these scenes. So the director of photography employed a polar screen density filter to darken the skies and, as is the custom with shooting night scenes by day, set the lens down 2½ stops to underexpose the film.

It took nine weeks to shoot in the Valley of Fire State Park, located fifty miles north of Las Vegas. In order to find the proper locations, Brooks, Hall, and assistant director Tom Shaw travelled the area by jeep, over an elaborate creation of twisted red rock. To facilitate the journey through the park, authorities accommodated the company by building a seven-mile-long dirt and gravel road. As it hadn't rained in the area virtually since the turn of the century, culverts were not created along the path. Tons of red clay had to be trucked to the site as the base for the construction of Raza's hacienda, which cost Columbia $200,000.

Technicians had to scale the cliffs of Coyote Pass in the Valley of Fire by driving into the rock steel parallels with special spikes. The devices were constructed to serve as a platform for the cameras. Small lamps were also hauled to the high site. Hall often found himself setting up camera angles from seventy-five to one hundred feet above ground, with the camera cocked at a forty-five-degree angle to put the rock slope into proper perspective. Director Brooks was extremely impressed with fifty-three-year-old Burt Lancaster's ability to scale the mountains when necessary. A fifteen-foot climb up the side of a cliff by rope was perhaps the most arduous task handled by the star.

At Indio, California, all the action took place at the train station and the goat keeper's camp, surrounded by a collection of abandoned box cars. Brooks lensed the scenes aboard the train using a process screen to achieve the correct balance of the interior of the car with the scenery speeding by as seen through the doorway.

There were many cold nights on location. Temperatures sometimes plummeted below freezing, accompanied by snow, hail, and rain. A flash flood stranded the cast in a box canyon of the Valley of Fire one evening. The company of 185 had to be rescued by heavy equipment. On other occasions the rain was so strong that trucks got stuck in the water-drenched dirt roads while travelling from camp to location. When everything else failed, director Brooks sent for bulldozers to fill the road so truck tires wouldn't be swallowed up. The filmmaker learned that his actors and technicians were made of steel—they adapted to the adverse conditions just as fast and expertly as Dolworth, Farden, Ehrengard, and Sharp would have reacted to any crisis.

Despite the myriad of problems created by weather conditions, Brooks and company spent only eighty-seven days in production. The camera crew averaged twenty different setups each day, an impressive figure. And the director didn't use a second unit for backup material either.

"*The Professionals* means excitement!" announced a Columbia poster for the Western. The list of stars followed: Burt Lancaster, Lee Marvin, Robert Ryan, Jack Palance, Ralph Bellamy, Claudia Cardinale.

Reviews were generally favorable:

Life, Richard Schickel:

Writer-director Richard Brooks, best known for his mixed-result attempts to meld literature with cinema *(Elmer Gantry, Lord Jim),* has here emphasized his natural gift for directing action instead of his dubious predilection for cultural uplift. . . . *The Professionals* is smartly paced, tough-minded and pleasingly acted; it has no real depth, but it has the breadth of outdoors.

Newsletter, Joseph Gelmis:

The Professionals is one of the best Westerns in years, gut-shaking, murderous, explosive-violence refined to art. . . . It is a film in the tradition of *Vera Cruz,* say, rather than *Shane.* The humor is broad, the action uncomplicated and the characterization simple—verging on burlesque at times. But it is hard to recall a recent Western in which the elements of suspense, action and laughs have been fused so well.

Newsweek, Joseph Morgenstern:

Rare is the Western that can boast political insights, intricate motivations, applied philosophy and some literary grace in the dialogue. Rarer still is the Western, like *The Professionals,* that succeeds in spite of that. . . . Richard Brooks, who wrote the screenplay, shoots high and often hits clouds. Richard Brooks, who directed, fires away at stunning scenery,

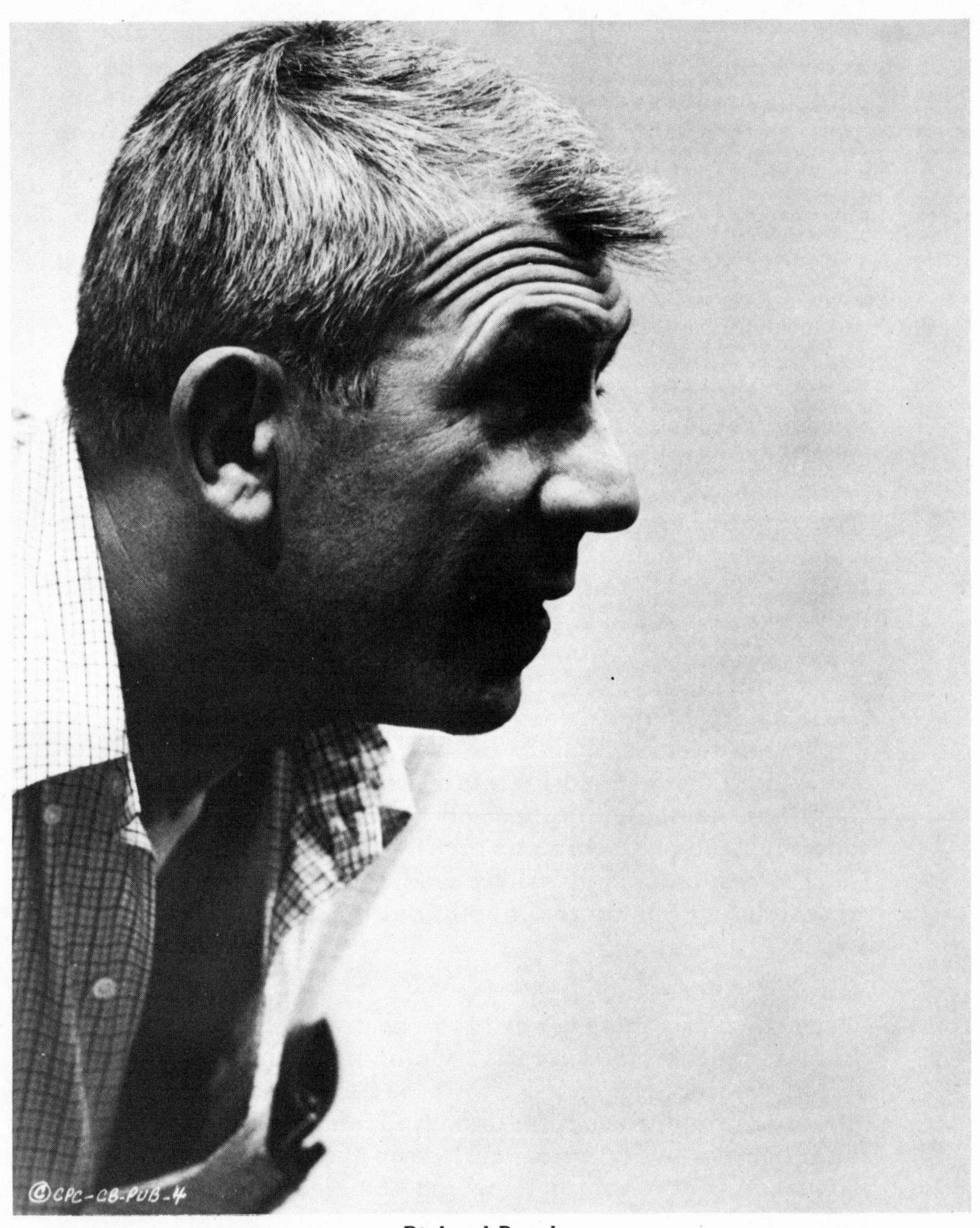

Richard Brooks

good faces and great action, and hits the bull's-eye almost every time.

Variety:

Exciting explosive sequences, good overall pacing and acting overcome a sometimes thin script. . . . Director Brooks has obtained sharp performances from Marvin, Lancaster and

> Bellamy, and other players. Scripting-direction relegate other principals to reactive postures. . . . Pictorial values are excellent, since Conrad Hall's Technicolor-Panavision camera has caught the dusty mood of the Southwest.

The stars of *The Professionals* all knew they had a box-office attraction and a fine film. Lee Marvin went so far as to state it should have received the Oscar for best picture of 1966. The Western garnered two nominations, for director and cinematography, but won in neither category. The film had to compete with Fred Zinnemann's *A Man for All Seasons* (Columbia), a penetrating study of Sir Thomas More, and Mike Nichols' adaptation of Edward Albee's *Who's Afraid of Virginia Woolf?* (Warner Bros.), both of which possessed deep, intellectual themes, and won many Oscars between them.

This turn of events isn't surprising, as Hollywood often forgets about the genre movies, the Westerns, crime films, comedies, and other staples of the American cinema which provide producers with the bread and butter to create more "serious" material. But *The Professionals* won favor with audiences. It made $8,800,000 in box-office rentals for Columbia. The tough-hided Western also found itself on *Film Daily*'s list of the ten best films of 1966.

The Professionals is a fine example of a Hollywood film made by dedicated artists and craftsmen who knew their business well. These are the men and women who have kept the American cinema on a higher overall level of quality than any other nation's motion picture industry.

John Wayne, Charlene Holt, and Robert Mitchum

CHAPTER TWENTY-SIX

El Dorado

Year Released: 1967
Studio: Paramount
Producer: Howard Hawks
Associate Producer: Paul Helmick
Director: Howard Hawks
Screenplay: Leigh Brackett, based on the novel *The Stars in Their Courses* by Harry Brown
Cinematography: Harold Rosson
Music: Nelson Riddle
Art Directors: Hal Pereira, Carl Anderson
Editor: John Woodock
Assistant Director: Andrew J. Durkes
Set Decorators: Robert Benton, Ray Moyers
Makeup: Wally Westmore
Wardrobe: Edith Head
Sound: John Carter, Charles Grenzbach
Special Effects: David Koehler
Special Camera Effects: Paul K. Lerpae
Process Camera: Farciot Edouart
Color, 126 minutes

Cast:

Cole Thornton	JOHN WAYNE
Sheriff J. B. Harrah	ROBERT MITCHUM
Mississippi	JAMES CAAN
Maudie	CHARLENE HOLT

"Doc" Miller	PAUL FIX
Deputy Bull Thomas	ARTHUR HUNNICUTT
Joey MacDonald	MICHELE CAREY
Kevin MacDonald	R. G. ARMSTRONG
Bart Jason	EDWARD ASNER
Nelse McLeod	CHRISTOPHER GEORGE
Maria	MARINA GHANE
Pedro	JOHN GABRIEL
Saul MacDonald	ROBERT ROTHWELL
Milt	ROBERT DONNER
Matt MacDonald	ADAM ROARKE
Jared MacDonald	CHARLES COURTNEY
Jared's Wife	VICTORIA GEORGE
Jason's Foreman	JIM DAVIS
Swedish Gunsmith	OLAF WIEGHORST
Dr. Donovan	ANTHONY ROGERS
Charlie Hagan	DEAN SMITH
Sheriff Bill Moreland	WILLIAM ALBERT HENRY
Deputy Joe Braddock	DON COLLIER
Saul's Wife	ANNE NEWMAN
Matt's Wife	DIANE STROM
Luke MacDonald	JOHNNY CRAWFORD

El Dorado isn't exactly a remake of *Rio Bravo.* But the Westerns are so much alike that they could be described as twins, with the later *Rio Lobo* a third, less successful variation on the story of a sheriff who, with a motley assortment of guns, battles a tyrannical family.

The powerful MacDonald clan is engaging in a lawless reign of a Western community. J. P. Harrah, the local sheriff, has become an alcoholic and is unable to thwart the aggression of the ruthless pack. Aging gunslinger Cole Thornton, an old friend of Harrah's, comes to the lawman's aid and, with the help of youthful knife-wielder Mississippi and the cantankerous deputy Bull, they rid the West of the MacDonalds.

At 126 minutes, *El Dorado* is fifteen minutes shorter than *Rio Bravo,* which accounts somewhat for the tighter plotting. The real difference is provided by the relationship of Thornton and Harrah, with roots in the strong screen personalities of John Wayne and Robert Mitchum. In fact, the disparity of the characters in the two

Westerns is caused by a simple exchange of traits and the peculiarities of the actors who play them.

In *Rio Bravo,* there is a huge gap between Wayne's John T. Chance and Dean Martin's Dude. Although both men measure up when it counts, Martin's ability as a romantic lead and light comedian has given him a much softer image than Wayne. Also, *Rio Bravo* features a Wayne who has, onscreen anyway, just touched that time when middle-age slows men down and makes them more reflective. The Wayne of *Rio Bravo* is much closer to the self-assured star of 1930s and 40s Westerns than the aching, pensive, but still tough, Wayne of *El Dorado.* Therefore, additional contrasts exist between Wayne and Martin, exceeding those of Wayne and Mitchum. In *El Dorado,* the drunk is the sheriff rather than a former gunman. Mitchum's screen identity has always been made of smouldering macho. The pathetic alcoholism which dominates his character in *El Dorado* strips him of the sexy look, but he retains a basic strength Dean Martin could never muster. Wayne's Thornton and Mitchum's Harrah both struggle to regain former power. Thornton hopes to at least temporarily throw off old age infirmities, while Harrah wishes to break through the alcoholic maze back into the spirit of the Hawksian hero, a man to whom professionalism is the ultimate goal and getting the job done is the *raison d'être.*

The professional at work is the theme that recurs constantly in the films of Howard Hawks. As in his other productions, *El Dorado* shows how men do their jobs. However, the Western is much more explicit about the nature of the work and the mutual respect engendered by those who share the same duties, whether they advocate the law or anti-social behavior. When detective Philip Marlowe admires the courage of the petty crook in *The Big Sleep* (Warner Bros., 1946), it is because the little man has followed the rules of the game.

Such spoken feelings in *El Dorado* not only give the production a more philosophical tone (if that is possible in a Hawks film, classically a creature which exists on a level of action, and little else) but bind the characters together. This union of professionals adds a real bite to the Western, especially in the dealings of Thornton and hired gun Nelse McLeod. McLeod is quickly depicted as a ruthless man, although he has the same code as good guy Thornton. McLeod discovers that one of his cohorts acted with two others in the murder of an elderly man. "It shouldn't a took three a you, Charlie," he chides the outlaw. McLeod allows Charlie to be killed because his sidekick broke that unwritten law of fair play. McLeod even saves Thornton's life at one point. Others want to shoot him in the back but McLeod vetoes the idea, opting instead for "professional courtesy." In the climactic shoot-out, Thornton blasts

James Caan, Robert Mitchum, and John Wayne

McLeod. Both men knew it had to be one or the other. "You didn't even give me a chance," McLeod utters before dying. It was a compliment. "You're too good to give a chance to," counsels Thornton.

In revamping *Rio Bravo,* the typical Hawksian black humor is also switched from character to character in *El Dorado.* While Ricky Nelson's Colorado is a relatively callow gunslinger in the former film, James Caan's knife-throwing Mississippi is a much tougher man. Caan has more range than Nelson; therefore Hawks makes Mississippi the butt of some humor which deflates the cowboy's male ego. Mississippi can't handle a pistol and, since a knife is useless when warring from a distance, Thornton teaches him to use a sawed-off, double-barrel shotgun. The weapon, which Mississippi carries in a holster, has the effect of a cannon but the man still can't hit a target. Courage and a grim sense of humor will carry him through.

Men do their jobs well in *El Dorado.* The production company of the Western has been equally professional in the creation of a slam-bang oater which brilliantly succeeds as entertainment but is also an incisive exploration of the passage of men from youth to middle age.

The Making of *El Dorado*

Rio Bravo wasn't supposed to be the first part of a Western trilogy. It just worked out that way.

A number of people were involved in making all three films, including director Howard Hawks, writer Leigh Brackett, and actor John Wayne. *Rio Bravo, El Dorado,* and *Rio Lobo* all bear the unmistakable signs of these three people.

Hawks had been an individualist ever since arriving in Hollywood after being discharged from the service in World War I. The producer/director/writer was blessed with the ability to make simple, straightforward, action-filled, and funny films which pleased both audiences and himself. As a proven moneymaker, Hawks was able to take more liberties than, say, a Stroheim or Welles, who didn't have the leverage of heavy box-office success.

Since the early 1930s Hawks had often produced the pictures he directed, which gave him more control. He was confident enough to violate one of the seminal rules of Hollywood's unwritten code: that one cannot remake a great film. Howard Hawks firmly believed that if a story is good once, it can be good again. And a third time.

The need existed for a second Western. Closing in on seventy years of age, Hawks slowed down a bit in the 1960s. After *Rio Bravo* opened in 1959, the director didn't finish another production until *Hatari* (Paramount), in 1962. Then came *Man's Favorite Sport?* (Universal) in 1964 and *Red Line 7000* (Paramount) the next year. The last two efforts were very different from most of Howard's previous work in two important ways: the critics didn't like them and neither did the public.

The question in many minds might have been whether Howard Hawks was losing his touch. *Man's Favorite Sport?,* a limp comedy, resembled the Hawksian farces *Bringing Up Baby* (Columbia, 1938) and *Monkey Business* (Fox, 1952). But could that kind of frantically silly comedy work in 1964? Apparently not, at least in the case of *Man's Favorite Sport?* or with star Rock Hudson, although the actor was an established light comedy performer. Was *Red Line 7000* thirty years too late? The production did combine two elements Hawks had used well in the past—a story about auto racing, which he learned about as a stock car driver, and new faces. Lauren Bacall, Montgomery Clift, and Joanne Dru, to name three, all became stars after working with Hawks. Had he lost the ability to sign promising unknowns? Having directed two less than successful films in a row and at the age where most men retire, Hawks needed a vehicle that would show that his talents hadn't diminished. The property became *El Dorado.*

In the late 1950s the director decided that moviegoers wanted good Westerns, so he asked friend John Wayne to star in some. Wayne agreed, and *Rio Bravo* resulted. Hawks always rewrote dialogue, sometimes whole scenes on the set, and concocted bits of business which couldn't be used. Consequently, the filmmaker had already penned material for *El Dorado.* He would unofficially remake *Rio Bravo* with John Wayne, institute plot and character alterations, and come up with a different picture.

Hawks had purchased rights to a relatively violent Western novel, *The Stars in Their Courses,* by Harry Brown, son of producer/director Harry Joe Brown. Leigh Brackett, who had collaborated with Jules Furthman on the script of *Rio Bravo,* agreed to pen the scenario for *El Dorado.* It would be the fourth time the filmmaker and writer worked together. She had previously contributed material to *The Big Sleep,* the aforementioned Western, and *Hatari.* With an increasing amount of *Rio Bravo* being inserted by Hawks into *El Dorado* as production progressed, less of Brown's original novel ended up being used.

As in *Rio Bravo* and some other Hawks productions, the director wanted *El Dorado* to begin on a serious tone, then mix in comedy and drama. In this way, Hawks hoped to get the audience's attention, then proceed to do what he did best: tell an entertaining story.

Rio Bravo, El Dorado, and *Rio Lobo* share a unique unity of plot and character. Casting *El Dorado* proved to be a strange problem for Hawks. He had to look for the same types in *El Dorado* (and in the future, for *Rio Lobo*) as appeared in *Rio Bravo.* But he didn't want to use the same actors again, aside from Wayne. So he might very well have been in a position of picking a performer for *El*

Dorado that he rejected while casting *Rio Bravo.*

Following is a breakdown of the casts for Howard Hawks' (unintentional) Western trilogy, plus *Red River,* his first Western, and *The Big Sky* (RKO, 1952), about the early 19th-century American wilderness. The chart is an expansion of Judith Bernstein's list which appeared in the useful but now defunct periodical *Focus!* (Autumn, 1972).

Roles	*Red River*	*The Big Sky*	*Rio Bravo*	*El Dorado*	*Rio Lobo*
Hero	John Wayne	Kirk Douglas	John Wayne	John Wayne	John Wayne
Second Lead	John Ireland*	Dewey Martin	Dean Martin	Robert Mitchum	Jorge Rivero
Young Man	Montgomery Clift	Dewey Martin	Ricky Nelson	James Caan	Chris Mitchum
Female	Joanne Dru	Elizabeth Threatt	Angie Dickinson	Charlene Holt	Jennifer O'Neill
Old Man	Walter Brennan	Arthur Hunnicutt	Walter Brennan	Arthur Hunnicutt	Jack Elam
Villain	John Wayne	Jim Davis	John Russell	Edward Asner	Victor French
Henchmen	Drovers	Davis' cohorts	Claude Akins	Christopher George	Mike Henry

*Ireland's role was cut down considerably during production.

Despite the uniform professionalism of the cast of *El Dorado,* Hawks complained about the general difficulty of finding suitable actors for circa 1960s adventure scripts. The director looked at several dozen performers before deciding on James Caan to play Mississippi. Caan was the only one of the newcomers featured in *Red Line 7000* to fulfill his screen promise and was Hawks' last "find."

The filmmaker blamed the lack of star power in the movies on what he considered to be the overtraining of student actors. By the time they arrived in Hollywood, aspiring players were too *experienced* and specialized to suit Hawks. While television should have provided a good learning environment, Hawks felt that anything an actor picked up working on the small screen would have to be undone for the cinema.

Rather than Russell Harlan, who lensed *Rio Bravo, Man's Favorite Sport?, Hatari,* and other Hawks pictures, the director employed veteran cinematographer Hal Rosson to shoot *El Dorado.* It was Rosson's first assignment since *No Time for Sergeants* and *Onionhead* (both Warner Bros., 1958). Rosson had begun as a cameraman in 1919, just about the time Hawks came to Hollywood.

The production company of *El Dorado* spent thirty-six days on location. Headquarters were in Tucson, Arizona. Hawks and Wayne stayed at a local Ramada Inn, while Robert Mitchum leased

Robert Mitchum (right)

Arthur Hunnicutt, Charlene Holt, John Wayne, Robert Mitchum, and Paul Fix

Robert Mitchum, Arthur Hunnicutt, and John Wayne

the home of former Senator William Nolan. The 200 member company trekked thirteen miles from Tucson each day to shoot at a site called "Old Tucson," built in 1940 for Wesley Ruggles' *Arizona* (Columbia). The large set had been used for fifty features and television shows by the time Hawks and company arrived. The eighty-four buildings making up "Old Tucson" underwent only slight alteration at the hands of the construction crew.

The cast and crew of *El Dorado* became a familiar sight to area residents. Each day the moviemakers drove to their make-believe town in a multi-faceted transportation fleet, twenty-five cars, and thirteen pieces of heavy equipment obtained locally. Hawks used a number of locations. The director had first employed the terrain for the film *Red River,* so he knew the geography. Some scenes were shot near the Senorita Creek on the Oak Bar Ranch, located between Nogales and Patagonia. Other locales included the Amado Ranch outside Amado, Arizona, the Pantano Creek, and Avra Valley, a cactus-rich site in Pima County.

Travelling to many different spots in one area allowed Howard to view the changes occurring over the past two decades. When he had begun filming in Arizona years earlier, equipment had to be transported by pack mule because the terrain was so hazardous. In 1967 Hawks had to make sure none of his images contained paved roads or a swimming pool.

Although making *El Dorado* brought up many situations which irritated the director, such as the dearth of properly leathery leading men and the unwelcome civilizing of the frontier, Hawks liked his actors very much and found the Western a perfect property for material he'd wanted to include in a film for twenty years.

A major change, or perhaps an expansion of an implication in *Rio Bravo,* involved the character played by John Wayne. Hawks felt that the star was getting too old to do the stalwart hero of Westerns past. So in *Rio Bravo,* Hawks made Angie Dickinson the sexual aggressor instead of Wayne, thus mellowing the actor's image with a striking complexity. Hawks wanted more of the same in *El Dorado.* First, he turned Wayne's character from a lawman into a gunfighter (Robert Mitchum played the hard-drinking sheriff in *El Dorado* in contrast to Dean Martin's town drunk in *Rio Bravo*). Then he made it quite clear that the gunfighter was extremely weary, tired of years of battle.

These switches were used by Hawks in 1970 as proof that he had never intended *El Dorado* to be a remake of *Rio Bravo.* The director insisted that the similarities resulted from having two choices with many of the elements in *Rio Bravo.* If the selections were both good, why not use one and file the other away for future reference?

Although James Caan was the filmmaker's first choice for the role of Mississippi, he had to be taught to throw a knife by Indian Rodd Red Wing. Red Wing also showed Michele Carey how to fire a rifle and instructed Christopher George on the tricky craft of the ambidextrous draw.

George was one of the new breed of actors Hawks grew to like. The director appreciated the performer's sense of humor and total willingness to cooperate. Consequently, Hawks led George to a fine performance as the villainous gunfighter who is quite human and even funny at times, in another contrast to his counterpart (Claude Akins) in *Rio Bravo.*

After the month-plus on location, Hawks spent nine weeks shooting interiors. *El Dorado* did not open until the summer of 1967 because Paramount executives felt those months would offer the most receptive audiences for an old-fashioned action Western.

Posters announced from theatre lobbies and in newspaper ads:*

It's the Big One with the Big Two!

They were friends. They were enemies. A passerby could not tell who was who.

Paramount issued *El Dorado* comic books, a puzzle, and a coloring contest. By the 1960s studios didn't indulge in as much gimmicky publicity. But, then again, traditional advertising fit perfectly the traditional Western, albeit a Western with twists of plot and character.

Many reviewers liked *El Dorado.* Some didn't.

London Observer, Philip French:

About every five minutes someone says, "Because I'm not good enough," "I just hope you're good enough," or "We didn't think you were good enough," and we even get that old favorite, "You were pretty good in there," a line that Hawks' mentor, Hemingway, once applied to the crucifixion. Furthermore, the picture is inordinately slow, and so talkative that the chief "classic" quality is the way the lengthy impositions of plot remind one of messengers in Greek tragedy.

Saturday Review:

But the curious aspect of *El Dorado* is the underplaying of the action. There are some wild brawls between the two stars,

*The "Big Two" are, of course, Wayne and Mitchum.

Robert Mitchum

but mostly in fun. There are no hot pursuits, and even in the inevitable barroom brawl, Wayne waits patiently before mixing in. Instead of action, the film proffers a rather pleasing rough-and-ready kind of humor—a man to man joshing that goes on between virtually all the members of the cast.

Variety:

El Dorado stars John Wayne and Robert Mitchum in an excellent oater drama, laced with adroit comedy and action relief, and set off by strong casting, superior production and solid directing.

Village Voice, Andrew Sarris:

Fortunately, *El Dorado* is a Western that sticks to its guns by affirming the spirit of adventure instead of trampling it in the fashionable dust of misanthropy. Humor and affirmation on the brink of despair are the poetic ingredients of the Hawksian Western. And now memory. Especially memory. Only those who see some point in remembering movies will find *El Dorado* truly unforgettable.

El Dorado also received some criticism for its camera technique. Hawks long had been known as the advocate of "eye level" cinema, a style of filming which doesn't call attention to such elements as camerawork and editing. Some film enthusiasts were particularly surprised at the director's handling of violence. While the shooting and punching went fast, as usual, the position of the camera caused comment. But Hawks wanted to show some actors falling into the camera and so he did. That was that.

El Dorado was the second of three Westerns Howard Hawks made with John Wayne between 1959 and 1970. *Rio Lobo* became the director's swansong. Many films reached the planning stages, but none was produced before Hawks' death in 1977.

John Wayne went from a fine performance in *El Dorado* to a number of solid characterizations in mediocre projects before finally receiving an Oscar for his great portrayal of Rooster Cogburn in *True Grit* (Paramount, 1969).

Mitchum continued in tough guy roles, changing once for David Lean's *Ryan's Daughter* (MGM, 1970). James Caan became a major star through such fine fare as *The Godfather* (Paramount, 1972) and TV's *Brian's Song* (1972). Charlene Holt, Michele Carey, and Christopher George have yet to climb to stardom.

But in *El Dorado,* everything is golden.

John Wayne

CHAPTER TWENTY-SEVEN

True Grit

Year Released: 1969
Studio: Paramount
Producer: Hal Wallis
Director: Henry Hathaway
Screenplay: Marguerite Roberts, based on the novel *True Grit* by Charles Portis
Cinematography: Lucien Ballard
Music: Elmer Bernstein
Production Design: Walter Tyler
Editor: Warren Low
Assistant Director: William Gray
Color, 128 minutes

Cast:

Rooster Cogburn	JOHN WAYNE
Mattie Ross	KIM DARBY
La Boeuf	GLEN CAMPBELL
Emmett Quincey	JEREMY SLATE
Ned Pepper	ROBERT DUVALL
Moon	DENNIS HOPPER
Colonel G. Stonehill	STROTHER MARTIN
Tom Chaney	JEFF COREY
Goudy	ALFRED RYDER
Captain Boots Finch	RON SOBLE
Lawyer Daggett	JOHN FIELDER
Judge Parker	JAMES WESTERFIELD

Sheriff	JOHN DOUCETTE
Barlow	DONALD WOODS
Mrs. Floyd	EDITH ATWATER
Dirty Bob	CARLOS RIVAS
Mrs. Bagby	ISABEL BONIFACE
Frank Ross	JOHN PICKARD
Mrs. Ross	ELIZABETH HARROWER
Yarnell	KEN RENARD
Harold Parmalee	JAY RIPLEY
Farrell Parmalee	KENNETH BECKER
Hangman	GUY WILKERSON
Undertaker	HANK WORDEN
Deputy	MYRON HEALEY

True Grit represents Hollwood at its twilight. The story of an aging legendary hero about to engage in one final battle is naturally filled with references to growing old and dying and reflections about how a life was lived. Made by star John Wayne, director Henry Hathaway, and producer Hal Wallis, among whom about 120 years of motion picture experience is represented, *True Grit* upholds the Hollywood tradition that the show must go on, and is as tough, funny, and action-packed as any other picture in their distinguished careers.

Teenager Mattie Ross' father has been killed by a cowhand named Tom Chaney, and the girl wants the murderer punished. She is told that one-time lawman, gruff Rooster Cogburn, has what it takes to capture Chaney and pays him fifty dollars to do the job. The next day Mattie meets Texas Ranger Le Boeuf, who joins the search. Although the men try to dissuade Mattie from tagging along, she is insistent. After learning that Chaney has joined the Ned Pepper gang, the trio makes an abortive attempt to capture the outlaws. Mattie is corralled by Chaney and she forces the other two to ride away. But Rooster returns, and, with guns blazing, wipes out most of the gang. Le Boeuf dies in the fight but Chaney is brought to justice.

There is little subtlety in *True Grit.* It offers nothing new. It is broadly played, sentimental, starkly violent, and firmly set in the mode of action productions of years past, where the good guys were sometimes crusty and cynical but always honest, the villains invariably mean and evil, and the children wise beyond their years. Yet it is the authority with which *True Grit* was lensed which makes it such a fine Western.

Wayne's Rooster Cogburn is superficially a curmudgeon. He doesn't want anyone getting close to him. Wayne plays his scenes with Kim Darby the way Wallace Beery used to act with Jackie Cooper. Like Lee Marvin's soused gunfighter in *Cat Ballou* (Columbia, 1965), Rooster is the source of the light-hearted frontier schtick of director Hathaway. Nevertheless, the one-eyed ex-lawman has tons of what Mattie calls "True Grit," the courage to do a job right despite the odds.

The scene which best typifies Wayne's performance comes during the wait for the Ned Pepper gang. Rooster and Mattie sit in the bushes. The camera closes in on John Wayne as he relates the history of Rooster Cogburn. All the humor, sentiment, idiosyncracies, and courage of the flabby old marshal are slowly revealed. Rooster can be laughed at when admitting that his son didn't like him and respected, disliked, and even loved as he tells Mattie about his marital relationship, and how he had to leave to maintain his independence. Nobody is going to get a grip on ol' Rooster's heart, he might be saying between the lines, but many have earned his love just the same. Cogburn's speech capsulizes his feeling for Mattie. Here Wayne reveals a touching sensitivity that he has rarely shown in other films.

While the final shoot-out in *Ride the High Country* is a more down to earth coda to the careers of two aging cowboys, the joust in *True Grit* between Rooster and the Pepper gang stands as a segment which brilliantly crosses wires with another type of legend. When Cogburn holds guns in both hands, clenching the reins of his horse between his yellowed teeth, he has become a grubby knight, and the battle is elevated from a graphic climax to a duel with frontier lances by a Western code of honor.

"Show your hand, you son-of-a-bitch!" Rooster challenges as he charges the outlaws with guns shooting a barrage of bullets. Director Hathaway repeatedly cuts to an extreme close-up of Rooster's worn face as he gallops, shotgun and pistol twirling, into an American valley of death. Tennyson's 600 man Light Brigade is here replaced by one lawman, with the young Le Boeuf more or less at his side.

The violence is graphic and bloody. Despite the comic leanings of Cogburn, the stiff, pouty-lipped sincerity of Kim Darby's Mattie, which resembles Shirley Temple's best, and the shallow sincerity of Glen Campbell's Le Boeuf, *True Grit* is tough when it counts. Earlier, Cogburn guns down some of Pepper's gang as if he were acting out a personal vendetta. The old man is properly vicious in his treatment of wounded outlaw Moon, played by Dennis Hopper. The feeling persists that Wayne would blow his head off at the slightest provocation.

John Wayne and Kim Darby

John Wayne, Kim Darby (second from right), and Myron Healey (far right)

In the end, however, sentiment arrives with a flourish. Mattie offers Rooster a spot beside her future grave, as the lawman has no one to bury him. Like every other older man John Wayne has played over the years, including such hard noses as Tom Dunson in *Red River* and Nathan Brittles in *She Wore a Yellow Ribbon* (RKO, 1949), Cogburn finally surrenders to that great need for affection each of the actor's aging characters hides so well but inevitably embraces. Rooster mounts his horse, leaps over a fence, asks Mattie to come see a fat old man sometime, then rides off across the prairie, like the archetypal Western hero.

True Grit uses ingredients of aging, youthful exuberance, violence, comedy, death, and sentiment with the same gusto which propels Rooster over the fence. That is its beauty.

The Making of *True Grit*

Charles Portis wrote a novel called *True Grit,* about a strong-willed girl named Mattie Ross who enlists the aid of old codger Rooster Cogburn and Texas Ranger Le Boeuf to capture the man who murdered her father. The book was published in spring 1968 but had aroused interest in Hollywood before then.

Unlike other writers, Portis, in this case anyway, had already visualized the actor he thought could best play Rooster Cogburn—John Wayne. Portis sent a set of galleys of his unpublished work to Wayne at his Batjac Productions.

The Cogburn character was gruffer than any Wayne had done in his forty-year career. Cogburn was getting on in years. He was mean. He looked like a derelict. He was fat. He had only one eye. But Rooster also possessed a penchant for telling the truth, for being honest, and, most significant, for understanding himself. Playing Cogburn would give Wayne a chance to indulge in comedy, something he had done with increasing frequency over the past ten years. And Rooster was a meaty role for any actor. Perhaps too meaty. It would take mighty discipline for a player to prevent Rooster Cogburn from descending to the broader, coarser, and ultimately less realistic aspects of the aging Westerner's personality.

John Wayne really wanted to act the part. He bid $300,000 for screen rights to Portis' novel. He decided to direct the property as well. After helming *The Alamo* (United Artists, 1960) and *The Green Berets* (Warner Bros./Seven Arts, 1968), the actor felt capable of directing it.

Others had the same idea. Paramount producer Hal B. Wallis had also read the galleys of *True Grit.* The studio purchased film rights for $500,000. Wallis had been making Westerns for many years. More recently he had produced Henry Hathaway's *The Sons of Katie Elder* (Paramount, 1965), starring Wayne, as well as Hathaway's *Five Card Stud* (Paramount, 1968).

Wallis approached Wayne with a deal. The actor would star in *True Grit,* at a salary of $1,000,000 plus thirty-five percent of the gross receipts. However, Wayne would have to leave the direction to someone else. Duke agreed.

Both Hollywood veterans were happy at the compromise. Like many other men who influenced the look of American movies in the 1920s, 30s, 40s, and 50s, Hal Wallis disdained the new permissiveness of the films of the 1960s. He didn't like much of the language, the plots (or lack of them), and some of the camerawork and editing which he considered tricky and detrimental to the growth of a good screen story.

Instead of signing a younger director to make *True Grit*, Wallis opted for the services of Henry Hathaway, another moviemaker with four decades of experience, a talent for getting what he wanted on the set, and the ability to bring out the best in John Wayne. Hathaway was one of the few directors Wallis employed in the 1960s with any sense of gut command, someone whose work always had individuality. With Wallis, Hathaway, and Wayne, the filming of *True Grit* would be a meeting of giants, men who were legends in their own time.

Marguerite Roberts, who had worked for Hathaway and Wallis before on *Five Card Stud*, wrote the screenplay for *True Grit*. As was his usual practice, Hathaway got together with Roberts after the scenario was completed and went about revising it to his satisfaction. The director felt there was too much repetition in the script (a carryover from the novel) so he scissored a number of scenes, but he did very little work on the dialogue. Hathaway usually trusted a writer's instinct for language. One particular scene Roberts added became one of the best in the Western—the one at the grave near the end of the film.

Unfortunately, relations weren't that close among some of the members of the production company of *True Grit*. Although Glen Campbell eagerly signed to make his film debut as Texas Ranger Le Boeuf in a non-exclusive five-picture contract with Hal Wallis, Dennis Hopper and Robert Duvall weren't always as happy.

Hopper's problems with Hathaway had started a decade earlier. The director had guided Hopper through a solid performance as the hard-headed, wet-nosed son of a big cattle rancher in the excellent Western *From Hell to Texas* (Fox, 1958). The twenty-two-year-old actor was on loan-out from Warners, where he had co-starred with James Dean in *Rebel Without a Cause* (1955). Dean influenced Hopper both personally and professionally. Both young men were method actors, having trained at Lee Strasberg's Actors' Studio in New York. That was the source of the friction between Hopper and Hathaway. The veteran director was known to be very tough on actors in general. Wendell Mayes, the scripter of *From Hell to Texas*, has commented that while Hathaway remained flexible with writers, he became stronger, more demanding on the set. Hopper felt that Hathaway was overdirecting him, telling him how to read the dialogue. In fact, Hopper has since related that Hathaway told him to do what the actor considered a bad imitation of Marlon Brando with mumbling, stuttering, and meandering speech. Their relationship got so bad during the making of *From Hell to Texas* that Hopper walked off the film three times.

Dennis pleaded with Hathaway to give him more freedom to interpret a scene. As a subscriber to "The Method," Hopper had to sense things about his characters, use his sight, smell, touch, feelings. He didn't want to lose that way of working because the performer had just overcome what he considered to be repressive early Shakespearean training.

On the final day of filming *From Hell to Texas*, Hopper had to do a ten-line scene. Both the player and his director came prepared. Hathaway brought in a pile of film cans, pointed to them, and told Hopper they would use up every foot of stock if necessary to get the bit right, the way the filmmaker wanted it. Reportedly Hathaway insisted on showing Hopper how to recite every line, when to move, and when to stand still. Never one to submit to such orders meekly, the individualistic Hopper decided to play the moments for all they were worth. He read the scene in as many ways he could devise. Once it was highly dramatic, another time comic, a third rendition would contain pathos. Jack Warner telephoned constantly, demanding to know what had happened to his actor. Finally Hopper finished the scene and left the set. He didn't work much for the next eight years.

Ironically, one of the films he did was directed by Henry Hathaway. The filmmaker respected Hopper's talent enough to cast him in a supporting role in *The Sons of Katie Elder*, another vigorous John Wayne Western with comic overtones. Hathaway, Hopper, and Wayne learned to work together.

"Hathaway was a very serious director about the business," assistant director Bill Gray told me. "He worked very hard himself and expected everybody else to do the same." Perhaps this is the key to the understanding achieved by Hathaway and Hopper. Both were unrelenting in the struggle to better their work. Naturally when two men with strong visions unite for a project, unless the ideas are identical, there is bound to be some conflict. Professionals work it out.

Henry Hathaway (right) in 1947

When Hathaway hired Hopper for *True Grit*, he told the performer in no uncertain terms what was expected of him. Hopper acquiesced quietly. The actor had learned it was possible to follow direction and still maintain artistic integrity. And with the generous salary Wallis offered, Dennis Hopper decided to keep a low profile during the making of *True Grit*.

In fall 1968, the *True Grit* company travelled to the Colorado Mountains to shoot the film. On the second day of production, a conflict erupted.

Robert Duvall, who played outlaw leader Ned Pepper, suspected even before the start of production that his relationship with Hathaway might run into trouble. Duvall was another New York-trained stage actor. For the most part, the films he had done up until then were of high quality or at least contained thoughtful scripts and good characterizations. He had been directed onscreen by Robert Mulligan and Arthur Penn, both of whom have reputations as being good with actors.

Duvall watched Hathaway berate Glen Campbell more than once and was prepared to receive some of the same. When the director gave him an order, Duvall blew up. According to reports, a heady argument ensued. Later, the actor said he simply did not like Hathaway's method of directing. Duvall considered the veteran to be too much a member of the old school of filmmaking, where a performer had to be positioned exactly before reading lines.

Bill Gray recalled that there "was a little personality conflict with Robert Duvall," but it evidently did not grow out of proportion. The filming proceeded as it should have. Gray went out each morning to a different location, planning for future work, scouting areas to make sure they could be passed through, keeping track of weather reports.

Charles Portis, author of the novel *True Grit*, accompanied the cast and crew on location. According to Duvall, Portis' suggestions were ignored throughout. Allegedly the author wanted the production lensed in a poverty-stricken section of eastern Oklahoma which more closely approximated the feel of the land as revealed in the book.

Hathaway and Duvall ultimately resolved their differences enough to continue shooting. And the film *True Grit* emerged as the raw, boisterous, graphic, yet picturesque, tale that Wallis, Hathaway, and Wayne had visualized. Wayne was particularly pleased with the director's ability to cater to the fantasy concept of an aging Westerner making that last heroic stand and maintain the script's basic honesty.

Hathaway could do that. He had been mixing fast action, slightly more real characters than was the norm in Hollywood's golden age, and fine pictorial quality for forty years. *True Grit* was his fifty-ninth film and eighteenth Western.

Hathaway may have learned how to construct expressive imagery without constantly moving the camera from fellow director Victor Fleming, whom he assisted on *The Virginian* (Paramount, 1929). Henry was an assistant director at Paramount for the next several years, then got a chance to direct one of a series of low-budget Westerns the studio planned to produce. One assignment turned into eight economical, fast, entertaining adaptations of Zane Grey novels, including *Heritage of the West, Wild Horse Mesa* (both 1932), *Under the Tonto Rim, Sunset Pass, Man of the Forest, To the Last Man, Thundering Herd* (all 1933), and *The Last Round-Up* (1934).

The director discovered how to deal with actors and technicians on these little hoss operas. Each night he took the script back to his dwelling and thought about the next day's work. He planned the shots thoroughly, then found that he often needed to rearrange a bit. But he acquired the skill to make films. By the late 1960s, Henry Hathaway had watched many Western fads come and go. He had some theories about why he was so involved in the genre and spoke of Hollywood's treatment of the West.

The director figured he was identified as a maker of Westerns essentially because there were fewer filmmakers dealing with the genre. And there were only so many stories that could be made. Hollywood shot the same plots, from the days of the one-reelers to *Shane* in 1953, which featured a gunfighter protecting farmers. When feature productions took over for one- and two-reelers after World War I, moviemakers already had to scramble to find new ideas. Instead of fresh stories, various cinema techniques gave aging narratives a new slant. Westerns without subtitles didn't work. Then came sound, which provided a new medium for the creaking plots. Color, Cinemascope, and Cinerama all made the good guys versus the bad guys seem different. Yet they all went back to the cowboy. It had started with Bronco Billy and had returned to Rooster Cogburn. Hathaway found to his delight that audiences were interested in the personalities of their protagonists, even if they acted out old-hat tales.

The director thought that *Butch Cassidy and the Sundance Kid* and *The Wild Bunch*, along with *True Grit*, were three of the finest Westerns to be produced in a long time. He liked the men in those pictures and he appreciated the more realistic telling of Western times.

Hathaway happily discovered that audiences liked Rooster Cogburn, despite the man's ornery character. Kim Darby was an essential element in the Western's believability, according to the

Alfred Ryder (center) and John Wayne

filmmaker, who agreed with producer Hal Wallis about the actress' potential.

Unquestionably, the production company of *True Grit* brimmed with thinking individuals. The conflicts may have arisen from old Hollywood veterans trying to come to grips with the new talents, the Hoppers and the Duvalls. But there was one solid relationship between the two generations which got better as the shooting progressed.

Like Kim Darby, Glen Campbell made his cinema debut (in a major role) in the Western. The singer had grown up on John Wayne movies and was highly respectful whenever he and the star met. As with so many other young performers over the years, Wayne was extremely gracious and helpful to Campbell, treating him more like a friend than an inexperienced actor, which undoubtedly added to the quality of Campbell's performance.

If Campbell had just begun his short-lived career as a movie player (at this writing, only a lead in *Norwood* has followed *True Grit*), Wayne was in a way wrapping up forty years as an action star with a performance which won him the Oscar he had always wanted. The actor felt the part was in many ways close to him and believed from the start he could give Rooster more believability than, say, Lee Marvin. And he was correct. John Ford had taught him to not act but react to words and action onscreen. Part of the lesson had involved using a spare acting style.

Reviewers seemed to like *True Grit*, although the Western has since been critized for being overly broad:

> *Kansas City Star,* Giles M. Fowler:
>
> *True Grit* blends a priestly respect for the old ritual with a marvelous flair for stylistic embellishment. The variations never hide the theme; they mainly give it a new freshness through all kinds of expertise and canny detailing. Even the one ghastly blunder, the casting of Glen Campbell in a role he wears like a pine coffin, does not alter my verdict that here is a great movie of its kind.
>
> *Variety:*
>
> Producer Hal Wallis, John Wayne, director Henry Hathaway, a walloping story line, and quality color photography should guarantee *True Grit* as one of the big ones domestically and across the waves. Pic debuts Kim Darby and Glen Campbell, plus action, action, action, are on the positive side in the venture, with a supporting cast, including the great outdoors of Colorado and Mammoth Lake, California adding to the engrossing film.
>
> *The Villager,* Donald Mayerson:
>
> Henry Hathaway has made Charles Portis' best-selling 1968 novel into a lonely and old-fashioned film which comes on the summer movie screen as a winner. . . . *True Grit* has much to recommend it. Big as all outdoors and magnificently filmed, it is violent and tender, brutal and funny. It is also totally unbelievable but very enjoyable.

John Wayne not only won an Oscar for playing Rooster Cogburn, but received a Photoplay Gold Medal Award as well, and later reprised the role in *Rooster Cogburn* (Universal, 1975). A TV pilot in 1978 using the Cogburn character starred Warren Oates. *True Grit* didn't win an Academy Award for Best Picture but was on the National Board of Review's ten best list of 1969.

In 1971 a newspaper story reported that some citizens of the village of Ridgeway, Colorado, which was converted by the *True Grit* company into a 19th-century town, complained that Paramount still hadn't restored the antique caboose from the Rio Grande Southern Railroad the studio had borrowed. Reportedly Paramount paid the community $700 to cover paved sidewalks with dirt, close a park and some streets, and build a gallows and stable. Assistant director Bill Gray told me the production company restored everything, with the exception of a number of roofs over privately owned porches, at the owners' request, and anything else the town decided they liked better. Gray remembered the many friends he made with the area residents during the making of *True Grit* and said he has communicated with those people many times since then.

True Grit shows what made Hollywood great and hints at the traits which will keep the American cinema at such a high level of quality. John Wayne, Henry Hathaway, and Hal Wallis, in their own ways, refined their nation's cinema, consolidating the star image, film technique, and production values. Dennis Hopper and Robert Duvall represent the vitality of those who still make commercial American movies. Both have gone their own glorious ways since *True Grit*. Hopper went on to collaborate with Peter Fonda on the blockbusting anti-establishment, very box-office *Easy Rider* (Columbia, 1969), then into virtual oblivion with the brilliant, apocalyptic film about film called *The Last Movie* (Universal,1971). Duvall continued to give fine performances and was finally recognized for the excellent actor he is in *The Godfather* (Paramount, 1972) and *The Godfather, Part II* (Paramount, 1974).

True Grit is the place where the old and the new met, skirmished, and made one of the most memorable Westerns of the 1960s.

Edmond O'Brien and William Holden

Ernest Borgnine, Warren Oates, William Holden, and Ben Johnson

CHAPTER TWENTY-EIGHT

The Wild Bunch

Year Released: 1969
Studio: Warner Bros.-Seven Arts
Producer: Phil Feldman
Associate Producer: Roy N. Sickner
Director: Sam Peckinpah
Screenplay: Walon Green, Sam Peckinpah, based on a story by Roy N. Sickner and Walon Green
Cinematography: Lucien Ballard
Music: Jerry Fielding
Art Director: Edward Carrere
Editor: Louis Lombardo
Assistant Directors: Cliff Coleman, Fred Gammon
Makeup: Al Greenway
Wardrobe: Gordon Dawson
Sound: Robert J. Miller
Special Effects: Bud Hulburd
Color, 134 minutes

Cast:

Pike Bishop	WILLIAM HOLDEN
Dutch Engstrom	ERNEST BORGNINE
Deke Thornton	ROBERT RYAN
Sykes	EDMOND O'BRIEN
Lyle Gorch	WARREN OATES
Angel	JAIME SANCHEZ

Tector Gorch	BEN JOHNSON
Mapache	EMILIO FERNANDEZ
Coffer	STROTHER MARTIN
T. C.	L. Q. JONES
Pat Harrigan	ALBERT DEKKER
Crazy Lee	BO HOPKINS
May Wainscoat	DUB TAYLOR
Lieutenant Zamorra	JORGE RUSSEK
Herrera	ALFONSO ARAU
Don Jose	CHANO URUETA
Teresa	SONIA AMELIO
Aurora	AURORA CLAVEL
Elsa	ELSA CARDENAS
German Army Officer	FERNANDO WAGNER
Bits	PAUL HARPER
	CONSTANCE WHITE
	LILIA RICHARDS

The Wild Bunch is a devastating chronicle of the death of the West and the end of Western chivalry. In his depiction of how man's instinct for survival and his greed erode dignity, Sam Peckinpah elevates the Western into an apocalyptic vision of America transforming from the wilderness into the industrial age.

A group of men, led by Pike Bishop, arrive in town to rob a bank. Deke Thornton, a former gang member, has allied himself with the railroad. The townspeople surprise the would-be robbers and kill many of them. Those few who escape flee to Mexico, where Bishop discovers it was Thornton who set the gang up for the ambush. "When you side with a man, you stay with him. And if you can't do that, you're like some animal. You're finished. We're all finished." The bandits are hired by a Mexican revolutionary to rob guns and ammunition. They pull off a heist only to be double-crossed by Mapache, the chief insurgent. To avenge the brutal murder of one of their members, the Bunch attacks the garrison. There are no survivors.

As the bandits ride into the village, they pass a group of children eagerly watching a scorpion battle some vicious ants. Impossibly overwhelmed, the scorpion dies slowly in the dust. The demise of the creature symbolizes the dirty termination which awaits all gunmen who live by firepower. Such Westerners will perish in the struggle with a multi-tentacled corporation called modern, organized society, where force is an amoral alternative, not a necessity. As the scorpion is vanquished by nature's command, so is the frontiersman defeated by the invincible might of progress, fueled by a violence which looms organically from beast and man, motivated by the need to survive.

To render the full impact of the horrific but logical procedure, Peckinpah divides his characters into two groups. The first is the honorable men, the Wild Bunch existing on the frontier by their wits, courage, and mutual loyalty. They may be outlaws, but nevertheless they possess cherished qualities. The second group is the civilized or organized man, the railroad officials, the revolutionaries, Thornton, or those who have compromised their ideals to achieve a complex goal, rooted in that need to live another day.

Peckinpah treats Pike Bishop like some sort of perplexed Don Quixote who is at tilting windmills every time he points a gun at a bank teller. It is the relative innocence of the Wild Bunch, the motivation of their violence, that the director extols over the conniving railroaders or Mapache. Like Ford, Peckinpah doesn't exclude those society considers evil from the ability to act honorably. While the Fordian hero tends to go through change or age strictly on a personal level, Bishop is treated as an anachronism, as if the great scheme of things is about to designate him obsolete. So the gang must fight back. Despite the fact that Thornton and the railroaders are in hot pursuit, Bishop agrees to rob the ammunition for Mapache, perhaps as a gift to the revolution, more likely as a nose-thumbing tactic to the 20th century.

But no one can be trusted. While the revolutionaries in *The Professionals* are forced to use deception to foster a realistic, grass-roots rebellion that is ultimately an affirmation of their ideals, Mapache and his gang are obviously as bad as those they wish to replace. When the Mexicans renege on the deal, they hold gang member Angel hostage and treat him sadistically. He is beaten, tied to the back of a car, and dragged around, as Achilles attached Hector's body to the chariot to dishonor the Trojan's memory. Children jump on the tortured man and he is yanked through the hot Mexican dirt, recalling the youngsters' fascination with the writhing scorpion. Ultimately Mapache murders Angel in one of the most brutal scenes recorded in the American cinema. This enrages the Wild Bunch and sets the tone for revenge.

The climatic gunfight between the gang and the Mexicans sets new standards for the depiction of screen violence. Lasting approximately twenty minutes in its best available form, the bloodletting and blowing apart of the human anatomy contains graphic details facilitated by slow motion. The spilling of life and the bursting of guts makes up an evil ballet designed to show the blackest side of

Ernest Borgnine and William Holden

The last battle

the human soul. The entire atmosphere of *The Wild Bunch* is chokingly arid, from the parched terrains to the cracked, pitted faces of the gang to the dusty clothes they wear, and life itself seems to be on the edge of explosion. The final battle detonates the bomb which has disarmed the gunfighter as a vital force in America.

The cast of *The Wild Bunch* is composed primarily of seasoned veterans as experienced in their craft as the men they enact. William Holden, Ernest Borgnine, Robert Ryan, Edmond O'Brien, Warren Oates, Jaime Sanchez, Ben Johnson, Strother Martin, L. Q. Jones, and the others perform as a cohesive unit the way John Ford's renowned stock company worked in the 1930s, 40s, and 50s.

But the men in *The Wild Bunch* have to die. The way they go makes for the greatness of the film.

The Making of *The Wild Bunch*

Sam Peckinpah hadn't directed a complete film in four years. After lensing two "B" Westerns, *The Deadly Companions* (Pathé-American, 1961) and *Ride the High Country* (MGM, 1962), it looked as though Peckinpah might become one of the most respected American filmmakers of the 1960s.

His next two projects were fraught with dissension. The director began shooting *The Cincinnati Kid* (MGM, 1965), a contemporary drama about a gambler, but was replaced by Norman Jewison. Peckinpah co-wrote the script for his next production, *Major Dundee* (Columbia, 1965), which promised to be a Civil War epic. The film went over schedule, over budget, and suffered at the hand of studio editors. The finished product pleased neither critics nor public.

Disenchanted with the filmmaking process, Peckinpah spent the next several years living day-to-day, picking up television assignments whenever possible. But his career was at a standstill. The promise had yet to be fulfilled.

During this time, the Western began looking like a has-been genre, a field of film slowly decaying under the weight of former grandeur. The best cowboy movies of the period tended toward simple constructions, veteran actors, and experienced directors such as Howard Hawks and Henry Hathaway, men with about eighty years in the motion picture industry between them. These Westerns generally stressed comedy a bit more than their predecessors and poked fun at the fallibility of heroes, heroines, and villains. Another short-lived cycle of the time was comic Westerns. *Cat Ballou* (Columbia, 1965), *The Hallelujah Trail* (UA, 1965), *The*

Rounders (MGM, 1965), and *Support Your Local Sheriff* (UA, 1969) took a lighthearted look at outlaws, the military, and lawmen.

Producer Daniel Melnick admired *Ride the High Country* and, when he decided to adapt Katherine Anne Porter's short story *Noon Wine* for television, he contacted Sam Peckinpah. The director turned *Noon Wine* into a tender video drama, one of his best televison pieces. Peckinpah was promising again.

Over the years Sam had read a number of scripts, considered ideas himself, and thought about adapting material. He believed a screenplay written by Walon Green, Roy Sickner, and actor Lee Marvin had great potential. He discussed the property with producers Phil Feldman and Kenny Hyman. Both were enthusiastic, Feldman particularly so because he was a fan of *Ride the High Country*. In fact, he regarded the Western as a masterpiece and Peckinpah a genius for having made it.

Feldman and Hyman had already gone over two other projects with Peckinpah, titled *The Diamond Story* and *North to Yesterday*. But the director pushed for the Western script, which would be called *The Wild Bunch*, and finally he got the go-ahead. As was the case with *Ride the High Country*, Peckinpah made extensive revisions in the script.

The credits of *The Wild Bunch* list Peckinpah and Walon Green as co-authors of the screenplay, with no mention of Roy Sickner or Lee Marvin. Although Marvin wasn't publicly associated with the picture, Sickner was its associate producer.

The Wild Bunch became Sam Peckinpah's vision. He had strong ideas about Western themes. The director once said he'd like to make Westerns in the way of Japanese filmmaker Akira Kurosawa. Two of Kurosawa's greatest works, *Rashomon* (1951) and *Seven Samurai* (1954), have been turned into two Hollywood Westerns, *The Outrage* (MGM, 1964) and *The Magnificent Seven* (UA, 1960), so the analogy isn't so far-fetched.

Peckinpah saw the frontier as a dirty, violent place, where honor among men could only occasionally be achieved. The filmmaker believed that the Westerner was not inherently noble but had to be taught the ways of civilization. The way he would illustrate this point helped provide the unique quality of *The Wild Bunch*. Co-star Robert Ryan opined that all Western stories have been filmed before, but the difference in Peckinpah's work came from its style.

That style had roots in an acute attention to detail and an incredible facility to turn minute aspects of frontier existence into microcosmic symbols of American Western culture. This talent, so aptly shown in *Ride the High Country*, which struggled for life in

Major Dundee, blossomed fully in *The Wild Bunch*.

The cast was extraordinary. William Holden headed the gunfighters (all familiar screen faces). The survivors of an attempted bank robbery are hired by a Mexican general (Emilio Fernandez) to steal arms and munitions. Robert Ryan acted the Judas of the Bunch, who has turned against his compatriots to align himself with Pat Harrigan (Albert Dekker), an unscrupulous railroad man.

William Holden's career had leveled off before Peckinpah cast him as Pike Bishop, leader of the Bunch. His previous four films, *The Seventh Dawn* (UA, 1964), *Alvarez Kelly* (Columbia, 1966), *Casino Royale* (Columbia, 1967), and *The Devil's Brigade* (UA, 1968) are not particularly memorable, although *Kelly* shows the actor's still-ample ability to render a gritty performance (such as the one he would give for Peckinpah). Like Burt Lancaster in *The Professionals*, Holden was the only leading man used in a list of equally talented craftsmen.

Borgnine, O'Brien, and Ryan could lend top-notch support to any production, good or bad. They were the ones who often made forgettable films palatable. When given a top quality script, like *The Wild Bunch*, their real talents emerged. The Borgnine of *Marty* (UA, 1955), the O'Brien of *Julius Caesar* (MGM, 1953), and the Ryan of *The Set-Up* (RKO, 1949) came back like a phoenix from the ashes of mediocre movies.

Warren Oates, Strother Martin, and L. Q. Jones form the core of a repertory company the quality of which hasn't been seen in American cinema since Victor McLaglen, Ben Johnson, Ward Bond, Harry Carey, Jr., George O'Brien, and others became stock faces in the Westerns of John Ford. Each of Peckinpah's "regulars" had a special respect for their director, which grew with their professional association with the man. They all worked together in television. Oates co-starred in *Ride the High Country* and *Major Dundee*. L. Q. Jones appeared in *Ride the High Country*.

The men behind the camera respected Sam Peckinpah as well. Lucien Ballard, director of photography on *Ride the High Country*, was assigned the same duties on *The Wild Bunch*. He and Peckinpah ploughed through many films and photographs concerning the Mexican revolution, finding that images often contained a rather shallow, flat tone, and choosing the lenses considered best for achieving that effect in *The Wild Bunch*. Whenever Ballard had a suggestion for a camera angle, movement, lighting, or anything else, Peckinpah was receptive. And the director wasn't one to blame the failure of an idea he accepted from somewhere else on that person. Like producer Darryl F. Zanuck, Peckinpah felt totally responsible for the films he turned out. When something went wrong, he took the blame. Such dedication can really bind a cast and crew into a fine unit of production.

Despite the problems he had had with Columbia over the making of *Major Dundee*, Peckinpah did not deny Warners the right to see sections of *The Wild Bunch* while production continued. Instead of showing rough cuts of certain scenes, the director polished the work with editor Louis Lombardo in the evening, after spending the day lensing new material. Peckinpah often worked fifteen to twenty hours a day for weeks at a time to get both jobs done. But with the studio exerting much pressure on him to finish the picture, and even considering terminating the entire project, the filmmaker must have felt it especially important to show executives good results from their hard work.

Since the director pushed his talents to the limits daily, he naturally expected his co-workers to do the same. Stella Stevens, co-star of Peckinpah's *The Ballad of Cable Hogue* (Warner Bros., 1970), has attested to that. L. Q. Jones has testified to the director's incredible attention to detail. He always insisted, for example, on checking over the costumes of extras who would only be seen at a distance in the film. And so it went. Authenticity was stressed in every aspect of *The Wild Bunch*. Everything had to be consistent if Sam Peckinpah's vision would come to the screen intact. This is certainly not an unusual stance for a filmmaker to take. Erich Von Stroheim alarmed executives by ordering extras playing army officers in *Merry-Go-Round* (Universal, 1923) to wear regulation underwear, despite the fact that no one would see the shorts. While making *McCabe and Mrs. Miller* (Warner Bros., 1971), Robert Altman insisted drawers which would never be opened in a scene be filled with artifacts of the narrative's turn-of-the-century environment.

When Peckinpah couldn't find the right kind of ants in Mexico, the director sent back to the United States for some. Of course, such dedication sometimes makes it tough on fellow workers. Striving for perfection is an arduous, time-consuming task. Things have to go exactly right. And they seldom do. At first Strother Martin had a difficult time with Peckinpah. The actor apparently wasn't giving the director the kind of emotion he wanted. But the difficulties must have been overcome, as Martin received a supporting role in Peckinpah's next film, *The Ballad of Cable Hogue*.

It wasn't until after the final scenes of *The Wild Bunch* were shot that the real controversy began. The Western's savagery and extreme violence, featuring a number of graphic gun fights (some shot in slow motion, making the shattering of bodies and the pouring of blood and guts more visible), shocked many. One particularly horrific scene features a throat-slitting.

Warner executives recoiled at Peckinpah's film and insisted he make extensive revisions, eliminating a portion of the brutality. The director agreed. He didn't like the pace of the film anyway. Peckinpah and editor Lombardo cut out the first battle in the production and scissored a disemboweling.

Lombardo was most grateful to Peckinpah for the opportunity to edit *The Wild Bunch*, his first major cinema assignment. Lombardo also edited Peckinpah's TV *Noon Wine*. The editor discovered that the filmmaker inspired him to heights he didn't know he could achieve. A necessary key to the success of any film is the relationship between the director and editor. If they agree on the overall concept of the cutting, a production can be greatly enhanced; if not, a work might look choppy and incomplete. It was of the utmost importance that Peckinpah and Lombardo get along, due to the complex nature of *The Wild Bunch* and to provide a united front in the war to drastically alter the length and content of the Western.

There were reportedly 3,643 cuts in the original version of *The Wild Bunch*, more than twice as many as in the average feature length film. It has been asserted that there are more separate shots in the Western than any other Technicolor production. A number of the shots are only three or four frames long. Much time and effort was spent by Peckinpah and Lombardo paring down the footage of the print to a work suitable to all. The two spent at least fifteen hours a day together. Lombardo later recalled that he spent more time with the director in this period than with his wife. Sometimes Lombardo added or subtracted as few as two or three frames per shot, which would surely test the mettle of any cutter. Lombardo found this kind of quest for perfection to be a tonic to his talents rather than a strain on his composure and sanity.

Peckinpah went over *The Wild Bunch* frame by frame. He did the first cut on location in Paras, Mexico. The director allowed Lombardo much freedom on the rough cut for each scene. Then he stepped in to make corrections, additions, and suggestions. While the filmmaker had a clear concept of *The Wild Bunch*, it didn't stop him from making alterations in the editing room. He never let preconceived notions dominate when intuition told him to follow another course.

With all the problems regarding the length and content of the Western, Peckinpah happily did not face the strife which fellow director John Sturges engaged in while trying to make *The Magnificent Seven* in Mexico about a decade earlier. It has been said that Sam Peckinpah's intimate knowledge of Mexico and Mexicans made it easier for him to film south of the border than, say, a moviemaker with no exposure to the land or customs of the country.

Warner Bros.-Seven Arts didn't handle *The Wild Bunch* well at

Sam Peckinpah

all. There were so many varying opinions about the film and the way it should be distributed that it almost drowned in its own publicity. Allegedly Warner executive Ben Kalmenson didn't like the film and as such gave the production a lackluster advertising build-up. Peckinpah was of course distraught over what he considered to be cavalier handling of the piece of art he had labored so long and hard to create. However, the director was pleased with the decision of Warner Bros. International head Norman Katz to book seventy-millimeter prints of the Western into theatres in Sweden, Great Britain, France, Italy, Japan, Spain, and Australia.

At one point, the director tried to put back two flashbacks and a raid on a Mexican town which were originally scissored. Whether or not he succeeded depends on the print available for a given screening. Even when first shown in 1969, *The Wild Bunch* seemed to list a different length every few months. Leonard Maltin's reliable volume *TV Movies* (Signet) gives a time of 134 minutes. Sixteen-millimeter rental houses offer the Western at about this length. But, in 1972, Warners offered a "TV version" to networks, with no pretense that they were getting the film as Peckinpah envisioned it. *The Wild Bunch* can be viewed as a classic Western or a foray into senseless, unmotivated violence. It all depends on the print.

Whatever the qualms of the front office, the cast and crew of *The Wild Bunch* supported the Western all the way. After a press screening in the Bahamas, star William Holden was shocked at the negative reaction of the viewers. He couldn't believe that members of the audience could accept violence in daily life and reject it on screen. Director Peckinpah was notably absent during much of the conference, having probably anticipated what was by then a stock reaction to his picture.

The reviews varied in tone and intent:

Kansas City Star, Giles M. Fowler:

Yet the film as a whole leaves a feeling of growing distaste, as the enormity of it seeps through other reactions. On the one hand, one discovers the picture's underlying tone of sententious preachiness, its heavy laying-on of moral points bracketed by savage action. On the other hand lies the negative effect of savagery carried beyond the level of horror to the level of numbing surfeit.

New York Morning Telegraph, Leo Mishkin:

It may be that with all its shocking savagery, with all its blood and gore spilling out over the screen—in slow motion yet—with all its brutality and sheer revulsion, *The Wild Bunch* may have opened up a new form of screen violence, one that may eventually prove much more beneficial in the end than what we've been objecting to up to now.

Manhattan Tribune, Clayton Riley:

Sam Peckinpah brings us back to death . . . thrusts the end

of life across the brink and into our anxious laps, gives the world *The Wild Bunch* crashing all silence, with a violence that is too purely stated to be anything else but a cherished, sensually pleasurable exercise in cinematic masturbation. . . .

Variety:

Film at 145 minutes is far overlength, and should be tightened extensively, particularly in first half. . . . Holden goes into character for his role and handles assignment expertly. Borgnine delivers his usual brand of acting as former's aide and Ryan is dramatically efficient as Holden's hunter.

Co-star Robert Ryan felt that America had a tradition of violence which was merely reflected in *The Wild Bunch*. The thinking performer couldn't guess if screen brutality would be a benefit or drawback in the future, but argued that Peckinpah's depiction of killing and maiming, while occasionally overdone, had been accomplished with great artistry.

Sam Peckinpah could not understand the negative reaction to his Western. He believed he was simply showing the reality of the human condition, nothing more. Perhaps some didn't want to come to grips with the notion that homo sapiens shared more with the animal kingdom than the earth they treaded. The filmmaker insisted that man was violent in order to survive. The instinct was as old as the human race itself. He wanted to render a depiction of the tough, sometimes cruel men who lived in the West. Sam Peckinpah wanted *The Wild Bunch* to have a cathartic effect on viewers. The director certainly didn't think the work would provoke moviegoers. The climactic gun battle was supposed to illustrate the reality of being ripped apart by a bullet. To the filmmaker, the Western made a statement against violence.

The Wild Bunch now is generally regarded as a classic. It is indeed an archetypal case of one man's battle to put an untouched vision onscreen in an industry which is today ruled by commercial considerations more than ever before. The old studios could afford to make an occasional "art" film, a work they didn't expect to make money, because their production lines assembled so many other profitable vehicles. In the 1960s and 70s, independent producers just didn't have the machines of yesteryear, and studios were often nothing more than distribution houses. One-picture contracts are the norm. There are comparatively few people on a movie company's payroll from year to year. The breakdown in the studio system in the 1950s was supposed to have freed film artists from the need to sign long-term, exclusive contracts which virtually gave away their power to accept or reject a given script.

Like Erich Von Stroheim, William S. Hart, and Orson Welles before him, Peckinpah fought movie executives for the right to control his own art. Since *The Wild Bunch* grossed $5,250,000 in America, the graphic Western wasn't his last film. He lensed *The Ballad of Cable Hogue* for Warners the next year, *Junior Bonner* (Cinerama, 1972), and *Pat Garrett and Billy The Kid* (MGM, 1973). But Sam Peckinpah was an honorable man, in the way of Pike Bishop, determined to do his job as he saw it. Bishop died, and fulfilled his fate. Peckinpah can go on breathing life into the American cinema as long as his work continues to make a profit.

Paul Newman, Katharine Ross, and Robert Redford

Robert Redford (center left), Paul Newman (center right), and the gang

CHAPTER TWENTY-NINE

Butch Cassidy and the Sundance Kid

Year Released: 1969
Studio: Twentieth Century-Fox
Producer: John Foreman
Director: George Roy Hill
Screenplay: William Goldman
Cinematography: Conrad Hall
Music: Burt Bacharach
Art Directors: Jack Martin Smith, Philip Jefferies
Editors: John C. Howard, Richard C. Meyer
Assistant Director: Steven Bernhardt
Second Unit Director: Michael Moore
Production Manager: Lloyd Anderson
Set Decorators: Walter M. Scott, Chester L. Bayhi
Makeup: Dan Striepeke
Costumes: Edith Head
Sound: William E. Edmondson, David E. Dockendorf
Special Photographic Effects: L. B. Abbott, Art Cruickshank
Special Still Photography: Lawrence Schiller
Graphic Montage: John Neuhart
Color, 110 minutes

Cast:

Butch Cassidy	PAUL NEWMAN
The Sundance Kid	ROBERT REDFORD
Etta Place	KATHARINE ROSS

Percy Garris	STROTHER MARTIN
Bike Salesman	HENRY JONES
Sheriff Bledsoe	JEFF COREY
Woodcock	GEORGE FURTH
Agnes	CLORIS LEACHMAN
Harvey Logan	TED CASSIDY
Marshal	KENNETH MARS
Macon	DONNELLY RHODES
Big Woman	JODY GILBERT
News Carver	TIMOTHY SCOTT
Fireman	DON KEEFER
Flat Nose Curry	CHARLES DIERKOP
Bank Manager	FRANCISCO CORDOVA
Photographer	NELSON OLMSTEAD
Card Player #1	PAUL BRYAR
Card Player #2	SAM ELLIOTT
Bank Teller	CHARLES AKINS
Tiffany's Salesman	ERIC SINCLAIR

Butch Cassidy and the Sundance Kid celebrates the last of the legendary Western outlaws in a warm and nostalgic way which depicts the West as it should have been. William Goldman's story of two fun-loving bandits to whom robbery is a way to make money, and not an obsession, is taken into various realms of parody, reality, and romance by director George Roy Hill, whose keen eye for character balance and graceful visuals helps create a truly charming Western with the precision of a pendulum.

Two outlaws rob banks and trains in the late 19th- and early 20th-century Southwest and, in their escapades, they meet a pretty schoolteacher named Etta Place who is looking for adventure. The three take off together and Sundance is soon romancing Etta. The trio performs as a well-knit unit of banditry, with Etta often going to a prospective bank and noting details. Whenever Butch and Sundance pull a job, it is always without violence. As their reputations grow, the law begins to pursue them with increased vigor. Etta eventually becomes tired of running, and the three decide to start a new life in South America. There the men change their names and take jobs in a mining camp, but the robberies begin again and Etta finally returns to the United States. The Pinkertons have located the outlaws in Bolivia and, with the help of the local militia, ultimately

Paul Newman and Katharine Ross

shoot down Butch and Sundance.

By 1969, there were a number of films which showed the final days of the West that once was. But *Butch Cassidy and the Sundance Kid* gives new life to the subject while embracing the notion that cowboys, gunfighters, and bandits had to disappear with the coming of modern civilization. Screenwriter Goldman and director Hill intertwine three perspectives of their outlaws to fully illustrate how legend and history view the men. The natural range of Paul Newman and Robert Redford blends these dynamics into combustible, whole men who can act like heroes or clowns.

Butch and Sundance were very real, but time and their talents have made them part of Western mythology. Unlike other criminals of the day, they always eschewed violence in favor of shrewd, bloodless planning. Yet Butch's quick wit and Sundance's fast gun can get them out of just about any situation. At one point, it looks like the two have pulled their last job when the pursuing posse has them trapped on a cliff where the only escape is the river far below. The wily Butch decides they should jump, even though Sundance can't swim. They grab hold of a single holster and leap into the water. Surviving such a dangerous stunt itself turns them into legends in their own time.

Yet the scene is funny and touching as well as adventurous. The two say goodbye in a subtle way, making a final affirmation of their friendship. It is a unique cameraderie in a frontier where a man would just as soon shoot another in the back or steal his horse as look at him. Sundance reveals an embarrassing secret. Redford's Kid looks hesitatingly at Newman's Butch, then shouts "I can't swim!" The laugh has a cathartic effect, breaking the poignant tension of the previous moment. The actors' ability to make the smooth transition from an heroic tenderness to an Abbott and Costello situation stemming from Sundance's relatively petty fear of water brings together the valiant aspect of their macho characters and a simple, sometimes awkward humanism which is always real.

Director Hill switches repeatedly from exciting adventures to comic antics and a touch of romance. Minor plot elements or character details are expanded to show what their lives are all about. The scene played out to Burt Bacharach's "Raindrops Keep Falling on My Head" developed from Butch's affinity for bicycling. Together, in an image filled with misty morning sun, Butch and Etta ride, smiling and laughing, without saying a word. Here Hill capsulizes the bandits' relatively carefree existence.

All three know the idyllic lifestyle must end. Hill and Goldman manage the extremely difficult task of switching the film to a deadly serious depiction of the price which is exacted for unorthodox living. After Etta leaves, the fate of Butch and Sundance is sealed. The two are hunted down at a mining camp. The situation is similar to the one on the mountain cliff. Boxed just inside the mine entrance, surrounded by dozens of well-armed men, they prepare to break out in a blaze of glory. They, of course, don't make it. But George Hill never lets us see them fall in the hail of bullets. As soon as the two thrust themselves out of the rock cocoon, they are caught by director Hill in a freeze frame that catches them hunched over, running for their freedom, against the sounds of massive fire power. A sepia tone imbues the image, as does the opening scene of the Western, forever coating Butch and Sundance like eternal tintypes in the golden mist of memory. The filmmakers don't want to tell of their deaths. But they must. No one mourns. The Western prefers to remember the outlaws as they were, as opposed to the bloody end suffered by the gangsters in *Bonnie and Clyde* (Warner Bros., 1967).

Butch Cassidy and the Sundance Kid is a radiantly individual film which looks at its protagonists as legends, as men, and as memories.

The Making of *Butch Cassidy and the Sundance Kid*

WANTED: Robert Leroy Parker, alias "Butch" Cassidy, George Cassidy, Ingerfeld, Lowe, Maxwell. Height: 5'9"; Weight: 155; Eyes: Blue; Hair: Light Brown; Distinguishing Marks: Two scars on back of head, one scar under left eye.

Robert Parker was born on April 6, 1866, in Cleville, Utah, the eldest of thirteen children of Mormon parents. Only Robert and his younger brother Daniel became outlaws. The rest of the children stayed within the law.

A bandit named Mike Cassidy was a neighbor of the Parkers and at an early age Robert became fascinated with the man. Like a 19th-century Western groupie, Robert rechristened himself "Robert Cassidy," after his hero. Mike taught Robert how to shoot a gun and elude lawmen. The education of Robert Cassidy fell to the "able" hands of one of the old masters of banditry on the American frontier.

Mike introduced young Robert, nicknamed "Butch," to the art of cattle rustling in the Colorado range. Butch learned quickly, and his easygoing style made him a natural leader. Soon he and Mike were running the gang together. Butch assumed complete control when Mike shot a Wyoming rancher and disappeared into the anonymity so easily achieved in the spacious West.

Butch and his gang held up at Robber's Roost, where he met the *creme de la creme* of outlawry—the McCarty Brothers and Matt Warner, among others. It didn't take long for such men to take up arms on the wrong side of the law with Butch Cassidy.

Their first job was robbing the Denver and Rio Grande Express on November 3, 1887. It failed because the vault guard simply refused to open the safe. The McCartys considered shooting the man.

Butch called for a vote. The "nays" won, the courageous guard stayed alive and the gang rode off empty-handed, but learned much about their leader.

For a variety of reasons, the men switched to robbing banks. They hauled in $20,000 without firing a shot by using wit and daring at the First National Bank of Denver on March 30, 1889. With growing success came more intense action by law enforcement agencies. Posses criss-crossed Wyoming and Colorado looking for Butch and his cohorts, who wisely decided to keep a low profile.

In the early 1890s Butch Cassidy temporarily became a law-abiding citizen, taking work as a cowboy and a butcher. Ultimately, he drifted back into banditry and, with Al Rainer, formed an organization which specialized in extorting money from local ranchers. As if Al Capone had set up business in the West, Butch told ranchers that they would have to pay him a "protection" fee against the possible loss of their cattle. Rainer and Cassidy were arrested by Sheriff John Ward of Wyoming, and Butch spent the next two years in prison.

In jail, he heard about Hole-in-the-Wall, one of the final robber hideaways located in Colorado. There Butch met many native desperadoes, and was crafty enough to recruit from them a group which consisted of top gunmen and thieves.

With George Curry, Harvey Logan, and Ezra Lay, Butch put another nail into his rapidly developing reputation during the Union Pacific Overland holdup of June 2, 1899. One of the gang members had to uncouple the car carrying the bank vault because the engineer refused to accommodate them. Butch and the others didn't realize the great danger they were all in while Lay unhooked the car alone. They forgot about a dynamite charge planted beneath the trestle where the stalled train rested and barely escaped with their lives.

Another stubborn guard later tried to thwart their plans by refusing to open a bank vault. Butch dynamited the door, knocking the guard unconscious in the process. Harvey Logan almost killed the man but Butch thought such courage should not be rewarded by death, so the gang simply left with $30,000.

The Pinkertons took up the trail of Butch and the Wild Bunch after this robbery. Several additional stick-ups followed, and, although Cassidy remained free, the gang membership changed, as usual, thanks to various hangings, jailings, killings, and occupational transience. In 1900, Butch met outlaw Harry Longabaugh, who called himself The Sundance Kid, at Hole-in-the-Wall. The Kid was reportedly the fastest gun in the West at the turn of the century, although his soft-spoken character belied the reputation. He and

Butch formed a true friendship, a rare occurrence in their line of work.

In 1901, the Wild Bunch robbed the Great Northern Flyer when it chugged to the outskirts of Wagner, Montana, netting $40,000 as well as the attention of a hundred-man posse. The gang hid out at a brothel in Fort Worth, Texas, and allegedly Butch learned how to ride a bicycle.

When the law slowly closed in, Butch, Sundance, and a schoolteacher named Etta Place fled to South America. The Kid and Etta became intimate. For a while the Pinkertons couldn't locate them, but when reports reached America of two cowboys sticking up banks in the manner long established by Butch and Sundance, the agency acted quickly. As a cover for their robberies, the outlaws worked by day as laborers for the Concordia Tin Mine in Bolivia. After two years, their employer discovered the identities of his employees and the pair fled. In 1907 Etta Place was taken to the United States by Sundance for an operation. She probably did not return to South America.

Sundance came back and the two continued robbing banks. Here the story of Butch Cassidy and the Sundance Kid veers off into several different trails. Some say that in 1908 the outlaws were surrounded by soldiers near San Vicente, Bolivia, and, as they ran for their weapons, Sundance was mowed down by a hail of gun fire. Realizing the situation was hopeless, Butch Cassidy blew his head off.

Or did he? Perhaps he made his way back to the United States, anonymously wandered the West while toiling at different jobs, and finally settled in Washington, where he died in the late 1930s. That was the fate of Butch Cassidy, according to his sister Lulu, the youngest of thirteen Parker kids. The eighty-five-year-old Mrs. Lulu Betenson said so in 1969. And she wrote a book about her brother's exploits to correct what she considered a lot of false impressions about his character. But nobody knows for sure what happened to Harry "Sundance Kid" Longabaugh, although recent findings have indicated he might have escaped death in Bolivia as well.

A half-century after Butch and Sundance may have died in the South American shoot-out, writer William Goldman became fascinated with their exploits. He spent more than a half-dozen years researching the subject, and pored over the actual records of the Pinkerton National Detective Agency, as well as many other sources in the preparation of a film script. Goldman realized quickly that the characters were not typical of the bad men who terrorized the 19th-century American West. They were friends. They didn't like to shoot or in any way maim people in the course of a hold-up. And they never had been the subject of a feature length

American Western, although Sundance had been portrayed often throughout the years.

It was almost too good to be true. While Jesse James, Billy the Kid, the Younger Brothers, the Daltons, John Wesley Hardin, the Ike Clanton Family, and other famous outlaws were included in many Hollywood productions, big and small, the studios for various reasons refused to explore the Butch and Sundance legend.

By 1968 Goldman fashioned a script called *Butch Cassidy and the Sundance Kid,* with many ideas as to how the film could be shot. Not that Goldman wanted to take over the director's job of devising the shot sequence of the Western. In Hollywood, movie executives often plan a production based on how many pages of a scenario can be filmed per day, not how difficult the shooting might be. At one point, writer Goldman gave his director extra time to polish the Western by including a virtual feast of direction from every angle—cinematography, mood, acting—just to "pack" the screenplay and make it seem a longer job than would appear if the material was submitted without the extras.

In any case, nobody would take the script. The same reason for rejection was given over and over again. To be sure, Butch and Sundance were colorful and unusual, but they weren't bad bad guys. They weren't normal cinema anti-heroes. Apparently, Goldman had "forgotten" to include a villain in the Western. He wrote the script with two heroes and nobody for them to fight, aside from some vague force called the law, usually seen only from a distance.

Yet the material was completely in stride with the kind of Westerns being produced in the 1960s, beginning with Sam Peckinpah's *Ride the High Country.* Peckinpah filmed two men, one good, one not so good. But both come through as heroes in a tale about the dying of the frontier. That's one of the concerns of Goldman's script. And Hollywood had been dipping notorious bad men in celluloid holy water and emerging with anti-heroes since the days of William S. Hart. King Vidor presented Billy Bonney as a not-so-bad guy in *Billy the Kid* (MGM, 1930). Henry King and Nunnally Johnson shed a sympathetic light on the James boys in *Jesse James* in 1939. Even Paul Newman's Billy the Kid movie, Arthur Penn's *The Left-Handed Gun* (Warner Bros., 1958), whitewashed somewhat the legend of the notorious outlaw. These infamous bad guys have been portrayed as heroes in any number of "B" Westerns.

Somehow Richard Zanuck of Twentieth Century-Fox was finally convinced of the merits of *Butch Cassidy and the Sundance Kid,* and advanced Goldman a record $400,000 for screen rights. Although he was a well-known author and playwright at the time, the writer's fee certainly reflected a lot of faith in the project on the studio's part.

After the movie opened, someone asked George Roy Hill why filmmakers had been so reluctant to deal with Butch and Sundance. Hill felt part of the reason made this Western different from past oaters. Formerly, sagebrush sagas were like "morality plays," where good was bad and bad was bad.

"Ours is more than even an adult Western; it's not a Western at all. It's a character study and a re-telling on the screen of the true adventures of a specific gang and their leader. And as a character study, Butch Cassidy's story couldn't have been put on the screen before. He was an affable man, who chose to be an outlaw as others decided to be lawyers and dentists."

It took several years before the script actually began production. William Goldman saw Paul Newman as the Sundance Kid, with Jack Lemmon playing Butch. Richard Zanuck immediately rejected Lemmon and planned the Western as a superstar vehicle. There weren't many stars bigger than Lemmon, but a number of actors were more immediately acceptable in a Western role. One was Steve McQueen. Zanuck wanted Newman as Sundance and McQueen to enact Butch.

Newman didn't know if he could portray Sundance. If he decided to sign for the role, however, the contract would have to stipulate that he get top billing over McQueen. Goldman couldn't see McQueen in his script at all. And when McQueen heard Newman's billing demand, the star of *The Great Escape* withdrew from the project.

By this time George Roy Hill had been offered the job of direction. After McQueen's departure, Zanuck, Goldman, and Hill met to discuss a replacement. Hill knew the man he needed right away. In 1962 he had tested a promising actor named Robert Redford for a small role in the director's first picture, *Period of Adjustment* (MGM). Zanuck was not impressed. He reportedly felt Redford had been given ample opportunity to demonstrate his abilities in such films as *Situation Hopeless, But Not Serious* (Paramount, 1965), *Inside Daisy Clover* (Warner Bros., 1966), *The Chase* (Columbia, 1966), *This Property Is Condemned* (Paramount, 1966), and *Barefoot in the Park* (Paramount, 1967), and all but the last, in which Redford recreated his Broadway role, received a cool reception from critics and moviegoers. The feeling persisted that Redford had received a chance to show his value and failed. And Zanuck wanted Goldman's serio-comic Western story to be bolstered by superstars.

The situation remained the same for some time. Others involved in the property realized director Hill was not going to be swayed from his belief that Newman and Redford would make a dandy team. *Butch Cassidy and the Sundance Kid* was to be Hill's

Robert Redford

first Western and in fact his first action narrative after *Period of Adjustment, Toys in the Attic* (UA, 1963), *The World of Henry Orient* (UA, 1964), *Hawaii* (UA, 1966), and *Thoroughly Modern Millie* (Universal, 1967). The last title had been the studio's biggest grossing production to that time. Being box-office gave Hill a leverage he probably wouldn't have enjoyed if his work had not shown a profit.

Zanuck finally relented, and Hill sent Redford a script. The actor was sure he could play Butch Cassidy, but preferred the role of Sundance. Newman worried about the comic quality of Butch. His previous film, *The Secret War of Harry Frigg* (Universal, 1968), an unsuccessful war comedy, made the star question his own comic activities. Hill persisted, Redford kept talking, and finally Newman agreed.

With the main characters cast, Hill started planning the production. He first screened about fifty Westerns to study the trends of the past. The director wanted to avoid cliches or any repetition. Plots, characters, and visuals were to be fresh. Hill chose Conrad Hall, who had photographed *The Professionals* and had worked with Paul Newman on *Harper* (Warner Bros., 1966) and *Cool Hand Luke* (Warner Bros.-Seven Arts, 1967), as his cinematographer.

Four months prior to the hiring of Hall were spent in seeking proper locations. A second trip taken by Hill and Hall checked out the sites again. Hill told Hall about the specific shots he wanted. The cinematographer then shaped the director's ideas into a workable form, sometimes adding dimensions to a concept or specific image. Today George Roy Hill considers his collaboration with Conrad Hall to have produced some of his finest work.

Conrad Hall appreciated being involved in the project early because the cinematographer felt the physical look of a picture to be his responsibility. By taking part in early preparation, he could make a more thorough and foolproof plan with Hill, which would help cut down the shooting schedule.

As usual, the director gave his ideas for the cinematography to a sketch artist, who roughed out approximations of the sequences. Hill then discussed them with Hall and other crew members, including assistant director Steven Bernhardt and second unit director Michael Moore. Although the drawings did not have to be strictly adhered to, they provided a frame of reference for all concerned and, in this case, allowed others to make suggestions.

Both Steven Bernhardt and Michael Moore told me that they enjoyed the freedom to contribute ideas of their own throughout the entire production, which some directors do not allow. "In the case of *Butch Cassidy,* I enjoyed it particularly, because George Roy Hill gave me quite a bit of latitude, in terms of working with the extras, setting up all of the background scenes," said Bernhardt. "The picture was basically a performance picture. Some people might not see it that way, but he concentrated very heavily on the performances, and all I would do is get an idea of what he wanted to see in the background." The assistant director's job was to work with other departments in verifying the authenticity of the film, from costumes to movement to continuity. He had to make sure everything appeared in the right place and at the right time.

"Thanks to George Roy Hill being the pro he is, he gives his second unit director much freedom and welcomes any ideas or suggestions either involving the second unit or, for that matter, situations involving the first unit," opined Michael Moore. "Speaking from a second unit director's viewpoint, one of George Roy Hill's best qualities is that he has no qualms about using a second unit. He knows that if it's done right, it can take nothing away from his being the director of the film. He knows that by using a second unit he can devote more time with his principals on the more intricate sequences, while the second unit is picking up footage using doubles that, if shot correctly, will intercut with his footage and no one will be able to determine what was first or second unit."

As Steven Bernhardt indicated, characterization and performance were the focal points of *Butch Cassidy and the Sundance Kid.* Director Hill wanted to impart this idea to the audience in the first scene of the film. So he began with close-ups of Newman and Redford, rather than panoramic long shots of prairie, mountains, and sky which opens so many Westerns. In this way, the filmmaker tried to equalize the stature of the actors in the eyes of the moviegoer. Newman was a superstar, Redford a talented, relatively fresh personality. Yet Butch and Sundance stood shoulder to shoulder, one as good as the other. Hill rejected the customary first lead, second lead Hollywood formula.

The mutual respect and admiration shared by Hill, Newman, and Redford aided the effort to make the characters into a balanced unit. Such a concept would have received a cool reception from many actors. Naturally, a big star does not ordinarily want to share the lead with a lesser one. It's something like the best house on the block being next to the most run-down dwelling on the street. There is always the fear that the mansion will go down in value. And of course the natural competition of performers who want to do a good job can sometimes spur a production to excellence. But just as Paul Newman realized he could successfully play the amoral title role in *Hud,* he was wise enough to know that being on the same level with Robert Redford would not in any way hurt him.

The only basic difference between the two actors was their way of working. While Redford preferred to do a scene with limited rehearsal, to maintain a certain spontaneity, Newman liked to go over lines a number of times, to get everything just right. Any problems were worked out by Hill.

"George is a very, very specific director," Steven Bernhardt recalled for me. "He is extremely bright and, when either Paul or Bob had a disagreement with him, they would stand in there and slug it out verbally. It was really kind of fun to watch because George always seemed to have an answer for whatever Bob or Paul would come up with—particularly Paul. I remember there were some scenes that were really unpleasant to shoot. In one instance, it was supposed to be a very hot day. They were ahead of the super posse and they were up on a hill. . . . Paul was supposed to take his hat off and fall backwards into a pool of water. It was absolutely freezing that day. I mean devastatingly cold. We were far away from any kind of encampment. The trucks were a long way down the road, and he had to do it time and time again. Each time Paul would come out shivering, and he had a line to read too, which was even worse. We would bundle him up in blankets, and he had other changes of clothes. . . . I kept hoping that George would say, 'OK, print it.' [Instead he said] 'Listen, can you try? . . .' Paul would just swear under his breath . . . and he would go back and do it again. He must have done it five or six times. But what it really represented was a tremendous amount of respect on the part of the actor. Both Bob and Paul, and Katharine, relied on George's judgment and would do pretty much anything he asked. I think that's the reason that Bob has worked with him so many times."

That sense of specificity equipped the production crew to handle a number of tricky scenes. In addition to the performers, George Roy Hill and his technical people also had to work around mother nature. For the "morning after" sequence, where Butch and Etta ride the bicycle, a set was constructed on location in Grafton, Utah, so that the director could film interiors and exteriors with ease. The camera remained inside, photographing Sundance and Etta in bed on the strength of a generator and lights placed strategically around the room. Hall also took shots outside from the same position, so artificial light augmented the sun rays which poked in, making the interior and exterior equally bright.

The filming of the second train explosion, which occurs after Butch plants some dynamite, was difficult to stage. A segment of the train was of balsa wood reconstruction, but interior footage featured a real car. Two stunt men placed themselves at the front of the balsa model, indicating to Hill how close they could stand to the source of the explosion without getting hurt. The explosion had to be shot at a different speed in each of the four cameras used to make sure that at least one would look realistic onscreen. Pieces of shattered balsa wood flew sixty feet into the air in less than half a second, so the cameras had to be cranked down. Filming at a normal speed of twenty-four frames per second would have given the scene a jumpy, Keystone Kops comedy look. Even though ex-

George Roy Hill

perts predicted that production could commence without danger, there is always an element of risk in such special effects. "There were a couple of explosions that were a little heavier than they were intended to be, which is always the case, because you never know precisely what's going to happen. You just want to make sure everything that goes up in the air is not heavy," related Steven Bernhardt.

Aside from the technical challenges successfully met by the production company of *Butch Cassidy and the Sundance Kid,* the effect of the scenes on the characters also had to be considered. Since Hill wanted the Western to feature its people, technique and narrative would have to coexist gracefully and blend into a unit. The entire bicycle scene, while presenting a lighting problem, also solved what the director considered a deficiency in the development of Katharine Ross' Etta Place. Nobody wanted Etta to be simply the girl who replaces the cowboy's horse as an object of affection. So it became obvious that something had to be done. Her role was noticeably skimpy. The filmmaker, whose work has been accused of reflecting a hardline male chauvinism, sketched out two scenes to help make Etta a more viable personality.

Hill felt Etta's best moments came when Ross didn't have any dialogue. This did not comment on the actress' ability but rather on the way the role grew. The segments in New York and the Bolvian bank robbery helped define Etta's relationship with Butch and Sundance. Hill needed more. On the morning after Etta makes love to Sundance, she also has fun riding a bicycle with Butch.

The director devised the wordless moments to flesh-out the bond between Etta and Butch. In place of dialogue, Hill inserted an original song. While cutting the Western, he used Paul Simon's "Mrs. Robinson" as an example of the kind of rhythm necessary. Hill then asked Bert Bacharach, composer of the film's soundtrack, to write a number with similar bounce. Bacharach's popular music possessed the bright, tuneful sophistication of the 1960s, a feeling Hill wanted to impart to the characters of Butch, Sundance, and Etta. They should act as if they had stepped out of that decade into the turn-of-the-century. The trio had a low-keyed, realistic view of life which the director thought very modern. So Bacharach composed the memorable "Raindrops Keep Fallin' on My Head." Pop/country singer B. J. Thomas sang it onto the record industry's Top Ten and the song and entire score won Academy Awards.

The vision of *Butch Cassidy and the Sundance Kid* shared by the cast and crew was complicated. Two 19th-century outlaws with 20th-century lifestyles would be recreated in a film which warmly remembered the times as they should have been and featured Butch and Sundance as men *and* legends. The film consistently had to echo that concept or it might turn into merely an incoherent mass of attitudes and styles.

The little black-and-white film of Butch holding up a train for the movie-within-a-movie he views in Bolivia is a good example of the overall harmony of the Western. "George had some definite ideas on how he thought the sequence should look," Michael Moore recalled, "but left it up to me to stage. I must say it was interesting to shoot this sequence and fun because we shot it trying for the look of early picture-making at twenty frames per second instead of the standard twenty-four."

Of course, in the silent movie days films did not look jumpy and characters did not run around the screen in fast motion. This only occurs when a silent picture is projected incorrectly or on a machine which cannot show it at the proper speed. The decision to shoot the black-and-white sequence so that things appear to be moving too quickly is in itself an acknowledgment of the dual temporality of the Western. *Butch Cassidy and the Sundance Kid* is both a nostalgic view through rose-colored glasses and a basically true-to-life illustration of two unique bandits. The film definitely peers at the outlaws from a modern viewpoint, and the black-and-white short is a funny consequence of that.

To keep the spark of legend about Butch and Sundance and to utilize the dispute about their ends, Hill decided that the bank robbers should not be blown to bits in the style of *Bonnie and Clyde.* The director wanted them remembered as the not-so-bad guys they were.

First what all considered to be a beautiful ending was shot. Two cameras rested side by side, one in fast and the other rolling in slow motion. A freeze frame stilled the action in a blur; then one camera came into clear focus and showed Butch's reaction to their imminent demise. A *tour de force,* this finish diminished the impact of the action. So it was scrapped. In its place a slow motion shot of Butch and Sundance running out of the mine into that barrage of gun fire ends in a freeze frame. The audience filled in their own ending.

George Roy Hill shot approximately 250,000 feet of 35mm film, printing about three out of every ten takes. It took seven days longer than the seventy-seven-day shooting schedule Fox allowed. But Hill brought in the picture for $6,270,000, $30,000 under the allotted budget.

"We felt in our hearts that we were working on an absolutely sensational film," Steven Bernhardt recalled. "Every member of the crew, dead tired at night, would be sitting watching dailies—each person looking at his own area, trying to see what he could have done better, or what he might alter . . . thinking ahead for the next day. It was really a labor of love and one of the nice things about it was the studio sent telegrams saying how sensational the picture was. . . . We weren't under pressure to get a tremendous amount of shots."

Twentieth Century-Fox decided to open the Western all around the country in a saturation booking. The strategy worked brilliantly. *Butch Cassidy and the Sundance Kid* has made $44,300,000 in distributors' box-office rentals as of this writing, the fifteenth highest earnings in the history of the cinema. This is more than any other Western.

Reviewers' comments varied greatly:

> *New York Daily News,* Wanda Hale, three and one-half stars:
>
> *Butch Cassidy and the Sundance Kid* is a laugh-in, a fun Western. Although we know they're headed for destruction . . . Paul Newman and Robert Redford make like a comedy team, playing their roles to the bitter end for laughs.
>
> *New York Post,* Archer Winsten:
>
> *Butch Cassidy and the Sundance Kid . . .* is a Western beautifully stylized halfway between melodrama and comedy, beautifully played by Butch (Paul Newman) and the Kid (Robert Redford), and beautifully directed and written by, respectively, George Roy Hill and William Goldman. And yet it's so packed with the artifice of finely designed entertainment that it would be silly to believe it.
>
> *New York Times,* Vincent Canby:
>
> There is thus, at the heart of *Butch Cassidy,* a gnawing emptiness that can't be satisfied by an awareness that Hill and Goldman probably knew exactly what they were doing—making a very slick movie. They play tricks on the audience, by turning a bit of melodrama into a comic blackout, and by taking short cuts to lyricism.

Although the Western remained popular with audiences, some critics in film journals took *Butch Cassidy and the Sundance Kid* to task for a variety of reasons. Much of the criticism centered around the filmmakers' alleged ignorance of the West. Goldman's script was considered to be more of a toy gun than a real reflection of frontier culture, while Fox was chastised for handing the directorial reins to a man inexperienced in the genre. Others were outraged because Burt Bacharach composed 20th-century pop tunes for a Western.

But there were those who appreciated the production. They realized that the theme of *Butch Cassidy and the Sundance Kid* reflects the warm memory of dime novel heroics with a realistic backdrop, and that the film is also historically accurate as it is nostalgic.

Butch Cassidy and the Sundance Kid is charmingly different. That holds the key to its triumph—the charm.

The inspired casting of Newman and Redford—in an extension of the well-proven "buddy system" so popular in films and especially in Westerns—was repeated later when George Roy Hill brought them together again to make *The Sting* (Universal, 1973). Redford and Hill also worked together on *The Great Waldo Pepper* (Universal, 1975), while Newman and Hill were reunited on *Slap Shot* (Universal, 1977). Katharine Ross again played Etta Place in the 1976 TV movie, *Wanted: The Sundance Woman,* which purported to tell what happened to her after Butch and Sundance were cut down in the climactic shootout. And Richard Lester's *Butch and Sundance: The Early Years,* filmed by Fox in the summer of 1978 as a "prequal" to the original film—containing events occurring long before and leading up to the action of the Newman/Redford movie—offered still another look at the outlaw pair.

Julie Christie and Warren Beatty

CHAPTER THIRTY

McCabe and Mrs. Miller

Year Released: 1971
Studio: Warner Bros.
Producers: David Foster, Mitchell Brower
Director: Robert Altman
Screenplay: Robert Altman, Brian McKay, based on the novel *McCabe* by Edmond Naughton
Cinematography: Vilmos Zsigmond
Music: Leonard Cohen
Art Director: Leon Ericksen
Editor: Lou Lombardo
Assistant Director: Tommy Thompson
Second Unit Director: Lou Lombardo
Special Effects: Marcel Vercoutere
Sound: John W. Gusselle, William A. Thompson
Color, 121 minutes

Cast:

John McCabe	WARREN BEATTY
Constance Miller	JULIE CHRISTIE
Sheehan	RENE AUBERJONOIS
Dog Butler	HUGH MILLAIS
Ida Coyle	SHELLEY DUVALL
Sears	MICHAEL MURPHY
Smalley	JOHN SCHUCK
Mr. Elliott	COREY FISHER
The Lawyer	WILLIAM DEVANE

Cowboy	KEITH CARRADINE
Bart Coyle	BERT REMSEN

McCabe and Mrs. Miller is a brilliantly elliptical Western covered in the veils of film technique. When one cuts through the grainy stock, color which resembles yellowed newspaper clippings stored too long in an attic, multi-layered sound, and enigmatic plotting, Robert Altman's version of the demise of the American individual is a glowing ember of clear truth. *McCabe and Mrs. Miller* remains one of the boldest Westerns ever because it gloriously emphasizes the reality of the moment over normal narrative development.

Free-lance businessman/gambler John McCabe rides into the town of Presbyterian Church, a turn-of-the-century village set on the Canadian border. He has plans to turn the unfinished community into a thriving enterprise. A saloon, bathhouse, general store, brothel, and other dwellings are constructed under McCabe's supervision. Prostitutes are imported, along with an English woman named Constance Miller as their madam. She proves to be such a shrewd businessperson that the townsmen have little to spend at McCabe's bar once they have patronized Mrs. Miller's establishment. While McCabe is all swagger and flashing teeth, it is Mrs. Miller who really builds the town into such a profitable enterprise that an aggressive business concern tries to buy them out. At her urging, McCabe refuses to sell his interest. Failing to reason with the enterprising man, the organization sends a debonair hired killer to shoot McCabe down. Learning this, Mrs. Miller finds herself torn between her business sense and a growing attachment for McCabe. McCabe ultimately is killed, and Mrs. Miller retreats to a crude opium parlor.

The most outstanding feature of *McCabe and Mrs. Miller* is the loose and elliptical structure of the story which fascinates despite its ambiguity. Director Robert Altan divulges just enough information about characters and plot to arouse curiosity, as the smell of a fresh-baked apple pie might whet the appetite. Both McCabe and Mrs. Miller are treated with the mystery of a deity as they separately enter Presbyterian Church. McCabe rides in first on a donkey, dressed in the suited, derbyed regalia of the gambler, to the tune of Leonard Cohen's gruff off-screen voicing of "The Stranger Song." Mrs. Miller makes her appearance on a locomotive-like contraption. Where did she come from? The question is never really answered.

As in the films of French writer/directors Alain Robbe-Grillet and Marguerite Duras, the viewers of *McCabe and Mrs. Miller* are forced to work at establishing relationships and motives. It is only after some time, for instance, that an inept looking youth played by

Keith Carradine, dressed in ill-fitting clothes and a floppy hat, is determined to be really a gunfighter. The roundabout tactics of the men who offer to buy out McCabe do not appear threatening, only vague. The tall, fur-coated gentleman who proudly rides into town is neither a statesman nor a poet, but rather a hired killer with the air of a Shakespearean actor.

Yet the enigmatic surroundings only bolster the positions of the gambler and the madam as the complex bulwarks of the script. Warren Beatty's John McCabe is basically a man with outmoded ideas about business and ego. In comparison with a possibly monolithic enterprise which evidently will go to any lengths to achieve a goal, McCabe the wheeler-dealer is like the pony express rider who was rendered obsolete by the railroad. The gambler is one of a dying breed, as were such cinema predecessors in *Tumbleweeds, The Gunfighter, Shane,* and *The Wild Bunch.*

The difference between the protagonists in those Westerns and McCabe is that Altman and Beatty have made the card sharp a gallant buffoon. The man is no match for Mrs. Miller, much less a big corporation. Yet in his mind, he is the one who has come down from the mountains to build Presbyterian Church into a gold mine and, as such, can do no wrong. The more sensible side of his character is filled with fear about having to face a professional gunman. Beatty plays McCabe as a fascinating mixture of Harry Langdon's timidity, W. C. Fields' bravura, and Gary Cooper's *High Noon* heroism. When McCabe finally dies in the snow, his demise, as it had to be, is a result of a hard-fought battle in which his opponent is also killed. The last image in the film is a long shot of McCabe slumped in the snow, flakes falling down and blurring an already white, grainy frame. Then Altman freezes the image as a monument to an honorable man who died for his convictions.

Along with Beatty's perceptive performance, there was fine work from Julie Christie as Mrs. Miller and the rest of the memorable cast of supporting players, including Shelley Duvall, Rene Auberjonois, Michael Murphy, Hugh Millais, John Schuck, and Keith Carradine. Even if their characters, excepting Christie's and Beatty's, are hardly developed, the personalities ring true because their screen moments are true to life—each has his own way of talking and looking. Julie Christie's ability to blend the tough heart of a business woman with the tender soul of a lover makes her performance one of her best ever, standing as one of the few woman's roles in early 1970s American cinema which is equal to that of the man's.

McCabe and Mrs. Miller is an unparalleled Western. It offers a sort of you-are-there truth to those willing to unravel the captivating mystery of sight and sound and follow the path led by the gambler and the madam.

Hugh Millais (center)

Warren Beatty

The Making of *McCabe and Mrs. Miller*

For a long time Robert Altman believed he had failed in his early years in the cinema to do the work he should have done. Yet he considered himself lucky.

The director began a movie career in Kansas City's industrial film industry. Altman entered features by producing and directing *The Delinquents* (UA) in 1957, from which he reportedly was fired for asking the actors to talk all at once. A documentary, *The James Dean Story* (Warner Bros.), followed that year. He spent the next decade in television, directing episodes of shows like "Combat," "Bonanza," and "The Whirlybirds," although unorthodox approaches made him unpopular with some network executives. Once, he wanted to establish a character in a series and then kill him off. That just wasn't done in 1950s and 60s video fare. It seems that Altman simply anticipated the mini-series, where no extreme continuity thoughts generally exist, as the program has a limited run.

Altman's next film chore didn't come until 1967's *Nightmare in Chicago* (Universal),* which he produced and directed. This low-grade thriller barely hinted at the pictures to come. In 1968, he lensed *Countdown* (Warner Bros.-Seven Arts), a routine drama about astronauts. No future genius there, people may have thought.

That Cold Day in the Park presented another idea. The 1969 Commonwealth United production opened to apathetic reviews, but was shown at the Cannes Film Festival—almost shown, that is. The projection room caught fire during the last reel and the ending was never seen. Nevertheless, the movie stayed in the memory. It is full of dazzling camerawork and strong performances by Sandy Dennis and Michael Burns, which keep interest throughout the rich density of sound that features actors talking all at once. Still, there was no sale as far as the American box-office was concerned.

Fourteen directors turned down Ring Lardner, Jr.'s comic script about soldiers who staff a battlefield hospital during the Korean War. Producer Ingo Preminger finally offered the job to Altman. Although *M*A*S*H** made $40,850,000 in distributors' domestic box-office receipts, the final product infuriated Lardner because producer/director Altman so radically altered the material.

It didn't really matter, at least in terms of Robert Altman's future in Hollywood. By 1970 being associated with Altman was like having an Indian to dinner. It was the thing to do.

*Filmed in 1964 in 16mm. for TV's "Kraft Suspense Theatre" and shown originally as *Once Upon a Savage Night* (4/2/64 NBC).

Although the director received the relatively small fee of $75,000 for his services on *M*A*S*H** when he preferred a five percent interest in the film, that money wasn't terribly relevant either. The director could live in the fun style he'd become accustomed to as a high-priced maker of television shows. But the success of the Korean War black comedy gave him something far more important. He had his independence as a filmmaker. Few American directors could claim the freedom of a Fellini, a Bergman, or a Godard. American filmmaking circa 1970 boasted two men whose positions were comparable to the Europeans', Stanley Kubrick and Peter Bogdanovich. After *M*A*S*H**, it was Kubrick, Bogdanovich, and Altman.

*M*A*S*H** was followed by *Brewster McCloud* (MGM, 1970), a strangely fascinating allegory which failed with many critics and moviegoers. Altman couldn't be dissuaded from making movies his way. *Brewster McCloud*'s inability to win interest did not give him any self-doubt. Like all smart people, the filmmaker learned from things that didn't go as planned. Being applauded for one work and criticized for another helped teach him the things he really wanted to do and those he did not.

Warners backed Altman's next project. The director bought a script by Brian McKay called *The Presbyterian Church Wager*, adapted from the novel *McCabe* by Edmond Naughton. It concerned a gambler named John McCabe who built a town with the help of a madam called Mrs. Miller.

As usual, Altman went to work refining the script, while Warners announced the movie's budget to be $2,400,000. The filmmaker decided to lens the Western in Vancouver, British Columbia, because he liked the overcast mood of the area, and had made *That Cold Day in the Park* there.

The stars of the film would be Warren Beatty and Julie Christie. While Donald Sutherland's performance in *M*A*S*H** had made him a top Hollywood name and Elliott Gould's growing reputation was confirmed under Altman's direction, this was the first time the filmmaker had to handle two solidly established personalities.

Beatty and Christie had undoubtedly heard the stories about Altman's relaxed direction of *M*A*S*H**. Some apparently thought him to be an incompetent trying to figure out how to deal with a big opportunity. Others knew better. Unlike a Fritz Lang, who molded an actor's portrayal to the smallest detail, sometimes even giving a performer eye movements, Robert Altman knew filmmaking was a collaborative process. Although the director wanted each film to reflect his vision, he realized that concept could only be executed with the help of others—actors, cameramen, set designers, writers, and all the remaining technicians. An ideal Altman film contains a

Julie Christie

little piece of everyone involved in its creation, and that is what he planned for *The Presbyterian Church Wager.*

Warren Beatty welcomed the responsibility given by Altman. After a fine start in the early 1960s performing in *Splendor in the*

Grass (Warner Bros., 1961) and *The Roman Spring of Mrs. Stone* (Warner Bros., 1961) among others, the actor showed his versatility by both producing and starring in *Bonnie and Clyde* (Warner Bros.-Seven Arts, 1967), one of the best American films of its decade. Beatty had a passion for detail and this trait set well with Altman although the pair would have numerous discussions about the Western's plot and characters. Julie Christie reportedly had qualms about the director's apparently easygoing approach to filmmaking. But soon she too became an integral part of the production unit.

The rest of the cast was composed primarily of what has come to be known as Altman's stock company. Each actor was relatively unknown at the time, but Shelley Duvall seemed like a whore, Keith Carradine a gunfighter, and William Devane an unscrupulous lawyer.

The great majority of Altman's actors are steadfastly loyal to their director. There is little ego-tripping during his productions, no "stars" lording over supporting or bit players. In fact, an actor who might have a lead role in one Altman film might have only a small part in another project.

Such was the case with Michael Murphy. He received his first real break in *That Cold Day in the Park.* Later in *Brewster McCloud,* Murphy performed a fine parody of Steve McQueen's laconic police detective in *Bullitt* (Warner Bros.-Seven Arts, 1968). In *The Presbyterian Church Wager,* Murphy signed to essay the small role of a representative of an unnamed organization trying to purchase McCabe's interests in the town. Murphy had absolutely no qualms about any possible repercussions on his career. Years ago an actor generally wouldn't consider taking a minor role once he had reached stardom unless he was under a very tight contract. Murphy's faith was rewarded by good parts in prestige pictures.

Altman discovered Shelley Duvall at a party. She had never acted professionally before *Brewster McCloud*. It certainly wouldn't have been difficult for her to obtain large follow-up parts, but she too was eager to do a minor role in the director's unusual Western.

By the end of 1970, Altman and part of his company were located in Vancouver. The filmmaker maintained a trailer office in West Vancouver's Cypress Park. Although his philosophy of moviemaking was that it should be an enjoyable experience, he did not look forward to starting *The Presbyterian Church Wager*. To Altman, beginning a film meant a total, twenty-four-hour-a-day commitment. Once the concept is clear, which may take anywhere from a few days to weeks, he commences work. Warners allowed Altman $750 per week living expenses during production, but he reportedly spent close to $4,000 every seven days to keep the company happy.

The making of *The Presbyterian Church Wager* literally began at the beginning. The film's title grew from the name of a partially constructed town complete with an unfinished church steeple which existed along the United States-Canadian border around 1902. And since, in the script, gambler McCabe masterminds the construction of the primitive community, the "Wager" was added.

Altman built a town. By December 1970, Presbyterian Church consisted of cabins, a sawmill, whorehouses, a bathhouse, two saloons, and a barbershop. The rooms stood as they might have seventy years earlier, with no provisions for the cameras or other film equipment. Altman wanted the filmmaking process to adjust itself to the reality of the town and its participants, not the other way around. Instead of using trained animals, he employed strays cared for by the cast and crew. Chickens kept in pens just as in the past were killed and eaten by the company.

The town cost $200,000 to erect. All the materials were real. The wooden creations looked as if they could have been transferred from the old Northwest, comparing in stark crudity to the sets of George Stevens' *Shane*. Altman's streets were every bit as muddy. Men and women sank up to their ankles as they traversed from one warped sidewalk to another. People who fought in the passageways found themselves covered with mud. The carpenters who came to build the town actually lived there and drank whiskey brewed from their own still. Other members of the company joined the living—and imbibing—later. There was such a communal feeling among those who spent much time there, that when co-star Rene Auberjonois arrived to begin his role, he felt like a stranger. But he became swept up in the energy of the townspeople.

Robert Altman's Presbyterian Church grew organically from the creative instincts of all concerned. When something in the script differed from its reality in town, one of the two was changed—sometimes the screenplay, sometimes the set.

Often the director found himself not knowing what he would film from one day to the next. At first, Altman's flexibility disturbed Warren Beatty, who found it difficult to work without a finished script. The filmmaker and star worked closely on the rewrites, often spending whole weekends changing dialogue, characters, or entire scenes.

Yet the process was a collective one—at Altman's insistence. This open attitude benefited him many times through production. Once, when he was looking for a hymn, his secretary suggested "Asleep in Jesus." Altman used it. The entire community was supposed to sing along. Then the director realized many of the men wouldn't have known the words to the song, but reasoned that the prostitutes might. So the women sang, while the menfolk shuffled about uneasily, and an actor named Brantley F. Kearns played the fiddle.

Despite his concern for reality in everything from wood construction to real money and period clothes in unopened drawers, the director emphasized emotional rather than literal truth. It wasn't necessary for the plot to follow the normal step-by-step format. There was of course much improvisation. Altman's belief is that his job is not to create art but to show the process of that creation. In doing so, much of the cogent narrative was scissored to make the viewer move from scene to scene on the strength of the characters rather than the force of a story which centers around the founding of a town and its leading citizen's battle to keep his property.

Robert Altman always had two cameras rolling at once, both equipped with a zoom lens. The excess footage technique was also used by George Stevens, who would film a shot repeatedly and from many angles in order to have a wide choice of material to edit together for the final print. Altman lensed with a pair of cameras to

Warren Beatty, Julie Christie, and Robert Altman

keep his actors working whether they were in reality being photographed or not. If a performer knew a camera lens might zoom in on him, even though he wasn't in the forefront of a shot, it would tend to keep him in character. The zoom lens is used prolifically throughout Altman's Western in the creation of a complex texture which emphasized the whole environment, not just one or two or three performers who supposedly dominate a moment.

Most of the script was shot with few retakes, although Altman varied his formula in scenes with Beatty and Christie. Since they seemed to get better with every take, he thought it wise to make as many as eight or nine takes of their scenes together.

One part of the scenario features a party thrown by the town prostitutes. The actresses asked Altman if they could make out the guest list. At first he refused but then decided that if emotional reality was to be stressed, the women would have to be allowed to decide who was going to be in the segment. But he did suggest that they drink real vodka at the party, rather than the usual cinema alcoholic beverage: colored water, weak tea, or the like. With their inhibitions slowly dying as the liquor slipped down their throats in the cold Vancouver winter, the performers naturally got more intimate and reacted to each other as people, not fictional characters.

It amounted to a cast party, filmed by Altman. After about five hours, the director called the merrymaking to a close. Very little of the part appeared in the film, but Altman didn't consider the time or the considerable cost of the four or five hours of shooting to be wasted. The actors learned more about each other and could respond henceforth in a truer fashion. It was not the kind of thing that the Warner front office was enthusiastic about.

Altman's alleged "excesses" weren't the only problems over which the director and the studio fought. When Robert Altman says he wants everyone in a production to be a member of a community of filmmakers, he takes it quite literally. He is offended by the attitudes of many of the union workers producers are forced to employ. To his mind, many art directors, sound men, electricians, et al., don't consider themselves part of the creative process, and often are not allowed to be by other directors. But to Altman, they are outsiders in an area where he feels everyone should know and be relaxed with one another. Consequently, he has often refused to hire such people. The art director of *The Presbyterian Church Wager* was Leon Ericksen, who had worked on Altman's *That Cold Day in the Park*. Altman considered Ericksen, who did not belong to the union, as important to the Western as Warren Beatty or himself. In order for the man to legally serve as an art director, he would have had to serve a long apprenticeship, but Altman didn't see any reason to wait. He had even less patience when a prop had to be moved. Normally, a union crew would take care of it. Altman sometimes moved the object himself and often paid fines for infractions of stringent Hollywood filmmaking rules.

Shortly after *The Presbyterian Church Wager* was finished in 1971, it was retitled *McCabe and Mrs. Miller*. The Western cost $3,000,000, which was $600,000 over budget.

Warners was not happy about the finished product. As always happens with a film which falls from the favor of a studio, *McCabe and Mrs. Miller* received little publicity and no national advertising campaign. The production was virtually dumped into theatres.

Reviewers penned widely different critiques of the Western:

> *New York,* Judith Crist:
>
> Robert Altman's *McCabe and Mrs. Miller* is also of the past, a sad and haunting frontier ballad about a gambler and a madam who could have made it big but didn't. With his first look into the past . . . Altman has wiped the knowing and sophisticated glint away and given us a raw and glowing glimpse of a mining town on the rise and two people meaningful only in their passing through it.
>
> *New York Daily News,* Rex Reed:
>
> What hell has Robert Altman, the once talented director of *M*A*S*H*,* showered upon us now. I was willing to dismiss his vomitous *Brewster McCloud* as a bad acid trip resulting in temporary brain damage, hoping he'd get the monkey shines out of his system and get back to serious work. But now there's *McCabe and Mrs. Miller*—an incoherent, amateurish, simpleminded, boring and totally worthless piece of garbage.
>
> *Variety:*
>
> *McCabe and Mrs. Miller*, Robert Altman's latest film, is a disappointing mixture which succumbs to its liabilities despite some key creative assets. . . . The David Foster-Mitchell Brower production suffers from overlength; also a serious effort at moody photography backfires into pretentiousness. . . .

Praise from magazine critics like Judith Crist came too late to save the Western from a disastrous first run in theatres. Warners readied the coffin for the latest effort of Robert Altman, a director who just two pictures earlier was the bearded genius. The dictum that you are only as good as your last film could have been put on Altman's tombstone, which might very well have been made of the reel cans of *McCabe and Mrs. Miller.*

Warren Beatty wouldn't accept the studio's treatment of the

Western and persuaded executives to give it another chance. With a new release, backed by a major advertising campaign, the production would be able to benefit from the many fine reviews it ultimately received.

Beatty's persistence paid off. *McCabe and Mrs. Miller* became hot box-office. It grossed $28,724 in New York City in its first week and then went on to take in $4,000,000 in distributors' rental fees, providing a small profit for Warners.

McCabe and Mrs. Miller was one more step in the building of Robert Altman's reputation as the major American directorial find of the last decade. From there, he went on to commercially questionable but rich and complex works such as *Images* (Columbia, 1972) and *The Long Goodbye* (UA, 1973) before *Nashville* (Paramount, 1975) confirmed him as a moneymaker once more.

Shelley Duvall, Keith Carradine, Michael Murphy, and William Devane have gone on to stardom. Rene Auberjonois and John Schuck appear regularly on television. But the feeling persists that they would take a bit part in a future Robert Altman film, as did Julie Christie in *Nashville*, just for the fulfillment. They would do it because *McCabe and Mrs. Miller* was that kind of experience.

Selected Bibliography

Behlmer, Rudy, ed. *Memo From: David O. Selznick*. New York: Viking, 1972.

Everson, William K. *A Pictorial History of the Western Film*. Secaucus, N.J.: Citadel Press, 1969.

Hart, William S. *My Life East and West*. New York: Benjamin Blom, 1929.

Higham, Charles. *Hollywood Cameramen*. Bloomington and London: Indiana University Press, 1970.

Horwitz, James. *They Went Thataway*. New York: Ballantine, 1976.

Kitses, Jim. *Horizons West*. Bloomington and London: Indiana University Press, 1969.

LaGuardia, Robert. *Monty*. New York: Arbor House, 1977.

McBride, Joseph. ed., *Focus on Howard Hawks*. Englewood Cliffs, N.J.: Prentice-Hall, 1972.

Mix, Paul E. *The Life and Legend of Tom Mix*. Cranbury, N.J.: A. S. Barnes, 1972.

Parish, James Robert. *Great Western Stars*. New York: Ace, 1976.

______. *Hollywood's Great Love Teams*. New Rochelle, N.Y.: Arlington House, 1974.

______. *The Tough Guys*. New Rochelle, N.Y.: Arlington House, 1976.

Place, J. A. *The Western Films of John Ford*. Secaucus, N.J.: Citadel Press, 1974.

Richie, Donald. *George Stevens: An American Romantic.* New York: Museum of Modern Art, 1970.

Sarris, Andrew. *Interviews with Film Directors.* New York: Bobbs-Merrill, 1967.

Schickel, Richard. *The Men Who Made the Movies.* New York: Atheneum, 1975.

Tornabene, Lyn. *Long Live the King.* New York: Putnam's, 1976.

Tuska, Jon. *The Filming of the West.* Garden City, N.Y.: Doubleday, 1976.

Walsh, Raoul. *Each Man in His Time.* New York: Farrar, Strauss, & Giroux, 1974.

Wellman, William A. *A Short Time for Insanity.* New York: Hawthorn, 1974.

Whitney, Steven. *Charles Bronson Superstar.* New York: Dell, 1975.

Zolotow, Maurice. *Shooting Star.* New York: Simon & Schuster, 1974.

Index

Numbers in italics indicate pages showing photographs of the individuals and movies mentioned. If the letter "*f*" follows a page number, the reference is to a footnote on the indicated page.